AutoCAD®

SECRETS EVERY USER SHOULD KNOW

DAN ABBOTT

BICENTENNIAL
BICENTENNIAL
1807
WILEY
2007
BICENTENNIAL
BICENTENNIAL

WILEY PUBLISHING, INC.

Acquisitions Editor: Willem Knibbe

Development Editor: Heather O'Connor

Technical Editor: Jon McFarland

Production Editor: Martine Dardignac

Copy Editor: Tiffany Taylor

Production Manager: Tim Tate

Vice President and Executive Group Publisher: Richard Swadley

Vice President and Executive Publisher: Joseph B. Wikert

Vice President and Publisher: Neil Edde

Book Designer: Caryl Gorska

Compositor: Chris Gillespie, Happenstance Type-O-Rama

Proofreader: Nancy Riddiough

Indexer: Ted Laux

Anniversary Logo Design: Richard Pacifico

Cover Designer: Ryan Sneed

Cover Image: GettyImages, Donovan Reese

To Herman Abbott, a
exceptional machinis
and fathe

Acknowledgments

Five of my colleagues at Southern Maine Community College played a vital role in making this book a reality. I can't possibly thank adjunct professor and applications developer Paul Richardson enough for his detailed technical advice, which improved every aspect of this book. I'm also very grateful to professor Meridith Comeau for her 3D expertise, her contributions to the curriculum materials, and her unflaggingly buoyant spirit. Adjunct professor and applications developer Scott Danis was generous with his AutoLISP insights. Professor Ed Fitzgerald filled many gaps in my knowledge of architectural design and technical graphics, and IT maestro Mike Cyr willingly discussed the arcane applications of DOS batch files whenever I asked. This is a remarkably talented group of colleagues.

This book also benefited greatly from Monica Wood's willingness to put her own writing on hold whenever I needed writing advice, which was shockingly often. I couldn't have finished (or started) without her support. I was also fortunate to have a wonderful team at Sybex. Willem Knibbe's enthusiasm was a surprise and a delight to me. Heather O'Connor, Jon McFarland, and Martine Dardignac kept the project moving relentlessly along, meeting a series of deadlines that seemed daunting to me at the beginning. I am especially grateful to Tiffany Taylor, whose astonishing skill raises copy editing to a fine art.

And a special thanks to the Maine Community College system and Southern Maine Community College for granting me a semester sabbatical to work on this book.

Table of Contents

Introduction

A program as ubiquitous as AutoCAD shouldn't have any secrets. But if you don't know something, it's a secret to you. I hope that *AutoCAD: Secrets Every User Should Know* will take some of the mystery out of AutoCAD and AutoCAD LT, and also remind you of some traditional knowledge that I fear is being slowly eroded.

This book includes useful tips, detailed instructions, general guidance, a few tutorials, many solutions to problems of all kinds—and yes, even some secrets—that can be applied to AutoCAD in any application.

Who Is This Book For?

I wrote this book for two groups: experienced users with some gaps in their knowledge, and recent users who want to maximize their understanding of this complicated and multifaceted tool. The more familiar you are with AutoCAD or AutoCAD LT, the more this book will help you avoid common problems and produce work that is consistent, reliable, and accurate.

For most of you, AutoCAD is just one of the many tools you use, and you don't have time to become an expert at it. You don't have to. In my professional life, I've worked with a wide range of AutoCAD users in a remarkable array of disciplines. I've done AutoCAD training for companies, presented workshops for vendors, offered expertise in corporate disputes, and taught college courses in AutoCAD for nearly 20 years. This book is a result of that experience, and I hope you'll use it to expand your knowledge and improve your efficiency.

What Release of AutoCAD Is Covered?

This book isn't release-specific, although AutoCAD 2007 is used throughout for the graphics. Many offices don't upgrade immediately to new releases, and I understand why. Upgrades cost money and take time, and the law of unintended consequences often kicks in at exactly the wrong time. Most of the material in this book applies to any release of AutoCAD or AutoCAD LT. Where it doesn't, I make that clear. The most obvious distinction occurs in Chapter 3, "Customizing AutoCAD's Interface," because of the introduction of the Customizable User Interface in AutoCAD 2006.

AUTOCAD OR AUTOCAD LT?

Despite the *AutoCAD* of the title, most of the advice in this book can apply to AutoCAD LT. And who knows? After you look over the AutoCAD-only chapters, you may find enough ammunition to get at least one seat of AutoCAD installed at your workplace.

What's Included?

Much of the material in this book was developed for the Advanced AutoCAD course at Southern Maine Community College and then used in presentations at Autodesk University over the past decade. The topics derive from the kinds of questions I've been asked over the years by people who use AutoCAD every day.

This isn't meant to be a comprehensive book about AutoCAD. I've tried to identify common problem areas and provide some advice on how to approach them. I'm also trying to preserve some traditional knowledge that is often overlooked by users: knowledge as simple as making proper centerlines, as arcane as using DOS to improve efficiency, as exciting as programming, and as dramatic as 3D modeling. Here's a brief review of what's covered in each chapter.

Chapter 1: AutoCAD Productivity In this chapter, you'll find general rules for using Auto-CAD that I believe should be universal. The chapter includes a review of often-overlooked AutoCAD features, many with options or applications that you may have missed.

Chapter 2: Managing Your System Most AutoCAD users are computer savvy, but if you're not, this chapter's for you. In addition to information about how to make your computer work well with AutoCAD, you'll get some advice on the AutoCAD search path, see the settings in Options that I consider the most significant, and find out how to actually use SV$ files.

Chapter 3: Customizing the AutoCAD Interface You can make a lot of simple changes to your interface that will improve your efficiency with AutoCAD or AutoCAD LT. Here's where you'll learn about the CUI, quick keys, creating macros, and so on.

Chapter 4: Applying Graphics Standards AutoCAD is used distressingly often to produce documentation that doesn't meet the most fundamental requirements of technical graphics. This chapter is a primer on how to make AutoCAD do the right thing, with a review of the kinds of standards that drafters used to know and that AutoCAD users still should.

Chapter 5: Symbols, Tables, and Fields This is an area that bedevils a lot of users. You'll find information about blocks, the WBLOCK command, adding attributes, extracting attribute values, and managing external references as well as helpful tips on AutoCAD Tables and Fields.

Chapter 6: Plotting Being able to control the output from an AutoCAD drawing can set you apart from the crowd. If you have any confusion about plotting, layouts, or Paper Space, this expansion of the "Lost in Paper Space" workshop I've been doing for years at Autodesk University should help you out.

Chapter 7: AutoCAD Scripts This often-overlooked tool is the basis for the biggest productivity tip in this book: the ability to modify thousands of drawings automatically. The lowly script has some other great applications as well. Don't skip this chapter—it could save you a bundle and make you the office hero.

Chapter 8: AutoLISP by Example: Getting Started AutoLISP is the programming language for users. Jump in. This chapter will have you programming in minutes.

Chapter 9: AutoLISP by Example: Getting Better Chapter 8 was designed to get you started, but I'm betting that once you see how logical, fun, and easy it is to create programs in AutoLISP, you'll want to get better. In this chapter you'll see examples of debugging techniques, error handling and annotation, creating and using new AutoLISP functions, getting and converting input, using conditional expressions, manipulating entities, opening and creating text files of data, and more than a few other tricks. The chapter doesn't cover everything about AutoLISP, but it'll keep you going for a long time.

Chapter 10: 3D for Everyone Any AutoCAD user will be able to create models after going through this tutorial. And there are two suggestions for using legacy data—one architectural, one mechanical—that may surprise you.

Chapter 11: AutoCAD Puzzlers I loved writing this chapter. It addresses 35 questions from puzzled AutoCAD users. If you're even a little bit of an AutoCAD geek, you'll have fun trying to figure them out. Don't peek, but solutions are at the end.

The Book's Website Check out this book's website at www.sybex.com/go/autocadsecrets where I've placed several other tools to help you utilize and understand AutoCAD. In Web Appendix A, I review the features I consider most significant in each release since AutoCAD 2000. Web Appendix B contains a DOS command reference, and Web Appendix C provides a listing of all the AutoCAD file extensions. You'll also find all the scripts, DOS files, and AutoLISP code used in this book; and, in particular, a useful script for restoring the default settings for AutoCAD variables.

Finally, if you have any new puzzlers, differences of opinion, suggestions, or comments, you can find my contact information on this book's site.

CHAPTER 1

AutoCAD Productivity

Considering the complexity of AutoCAD, it's not surprising that many people who use it miss something important along the way. Many users had little training on the software before being expected to start producing useful work, and these users in turn have trained others based on what they figured out on their own. Even the most experienced AutoCAD users have likely forgotten some useful things they once knew.

This chapter is the result of the many questions I've been asked by AutoCAD users over the years while teaching, training, consulting, and responding to e-mails and phone calls. Here I'll offer advice on using AutoCAD, with an emphasis on features and techniques that are often overlooked or forgotten by users. I'll include general design advice that applies to the use of any CAD system, providing my recommendations for universal standard practice in using AutoCAD, reviewing techniques and commands that apply to all releases of AutoCAD.

This chapter isn't meant to be a comprehensive review of AutoCAD—many excellent books already provide that—nor is it a replacement for learning how to use the software. What I've selected here are items that people often overlook.

- **Design Standards**

- **AutoCAD Best Practices**

- **Feature Review (All Releases)**

Design Standards

CAD software is used in so many fields of design that it would be impossible to develop extensive standards that apply to all of them. I've trained people who use AutoCAD to design quilts, hearing aids, doll clothes, houses, barns, commercial buildings, M16s, submarine hatches, and the myriad components of machinery. But there are some foundational rules that represent a consensus among serious users of CAD. You'll find exceptions to these rules, of course, but think of them the way you think of the rules for dimensioning drawings: You follow them *if possible*. The fact that a rule has rare exceptions doesn't reduce its value as a guide. You certainly follow the rules requiring you to drive on the proper side of the road all the time—except when a dog darts out in front of you, or the road is washed away by a flash flood, or you're passing someone. So, here are some of my rules for using AutoCAD.

Draw Everything Actual Size

Unless you have a very good reason not to, draw everything at its actual size. Even details can be drawn full size, if you use layouts. They may not look right to you in the Model Space tab, but you can display them in Paper Space viewports and give them any scale you want. At one time, you would have used the SCALE command and then set DIMLFAC to compensate for dimensions, but that's *not* a good idea now. You know why. At some point, you'll forget that your dimension style is multiplying every dimension by 2; or you'll dimension a detail and forget to change DIMLFAC, and all the dimensions will be half their actual size. You have a complex enough job as it is, keeping track of so many details. Why not simplify your life by drawing everything the size it's supposed to be? You're not at a drafting table. Worry about how something will plot when you set up a layout.

I've done a lot of training for different industries and have looked for situations where it was impossible to draw full size; I haven't found an instance yet that couldn't be addressed using Paper Space. At one shop I worked for, two groups of designers who used AutoCAD had a difference of opinion about full size versus scale. One group of designers thought they couldn't draw full size because they were designing long pieces with almost no detail along their lengths but a lot of detail at the ends. They only drew the ends, and then they broke the piece with a conventional break and plotted it for the fabricators. The dissenting designers wanted to draw parts at their actual lengths so they could use them in assembly drawings without re-creating them.

The solution I offered was to draw the pieces full length, with proper end detail, and then create a layout with two viewports to represent each end of the object. As long as the two viewports were at the same scale and aligned, they could be separated for a break symbol to be added in Paper Space. Even the dimension of the overall length was correct, because it was in Model Space (where I think it normally

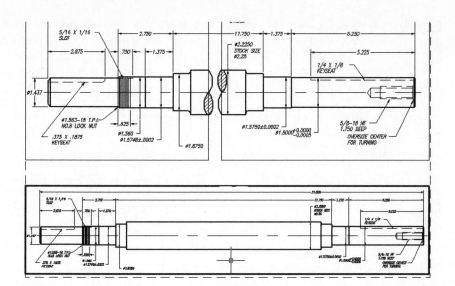

Figure 1.1

**Conventional break
for long part**

belongs). They could drag the value right or left so it could be seen in one of the viewports. (See Figure 1.1.) The entire part is shown at the bottom, with the conventional break created with two floating viewports above.

Draw Existing Features "as Built"

This tip probably seems obvious, but I've been asked more than once what I recommend when designing for renovations or additions to existing structures. The question is usually in this form: "I have the original drawings of the building. Should I use them to create an AutoCAD drawing of the existing structure, or should I create the AutoCAD geometry 'as-built'?"

Clearly, creating geometry "as built" rather than "as designed" permits you to solve problems in the software instead of in the field, because few actual structures didn't change in some way from the original plans. You can use the original plans to create a base drawing and then check key locations and dimensions for changes. This is one of the great benefits of using such a precise design system. You can reduce what some builders call *on-site engineering* by drawing everything as accurately as you possibly can. That way, the results are much more likely to match the plans. Who knows: Someday "as built" and "as designed" may become the same thing.

Draw Mechanical Parts at MMC

My advice to draw mechanical parts at Maximum Material Condition (MMC) may be less obvious than my "as-built" advice, because mechanical parts always have a specified tolerance—at least, they're supposed to. The question is, where in that range should you create your accurate-to-15-decimal-places geometry when using a CAD system? (You know it's impossible to make anything an exact size. If you think you can, you're not using a precise enough measuring tool.)

There are several possibilities. Some people draw objects in the middle of their size tolerance range. Others use what they consider the design size or nominal size—the base size given before the plus/minus sign. After all, isn't that the ideal size? Well, it may be the ideal size, but neither of these approaches is good practice, whether you're creating a 2D drawing or a 3D model. The fact is, a mechanical part has no ideal size. If a part is designed properly and given a functional tolerance, as required, it will work fine as long as its dimensions fall within that tolerance. No size in that tolerance will make the part perform better than any other size. As a machinist, you may aim for the middle of a range, but not because that makes a better part. You do that to reduce the chances of making the part too small or too large and having to throw it out.

Draw all parts and create all solid models at MMC unless it's one of those rare features that are controlled at Least Material Condition (LMC) in a tolerance frame. Features with outside dimensions, like a shaft or a pin, should be drawn at their largest acceptable size. Features that have inside dimensions, like a hole or a slot, should be drawn at their smallest possible size. In both cases, the result is a part with the maximum amount of material in it. That's usually when parts are least likely to go together; this approach allows you to draw parts in the situation where they're most likely to fail and to check for interferences more readily. It's also easier to be consistent this way, because the rules for Geometric Dimensioning and Tolerancing assume MMC for many of the specific situations where the rules apply. I recommend this approach for both 2D and 3D modeling, including when you're using Mechanical Desktop, Inventor, or any other CAD package.

Use Logical Increments

When designing something, you can use any size increment you wish. If you choose increments that are easy to work with, or that result in less waste during fabrication, you save both time and materials. During the early design stages, you can set a SNAP to that increment in AutoCAD, with a GRID set to twice the increment. Doing so can speed up the initial layout.

For architectural design, I recommend using the largest increment possible, such as whole inches, one foot, two feet, or four feet. Doing so makes it much easier to use standard-sized sheets of material during construction. For mechanical parts, use increments of 2mm or 0.1 inches if possible.

METRIC IS EVERYWHERE

I've been predicting since 1976 that the U.S. was about to go fully metric. I keep making that prediction, and I'm getting less and less wrong. That may not be as good as being right, but it's possible that you'll have to deal with the metric/inch conflict at some point.

I've assisted both mechanical designers and architectural designers in converting existing designs from inches to metric, and if this is done as a hard conversion, it often results in dimensions that aren't logical to people who are used to working in the metric system. Sometimes that can't be helped—it may not be possible for a precision mechanical part to be redesigned to use even values. It may be possible, however, for an architectural design to be soft-converted to millimeters (yes, millimeters) without any ill effects. Does anyone in the Architecture Engineering and Construction (AEC) field use metric units? Well, yes. The whole rest of the world does, and some companies in the U.S. are beginning to find that out—for example, cabinet makers whose cabinets won't fit into the space available except in U.S. houses, and plywood makers who have no market for 48×96″ sheets anywhere but here.

In one case, a log-home builder in Maine sold a home to a company in Japan. The builder boxed it up, put it on a container ship, and then got the fax: What the heck are these numbers, and how soon can we get drawings in millimeters? When they contacted me, I suggested that they convert their shop drawings to millimeters by changing DIMLFAC to 25.4 and then setting DIMRND to 2. All dimensions were then in whole, even millimeters. Nothing was off by more than one millimeter, so the design wasn't compromised, but the drawings looked better to the Japanese crew who had to read them. Imagine how confusing it must be to see 7′8¾″ when you're used to values like 2356.

AutoCAD Best Practices

I've been training people to use AutoCAD for technical graphics and design since the late 1980s. At that time, I frequently got resistance from drafters and designers who felt I placed too much emphasis on absolute accuracy. They would point out that once a drawing is plotted, the absurd 15 decimal places of precision that AutoCAD uses for calculations become meaningless. Once you plot a drawing, even significant errors are difficult to detect, as long as you carefully replace any key dimensions with those you typed in.

I believe all industries that rely on computers for design and documentation should share common standards when using CAD software. In this section, I offer advice on accuracy and other aspects of AutoCAD that should be standard practice across all disciplines. If you understand AutoCAD, it's faster to produce an accurate drawing than an inaccurate drawing. You or your company have probably invested upwards of $7,000 to put you in an AutoCAD seat, so why not produce as accurate and useful a drawing file as possible?

Use the Help System

The AutoCAD Help system has become one of the best Help systems available in any software. If I had to identify one AutoCAD feature as the single most underused, this is it. I've gotten many phone calls from people who have an AutoCAD question that I answer by simply going to the AutoCAD Help system. Use it. It keeps getting better and better. It's a model for what a Help system should be.

Use Blocks as Often as Possible

Blocks can dramatically reduce file size, allow you to quickly update large amounts of work, and make your drawings more consistent. Any time you create a symbol, standard detail, title block, or other collection of objects that you may ever want to use again, consider creating a block definition.

Once you've used a block, don't explode it unless you have a good reason. This is especially true for dimensions. Once you explode it, the block entity no longer exists. You lose the ability to update the dimensions, and you increase the file size (sometimes dramatically). Dimensions will no longer update values when you modify geometry, and you can't update dimension appearance with changes to dimstyles. Don't explode hatch patterns, either, for the same reason.

Never Override Dimension Values

When you're adding dimensions to drawings, it's tempting to type in the correct value when a dimension is wrong. Unless you absolutely don't have the time to do it, redraw the geometry so it's correct, and then add an associative dimension. Otherwise, you and everyone who ever uses your drawing will assume it's correct—with potentially dire results.

If you do override a dimension because you just can't help it, then make sure you flag the change, or note it so you can go back and re-create the geometry later when you have time.

When I'm dimensioning architectural plans, I set precision to an increment of $1/256$ in the Primary Units tab of the Dimension Style dialog box. That's ridiculously small for a dimension, but by using such a small increment of precision, I know immediately if there's an error in the geometry as I'm adding dimensions. If there are no errors, the proper dimension value is displayed. If you set the increment to a whole number, for example, small errors are masked by being rounded to the nearest inch.

HELP SYSTEM

I'm not exaggerating when I say I answer many questions from confused users by bringing up the AutoCAD Help system—often while I'm on the phone with them. The most recent was a call from a frustrated user who was using AutoCAD 2006 to edit text in a vertical title block. The version of AutoCAD they had upgraded from displayed the text horizontally; but Auto-CAD 2006 displayed the text in place, which meant he had to tilt his head to the side to read it. He was about to rotate the title block for editing when he decided to call me.

I knew the MTEXTED variable would allow him to change the MTEXT editor to the previous version so he could use horizontal text, but I didn't remember the correct setting for doing so. As he was asking the question, I used the Help system to look up the MTEXTED variable, and then I told him to set it to OldEditor. He sighed and asked, "How can you know everything about AutoCAD?" When I admitted that in this case my secret was the Help system, I think I heard him slap his forehead.

No one can know everything about AutoCAD, but if you want to be the indispensable AutoCAD go-to user in your office, become familiar with Help. Whether you reveal your secret source is up to you!

Use Layers with Logical and Consistent Names

Using layers with logical names allows you to separate different kinds of geometry and different functions. Don't be one of those people who produce nightmare drawings by placing all or most entities on a single layer. Layers give you control over a drawing that's essential to efficient management. If your layer names are logical, it's easy to manage multiple layers.

That logic should be embedded in an office standard and reflected in the use of standard drawing templates, and a .DWS standards file. There have been many attempts to standardize layer naming across disciplines. See Chapter 4, "Applying Graphics Standards," for more information.

Set All Properties to ByLayer

Unless you have a good reason, avoid the urge to use multiple colors, linetypes, or lineweights on a single layer. If you get a drawing from someone who has done this, use FILTER or QSELECT to select and move objects to different layers, and then change their properties to ByLayer.

Good reasons may include the desire to create a symbol or detail that contains multiple linetypes and colors. Although this can be done by using objects on different layers, many users prefer to have all elements of a block definition reside on a single layer so *only* that layer controls the appearance of the block. In this case, you can apply a specific color or linetype to an element before including it in a block definition.

LAYER MANIPULATION

Consider the following example from a residential floor plan. Layer names all begin with a field that designates the floor of the residence: FL1, FL1-DIM; FL2, FL2-DIM; FND, FND-DIM. Each floor has a number of associated layers for hidden lines, center lines, dimensions, appliances, electrical, and so on.

Because the layer names are uniform, you can use the following syntax either at the command prompt or within a menu to make the following changes to the layer:

- Thaw all layers.
- Set layer FL1 as the current layer.
- Freeze all layers that don't start with the characters *FL1*.

Your code should look like this:

```
-Layer;T;*;S;FL1;F;~FL1*;;
```

The * is a wildcard meaning *all*. The ~ (tilde) is a wildcard meaning *all except*.

If you find it necessary to apply a color or linetype directly to an object rather than to ByLayer, I recommend doing so with the Properties palette *after* the object is created. If you select the color in the Properties toolbar, you may forget to set it back to ByLayer and continue drawing. You should close the Properties toolbar to avoid using it. See Figure 1.2.

Use the Drafting Tools

Learn to use direct-distance entry, osnaps, object tracking, temporary tracking, and polar tracking. They're great tools that can dramatically speed up your work once you understand how they work together. Check out the newer osnaps, like M2P, Temporary Track Point, Parallel, and Extension. However, don't overdo the running osnaps. Open the Drafting Settings dialog box, and uncheck as many as possible in the Object Snap tab.

If you're drawing lines at unusual angles, and you want to be able to continue with lines that are perpendicular *from* the last line segment you drew, set PER as a running osnap and hover over the end you just selected.

Figure 1.2

Set properties to ByLayer.

Plot from Layouts in Paper Space

Read Chapter 6, "Plotting," for the full story; but for now, follow these steps in sequence when you create a new drawing file:

1. Create your geometry full size in Model Space, but don't add dimensions, text, or hatches.

2. Set up a layout with all views at the proper plot scale.

3. Add dimensions, text, hatches, and schematic symbols to your drawing from a layout with a properly scaled viewport.

> Use the command CHSPACE (an Express Tool before AutoCAD 2007) to move objects between Paper Space and Model Space. If you put something in the wrong spot, it's easy to change it and have it scaled automatically so it plots as you intend.

Draw Perfectly—Somebody Will Assume You Did

I've heard some horror stories about AutoCAD drawings that were done using the Etch-A-Sketch® method and then reused later by someone who assumed they were done accurately. Most of these stories involve hapless users stuck with their predecessors' drawings, but in some cases users run into trouble by relying on their own inaccurate drawings. In one case, which involved a lawsuit and a lot of money, a bid was made on a structural design based on the assurance that accurate AutoCAD drawings of the existing structure would be provided by the client. Unfortunately, those drawings were facilities drawings—done to show egress and general locations—and were unusable for the intended purpose.

How does this happen? Because most AutoCAD drawings *look* accurate even if they aren't, we forget that we created something quickly by sketching and then saved the file.

> It's quicker to use the accuracy tools built into AutoCAD than to draw by eye, so why not use them?

Set Text Height to 0

If you set the height to a fixed value when creating a new text style, the text can be used only at that height no matter how you set the text height in your dimstyle. Setting a height of 0 gives you control over text height every time you enter the height. If you can't read a dimension because the text is too small, but you can see the arrowheads, you've specified a fixed height in your text style.

Don't Use the Name *Standard*

The name *Standard* is used as a default name for the text style, dimension style, table style, and probably a few other things in AutoCAD. It's misleading, because it's a standard only in the sense that it always shows up in an AutoCAD environment. Never does the name represent a real standard in any discipline. To avoid a nasty surprise down the road, build a template file that banishes *Standard* as a name for anything.

I suggest naming text styles for the fonts they use. If you set their height to 0, you won't need all those Romans48 type names; Romans will work fine. For dimensions, give the styles names that represent their disciplines, or the name of the client. For tables, use names that represent their use. Or, use the names of your favorite pets—just don't call anything *Standard*.

Be Cautious When Using REFEDIT

REFEDIT is used to edit block definitions or external reference drawings; it replaces the originals if you tell it to. If you click Save Reference Edits, you'd better mean it. You can protect a drawing that will be used as an external reference (XRef) from being edited with REFEDIT by setting the variable XEDIT to 0 before saving the intended XRef. Before AutoCAD 2006, double-clicking a BLOCK insertion opened REFEDIT. Users who didn't understand what REFEDIT was would close the resulting toolbar and keep working. Unfortunately, they were still reference-editing without knowing it, and eventually they got the *not in the working set* error. If you get this error, type REFCLOSE at the command line.

Beware When Moving or Renaming Files

Don't change filenames or locations for hyperlinks, XRefs, XRef images, menu files, icon BMP files, or other support files unless you know how to redefine the path used to locate them. Otherwise, you'll get blank rectangles for images and a line of text for XRefs, your menus won't load, many commands won't work, or you'll see clouds or questions marks on your custom toolbars. Using the Relative Path option can help for images and XRefs.

THE PROBLEM WITH *STANDARD*

Every AutoCAD drawing uses *Standard* as the default name for styles. At some point, you may insert your drawing into another host drawing. If you never bothered to rename the style you use, you'll have a conflict in the host drawing between its dimension style and yours. Only one of the two styles named Standard can win this fight. Will it be your drawing, or the drawing into which it's inserted? Hint: Your drawing will lose this fight, and all your dimensions will look awful if you explode the resulting block.

Control Imperial vs. Metric Settings

Starting from scratch with either an imperial (`acad.dwt`) or metric (`acadiso.dwt`) template controls the files used for linetypes and hatch patterns. `ACAD.lin` and `ACAD.pat` are used for imperial, and `ACADISO.lin` and `ACADISO.pat` are used for metric. You can change this using the MEASUREMENT variable. The imperial setting is 0; the metric setting is 1.

Changing this doesn't change the limits or the default dimstyle after the fact. When you're plotting a metric drawing, change the drawing area to Metric in the Plot dialog box if you are using a release prior to AutoCAD 2005. AutoCAD 2005 made a change in the plotting process: When you plot a drawing starting with the metric template (or when you've changed the setting for Measurement to 1), and you select a paper size measured in inches, the plot scale is automatically set to 1:25.4. If you get odd results when plotting, check this value.

Learn to Use QSELECT

QSELECT is *very* useful when you're trying to fix a problem drawing. I once received a DXF file from the engineer of our city hall. He had generated a large number of points using GPS equipment to map the location of sewers, drains, manhole covers, and so on. The problem he had was that all the points and all the text were placed on one layer. The text height was so large that the text overlapped and was unreadable. See Figure 1.3.

To fix the problem, I did the following:

1. I used QSELECT to select all the points and put them on their own layer, which I immediately locked to protect the valuable locations generated by the GPS software.

2. I used QSELECT to select all the text (height 294) and change its height to 5 so it would be manageable.

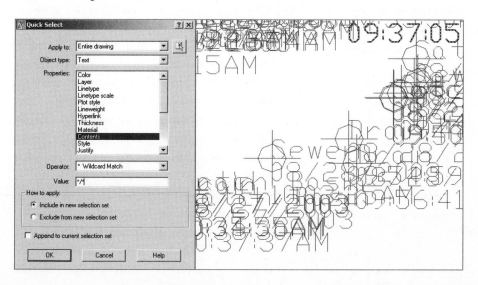

Figure 1.3

Using QSELECT

3. I used QSELECT to select all text containing a front slash (all the dates) and put them on their own layer. This required using the * wildcard match operator (nice to know some DOS). By placing */* in the Value window, you get all text containing a front slash anywhere in the string.

Create Tool Palettes to Enforce Standards

Using AutoCAD DesignCenter (ADC), you can create a tool palette that contains all the blocks from a symbol-library drawing with a single selection. Locate the drawing in the browser window of ADC, right-click it, and select Create Tool Palette, as shown in Figure 1.4.

Once you've created a tool palette, you can use it to enforce standards by setting the properties of any object on the palette, including the layer it's on (all tools), the scale (blocks and hatch patterns), and rotation angle (blocks and hatch patterns). To add a hatch pattern, use ADC to locate the file ACAD.pat or ACADISO.pat, and drag and drop a pattern to the palette.

Feature Review (All Releases)

One of the difficulties with an application as complex as AutoCAD is that everything seems to change with each release. It can get a little discouraging. Why learn the nuances of anything, when that knowledge may be worthless in 12 months? And if you do dig into a release and learn to use it productively, can you keep doing those things after the next release?

The fact is, many things about AutoCAD haven't changed over the years, including fundamentals like the underlying Cartesian coordinate system, the basic command structure, the way menus and toolbars work, the methods for creating and modifying most objects, and how files are saved. This section reviews the functionality that has been fairly constant in AutoCAD across many releases and is likely to stay that way. No matter how much things change, you'll still be able to save a specific screen display using the VIEW command; in fact, that command gets more and more useful with the development of sheet sets. There can be a big difference in drawing efficiency between one user and another that has nothing to do with new features.

Earlier in this chapter, I discussed some rules and standards for using a CAD system. Here I'll point out general AutoCAD features, big and small, that a lot of users have missed. They aren't secrets; they just seem that way if you don't know about them. And because they aren't new features, they don't show up in the New Features Workshop as spiffy and new. I think of these elements as spiffy and old. I don't care what release of AutoCAD you use, there's something here for you.

Figure 1.4

Creating a tool palette from a symbol drawing

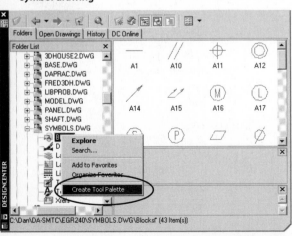

Drawing Efficiency

At the heart of a CAD system is the ability to create accurate geometry. Speed is always secondary to accuracy, but it's possible for one user to be much more efficient than another in creating geometry while still maintaining accuracy. That efficiency isn't merely the result of being fast with a mouse and keyboard—it's the result of planning strategies for approaching each new object to be drawn. And, of course, you must be able to get information from the drawing to check the accuracy.

The following suggestions may improve your speed and accuracy in drawing and improve your ability to get information from a drawing quickly.

COMMAND-LINE VERSIONS OF COMMANDS

One technique for becoming more efficient with AutoCAD is to type aliases and commands at the keyboard. If you can't type, you may be out of luck; but when I watch keyboard jockeys use AutoCAD, I see countless places where they save a few seconds here, a couple of seconds there, and pretty soon it adds up to real time. But what happens if the command brings up a dialog box? You have to wait for the dialog to display, grab your mouse, make some picks, click OK, and get back to work.

It may be faster if you don't have to deal with a dialog box, and many AutoCAD commands have both a dialog-based version and a command-line version. When they do, you can issue the command-line version by placing a minus sign in front of the command name or its alias: for example, -AR or -ARRAY. This behavior is in AutoCAD to protect legacy applications written by users of past releases, but you may find it more efficient than toolbars, tool palettes, or pull-down menus.

Knowing how to bring up a command-line version of a command is a godsend when you write AutoLISP programs. You can check the sequence for creating layers, for example, by typing **–LA** or **–LAYER** to avoid the dialog box and see the prompts.

Speaking of the LAYER command, let me use it as one example of efficiency. When I need a new layer—say, one named newlayer—for something I'm about to draw, I almost always type something like this: **–la↵m↵newlayer↵**. I just timed it: It took me six seconds. Newlayer is now the current layer, and I'm drawing away. I did the same thing using the Layer Properties Manager dialog box, and it took me 16 seconds. You may see that as saving only 10 seconds. I see that as a 267 percent improvement in my efficiency.

This technique doesn't suppress all dialog-based commands. If you want the command-line version of the SAVE command, for example, you need to first set the variable FILEDIA to 0. Then, typing **SAVE** (no minus sign needed) won't display a dialog box, but will give you save options at the command prompt.

Rectangular Arrays

When you're creating a rectangular array, it's easier than you think to confuse columns and rows when you're asked to specify their distance. Columns are vertical, and the icon illustrates that in the dialog box. Keep in mind that the distance between rows and columns is the distance from a point on one item to the *same* point on the next item.

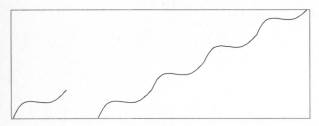

A rectangular array can be created at any angle by selecting the Angle Of Array option in the Array dialog box, even if you don't know the angle. Suppose you want to array the shape on the left in Figure 1.5 to form the shape on the right.

In the example, both the angle and the size of the object are randomly assigned. In other words, you

Figure 1.5

Precision array at an angle

don't know the exact size or angle, and you can't estimate because you want the result to have no gaps or overlaps of the objects as they're arrayed. You can approach this situation using two methods, one of which works with either the command-line version or the dialog-box version of ARRAY.

DIALOG BOX ARRAY

To create the shape in Figure 1.5, follow these steps:

1. Run the ARRAY command, pick the Select Objects button, and select the spline object.

2. Enter **1** for the number of columns and **4** for the number of rows.

3. Pick the Angle Of Array button shown in Figure 1.6; The dialog box will close temporarily to allow you to select two points in response to the prompt `Specify angle of array`.

4. Using the Endpoint object snap, select each end of the spline. Doing so returns an angle and places that value in the window.

Figure 1.6

Array dialog box

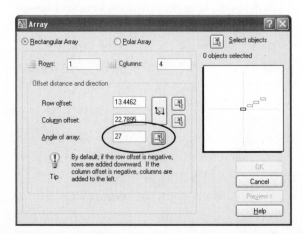

DISPLAY PRECISION

Don't be fooled by the integer of 27 shown for the angle in Figure 1.6. The actual angle may be different. Why? Because the default precision for angle display is 0, which means all angles are rounded to a whole number for display purposes only. If you change the angular precision using either the variable AUPREC or the Units dialog box, you'll see the angle in this case is actually 27.37591770°. This often fools people when linear distances are displayed, as well. (Linear precision can be set with the LUPREC variable or the Units dialog box.) Display

This doesn't affect the actual precision AutoCAD uses for calculations. All calculations are done to 15 decimal places no matter how the results are displayed.

5. Pick either the Column Offset or Unit Distance button, which results in the prompt `Specify distance between columns`.

6. Using the Endpoint object snap, select each end of the spline once again. Doing so returns a *distance* this time and places that value in the window. Click the Preview button; if you like the results, you're done.

COMMAND-LINE VERSION OF ARRAY

You may decide to automate a process like this using AutoLISP. In that case, you need to follow these steps, using the command-line version of the ARRAY command:

1. Run the UCS command, and type **Z⏎** to rotate a UCS around the Z axis. You may have noticed that Z isn't displayed as an option. It's a hidden option of UCS.

2. Select the two endpoints of the object, in this case a spline, to indicate the angle of rotation.

Any time you're prompted for a distance or an angle in AutoCAD, you can select points on the screen instead of typing them in. Doing so is both fast and accurate. When you start creating your own commands in AutoLISP, you can use specific functions to make your programs behave the same way.

3. Run the ARRAY command at the command prompt (**-AR**), and select the spline you want to array at an angle.

4. Press the Enter key at the `Enter the type of array [Rectangular/Polar] <R>` prompt.

5. Specify one row and four columns, and you'll be prompted to give the distance only between columns.

6. Select the two endpoints of the spline again to give the exact distance.

7. Use the UCS command to return to the World Coordinate System (WCS).

Because WCS is the default, you can type **UCS** and press the Enter key twice—once to execute the command, and once to accept the default.

Polar Arrays

Geometry with a repeated angular pattern is often found in mechanical applications and sometimes in architectural and civil applications. To create polar arrays efficiently, avoid repeating the same set of editing operations for each feature arrayed. Start by identifying a *repeatable pattern* on the object. Draw the whole pattern once, and then array the result, rather than arraying each of the components of the pattern separately. Be careful. It's easy to select an extra entity when you use the Polar option of ARRAY. The result looks fine, but you have entities on top of each other. The image in Figure 1.7 illustrates an efficient technique for using polar arrays by identifying and creating the *repeatable* pattern *before* arraying anything. The repeatable pattern is shown on the left, and the result of doing a single array of that pattern is on the right. The alternative involves multiple construction lines and six times more editing for each feature.

PEDIT

After using ARRAY to create geometry from lines and arcs, you can determine whether the result is perfect using the PEDIT command. If you use PEDIT to join lines into a closed object, they can only be joined if they connect perfectly at all intersections. Your geometry is perfect if the first option of PEDIT, Close, changes to Open after you've joined all your lines. If the geometry isn't perfect (and sometimes that can't be helped), you can still join the segments into a single object using the MPEDIT command.

_____
Figure 1.7

**Arraying the
repeatable pattern**

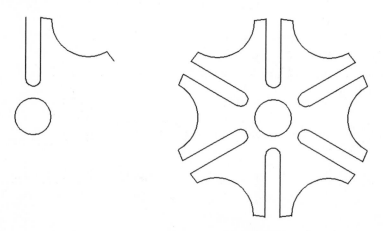

REDUCE CONSTRUCTION LINES

Try to use as few construction lines as possible when creating geometry. The more lines you use to locate points or edges, the more chances that you may confuse one or more for actual lines, or leave lines behind that are on top of each other. I've seen this lead to subtle, but often important, errors.

The often-related problem of lines on top of lines may seem like no big deal, because everything plots fine; but if you have a short line segment on top of a longer one, it's possible to snap to the wrong endpoint or midpoint without noticing it and create inaccurate geometry. The OVERKILL Express Tool can help fix this problem.

MPEDIT was once an Express Tool. It allows you to set a fuzz factor for combining lines, arcs, or plines into a single object. To use it, run MPEDIT, and then select all the objects you want to join. You're prompted for a fuzz factor. Enter a number that is greater than your likely error, and MPEDIT cleans up the mess. (I hope you're working on someone else's mess, because you should be able to avoid sloppy drawing if you use the accuracy tools available in AutoCAD.)

There are also some alternatives to PEDIT for finding areas, even if your closed geometry has overlapping lines. Using the BOUNDARY command, you can select a point and have a closed pline or a region created automatically. This works great for interior spaces, but you can use this command even in situations that are less obvious. For example, when you have overlapping construction lines and want to create a clean set of double lines (a floor plan, for example), use the technique shown in Figure 1.8: Enclose the entire group of lines with a circle, and select a point inside the circle but outside the lines.

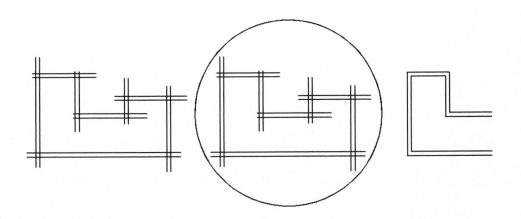

Figure 1.8

Using BOUNDARY for quick shapes

ALTERNATIVE TO PEDIT

You can create regions with the BOUNDARY command or with the REGION command. Either way, you can also use regions to create complex objects quickly by using the SUBTRACT, INTERSECT, and UNION commands. The shape shown in Figure 1.9 was created in under one minute (actually, 38 seconds).

To create regions from existing closed plines or circles, use the REGION command and select the objects. You can create a new object using SUBTRACT, UNION, or INTERSECT, and that object is also a region. If you need to work with individual lines or arcs, use the EXPLODE command to break the region into entities.

> If you have trouble understanding what a region is, think of it as a flat 3D object with a thickness of 0. The 3D Boolean editing commands will work with any region; the REGION command can be useful for other applications as well, including creating floating viewports in a layout.

Drawings with Interior Angles

For many drawings, you know the length of each line and the angles between lines. However, you probably don't know the absolute angle of each line in the X-Y plane (angle from 0°–East). There is a strategy for doing drawings of this kind; it involves recognizing that supplemental angles form a straight line (180°). It also involves using the often-overlooked Relative option of AutoCAD's polar tracking feature.

To set polar tracking to Relative, right-click the POLAR button at the bottom of the screen, and select Settings. Select the Relative To Last Segment radio button in the Polar Tracking tab of the Drafting Settings dialog box. Select the Track Using All Polar Angle Settings option as well, as shown in Figure 1.10.

Figure 1.9
**New shapes
from regions**

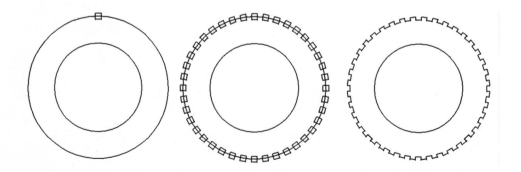

Note that in this case, Increment Angle is set to one (1). This is a small angle, and it isn't easy to work with, but it can be used. If the angles you're using are based on larger increments, use them. It's much easier to use an angle increment of 5, 15, or 45; but *any* increment can be typed into the window, including values so small they are completely unusable as angles. That's one of the things I love about AutoCAD. It doesn't restrict what you can do by overprotecting you from the results of commands.

In Figure 1.11, supplemental angles are determined from the interior angles and used to calculate the resulting relative angle of the next line segment. As you draw, use the readout from polar tracking to determine the relative angle for the next segment. Sometimes it will be reported to you as 299 instead of 61, for example, because it's increasing in the clockwise direction rather than the default counterclockwise direction.

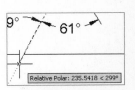

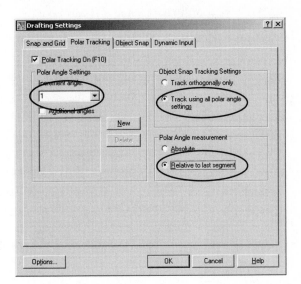

Figure 1.10

Polar tracking settings

Figure 1.11

Supplemental angles with relative tracking

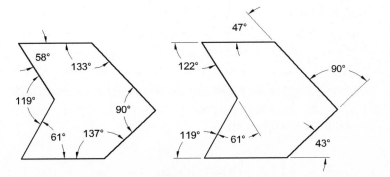

You can change the default direction of angles from counterclockwise to clockwise to do this kind of drawing when it's easier to draw clockwise. But if you change the angular direction from counterclockwise to clockwise to simplify drawing a single shape, make sure you change it back to avoid confusion later.

Use From, Auto Tracking, or @ to Begin Drawing

If you know that you need to start drawing an object a specific distance from an existing object, use the From osnap and the @ symbol. For example, if you want to start a rectangle 10 units over and 45 units up from an existing endpoint, do the following:

1. Start the RECTANG command.

2. Use the From osnap.

3. Select the starting point.

4. Type the coordinates for the first corner of the rectangle as **@10,45**.

Figure 1.12

Hover over an osnap to acquire a point

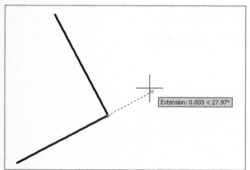

If you have POLAR, OSNAP, and OTRACK on, and the Extension osnap is set as a running osnap, you can pause over any running osnap, acquire a temporary tracking vector, and use it with direct-distance entry to quickly draw an object relative to another object. See Figure 1.12.

Even better, play with the Temporary Track Point osnap until you understand how to use it, because it allows you to chase points all over the screen by typing **TT** prior to acquiring a tracking point. The new tracking point is temporary until you actually select it. I use TT a lot, and if you haven't figured it out, it's worth trying.

The @ symbol can be used by itself to select the last point you entered.

Using CIRCLE and FILLET to Create Tangent Arcs

Another common shape involves tangent arcs. The quickest way to create an *inside* (concave) arc between two circles is to use the FILLET command with the proper radius set. However, an *outside* (convex) arc can't be drawn between two circles or arcs using FILLET. You must use the CIRCLE command with the TTR option and trim out the unwanted portion of the circle. The location of your cursor on the circles when you select tangent points determines whether a concave or a convex arc result. (See the Deferred Tangent tooltip in Figure 1.13.)

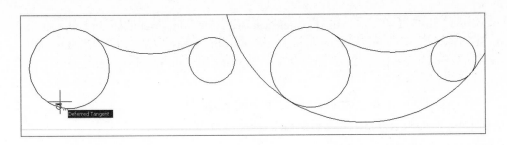

Figure 1.13
**Circle TTR for
tangent arcs**

One overlooked feature of the FILLET command is its ability to quickly close two par-allel lines with a tangent arc. Select both lines, and AutoCAD will calculate the size of an arc that it will use to join them on the end nearer your selection.

DTEXT

Most justification options are logical. Every line of text has four vertical locations for justi-fication: Top, Middle, Baseline, Bottom, in that order. The Bottom is a line running through the lowest point on a lowercase letter with a descender (j, g, p, y). These locations are shown in Figure 1.14. The Justify options of DTEXT are [Align/Fit/Center/Middle/Right/TL/TC/TR/ML/MC/MR/BL/BC/BR]. The two-letter combinations match the locations: TL is Top Left, ML is Middle Left, and so on.

Extracting Information from Drawings

You can use geometry created in AutoCAD to get information accurate to 15 decimal places. However, the information you get out of AutoCAD is only as good as the accuracy of the geometry you create. Following are some tips on using inquiry commands.

AREA

It's easier to work with circle, pline, or region entities when determining areas, particularly if you're trying to add or subtract areas to get a final total. This section will give you some advice about using other entities to create plines or regions so you can easily find their areas.

Figure 1.14
**Understanding
DTEXT justification
options**

PEDIT

You can use the PEDIT command to create a closed pline from several line and arc segments. To do so, issue the command, pick one of the lines, answer Yes when asked if you want to turn it into a pline, select the JOIN option, and pick the other segments with a window. Remember:

- All segments must be touching but not overlapping.
- You can't have segments on top of each other.
- The resulting pline should be closed.
- Use the Fuzz option of MPEDIT if your geometry isn't exact.

The variable PEDITACCEPT was added to AutoCAD 2005. If it's set to 1, the user isn't prompted with the question `Object selected is not a polyline. Do you want to turn it into one? <Y>`. Instead, the object is automatically turned into a pline. It's possible that 1 will become the default setting in a future release.

ENTITY SELECTION

When you use the AREA command, it's easier to select objects than it is to pick points. To find the area of a large object minus the areas of several smaller objects, you can use the Add and Subtract options of the AREA command. Pay attention to the command prompts. Type **AREA**↵**A**↵ followed by **O**↵, select the largest entities, and then right-click when you finish; doing so adds the areas of all the objects you picked. Type **S**↵ to select the Subtract option, followed by **O**↵ for Object, and select each object whose areas you want to subtract.

The alias for the AREA command is AA, which doesn't follow the normal pattern used for other commands. Why not? A (ARC) and AR (ARRAY) are already taken. RENDER (RR) is the only other alias with this format.

QUICK AREA CALCULATION FOR COMPLEX FEATURES

It's not unusual to want to find the area of an object with a large number of features removed. It's easy to miss one or more objects in the process. The quickest way to get a total area when you have many areas to subtract is to create regions. If all the objects are circles or closed plines, you can do this with the REGION command. If the shapes are composed of anything else—lines, arcs, overlapping segments—use the BOUNDARY command. Once all the shapes are regions, use the SUBTRACT command to create a single region. Then you can select a single entity when using the Object option of the AREA command.

In Figure 1.15, it took 25 seconds to get the total area of the object with all internal shapes removed. Here are the steps:

1. Create regions from the existing geometry using the BOUNDARY command.

2. Use the SUBTRACT command to remove the holes from the large object by selecting them all with a window.

3. Use the Object option of the AREA command, and select the resulting region. You can also find the area as a property of the region in the Properties palette.

DIST

The DIST command gives you an accurate distance if you use object snaps to pick the points. It's also the quickest way to get an angle in the X-Y plane. Pick the points in the proper order, or the angle will be off by 180°. To get the angle between two lines, use DIMANGULAR (DAN). The lines don't have to exist; you can select three points with DIMANGULAR and get the angle between the segments defined by the points.

PROPERTIES and LIST

Both these commands give you information that varies by entity selected, including the arc length of an arc. PROPERTIES can be used to change the properties of multiple objects as well as individual objects. For example, you can change the height of all text in the drawing without changing the locations.

One piece of information that you can get from the LIST command that you can't get from the Properties palette is an object's handle. This may seem meaningless to you now, but the handle can be useful because it's the unique identifier of an object and never changes.

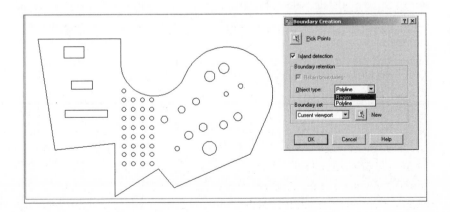

Figure 1.15

Using regions to calculate a complex area

TIME

TIME gives you the total time during which a drawing has been open for editing. You can also use it as a running timer by selecting the Reset option before beginning something new. Use this timer as you try to develop more drawing speed. Pick one object, and draw it several times using different strategies. The TIME command can tell you if you're getting any faster. I've also used the TIME function to see if one computer in an office really is slower than another, or if it's just the perception of a frustrated user. See Chapter 7, "AutoCAD Scripts" for a benchmark system to test computers with no user input.

The Save Options

You can save drawing files using any of the following commands: SAVE, QSAVE, SAVEAS, and WBLOCK. Each of these commands creates a DWG file in different ways, but each has its own advantages:

SAVEAS When you select Save As from the pull-down menu, or type **SAVEAS**, AutoCAD saves to a specified path with a specified name and makes the resulting path and filename the default. The next time you use a save command, including QSAVE (Ctrl-S), this name and location will be used.

SAVE The SAVE command, if it's issued by typing at the command prompt, allows you to save to a different location or name *without* redefining the default drawing. (The Save option on the pull-down actually calls the QSAVE command. I change this whenever I upgrade AutoCAD.) I wish all Windows software had this kind of save option.

QSAVE The QSAVE (quick save) command automatically saves to the default location and name. Ctrl-S issues the QSAVE command.

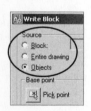

Figure 1.16

WBLOCK options for saving a DWG file

WBLOCK WBLOCK is a save command. It lets you save part of an existing drawing, using one of three methods. Select the option you want from the dialog box, as shown in Figure 1.16. Because dialog boxes can't be used in AutoLISP programs, you should know the command sequence for WBLOCK. When issued from the command line with FILEDIA turned off, the -WBLOCK command allows you to make the same selections. See Chapter 5, "Symbols, Tables, and Fields," for more information on the WBLOCK command.

Backup copies The best method for making backup copies to removable drives (CD, flash, DVD) as you're drawing is to type the SAVE command at the command line or use the Send To function of Windows. Otherwise, you redefine the default name and location. Right-click any filename in a windows file-management dialog box to select Send To. You can add a location by creating a shortcut and placing it in the folder C:\Documents and Settings\%username%\SendTo. Replace %username% with your login name. See Chapter 2, "Managing Your System," for automated backup techniques.

GROUP The GROUP command should be used more often, in my opinion. It allows you to name a selection set so that you can use it again. Once a group is created, you can type

G↵ at any selection prompt followed by the name of the group you created (make the names short and memorable). However, the group must be selectable. You can change whether a group is selectable using the Group dialog box.

PICKSTYLE The settings of the AutoCAD variable PICKSTYLE determine how other members of a group are treated, including associated hatch patterns, whenever any member of the group is selected. PICKSTYLE has four settings that you can toggle using the Ctrl-H keys (the Ctrl-A keys in AutoCAD 2000 and AutoCAD 2000i).

- PICKSTYLE = 0 allows selection of individual members of the group.
- PICKSTYLE = 1 allows the selection of the whole group but not boundaries.
- PICKSTYLE = 2 groups the selection of hatches with boundary objects.
- PICKSTYLE = 3 allows the selection of whole groups and group selection of associated hatches with their boundaries.

> If you find that a hatch boundary is erased when you erase the hatch, check your PICKSTYLE setting. It's probably set to 3.

Edit Commands

One of the most underused editing functions in AutoCAD is the Properties palette. Some editing functions can be used in ways they weren't necessarily designed for, and there are other options that a surprising number of people overlook—most notably the Through option of the OFFSET command and the Reference option of the SCALE and ROTATE commands.

PROPERTIES

This command displays the Properties palette of selected entities. If more than one object is selected, the properties common to all are displayed. Properties of similar objects can be changed simultaneously.

Using the Quick Select button, you can filter out objects based on multiple criteria by applying each criterion once and then selecting the current selection set for the next application. This is a great way to clean up problem drawings that you get from someone else. You can change the layer of all text, for example, or the style used for all text with a height less than 3. This is a powerful function that you should absolutely understand how to use.

Let's walk through an example. Let's say you have a drawing that has a lot of text. Every text entity must stay in its current location, but the height must change for all. At one time, that was a difficult problem, but not any more. Open the Properties palette, and click the Quick Select icon (the button with the funnel icon in the upper-right corner). Select text in the window, and all the text entities are highlighted (but not the MText entities). Now, change the text height in the Properties palette; the height of all the text changes. You can change any of the properties of the entire group. You could do the same for all the circles in a drawing or within a selection set, and change their diameters.

CHAMFER and FILLET

You can use either of these commands to clean up sharp corners or extend two unconnected lines into sharp corners by setting their values to 0. As of AutoCAD 2006, you have the following option: Hold down the Shift key while selecting the second line to create a sharp corner.

If you're having trouble snapping to what you think is an intersection between two lines, use FILLLET with a radius of 0, select the two lines, and then try again. If that works, you don't have to take the time to zoom into the intersection to see if there's a gap.

> You can quickly create a slot by selecting two parallel lines when prompted by the FILLET command.

DIVIDE and MEASURE

These commands behave similarly. The difference is that DIVIDE results in an entity divided into a specified number of segments, all the same length. MEASURE divides the entity into segments of a given length, with one shorter segment (usually) at the end. Entities aren't actually segmented; instead, a point is placed at each division.

> The appearance of all the points in a drawing (except those on the Defpoints layer) is controlled by the variable PDMODE. You can set this variable using the Point Style dialog box.

It's also possible with either DIVIDE or MEASURE to have a block inserted at each division instead of a point, which is a useful and often overlooked feature. You can quickly approximate a complex linetype, for example, by placing any block along a line, pline, or spline object. This works well for placing arrows on an egress map (see Figure 1.17).

Figure 1.17

Using MEASURE to place blocks

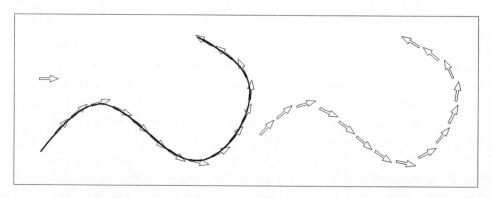

EXPLODE

You can use EXPLODE with the following entities: blocks, hatches, mlines, plines, solid objects, and blocks of text created with the MTEXT command. Any blocks can be exploded except those placed using the MINSERT command. For that reason, MINSERT should not be used unless you want a block that can't be exploded. When you use EXPLODE, be careful not to select more objects than you want.

> The TXTEXP Express Tool can explode individual pieces of text into vectors. The results aren't always pretty, but I've used this technique successfully to create cutting-tool paths for CNC machines used to mill letters in either metal or wood. The results differ between SHX fonts and TTF fonts. Shape fonts, which are vector-based, are exploded into line segments, whereas TrueType fonts are exploded into closed polylines. Usually a single letter requires multiple closed polylines that can be edited into a single outline.

> You can form 3D block letters by using TXTEXP to explode a TrueType font and then using EXTRUDE to create 3D solids out of all the segments used for each letter. Use UNION to create a single solid.

OFFSET

This command has always had two options: Distance and Through. The Through option allows you to offset an object through a selected point, even if the object isn't long enough to actually pass through the point.

AutoCAD 2006 added some nice features to OFFSET. You can offset an object onto the current layer. You can also elect to erase the source object after using offset. That sounds like it would just become the MOVE command, which it would, except that a multiple option was also added that lets you continue picking through points or offsetting the same distance multiple times.

OOPS

People use UNDO sometimes when they really should use the OOPS command. OOPS can be used at any time to restore all the entities erased as a single selection set the last time the ERASE command was used. It doesn't have to be issued immediately after the entities are erased. More often than I should, I erase objects that are in the way of a delicate editing operation, and then I use OOPS to get them back after I'm done editing. I don't recommend this approach, but I do it.

> OOPS restores objects even if their layer is currently frozen or turned off.

ROTATE

The remarkably useful and often overlooked option of ROTATE is Reference. You can use the Reference option by entering any angle at the keyboard or by picking two points on the screen. You then type the angle to which you want the selected points to align.

Instead of typing the new angle, you can also make one more selection. It becomes the second point on a new angle, using the first point selected as a reference for a base point.

SCALE

SCALE also has a Reference option that's similar to ROTATE's but that may be even more useful. I use it frequently to resize an image using a feature on the image that I know the size of—this can be a photograph of landscape, nautical charts, a mechanical part, or anything else that's not to scale when inserted. In the example in Figure 1.18, a National Oceanic and Atmospheric Administration (NOAA) nautical chart has been referenced as an image. Scaling it using the Reference options involves the following steps:

1. Issue the SCALE command.

2. Select the edge of the image.

3. Give a base point.

4. Type **R** or use the down arrows to select Reference, as shown.

5. Select a start point. In this example, the latitude line showing 17′ is the first point.

6. Select a second point. In this example, the latitude line showing 18′ is the second point.

7. Type **1** for one nautical mile, the base unit of this drawing. Because the distance from 17′ to 18′ is one minute of latitude, which represents one nautical mile on the earth, the image scales correctly.

Figure 1.18

Using the Reference option of the SCALE command

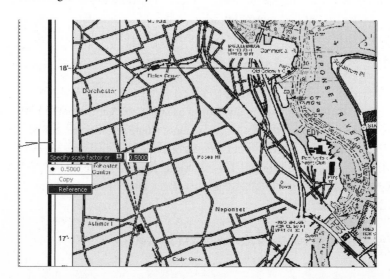

UNDO

The UNDO command displays the following options at the command prompt:

Auto/Control/Begin/End/Mark/Back<Number>:

Auto Auto requires an additional specification of On or Off. When Auto is on, any operation taken from the menu, no matter how complicated, is treated as a single command, reversible by a single U command.

Back Back takes the drawing back to the state it was in when the most recent mark was entered. If you don't enter a mark, the drawing goes back to the beginning of the editing session. AutoCAD automatically places marks when some commands are used, but normally you must place them yourself. You can place multiple marks and UNDO each.

Control Control limits the UNDO operation or disables it completely. It offers the following options:

- All enables the full UNDO feature.
- None disables U and UNDO commands.
- One limits U and UNDO to a single operation.

BEgin and End BEgin and End cause a group of commands to be treated as a single command for the purposes of U and UNDO. A group, once ended, is always treated as a single, indivisible operation.

> This is useful when you're writing an AutoLISP program. Place an UNDO BEgin at the beginning of the program and an UNDO End at the end. If the user doesn't like what the program did, it only takes one U to undo it. Otherwise, a separate UNDO is required for each step executed by the AutoLISP program.

Mark Mark makes a special mark in the undo information, to which you can later back up with the Back option. If you're about to go off on a design tangent, you may want to set a mark with UNDO so you can return to that point quickly if the tangent doesn't work out.

Number Number (default is 1) specifies the number of preceding operations to be undone. UNDO 1 is the equivalent of the U command. When you use a different value, 20 for example, 20 operations are undone at once. Typing REDO restores all 20. Using this option allows you to search back through the drawing history (only during the current editing session) for a specific point in the design process by typing in large values. Don't forget to save the drawing before doing this.

> You can click the down arrow next to the Undo button to see a command history and select the command you want to go back to. The Redo button has a similar command history.

LENGTHEN

This interesting command can be used to change the length of a line, polyline, or an arc. It's the only way to quickly create an arc with a specific arc length. To do that, create the arc, and use the Total option of LENGTHEN to change the total length to whatever you want.

LENGTHEN's options include the following:

DElta DElta allows you to add a specific amount to the length of an existing line or arc, or to add a specific angle to the existing included angle of an arc.

Percent Percent allows a specific percentage increase in the length of a line or pline or the included angle of an arc.

Total Total lets you set a new overall length for a line, a pline, or an arc.

DYnamic DYnamic allows you to change the length of a line (but not a pline) or the included angle of an arc by picking a new point and watching it change.

<Select object> <Select object> gives the existing length or angle of a line or arc.

Dimensions

Dimension styles are discussed at length in Chapter 4 because they're critical to applying technical graphics standards correctly. Here I want to point out some aspects of the process of dimensioning that people often get wrong, starting with a difference that almost nobody seems to understand: aligned versus rotated dimensions

Aligned vs. Rotated

In my experience, most users don't understand rotated dimensions. All linear dimensions are either aligned or rotated, but most are rotated. Vertical dimensions are rotated to 90, horizontal dimensions to 0. Because those angles are built in, users often overlook the possibility of rotating dimensions to other angles and frequently attempt to use an aligned dimension where a rotated one is needed. Figure 1.19 shows the problem with trying to use DIMALIGN.

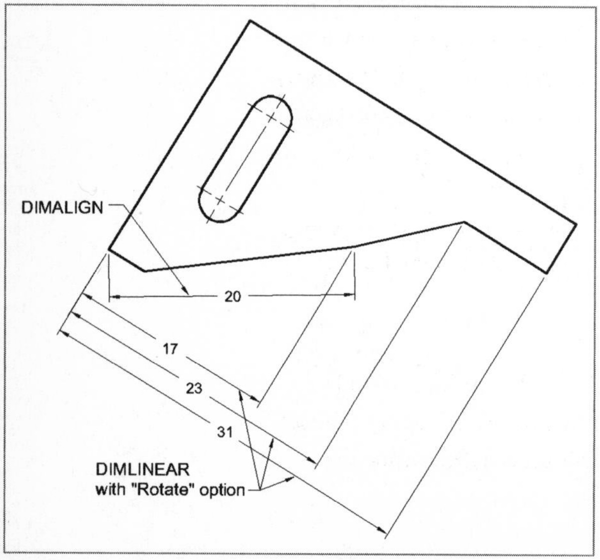

To place a rotated linear dimension between two points at any angle, use DIMLINEAR and select the Rotated option. You can specify a rotation angle directly or by picking any two points that are at the desired angle of rotation.

Figure 1.19
Rotated dimensions versus aligned

ORDINATE

Ordinate dimensions are used to set dimensions as coordinates in the X and Y axes. Ordinate dimensioning is used most often in mechanical drawing, but it's increasingly being used in architectural and other fields as well. When I draw a structure that I'll be building myself, I always dimension it with ordinate dimensions rather than with continuous dimensions, which is the traditional method. That way, I can hook a tape to one end of a sole or top plate and mark all locations of openings from a fixed point.

Although there's a DIMORD command, the quickest way to place ordinate dimensions is with QDIM. Select the points you wish to dimension, and then select a new datumPoint for 0,0. Now you can choose the Ordinate option, select your objects, and place all ordinate dimensions with one pick. If you have objects with different base points, use the datumPoint option again.

> To facilitate the use of ordinate dimensions, you can place points using the POINT command at every location you wish to use as an origin. Using either the FILTER or QSELECT command, you can now select only points. Doing so prevents you from inadvertently selecting too many objects.

If you don't use QDIM, you must first establish a new base point by setting a UCS with its origin at the 0,0 location on the part you're dimensioning. Use the UCS command, select the Origin option, and then select the 0,0 point on the part. If UCSICON is ON and set to ORigin, the icon representing the UCS moves to the new origin point. AutoCAD automatically places the correct distance in the X or Y direction, depending on which direction you move from the dimension origin point you pick.

These dimension values are associated with defpoints, *not* the objects themselves, if DIMASSOC is 1 or 2. This association is maintained for the UCS that was current when the dimension was placed. Stretching the defpoints of the dimensions results in the values being updated correctly, even if a new UCS has been set since the dimension was created.

Dimension Variables

AutoCAD 2007 includes 79 dimension variables. The easiest way to change them is using the Dimension Style Manager dialog box. You don't have to know all of them, but there are two you should understand.

DIMASSOC

This variable was added to AutoCAD 2002 to control associative dimensions. It replaces DIMASO, but not completely, because earlier drawings can be opened in current releases. When an earlier drawing is opened, the setting for DIMASO is used to determine the value of DIMASSOC.

DIMASSOC has three settings:

- *0*—Dimensions are exploded as they're placed, which is a bad idea unless you have a very good reason.
- *1*—Dimensions have the traditional defpoint association, but they're not associated with objects and aren't connected to Model Space when a dimension is placed in Paper Space.
- *2*—Dimensions move with objects and reflect true size when placed in Paper Space.

DIMSCALE

This variable controls all size dimension variables, such as DIMTXT, DIMASZ, DIMEXE, DIMEXO, DIMTVP, DIMTSZ, and DIMGAP. In the past, for Model Space plotting, DIMSCALE was set to the reciprocal of the plot scale to be used. If plotting will reduce a drawing 48 times to fit on a sheet of paper, you must first increase the size of the dimensions 48 times so they'll be readable. DIMSCALE is set to 1 if dimensions are placed in Paper Space (which I don't recommend).

The system that I do recommend is to place dimensions in Model Space and to plot from Paper Space. For that purpose, setting a DIMSCALE of 0 before dimensioning allows you to add dimensions in viewports with different zoom magnifications and have them all come out the same size. Select Scale Dimensions To Layout in the Dimension Style Manager dialog box on the Fit tab. See Chapter 6 for detailed information on plotting.

> Many offices still use the once-standard practice of setting DIMSCALE to a value that reflects the reciprocal of the plot scale. This is a legacy of the old days of AutoCAD when such practice was required. If you choose to change this practice, you should do so in the context of a complete overhaul of office standards. Such an overhaul should, of course, include all affected parties.

Settings Commands

This section discusses some of the system variables (the setvars) in AutoCAD, but certainly not all of them. What follows are the settings that people sometimes overlook or that I have specific recommendations about.

System variables control the appearance or behavior of AutoCAD. You normally set these by making a selection in an appropriate dialog box, but they can also be set from the command line. Old-time users probably do this a lot by typing the variable name quickly. If I want to change my linear unit precision to check something, I type **LUPREC** and then type **8**. When I have the information I want, I undo that action or type **LUPREC** again.

Not everyone can touch-type; however, I appreciate being able to. (This may be a good time to thank my mother for insisting that I take high school typing in 1967—an era when the manual typewriters used in classrooms had blank keys so you wouldn't hunt and peck.)

The OPTIONS command (see Chapter 2, "Managing Your System") allows you to set all drawing aids, file search paths, the appearance of the screen, and the variables affecting saving and opening drawings, and also lets you save these settings in a user profile. The profiles can be exported for use on other computers.

> There has been pressure over the years to eliminate the AutoCAD command line because it's seen by some people as outdated. I've always found this suggestion alarming, because a keyboard jockey can be much faster and more efficient than a toolbar user with comparable skills. For us keyboard users, Autodesk's decision to make the command line one more optional aspect of the interface was a welcome response to this pressure.

APERTURE

The APERTURE variable allows you to control how close you must be to an object, measured in pixels, when using an osnap. It can also be set using the Drafting tab of the OPTIONS dialog box. If you're having trouble isolating an object in a cluttered area, try setting this value to a smaller size—I prefer a setting of 3. If you're having trouble picking an object because you have to get too close to it, try a larger size.

PICKBOX is similar, but it controls the size of the box that shows up when you're asked to select an object for editing. You can also control it visually using the Drafting tab of the OPTIONS dialog box. I like a setting of 3 for this one, as well.

LTSCALE

In the past, it was common to set this variable to the reciprocal of the intended plot scale. If you use layouts properly, however, you shouldn't use LTSCALE to control the appearance of linetypes, because it's global and affects all lines in a drawing. Instead, set LTSCALE, CELTSCALE, and PSLTSCALE all to 1 and ignore the appearance of your linetypes until you set up a layout. With PSLTSCALE set to 1, your linetypes scale automatically in Paper Space, so they plot the same regardless of the ZOOM factor used for the viewport in which they appear.

> Some people don't like drawing in the Model Space tab unless their linetypes display correctly. I don't think it should matter. If you put entities representing each linetype on a different layer and use different colors for those layers, you can easily identify the type of line it represents without seeing the segments. Once you have a layout, everything will look great.

If some of your entities have linetypes that aren't scaled to your liking, instead of changing that with LTSCALE, use PROPERTIES to make changes to each individual object in a viewport in the layout.

Linetype problems are often the result of confusion between metric and imperial units. If you need an LTSCALE of 25 or so to see linetypes properly in a layout, you've probably started your drawing in imperial units but are drawing objects measured in millimeters. If you need a small setting, say .04, then it's likely that you have the opposite problem: You started a drawing in metric units but are drawing in inches. See the earlier section "Control Imperial vs. Metric Units."

Layers

A number of things about layers can give you problems. Here are a few of them:

- Locking allows you to lock a layer so that it's visible but not changeable. You can still use osnaps on the visible entities. Most users would benefit from using layer locking more often to avoid inadvertent changes to their drawings.

People sometimes confuse layer locking with viewport locking in a layout. They do different things and aren't related. Locking a layer doesn't affect the display of objects in any way. Locking a viewport doesn't prevent you from changing objects in that viewport.

- Layer filters, and freezing layers by viewport (VPLAYER) are useful advanced commands in the Layer Properties Manager dialog box.

- You can change layer names in the Layer Properties Manager dialog box; but the RENAME command is faster when you're changing names of layers from a bound XRef, because you can use wildcards. Layer 0 is the only layer you can't rename.

- Plot/No Plot settings can be made for layers, so there's no longer a need to use the Defpoints layer for that purpose. Don't make Defpoints the active layer, because any objects you add to it won't plot.

I've seen two cases of odd behavior with objects placed on the Defpoints layer: One user was unable to select a viewport even though it was visible, and another placed points on that layer but couldn't change their appearance. In the viewport case, freezing layer 0 created the problem. And points can't be displayed as anything other than a single pixel on the Defpoints layer. The only reason to place objects on the Defpoints layer is the security of knowing that no one will accidentally plot them.

- Lineweight should be set to BYLAYER. A default value of .20mm and an object-line value of .40mm usually give a good lineweight distinction.
- A button on the Layers toolbar makes the layer of a selected object current.
- A button on the Layers toolbar restores the previous layer state.

Display Commands

I'm sure you frequently use the All, Extents, and Window options of the ZOOM command, but have you ever saved the results with a name so you can return to it quickly? If you have to connect two small features that are widely separated, have you ever used VPORTS to place two views in the Model Space tab and drawn from one to the other? Read on.

VIEW

It surprises me how few people use this feature. It allows you to save a specific view on the screen, or as defined by a window, so that you can immediately call it up later. This approach reduces the number of regenerations necessary. It's particularly useful in 3D drawings, and some people use this feature for plotting a specific view. If you haven't ever tried saving named views, try it. You'll be surprised at how useful it can be, particularly when using AutoCAD sheet sets.

VPORTS

This function is essential in 3D drawing and often useful in 2D drawing as well. It allows you to divide your screen in Model Space into multiple views. In 3D, this permits you to create geometry while seeing it in a front, top, right side, and iso view. You can then have a different UCS in each viewport and get a different view of the same geometry.

To create a set of standard views for 3D, select the 3D option in the Viewports dialog box. Don't forget to use the SAVE option to save a configuration you've set up. Don't confuse saving viewports with saving views. You can restore saved views within any Model Space viewport and then save the viewport configuration. Now, whenever the viewport configuration is restored, it will contain the views exactly as they appeared when the viewport was saved.

The Middle Scroll Wheel

Roll the middle wheel away from you to zoom in or toward you to zoom out. The increment is controlled by the variable ZOOMFACTOR—the larger the value, the bigger the jump when using the wheel. If you hold down the scroll wheel, you can pan. If you hold down the wheel while holding the Ctrl key, you get a joystick pan—not that useful, but kind of fun.

Because holding down the middle wheel allows panning in all directions, the Windows scrollbars aren't useful and often get in the way. Turn them off under the Display tab of the Options dialog box, and you'll get a 4 percent increase in screen area. If you paid $400 for your monitor, that's like getting $16 just for changing a setting!

VTENABLE (View Transition Enable)

AutoCAD 2006 added a view transition feature that smoothly changes magnification or location when zooming or panning. This replaced the abrupt transitions of prior releases. Some people love it, and some people don't. VTENABLE allows you to turn it off for everything, for panning only, for zooming only, for scripts only, or for some combination. The VTFTS and VTDURATION variables control the threshold and speed of the transition. Personally, I turn it off to speed things up a little.

Utilities

Utilities allow you to do things like rename files and purge unused layers. There are just a few things here, but one that could be a huge timesaver is the use of wildcards in the RENAME command, particularly when you bind an XRef.

PURGE

The PURGE command is used to selectively remove unused layers, blocks, styles, linetypes, and dimstyles. You can do this by name or using the Purge All option (ALL at the command line). If your drawing has nested block definitions (blocks used to create other blocks), you can select Purge Nested Items starting with AutoCAD 2002. In earlier releases, use the PURGE command as many times as there are levels of nesting in your block definitions in order to ensure that you're purging everything. The Purge dialog box also allows you to select individual entities individually or in groups. To select a consecutive list of entities, select the beginning item, hold down the Shift key, and select the last item in the group. The Ctrl key lets you add or remove items from the selection set. See Figure 1.20.

Many people still use the WBLOCK command as a quick and complete PURGE command. That requires you to use the Entire Drawing option in the dialog box for WBLOCK, or the * option at the command line.

RENAME

This is a great way to rename blocks, dimension styles, layers, linetypes, materials, table styles, text styles, UCSs, views, and viewports. You can use wildcards, allowing you to quickly change all names created when binding external references (if you used the Bind option for binding, which I recommend you do, and not the Insert option). For example, if you bind an externally referenced drawing named STP123.dwg to a host drawing, the block definitions have names like STP123$0$BLOCK1, STP123$0$BLOCK2, STP123$0$BLOCK3, STP123$0$BLOCK4, and STP123$0$BLOCK5. If you want them to have the names BLOCK1 and so on, type **STP123$0$*** in the Old Name field and * in the Rename To field, as shown in Figure 1.21.

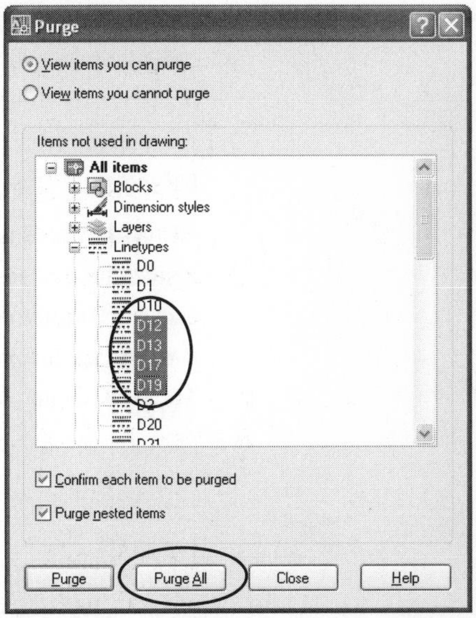

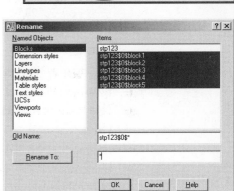

Figure 1.20

Purge All

Figure 1.21

Using wildcards when renaming objects

PARTIALOPEN

You can elect to open part of a drawing to reduce regeneration time on large drawings. Highlight a file and then select the Open button in the lower-right corner of the Select File dialog box that's used to open an existing drawing. The Partial Open dialog box that's displayed can be used to select only those layers or views with which you want to work. Once you've used PARTIALOPEN to open part of a drawing, you can use the PARTIALLOAD command (found on the File pull-down menu) to select different layers. There is a design flaw in PARTIALLOAD: You must reselect all layers each time you do a partial load. The layers you first selected aren't remembered. This issue wasn't addressed in AutoCAD 2007, but I'm hoping it will be fixed someday.

Express Tools

The Express Tools, which started as Bonus Tools, have always been popular with AutoCAD users. Many users haven't found them or haven't taken the time to understand them, or these tools aren't loaded on their workstation. Some afternoon when you have a little time, go to the Express pull-down menu and select Help. Now you can read about each tool and get inspired:

If you don't have the Express Tools loaded on your workstation, try typing the command **EXPRESSTOOLS** at the command line. They may show up. If they don't, the tools may not have been loaded by whoever installed AutoCAD. This is likely to be the case if you use Architectural Desktop (ADT) prior to Release 2007, because loading Express Tools isn't listed as an option during the install. You have to have the install CD, know where on the CD the Express Tools are stored (a folder named Express), and then load them manually. This is because CHSPACE will corrupt some pre–Release 2007 ADT objects.

CHSPACE

This command is indispensable, and it has finally evolved from an Express Tool into a native command in AutoCAD 2007. It lets you change objects between Paper Space and Model Space while retaining their relative scales. This makes it possible to place text or dimensions wherever it's convenient while working and then move them to their permanent home later. If you ever decide you placed something in the wrong space, you need this command.

LAYWALK This tool allows you to walk though the objects on various layers to give you a visual clue as to what you've placed where. It's valuable when you're dealing with someone else's disaster drawing. The objects on each layer are isolated temporarily while you cycle through the layers. Like CHSPACE, LAYWALK is now a native command in AutoCAD 2007.

TXT2MTXT TXT2MTXT is used to combine individual lines of text into a single MTEXT object. It doesn't format the final result as individual lines, so you almost always need to do some editing; but if you want to group text from older drawings into a single object, it's nice.

FLATTEN I've recommended this command to a lot of people in companies that do civil design. They call me because they're having trouble with a drawing from someone else. Object snapping to endpoints produces odd results because, it turns out, the elements aren't all at the same elevation. FLATTEN quickly and thoroughly places every object at an elevation of zero.

MKSHP and MKLTYPE These commands give you the ability to create complex linetypes: those containing text or shapes. This process requires that a shape be created first (MKSHP) and then the linetype (MKLTYPE).

LAYMERGE I often advise new users and companies to use as many layers as they *may* need so they'll have control over the related elements of a drawing. Sometimes this results in too many layers, which is always easier to fix than too few. When you do have too many layers, this command lets you put them together into one. This is another of the Express Tools that have become actual commands.

DIMEX and DIMIN These are related commands that allow you to export dimension styles and then import them into a different drawing. You can do this through AutoCAD DesignCenter or by inserting a drawing that contains the dimension style, but these Express Tools make it a little easier.

DIMREASSOC This is a nice tool. It permits you to individually or globally update dimensions that have been overridden by the operator. In other words, the value in the dimension and the actual size of the object don't match. My favorite application of this command is to find any dimensions that were overridden. I have overridden a dimension purposely on rare occasions when I had an imminent deadline and had to plot something out immediately. With DIMREASSOC, I can find those places and go back and fix the geometry.

You can also change the overwritten dimensions automatically, which may cause even more problems if you don't notice what got updated. The problem is that the value is probably overridden because the geometry is wrong.

SYSVDLG The System Variables editor is a wonderful tool. It gives you a concise list of each system variable, tells you where its value is stored, and describes what it does. The best thing is that you can save the settings to an SVF file and restore them if you ever have to. If you do any training using computers that aren't your own, take this file with you; it will reduce the number of surprises you may encounter.

OVERKILL This command gets rid of overlapping lines, line segments that connect in what appears to be a single object, and duplicate objects on top of other objects. It can clean up a mess of a drawing in a hurry; see Figure 1.22.

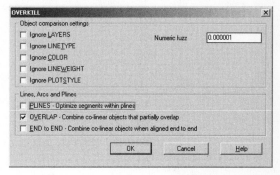

Figure 1.22

Overkill dialog box

> OVERKILL doesn't always work correctly. I've found that it works best if you use it for one kind of cleanup at a time (pline, overlaps, end-to-end) even though the dialog box allows you to check every type at once. Run it for each type separately to get the results you want.

CHAPTER 2

Managing Your System

I'm a teacher and trainer, and my experience with AutoCAD users tells me you should know some things about your computer system that affect how AutoCAD functions. I often find that even experienced AutoCAD users run into confusing situations when they try to use backup or Autosave files. That's why I'm focusing this chapter on managing the system you use to work with AutoCAD. In this chapter, I'll take you through the Options dialog box and discuss the relationship between profiles and workspaces.

I'll also take you on a brief trip into the past, with a discussion of how knowing some old-fashioned DOS can save you a huge amount of time. (If DOS is too antique for you, call it Windows Scripting Language.) I want to encourage you to preserve knowledge that's fast fading away; fewer and fewer AutoCAD users remember (if they ever knew) how powerful these functions are.

I'll conclude this chapter with a discussion of the ACAD.PGP file: a humble little thing that still has some utility and provides the only hook to certain operating system features from the AutoLISP processor.

- **Managing Files**
- **Managing AutoCAD**
- **Directories**
- **Why DOS Isn't Dead Yet**
- **External Commands**

Managing Files

AutoCAD uses many different file types. Two of them are useful to you because they're backups or automatically saved versions of your current drawing. When you're in a bind because you've lost a drawing, AutoCAD has stopped responding, the computer has crashed, or you tried to open a corrupted file, you should know how to use the backup files and the Autosave files that AutoCAD creates. It's not as obvious as you may hope.

Backup Files

When you save a drawing, any existing file of the same name is renamed by changing the .dwg extension to .bak before your drawing is saved. It's in the same folder as your .dwg file. To use a backup file, change the extension to .dwg, and open the file. If that results in a file with the same name as another file, you must also change the filename. Although some data may be missing, it's better than nothing. By the way, it's possible to turn off the backup feature in OPTIONS; doing so saves hard disk space at some risk of data loss.

Autosave Files

AutoCAD automatically saves your drawing every 15 minutes by default. Unfortunately, if you don't change the default settings for Windows, you won't be able to find the resulting file; and even if you could, you wouldn't be able to open it. This section shows you how to fix that surprising glitch. OK, it's a Windows *feature*, not a glitch, but why should it be so hard to find a critical file?

The file created by the Autosave function does not have the same name, extension, or path as the drawing. The name given to the file created by Autosave starts with the drawing name and contains incrementing characters. The extension is always .sv$. As with BAK files, the extension must be changed to .dwg before the file can be opened as a drawing.

> Note the dollar sign used as the last character of the extension: It indicates that this file is temporary. An SV$ file is available for a drawing *only* if AutoCAD terminates abnormally. Otherwise, it's deleted when AutoCAD closes. Don't rely too heavily on this feature—you must save your files regularly to avoid losing data.

By default, Autosave files are in C:\Documents and Settings\%username%\local settings\temp. To change the name of an Autosave file, you must do two things.

- The default location is a hidden folder, so you must make hidden folders visible in order to display the filename in Windows Explorer.

- The file extensions for AutoCAD are known file types, so they're hidden by default. To change the extension of an Autosave file from .sv$ to .dwg, you must clear the Hide File Extensions For Known File Types check box.

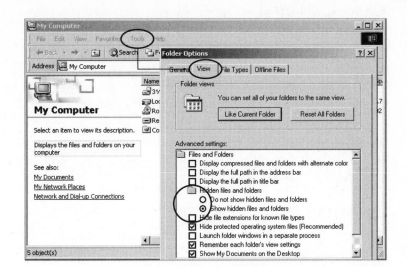

Figure 2.1

Changing folder options

You can do both of those things in any Windows file-management dialog box, such as Windows Explorer, by choosing Tools → Folder Options → View. Select the Show Hidden Files And Folders radio button, and clear Hide Extensions For Known File Types check box, as shown in Figure 2.1.

One you make these changes, you can both find the files created by Autosave and change their extensions. However, I recommend that you change the location of Autosave files from this default to a custom folder, using the Files tab of the Options dialog box (see Chapter 3, "Customizing AutoCAD's Interface"). I also recommend that SAVETIME be set to an increment of 15–30 minutes so you won't lose too much work if you ever need the Autosave file.

> SAVETIME is saved in the system registry, not in the drawing, so its value stays the same for every drawing once it's set.

AutoCAD 2006 added a Drawing Recovery Manager that pops up the next time you start AutoCAD if the last session ended abnormally. This makes it much easier to use the Autosave files, because you can open them from this window. Earlier releases don't have this function. To run the Drawing Recovery Manager manually, use the DRAWING-RECOVERY command, which you can access from File → Drawing Utilities → Drawing Recovery Manager.

Working with Files on Removable Media

Did you know that you shouldn't open DWG files directly from any removable media? Nor should you use SAVEAS to save a drawing directly to any removable media, including flash drives, CD burners, or floppy disks. Why? Because if you do, the default location for your drawing files is the removable disk. This can slow your work considerably, because the removable disk can fill up with BAK files, and the computer does frequent searches on it while you're working. Instead, to use a file from a removable disk, first copy it to the hard drive, and then open it from there. When you save files, even backup files, first save them to the hard drive, and then copy them to the removable disk.

To save a backup to a removable disk, right-click the filename in any file-management dialog box, and select the Send To option, as shown in Figure 2.2. Files copied from a CDR or DVD+R disk will probably have the Read-Only property checked. To change that, right-click the filename, select Properties, and then clear the Read-Only attribute.

Archiving Files

When you archive drawings on servers or local hard drives that have a limited capacity, reduce the file size as much as possible by using the PURGE or WBLOCK command. If you have limited file space, use compression software to reduce the drawings' sizes even further. You may even ask whether you really need all those files, but I err on the side of saving everything.

Don't rely entirely on keeping files on a single computer, or even in a single room. Writers often refer to *fire copies* of their manuscripts. You might think the same way. What if your office burns down? Invest in a DVD burner, determine which files would cost you money if you lost them, and put those files on DVD. Then, store them in another building.

Figure 2.2

Using Send To to save backup files

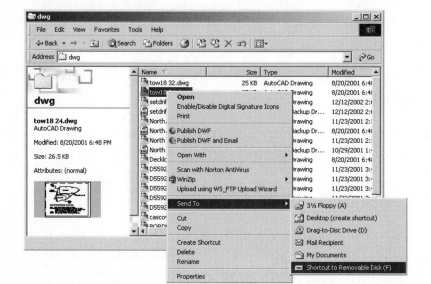

Set a Default File-Saving Location

Set the path for starting up AutoCAD in the Properties window for the AutoCAD desktop icon. Display the Properties window by right-clicking the icon and selecting Properties at the bottom of the list. Type in the location of the folder in which you want AutoCAD to start. Now you'll go directly to the folder you specify when you save new drawings for the first time.

Note that the example in Figure 2.3 also includes a startup template file, a startup profile, and a startup script. See Chapter 7, "AutoCAD Scripts," for more information.

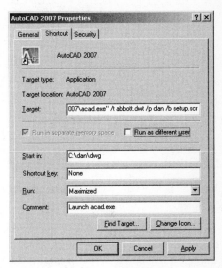

Figure 2.3

Desktop icon properties

Creating and Using Template Files

You can save a lot of work if you create and use AutoCAD template files. To create a template file, open a drawing that is set up the way most of your drawings in each discipline should be set up—with proper layer names, dimension styles, text styles, variable settings, layouts, and block definitions. Save it using the SAVEAS command, by selecting AutoCAD Drawing Template File (.dwt) from the Files Of Type field. Give the drawing a name that's logical, and save it in either the default location given (the default is C:\Documents and Settings\UserName\Local Settings\Application Data\
Autodesk\AutoCAD 2007\R17.0\enu\Template, which is, believe it or not, yet another hidden folder) or a custom folder. Now, erase all the objects in the drawing, and save it again. See Chapter 4, "Applying Graphics Standards," for suggestions about what should be included in a template file.

I also recommend creating a template folder of your own. In the next section, I'll discuss using OPTIONS to set the path for template files to your custom folder.

Managing AutoCAD

AutoCAD's interface is complex and can be cluttered. When you do a default installation and start AutoCAD, you barely have any room to draw. Most users immediately start changing the interface by turning off toolbars and tool palettes, but you have a lot more control than that. This is one of my favorite AutoCAD features: You have a lot of control over how the program looks and works, so it's easy to adapt it to your personal style of working.

One feature that helps users manage AutoCAD is the Options dialog box. By optimizing specific settings, you can improve your efficiency and make your AutoCAD experience easier and more pleasant. In this section, I'll show you how you can combine the use of saved workspaces and profiles, and I'll give you a little advice on maintaining AutoCAD.

If you want an uncluttered drawing editor, but you don't want to turn off all the toolbars and palettes, use the CLEANSCREENON and CLEANSCREENOFF commands. What, they're too hard to type? Well, this is AutoCAD, so you know there are three other ways to do it. The quickest is Ctrl+0 (that's zero, not O), which toggles clean screen on and off. Now you can have all those aids and room to draw, as well. There is also a button that controls Clean Screen at the right end of the status bar, but it's not a toggle since once it's selected, it disappears—you can only use it to turn CLEANSCREEN off. Use Ctrl+0 to turn it back on.

Options and Profiles

You can customize the interface by changing things like the background color, the behavior of right-click menus, the locations of default files, and so on. Use the Profiles tab of the Options dialog box to save the resulting profile with a specific and logical name, and export it to an ARG file so you can use it on another computer (or restore it on your current computer if your settings change). You may find that having multiple profiles is helpful, either because others use the same workstation you do, or because you use AutoCAD for different kinds of projects that benefit from different settings.

This section includes recommendations for changes to settings in each of the 10 tabs of the Options dialog box:

The figure of each tab illustrates the settings I recommend you change.

Files Tab

I have found that a great deal of confusion among AutoCAD stems from not understanding the notion of a *search path*. When any software needs a file, it looks for it in either the specific location you give (such as C:\dwg\mydrawing.DWG) or a predetermined set of folders. AutoCAD won't search an entire computer looking for the application files it needs, because that would take an enormous amount of time.

The order in which AutoCAD searches for folders also matters, because if it's looking for a file named ACAD.LIN, for example, it stops at the first such file it finds. It's possible that there are other files with the same name on your system, and they could even be in a folder that is specified as part of the search path; but if AutoCAD finds another one first, that's the one it uses.

If your custom linetypes, aliases, or AutoLISP commands aren't working as you hoped, it's possible that the file that contains them isn't early enough in the AutoCAD file search path, and that some *other* version of the file is being found first. That's why all the sections of the Files tab include a Move Up button. You can create new folders, if you desire, and then use this button to move them into the location along the path that suits your needs—usually at the top.

> To find the location of any specific support file that AutoCAD is currently using, replace `file-name.ext` in the following line of AutoLISP code with the name of the file you're looking for, and type it at the command line, including the parentheses: **(findfile "filename.ext")**.

I recommend that you create a folder in which you place all the files you use to customize AutoCAD, *except* the CUI files. This folder should *not* be located in the C:\program files\Autodesk\Autocad 2007 folder. Otherwise, you may inadvertently delete it when you upgrade to a new version of AutoCAD.

Once you have a folder for your customization files, add it to the Project Files Search Path. This setting identifies the folders that AutoCAD searches by default when it needs a file. This folder can be your personal folder or a network location that allows all users to have access to office-wide customization files. After you add the folder to the search path, move it to the top of the search path list so that your files are the first ones AutoCAD finds.

The Customization Files section shows the default location of both the Main and Enterprise CUI files. You should customize only the Main file for personal settings. The Enterprise file is to be created and managed by a CAD manager. It's generally used over a network for customization files to be used by everyone, and it's read-only to most users.

You can also set a new location for Autosave files in this tab using the Browse button. I recommend saving them in a folder that you've created. Doing so eliminates the problem of the hidden folder into which those files are placed by default. I recommend that you also create a location for your own custom DWT files and add that folder to the Drawing Template File Location path under Template Settings. The folder can be local or a shared folder on a network. If you're networked, you may want to point to a different location for plotters or pen style tables as well. See Figure 2.4.

Display Tab

The Display tab is where you can get creative about your personal preferences: the colors of backgrounds, the command line, the layouts, and so on. You should hide scroll bars; doing so gives you more screen space and prevents the sudden shift in the screen display that sometimes happens when you grab a scroll bar by mistake as you try to make a selection near the edge of your screen. You can also change your background color to white, which you may want to do if you use an earlier release of AutoCAD and are doing screen captures or using the WMFOUT command to create a raster image. If your eyes are going bad, increase the font size in the command line. If you think a magenta background would be soothing, change it.

Figure 2.4

**Files tab of the
Options dialog box**

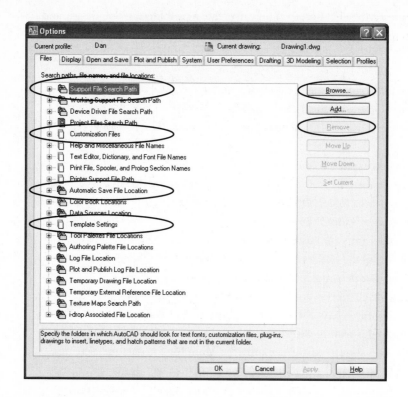

PRESENTATIONS

If you do any presenting with AutoCAD, create a presentation profile that includes a background color that shows up well with the equipment you're using. I normally use white, but others find that a gray, black, or even yellow (not me) background works better. If you do change the background color, particularly if you choose a gray color, make sure your tracking vectors and cursor display with enough contrast to be visible to an audience. You may have to change their colors as well.

You should also change the font. I use Lucinda Console at 14 points if I want my command line to show. And with AutoCAD 2006 or AutoCAD 2007, I usually change the size of the Drafting Tooltip Settings in the Drafting tab when presenting.

When you're doing a presentation, it also helps if the projector has a zoom function, as most do. You generally need the remote to make it work. If you use the projector zoom when you're displaying text on the screen, don't forget to set the view back to full-screen when you're done.

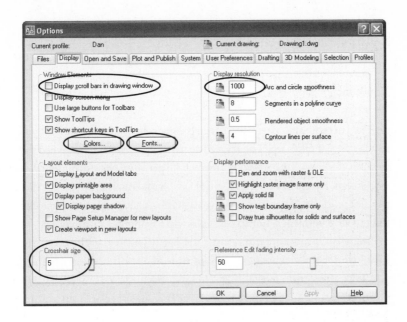

Figure 2.5

Display tab of the Options dialog box

Other things of note in this dialog box include the controls over layouts. By default, a floating viewport is added automatically to a new layout. If you don't like having a viewport created automatically, clear that setting. Set Arc And Circle Smoothness to at least 1000. On earlier releases the default value of VIEWRES is set to 100. The size of the crosshair can be increased from 5 percent up to 100 percent if you just have to have an R14 retro look. See Figure 2.5.

Open And Save Tab

By default, AutoCAD uses the file format of the current release when saving. Set the Save As option to an earlier release if you exchange drawings with other companies. I've gotten stuck more than once when I produced some work for someone and sent it off, only to find that they used an incompatible release.

> If you have a file you can't open because the format is incompatible with the release you are using, download a free conversion utility at www.autodesk.com. Search the Autodesk website for "DWG TrueConvert." While you're there, you may also want to download the utility "DWG TrueView." You can use this to view any AutoCAD DWG, DXF, or DWF on a computer that doesn't have AutoCAD installed.

Set Automatic Save to 15 to 30 minutes to reduce the number of interruptions. I find that 10 minutes is a bit too frequent for complex drawings, because the save takes time and system resources.

If you use an increment of 15–30 minutes, then when an Autosave takes place, look at an object some distance from the monitor and stretch your hands and wrists. If you're diligent about doing this every 15 minutes, you're much less likely to experience eyestrain or repetitive-motion problems.

The Incremental Save Percentage balances how quickly the drawing saves with how much space it takes up. The larger the value, the less time required for saving each drawing; but the size of the drawing is much larger until the estimated wasted space exceeds 50 percent. Once that happens, a full save with smaller file size takes place. I find that 50 percent works well because most workstations have ample storage capacity. If it takes too long to save your files, bump this value up to a higher number.

Security Options are interesting, primarily because of the opportunity to add password protection to your drawings. I don't know of any offices that use the digital signatures or password protection available by clicking this button. If I were a CAD manager, I'd turn it off just to prevent users from locking a drawing. Of course, an automated backup system should also be in place, with rights carefully controlled.

If backup files take up too much room on your hard drive, you can disable them here. I've done that in the past in student computer labs, but large-capacity hard drives are so cheap that I haven't bothered to do so for a while.

If you're using an earlier release of AutoCAD, increase Number Of Recently-Used Files To List from 4 to the maximum of 9. It would be nice if the history function of the much-maligned AutoCAD Today had been retained, but it wasn't. Setting this value to 9 is the closest you can come.

Demand Load Xrefs Enabled With Copy is generally the best setting for external references, but you may want to clear the Allow Other Users To Refedit Current Drawing check box if you're a CAD manager. It's easy for someone using an XRef to change it and save the result. I prefer to have someone open an externally referenced drawing directly if it needs to be edited. Clearing the check box sets the variable XEDIT to 0. See Figure 2.6.

Plot And Publish Tab

The Plot And Publish tab has a lot of things worth changing. Begin by selecting a default plotter. Doing so reduces the likelihood of someone using the wrong device. If you use the Plot To File option, as I often do to create raster plot images, you may want to create a different default location for plot files. By default, background plotting is used only when you plot using the Publishing functions. If you add the Plotting setting, it will speed up your plotting somewhat. If you use different plotter configurations for different sheet sizes, as is common, I suggest that you change the setting for Paper Size to Use The Plot Device Paper Size.

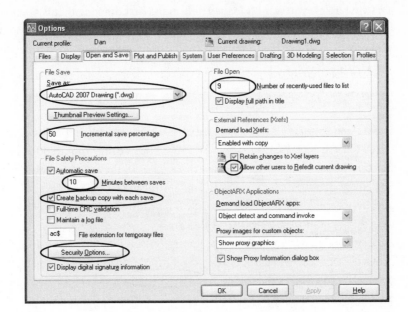

Figure 2.6
**Open And Save
tab of the Options
dialog box**

I also check the Hide System Printers box so that every print device available to a particular workstation doesn't show up as an available plotter. That way, output can be controlled by specific plot styles, and it's less likely that users will select a plotter for a new configuration. This tab is also the place to set up default plot stamp data.

Clicking the Plot Style Table Settings button gives you some control over plotting with color tables or style tables. Plotting is discussed in Chapter 6, "Plotting," at length, including a discussion of the merits of color tables versus style tables. If there wasn't such a long legacy of plotting by color, we wouldn't be faced with this choice—we'd be using style tables. But in my experience, most offices use color tables. I suggest specifying a default Plot Style Table here to avoid the None option being left on by mistake. When the Plot Style Table is set to None, you get a color plot that matches object color, which may not be what you want. See Figure 2.7.

System Tab

I have suggestions about only two options on this tab. The 3D Performance settings depend a great deal on your hardware, and I don't have enough experience with the options to advise you. You can find out whether your graphics card is certified by selecting View Tune Log and clicking Check For Updates, which takes you to the Autodesk website's certified hardware URL.

Otherwise, if you want the startup dialog box, this tab is where you can change AutoCAD's current behavior. If you use a legacy ACAD.LSP file, check Load acad.lsp With Every

Drawing unless you want it loaded *only* in the first drawing that is opened or started in an editing session. If so, you can create an ACADDOC.LSP file that will load in each drawing, and use the ACAD.LSP file to start up applications you want loaded only once. See Figure 2.8.

Figure 2.7

Plot And Publish tab of the Options dialog box

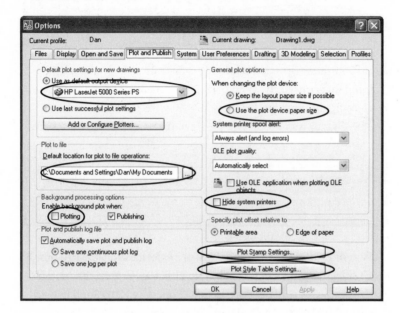

Figure 2.8

System tab of the Options dialog box

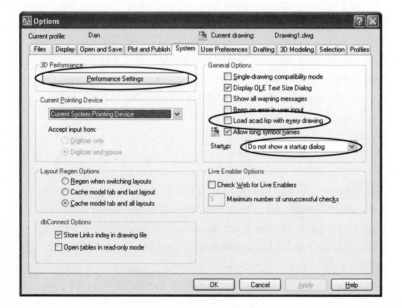

User Preferences Tab

The User Preferences tab contains some great stuff. I like the double-click functions of AutoCAD, but I know a lot of users who don't. If double-clicking an object and having its editing function pop up is annoying, you can turn off double-click editing here. Far more useful to me is the time-sensitive right-click available via the Right-Click Customization button. See Figure 2.9.

If you've been using AutoCAD for some time, you undoubtedly got used to right-clicking to end a command and then right-clicking to repeat a command you just exited. Drawing lines involved doing that constantly. When right-click menus became important in AutoCAD 2000, it was a difficult transition for some of us. We didn't like the menu popping up with Enter as the first option every time we right-clicked. With time-sensitive right-click, you can a get different behavior from a quick right-click than from a slow one. A quick click issues the Enter command, and a slow click brings up a menu. If you haven't tried this feature yet, you should, even if you're not an old-timer. The default setting of 250 milliseconds is OK, but you may want to lower the value so the time necessary to bring up a menu is reduced.

Priority For Coordinate Data Entry should be left the way it is. Otherwise, a specific absolute coordinate you type in may be overridden by a running osnap. That was a significant problem in AutoCAD before this feature was added. Scripts are exempted by default because people sometimes write script files in which they intend a running osnap to override absolute coordinates.

Figure 2.9

User Preferences tab of the Options dialog box

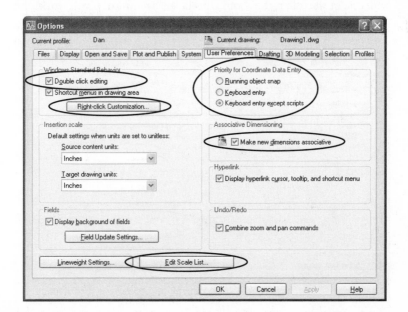

I have one other caution about the User Preferences tab. If you clear the Make New Dimensions Associative check box, the value of DIMASSOC changes from 2 to 1. This means dimensions will be associated with definition points, not with geometry, so they won't move when the geometry moves. They also won't give accurate values in Paper Space, except when the viewport being used is scaled 1:1.

The big news in this tab since AutoCAD 2006 is the Edit Scale List button. You can add or remove any scale from the Viewport Scale Control drop-down list that appears on the Viewports toolbar. You may remove scales to prevent users from selecting a plot scale that doesn't conform to your office standards. This drop-down list is used for selecting plot scales for viewports in layouts. If you've deleted some scales that you want back, you can reset the list to the defaults.

Drafting Tab

I have two recommendations for the Drafting tab: Reduce Aperture Size to make selecting objects with running osnaps more precise, and use Drafting Tooltip Settings to increase the size of the dynamic input cursor text. If your eyes are good, and you don't do presentations, you can leave it the way it is. See Figure 2.10.

3D Modeling Tab

The only thing I recommend regarding the 3D Modeling tab is selecting the Reverse Mouse Wheel Zoom option if you also use Autodesk Inventor. When I've been working with one or the other, the zoom wheel feels backward. If you work with both AutoCAD and Inventor, this adjustment is surprisingly helpful. See Figure 2.11.

Figure 2.10

Drafting tab of the Options dialog box

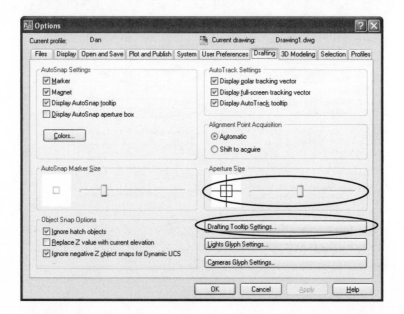

Figure 2.11

**3D Modeling tab
of the Options
dialog box**

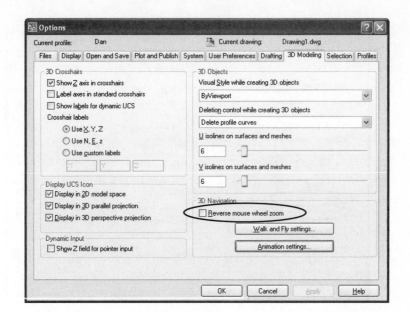

Selection Tab

The Selection tab, not surprisingly, is where you can control AutoCAD's behavior when you're selecting entities. See Figure 2.12.

Three options on this tab often go awry:

- Make sure Noun/Verb Selection is checked so you can select an object first, and then identify an action to apply to it. You undoubtedly use this feature whenever you change an object's layer with the Layer Control window on the Layer toolbar. This option controls the PICKFIRST variable, which sometimes gets changed without the user realizing it.

> Historically, AutoCAD has used a verb/noun syntax for commands. A user first started a command, like MOVE (verb), and then selected an object (the noun). Noun/verb syntax was added to AutoCAD because many other CAD programs let a user first select an object and then select the action to be performed on that object. Whenever you select an object and then select a layer to move it to, you're using noun/verb syntax.

- You may want to increase or reduce Pickbox Size to make object selection easier. You may also want to decrease the number of selected objects for which grips are shown, because the default is 100; I certainly wouldn't increase this value.

Figure 2.12

**Selection tab of the
Options dialog box**

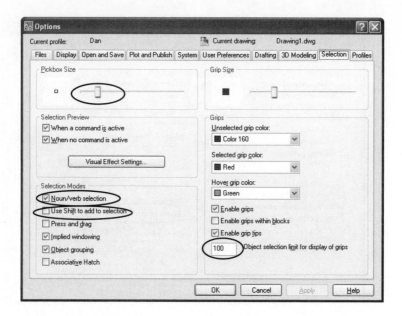

- You may also find that PICKADD, the variable that controls the Shift To Add option, mysteriously changes. If so, the Properties palette toggle is the likely culprit. Users sometimes try to close the Properties palette by selecting the + sign, which apparently looks too much like the X used to close a window. Why we needed a means of changing PICKADD there, I can't say.

Profiles Tab

The Profiles tab allows you to save a named profile once you've gone to the trouble of setting up the interface exactly the way you want it. A named profile is saved in the system registry and can be set current at any time, including on startup if you use a desktop icon and place the /p switch in the Target window. The only settings that are saved in a named profile are those that can be changed in the Options dialog box.

If you want to use a named profile on another workstation, or you want to back up the profile, export the result to an AutoCAD Registry file (.arg) using the Export button. You can import the file using the Import button. See Figure 2.13.

Setting a profile current may change the search paths used by AutoCAD. If you import an ARG file that was created by another user or for a different release or installation of AutoCAD, you may not have the correct search path for your workstation. Always save the current profile before importing a new one so you can quickly and easily return to the current settings if things go wrong.

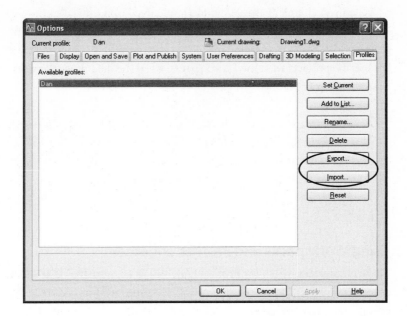

Figure 2.13
**Profiles tab of the
Options dialog box**

Workspaces

Workspaces were added in AutoCAD 2006. You should use them to save the appearance, properties, and location of the following elements:

- Advanced render settings
- Command line
- Dashboard
- dbConnect Manager
- AutoCAD DesignCenter
- External References Manager
- Info palette
- Materials palette
- Markup Set Manager
- Properties palette
- QuickCalc
- Sheet Set Manager
- Toolbars
- Tool palettes
- Visual Style Manager

When you change these elements, the changes aren't saved to the current workspace. You must manually save them by clicking Save Current As on the Workspaces toolbar and giving the workspace a name. This allows you to save custom toolbar and palette settings for specific projects to named workspaces. Keep the default workspaces intact so you can return to them if you need to.

Workspaces may have some tiny glitches. The state of the AutoCAD DesignCenter (ADC) sometimes changes if you exit AutoCAD with one workspace active, open it again and change to a different workspace. The display of custom toolbars isn't always predictable either. However, those little issues will be worked out—and even with them, workspaces are very much worth using.

Using Workspaces and Profiles Together

There is a startup switch for profiles (/p), and as of AutoCAD 2007, there's one for workspaces as well (/w). If you're using AutoCAD 2006 and want AutoCAD to start with a specific profile (dan, for example) and a specific workspace (abbott, for example), create a script file (see Chapter 7) with the line WSCURRENT abbott, and then save the file with the extension .scr (startup.scr, for example). Make a copy of the AutoCAD desktop icon, and add the following to the startup line in the properties window after the call to ACAD.EXE:

```
/b startup.scr /p dan
```

The entire startup line looks like this for a default installation of AutoCAD:

```
"C:\Program Files\ AutoCAD 2007\acad.exe" /b setup.scr /p dan
```

When you start AutoCAD by clicking this icon, you load both your profile and your workspace. In AutoCAD 2007, the same thing can be accomplished by adding the /w to the line, which looks like this:

```
"C:\Program Files\ AutoCAD 2007\acad.exe" /p dan /w abbott
```

Startup Switches

Speaking of startup switches, you can use others with AutoCAD either from an operating system command prompt or in the target window of a shortcut icon. Some of them—/b, /t, /p, and /w—I use regularly, but others I have never personally needed (I know that a lot of people use the /nologo switch). Table 2.1 identifies each switch and the use it serves in AutoCAD.

Maintaining AutoCAD

As with most software, a few problems get through the beta process for each version of AutoCAD. Usually, at least one service pack is required after each release. You can do several things to maintain your installation of AutoCAD and find workarounds for software bugs that get through.

Use the Communications Center icon in the status bar in the lower-right corner of your screen to check for updates (see Figure 2.14). If you have a live Internet link, you can set this feature to notify you of updates on a daily, weekly, or monthly basis. I set it to notification On Demand because this feature occasionally locks up and requires that I shut it down manually using the Windows Task Manager. I do a manual check periodically by double-clicking the icon.

SWITCH	NAME	PURPOSE	
/b	Script	Followed by a script name, runs a script (see Chapter 8, "AutoLisp by Example: Getting Started")	**Table 2.1** **Command-Line Switches**
/t	Template	Followed by the name of a DWG or DWT file, starts AutoCAD using that file as a template	
/c	Configuration	Sets the hardware path for a CFG file	
/v	View	Starts a drawing with a named view	
/ld	Load	Loads an ARX or DBX application	
/s	Support	Identifies support folders for the search path	
/nologo	No AutoCAD logo	Eliminates the AutoCAD logo on startup	
/p	Profile	Specifies a named profile on startup	
/nossm	No Sheet set	Prevents the Sheet Set Manager from displaying	
/set	Sheet set	Loads a named sheet set	
/w	Workspace	Specifies a named workspace (new in AutoCAD 2007)	
/pl	Plot	Plots a drawing set from a file	
/r	Configuration	Restores the default pointing device (usually a mouse) by changing the AutoCAD configuration in the acad2007.cfg file	

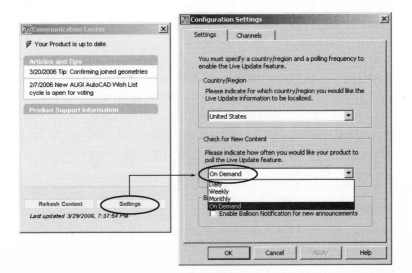

Figure 2.14

Communications Center Settings

You can find out about many AutoCAD bugs by reading Cadalyst, which you can find online at `www.cadalyst.com`. Look for the Bug Watch feature written by Steve Johnson.

Keep backup copies of key customization files, particularly `ACAD.CUI` (AutoCAD 2006 and 2007), `ACADDOC.LSP`, and `ACAD.MNS` (prior to AutoCAD 2006), in a folder that is *not* in the AutoCAD `Program Files` folder. If your menus change unexpectedly, you can replace the appropriate files.

Directories

The terms *directory*, *subdirectory*, and *folder* are used here interchangeably to refer to any named digital location that isn't a drive letter. In DOS, those locations are usually referred to as *directories*; directories contained inside another directory are called *subdirectories*. In Windows, they're called *folders*. Same thing.

Competent CAD work requires that you understand the fundamentals of your operating system. Among the most important of these fundamentals are subdirectories and path statements. I have a few tips about mapping drive letters, understanding what a path is, and understanding the confusing filenames that sometimes result from a conflict between the old and the new rules for naming files and folders.

Paths

Files used on computers must have a name and a location. When you save a file, you must identify both the filename and its location. A file's location is sometimes referred to as a *path*. A path starts with a drive letter, which can be any letter of the alphabet. Generally, the A: and B: drives are floppy drives, and the C: drive is the first hard drive. It's possible to partition physical hard drives into two or more drives (D:\, E:\, and so on). You can also have more than one physical hard drive in a computer. In addition to physical hard drives, you undoubtedly have one or more CD or DVD drives, and you may have multiple thumb or flash drives or even digital cameras attached via USB ports. They all have drive letters assigned to them.

To complicate matters further, if you're attached to a network, you have access to additional physical drives, some of which may be partitioned into more than one drive. Even worse, network directories are often mapped with drive letters, even though they're directories and not drives. And just to make things just slightly more involved, a drive letter can be assigned to any folder on a local workstation. Don't get thrown by all the drive letters you're likely to encounter, particularly in a networked environment: A drive letter is simply the start of a path.

You can easily map drive letters to a network folder in Windows by right-clicking the My Computer icon and selecting Map Network Drive, but it isn't so easy to map a drive letter to a folder on the local computer. To do that, use the DOS `subst` function at the Operating System command prompt or in a batch file (see the section "Why DOS Isn't Dead Yet," later in this chapter). Here's the syntax: `subst S: c:\sybex\ASTEUSK\ch01`. Now you can use the drive letter S: to go directly to the specified folder.

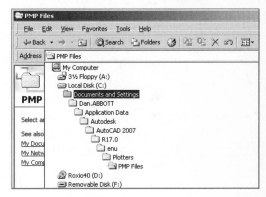

Figure 2.15

Directory or folder tree

Think of your computer as a file cabinet with multiple drawers: an A:\ drive drawer, a C:\ drive drawer, a D:\ drive door, an E:\ drive drawer, and an X:\ drive drawer. It's nice to have five places to store files, but you would never just throw a pile of papers into one drawer in a file cabinet. As with a file cabinet, in order to organize your work, you need separate folders within each drive and separate folders within those folders, and often you need folders within folders within folders. That's the tree you see in Windows when you're using its file manager. See Figure 2.15.

Naming Requirements

The lengths of file and folder names were limited in the distant past to no more than eight characters, with an extension of no more than three characters. This was known as the *eight-dot-three* (8.3) convention. Sometimes your computer treats folders and files with long names differently from those that follow the 8.3 standard.

LONG FOLDER NAMES	8.3 FOLDER NAMES
MyPhotos Cats	MyPhot~1
MyPhotos Dogs	MyPhot~2
MyPhotos Kids	MyPhot~3
MyPhotos Mom	MyPhot~4

Table 2.2

Comparing long folder names to their 8.3 names

Depending on the operating system, if a name includes spaces, you may have to enclose the filename in quotes so it can be read as a single name. If a folder or file has a long name that must be shortened to an eight-character name, the first six letters followed by the tilde and a number can be used to represent the folder, as in `PROGRA~1` for `Program Files`. See Table 2.2 for examples of how folders that start with the same six letters would be named.

Sometimes AutoCAD uses the 8.3 naming convention for search paths, but not usually. Check out the Automatic Save File Location used by AutoCAD in the Files tab of the Options dialog box for an example (see Figure 2.16). You may run across this convention in other situations as well, so don't let it throw you. Just recognize that the actual folder names are longer.

Figure 2.16

8.3 naming convention

Why DOS Isn't Dead Yet

You may wonder why anyone would put a section on DOS in a book about AutoCAD. It's simple: Knowing DOS, or what is now often referred to as Windows Scripting Language, has saved me hundreds of hours of time over the years (and that's no exaggeration). Chapter 8 contains a description of a system I use for batch-processing drawings that has saved companies thousands of hours of work—and it depends on a single DOS function to work.

Let's start with one example of how useful DOS can be. How would you go about creating a file that lists all the files in one of your folders? That should be easy, shouldn't it? Let's make this problem more useful and more challenging. How would you create a file that contains the locations and names of every single drawing file on your *entire* hard drive? If you can figure out a way to do that in Windows, please let me know.

Here's how you can do it in DOS:

1. In Windows, choose Start → Run.

2. Type **cmd** in the Run window.

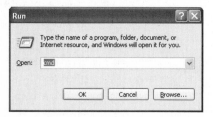

3. Click the OK button. A window with a black background opens; it's normally referred to as the *DOS screen*.

4. Enter the following at the DOS prompt: `dir c:\*.dwg /s /b > c:\dwglist.txt`. You may have to wait several minutes while your computer searches for every DWG file, so be patient. It would take a lot longer to do it manually!

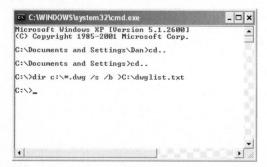

5. Open the file named `dwglist.txt` in Notepad. It's in the root of the C:\ drive.

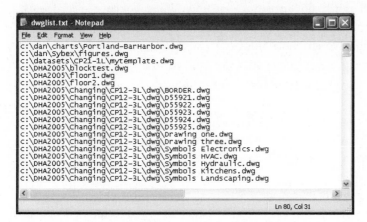

I just did this on my desktop computer. It took less than 30 seconds to go through the steps shown here. It took the computer only minutes to create the text file, which lists thousands of DWG files. Imagine how long it would have taken to create such a list without this little line of DOS code. Table 2.3 illustrates what each element does:

> Jon McFarland, the technical editor for this book, reports that he saves a ton of time by using the DOS Rename command to update the names of a large group of files. Type `rename C:\Sybex\???DCD.dwg ???AVM.dwg`↵ at the DOS prompt if you want to replace the last three characters of every six-character drawing name that ends with "DCD." "DCD" will become "AVM" for each DWG file.

DOS ELEMENT	PURPOSE	
DIR	Creates a list of files in a folder	Table 2.3
C:*.dwg	Identifies the files to be listed as having any name and the file extension .dwg	**Elements of the** dir c:*.dwg /s /b >c:\dwglist.txt
/s	Indicates that the search should include all subdirectories in addition to the root of the C:\ drive	
/b	Indicates that the listing should be bare, including only the filename and location, and not the file size, date, and attributes	
>	Directs the output into a file	
C:\DWGLIST.TXT	Creates a file with this name, and places the output of the DIR command into it	

DOS Batch Files

A DOS *batch file* is an ASCII text file containing a series of DOS-level (operating system–level) commands. Using a batch file allows you to control one or more computers without having to type a series of commands repeatedly.

An *ASCII file* is a plain text file containing only the 94 characters that can be typed directly from a keyboard with no formatting—no underlining, boldface, special fonts, and so on. Much of this book deals with ASCII files, and they must remain in that format. To ensure that happens, use Notepad, the AutoCAD VLISP editor, or a third-party plain text editor to modify or create them. Do *not* use a word processor for any file identified as an ASCII or text file, so you don't corrupt the file unintentionally.

> ASCII stands for American Standard Code for Information Interchange, by the way. It's the means by which different computer systems can communicate. If they ever ask you that question on Jeopardy, send me a thank-you note.

I've always used batch files to manage the network and labs at Southern Maine Community College, where I teach. I have a batch file that cleans out directories, deletes them, re-creates them, assigns new users, and gives those users rights to their directories. I could do this using the Windows dialog boxes, but I have more than 300 users who need more than 600 directories. I also need to assign rights to each directory to myself, the other instructors, and the individual students. That would take a lot of mouse clicks.

I also use a batch file to manage the computers in the labs. A logon batch file runs every time a student logs on to the network. Old drawing files can be removed from each computer, new AutoCAD support files can be copied to each computer, custom files can be copied to each computer, new plotter configurations can be copied to each computer, network paths can be mapped, and so on.

Without batch files, I would spend days doing these things manually. Once I write a batch file, I start it running, and it does everything without making a single error. That way, I can spend my time doing more interesting work.

DOS Commands

DOS commands, also known as operating system (OS) commands, are issued at an OS command line. You can get to that command line two ways in Windows:

- Type **SHELL**↵↵ at the AutoCAD command prompt. The second ↵ gets you past the prompt asking for an OS command. You see a blinking cursor on a black screen, with the name of the current directory in front of it. To leave this active shell and return to AutoCAD, type the word **EXIT**.

- Select Start → Run, and type **CMD**↵ in the window. The OS prompt opens in a window named cmd.exe.

> For those of you with a longer computer history, this is the Windows 2000 OS command interpreter. You can also get the old DOS 6 interpreter by typing **COMMAND** in the window; but if you do, you have to use the 8.3 filename convention, including **progra~1** for program files, and you lose some new functions.

To get a list of all DOS commands, use the Windows Help system and type **DOS** in the Index window. You can also type the word `Help` at the DOS command line to get a partial list.

> Many websites offer more information about using DOS. Search on DOS in your favorite search engine, and sit back. When I did a search at `www.ask.com`, it returned 19,490,000 hits.

Sample Batch Files

To write a batch file, start Notepad or another text editor, and type separate lines of DOS commands. When you're done, save the file with any name and the extension `.bat`, as in `BACKUP.BAT`.

> A batch file is a program file. If you double-click it or open it in a file list, the program is executed. To change the contents of a batch file, right-click it and select Edit from the cursor menu.

In each of the following tables, the actual DOS code that would appear in a batch file is shown on the left, and the explanation for each line appears on the right.

Creating Folders

Table 2.4 contains several lines from a much longer `FOLDERS.BAT` batch file that I use to create directories for multiple users. You don't need to see all the lines, because they're similar. The batch file contains only the lines in the column labeled DOS Code. The Purpose column explains what each line does.

Logon Batch Files

You can use batch files as logon scripts on a Windows network so that when someone logs on, the batch file runs automatically. Table 2.5 contains several lines from a `LOGAED.BAT` batch file used to manage the logon process. In this case, a drive letter is mapped to a folder named for an individual user, and another is mapped to a shared resource folder available to all users.

DOS CODE	PURPOSE
S:	Makes the S:\ drive current
CD\	Changes to the root of the current drive
CD acad1	Changes to the directory name acad1
MD grade	Makes a new subdirectory named grade in the directory named acad1
MD templates	Makes a new subdirectory named templates in the directory named acad1
MD custom	Makes a new subdirectory named custom in the directory named acad1

Table 2.4

`FOLDERS.BAT`

	DOS CODE	PURPOSE
Table 2.5	`rem -- ACADLOG.bat file`	rem means *remark*; allows notes to be added to the batch file
LOGAED.BAT	`net use S: \\tech\users\%username%`	Maps the drive letter S: to a folder with the same name as the user's logon name, which is located in a folder named users on the network server named tech
	`del c:\*.bak`	Deletes all BAK files in the root of C:\
	`del s:\%username%\*.bak`	Deletes BAK files from the user's directory
	`del s:\%username%*.ac$`	Deletes AC$ files from the user's directory
	`cd\`	Changes to the root of the current drive
	`net use R: \\tech\resources$`	Maps the drive letter R: to a hidden, shared folder named resources on the network server named tech

The NET USE command is a network OS command and won't be listed in the DOS help system. To see a list of other network commands, type net help↵ at the DOS prompt. To get help with net use, type net use /help↵.

Backing Up Files

I use batch files to manage my own backup process, independent of the process available on my school's network—in fact, my backup process is redundant. It's not that I'm compulsive; I just don't like the idea of losing work. I use a similar system on my personal computer. The batch file shown in Table 2.6 copies all DWG files from the H:\ drive (a network drive on different server) to the network directory mapped as S:\ *if they are newer than those that are already there*. It then copies all DWG files on the S:\ drive to the H:\ drive, but again, only if they're newer than the versions that are already there. This type of batch file can be used as a way to make sure you have the latest versions of all DWG files on both network drives. It uses two switches:

- The /d switch is the date switch, limiting XCOPY to those files that are newer than those with the same name on the destination drive.

- The /s switch includes all the directories on both drives that contain any DWG files. Otherwise, only DWG files in the root of each drive would be copied.

	DOS CODE	PURPOSE
Table 2.6	`xcopy H:\*.DWG S:\*.DWG /d /s`	xcopy (extended copy) copies all files on the H:\ drive with a .dwg extension to the S:\ drive. Files of the same name are copied only if they're newer than the versions in the destination drive.
H2S2H.BAT	`xcopy S:\*.DWG H:\*.DWG /d /s`	xcopy copies all files on the S:\ drive with a .dwg extension to the H:\ drive. Files of the same name are copied only if they're newer than the versions in the destination drive.

The batch file shown in Table 2.7 has a slight twist: It backs up to a removable DVD that doesn't have enough capacity to store all the files I want backed up from my hard drive. BACKUP.BAT lets me keep ongoing backups of new files. The D:\ drive is my DVD burner. The date switch here is used to copy only files created *after* a specific date—in this case, December 1, 2007. After the computer is done copying, the batch file opens in Notepad, and I change the date. When the DVD gets full, I start a new backup disk.

The second line of the batch file in Table 2.7 is interesting. It actually opens the batch file so I can change the date each time it runs. Once I save the new version of the batch file with the new date, the DOS window closes.

DOS CODE	PURPOSE	
`XCOPY C:\dan\*.* /s /d:12/1/07 D:`	Copies all files created after 12/1/2006 from the folder named dan on the C:\ drive to the D:\ drive	Table 2.7
		BACKUP.BAT
`start /wait notepad.exe c:\bat\backup.bat`	Starts the Windows application NOTEPAD.EXE, opens the file named BACKUP.BAT located in the folder named bat on the C:\ drive, and waits for the file to be closed before returning to the OS command line	

Running Batch Files Automatically

You can run a batch file manually by right-clicking the filename and clicking Open. You can run one automatically by making it the logon script for a network. But you can also run a batch file automatically by identifying it as a scheduled event in Windows. That's what I do for the backup batch file shown in Table 2.7. To make a batch file a scheduled event, follow these steps:

1. Create the batch file, and save it. (I have a folder named bat in which I keep all my batch files. That way, I'm a little less likely to double-click one by accident.)

2. Double-click the Scheduled Tasks icon in Windows Control Panel.

3. Double-click the Add Scheduled Task option to start the Scheduled Task Wizard, and then click the Next button.

4. Click the Browse button, and add your batch file.

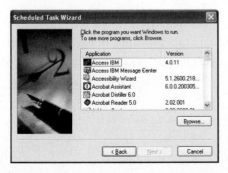

5. Set the frequency with which you want the task to run. I have mine run every day. You'll also get a chance to enter a password. (That's the password you log on with, if you use one.) Now the task will run even if you're logged on under another user name that has fewer rights to run programs.

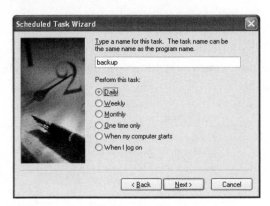

External Commands and Command Aliases

AutoCAD uses the ACAD.PGP file to define two kinds of commands: *external commands* (DOS commands to be issued at the AutoCAD command prompt) and *command aliases* (shorthand commands used to issue standard AutoCAD commands).

> Some people have discovered that they can type **START** at the AutoCAD command prompt followed by a filename like ACAD.PGP and have the file open. Don't do it. The START command is an operating system command, and it uses the Windows search path, not the Auto-CAD search path, to find the referenced file. If you have multiple versions of the file, you may open the wrong one. Use the AutoLISP findfile function, instead, as shown in Figure 2.18.

You have to go deep into the Documents and Settings folder, or use the Windows Search function, to find this file. The default location for the ACAD.PGP file for each user login name is shown in Figure 2.17. Your own login name will appear instead of Dan. Abbott, which is the logon name I used for this example.

Even knowing this, however, you're unlikely to find this file because you must navigate through another hidden folder, Application Data, in order to locate it. For a shortcut, you can type at the AutoCAD command line to open the file *without* navigating the long folder tree, as illustrated in Figure 2.18. As of AutoCAD 2006, you can also open this file from AutoCAD using Tools → Customize → Edit Program Parameters (acad.pgp).

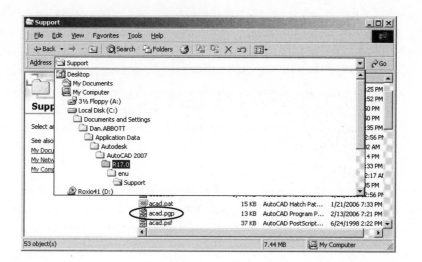

Figure 2.17

**AutoCAD
support path**

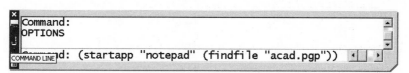

Figure 2.18

**Opening a file in
the search path**

If you don't know how to make a hidden folder visible, see the earlier section "Auto-save Files."

When you open the ACAD.PGP file, the header information looks like this:

```
;  Program Parameters File For AutoCAD 2007
;  External Command and Command Alias Definitions
;  Copyright (C) 1997-2006 by Autodesk, Inc.  All Rights Reserved.
;  Each time you open a new or existing drawing, AutoCAD searches
;  the support path and reads the first acad.pgp file that it finds.
...
;  The bits of the bit flag have the following meanings:
;  Bit 1: if set, don't wait for the application to finish
;  Bit 2: if set, run the application minimized
;  Bit 4: if set, run the application "hidden"
;  Bit 8: if set, put the argument string in quotes
```

The semicolons represent remarks. The section that follows the ellipses describes the bit-flag settings that can be used for external commands. Although it's not shown in the file, I've occasionally had to use a value of 0 as a bit flag, which forces the OS to wait for an application to finish before returning to AutoCAD.

You can add bit-flag values together to force more than one condition. A bit flag of 12 (4 + 8) runs the application hidden and requires that the argument used be placed in quotes. Using a numbering system where each value doubles to form the next value should be familiar to you: 1, 2, 4, 8, 16, 32, 64, 128, 256, and so on. It's used because the sum of any group of values is always unique and allows multiple conditions to be represented by one number. The variable that controls object snaps works this way. Each of the object snaps is assigned one of the bit-code values: 1 for END; 2 for MID, 4 for CEN, 8 for QUA, and so on. If you turn on all four of them, the OSMODE variable is set to 15. If you turn on END and CEN only, OSMODE is set to 5.

External commands are defined using five fields. The fields are shown in the lines in the next text box, which define external DOS commands supplied by Autodesk in the default ACAD.PGP file. If you type any of the commands listed in the first column at the AutoCAD command prompt, the associated DOS function is executed:

```
CATALOG,    DIR /W,        8,File specification: ,
DEL,        DEL,           8,File to delete: ,
DIR,        DIR,           8,File specification: ,
EDIT,       START EDIT,    9,File to edit: ,
SH,         ,              1,*OS Command: ,
SHELL,      ,              0,*OS Command: ,
START,      START,         1,*Application to start: ,
TYPE,       TYPE,          8,File to list: ,
```

The next group of lines from the default ACAD.PGP file defines external commands that use the START function to run any Windows program. You must know the name of the executable file to call it from AutoCAD. For example, the application file that starts Microsoft Word is named WINWORD.EXE. (See the next section for an example of how to use this filename to start Word from the AutoCAD command line.) The reference to (STARTAPP) indicates an AutoLISP function that can also be used to start a Windows program. That's one of the functions used in Figure 2.18 to open the ACAD.PGP file directly from AutoCAD:

```
; Examples of external commands for Windows
; See also the (STARTAPP) AutoLISP function for an alternative method.
EXPLORER,   START EXPLORER, 1,,
NOTEPAD,    START NOTEPAD,  1,*File to edit: ,
PBRUSH,     START PBRUSH,   1,,
```

This last group of lines from the ACAD.PGP file defines command aliases:

```
; Command alias format:
;    <Alias>,*<Full command name>
3A,         *3DARRAY
3DMIRROR,   *MIRROR3D
3DNavigate,*3DWALK
3DO,        *3DORBIT
```

```
3DW,        *3DWALK
3F,         *3DFACE
3M,         *3DMOVE
```

External Commands

To add your own external commands, follow the same format used for the default ACAD.PGP commands. Here is an example from my ACAD.PGP file:

```
WORD,        start winword,                          1,    ,

EXCEL,       start excel,                            1,    ,

ACCESS,      start msaccess,                         1,    ,

CALC,        start calc,                             1,    ,

AU,          start iexplore www.autodesk.com/au      1,    ,

WORK,        start explorer c:\dan\da-work,          1,    ,

LISP,        notepad c:\da\autocad\custom\acad.lsp,  1,    ,
```

Each of these lines has five fields separated by commas:

- Field 1—The name of a new AutoCAD command you're creating
- Field 2—The external command you want to run when the new command name is typed at the keyboard
- Field 3—A bit-flagged number that is explained at the top of the file, but which for our purposes can be 1
- Field 4—A prompt if it's needed, or a blank if a prompt isn't needed
- Field 5—A legacy blank space

Long Path Statements

There's a limit on how many characters AutoCAD can read from a single line in the acad.pgp file, and blank spaces in folder names and filenames can cause problems. You may also run into this problem in other situations.

To avoid surprises when referring to a long path, use the 8.3 naming convention if you want to write a new AutoCAD command. For example, the acad.lin file, which is located in the Documents and Settings folder, could be opened with the new command LIN if it were defined as follows. Note that the line is broken here because it is too long to fit on the page of this book, but it must be entered as a single line in the actual acad.pgp file:

```
lin,notepad c:\docume~1\dan\applic~1\autodesk
\autoca~3\r16.2\enu\support\acad.lin,1,,
```

Here is a situation where an existing long folder name or filename must be represented using the 8.3 convention. In this example , autoca~3 is the third folder, alphanumerically, in that location beginning with the characters *autoca*. The other two are earlier versions of AutoCAD that are installed on my computer.

Aliases

To create new command aliases, add lines in the following format or use the Express Tool ALIASEDIT (Express → Tools → Command Alias Editor…). The following are three commands from my ACAD.PGP file:

```
RI,    *REINIT
CY,    *CYLINDER
K,     *CAL
```

Each of these lines has two fields:

- Field 1—The name of the alias you're creating.

- Field 2—The name of the AutoCAD command, preceded by an asterisk, which lets AutoCAD know that this is a native AutoCAD command and not an external command. Because it's not external, the remaining fields aren't used. If a command can be issued transparently, like CAL, then the alias can be, too.

You can create as many aliases for existing commands as you want. You can even create an alias using a version of a command you often mistype. I once resorted to creating the alias CHAGNE for the CHANGE command.

Place your additions at the bottom of the file using lowercase letters so you can find them easily. If the same alias is used more than once, the one closest to the bottom of the file is the last one loaded. As of AutoCAD 2006, there's an area at the bottom of the file for user-defined aliases. If you place your definitions there, migrating them to future releases will be easier—at least, that's what it says at the end of the acad.pgp file.

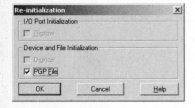

Figure 2.19

**Re-initialization
dialog box**

The ACAD.PGP file is loaded when you start AutoCAD; if you change it, you have to save the result and use the REINIT command to reload it into AutoCAD. This is the only file that can be reinitialized this way. Figure 2.19 shows the Re-initialization dialog box as an example.

If you want to reload the ACAD.PGP file from a Lisp program, reset the variable RE-INIT to 16 using the following AutoLISP code, including parentheses: (setvar "re-init" 16).

To load this file, it must be in the search path, so don't move it without adding its location to the default path used by AutoCAD. Read this entire file for a review of most of the AutoCAD commands. There's no reason not to use the entire alphabet for single-letter aliases. And some commands don't yet have an alias.

The ALIASEDIT Express Tool automates this process, but I think it's good practice to edit the file directly. Doing so helps you understand the role of text files in customizing AutoCAD.

CHAPTER 3

Customizing the AutoCAD Interface

You may be working in an office that's conservative about upgrades, and probably for good reason. Because of the fairly recent introduction of the Customizable User Interface (CUI) in AutoCAD 2006, this chapter will contain some sections that apply to most releases, but others that apply only to AutoCAD 2006 and later.

Why should you bother to customize AutoCAD's interface? There are three primary reasons:

- To make yourself more efficient
- To encourage the use of office standards
- To create linetypes that don't already exist in AutoCAD

Efficiency comes from eliminating some steps in using AutoCAD commands and reducing the clutter of toolbars and tool palettes that contain tools you never use. How about making your own toolbar? And while you're at it, how about creating personal commands that eliminate mindless repetition? If you haven't done any customizing before, you'll be surprised at how much easier it is to work when you've streamlined AutoCAD. Face it: We're all a bit lazy, so every little thing that keeps us from working hard is welcome. Sometimes I think the best AutoCAD users are the lazy ones.

In this chapter, I'm covered the areas I think give you the biggest return on your investment of customizing time. Take a look, and I'm certain you'll find something in this chapter that makes the time spent customizing worthwhile.

- **Tool Palettes**
- **Menus**
- **Accelerator Keys**
- **Custom Linetypes**

Tool Palettes (All Releases)

Tool palettes began as a place to store blocks and hatch patterns, but they eventually evolved into a useful system for organizing tools and content that you use regularly, including Lisp programs and commands. I particularly like them as a way of organizing and accessing groups of block definitions.

Tool palettes are also an excellent means of helping people enforce standards in an office, because you can set the properties of anything on a tool palette, including the layer it uses when you select it. Don't get too carried away with tool palettes—they're useful only if you streamline them enough that you can easily find what you want. If you create a lot of tool palettes, consider using the group function to combine related palettes into groups.

Open the Tool Palettes window from the command line (TOOLPALETTES or TP), from the menu (Tools → Palettes → Tool Palettes), or by pressing Ctrl+3.

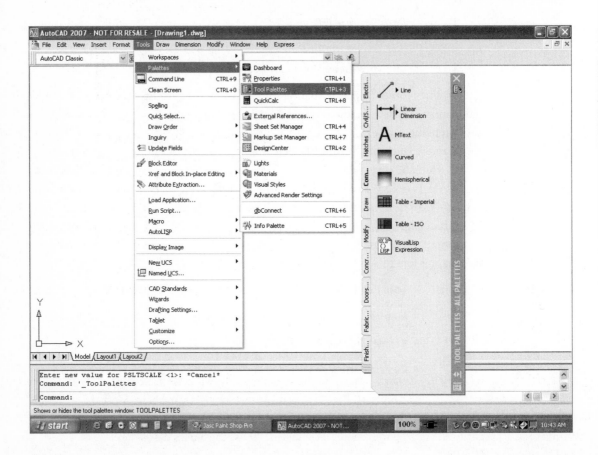

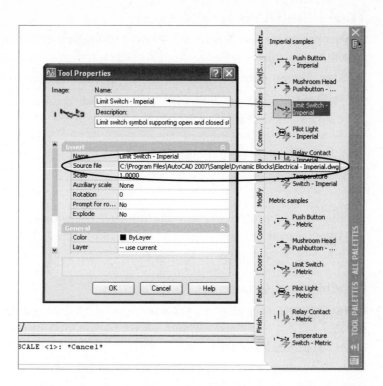

Figure 3.1

Block reference to a source file

It's important to remember that tool palettes contain references to a wide variety of AutoCAD operations, all of which are known as *tools*. A block reference on a tool palette is a reference to a block definition in a saved drawing file. If you move or rename the drawing that contains the block definition, you break its connection to the tool palette. Figure 3.1 shows the Tool Properties dialog box that results from right-clicking the Limit Switch-Imperial block reference. The Source File field contains the name and location of the drawing in which the block definition resides. The block isn't defined in your drawing until you insert one of the block references from a tool palette.

In this section, I'll discuss the specifics of placing block references, creating new tool palette groups, changing the properties of the tools on a tool palette, adding new tools to tool palettes, and exporting tool palettes. Let's get to it.

Adding Block References to a Tool Palette

One of the most powerful features of tool palettes is the ability to create a palette that contains references to all the block definitions in a single reference drawing. Because you undoubtedly already have one or more symbol library drawing files, let's start there. Most of you have a set of sample files that were copied into the C:\Program Files\AutoCAD 2008\ Sample\DesignCenter folder during the default installation. I'll use the blocks defined in one of those files—Landscaping.dxf—for this example, so the resulting tool palette is named Landscaping. The following steps walk you through a number of things you can do with tool palettes:

1. Start DesignCenter (DC, Tools → Palettes → DesignCenter, or Ctrl+2).

2. Navigate through the folders list to find a file that contains the block definitions you want on a tool palette.

> You can obtain content from any drawing file (DWG), template file (DWT), Drawing Interchange File (DXF), or even standards file (DWS).

3. Right-click almost anywhere on the AutoCAD DesignCenter (ADC) palette, and select the menu option Create Tool Palette (see Figure 3.2). AutoCAD automatically creates a single new tool palette that contains all the block definitions in that drawing.

Creating New Groups for Tool Palettes

It's easy to create a new tool palette containing all the block definitions in a symbol-library drawing—so easy that it probably makes sense for you to create one for each of your symbol drawings. You may notice that AutoCAD 2007 displays a lot of long tool palettes. To reduce the clutter on the screen, you can make a new group for the tool palettes you're creating and turn off all the others. Here are the steps:

1. Open the Customize dialog box by right-clicking an empty area of the tool palette and selecting Customize Palettes (see Figure 3.3).

2. Right-click in an empty area of the Palette Groups pane, and select New Group to create a group for your new tool palette (see Figure 3.4). Name this new group **Sybex**.

Figure 3.2

Adding block definitions to a tool palette

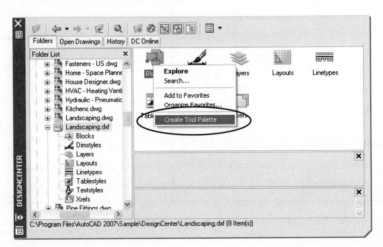

3. Select the name of a tool palette that you want to make part of a group. Hold down the left mouse button while you drag the tool palette into position under the group name; drop the tool palette by releasing the left mouse button. A horizontal black bar shows you where the palette will be placed in the group list. This adds your new tool palette—in this case, Landscaping—to its own group so you can turn off the default tool-palette groups that come with AutoCAD 2007 (see Figure 3.5).

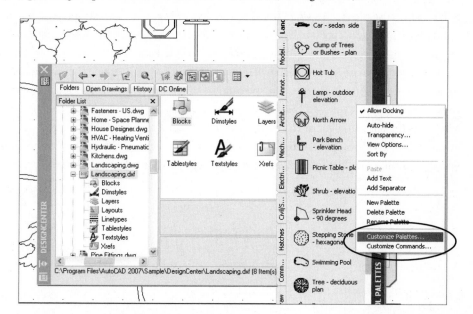

Figure 3.3

Customize Palettes

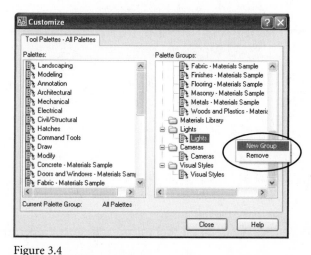

Figure 3.4

Creating a new palette group

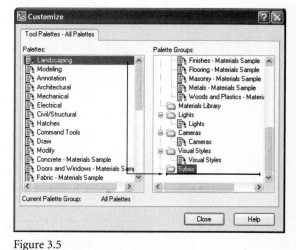

Figure 3.5

Adding a tool palette to a group

4. Close the Customize dialog.

5. Right-click the title bar of the tool palette, and select only your new group for display. Doing so turns off the 30 tool palettes that ship with AutoCAD 2007. (See Figure 3.6.)

Changing the Properties of Tools on a Palette

Now that you have a new palette that contains block references, let's control the properties that one of those blocks has when inserted into a drawing. For this example, use the block named Tree - Deciduous Plan. The tree symbol as drawn measures 120 units across. It would accurately represent a tree 10 feet across if I were using it in an architectural drawing where the basic units were inches. However, I want to use it in a civil drawing, where the units are feet. A tree 120 feet across would be much too large. I'd also like the symbol to be placed on the layer L-PLNT-DEMO automatically, so I don't have to remember to set that as my current layer or to change it after the fact. I also don't like the rotation angle at which it the symbol was created, because it looks too regular with the horizontal and vertical lines used for the symbol. Here are the steps you can take to change the properties:

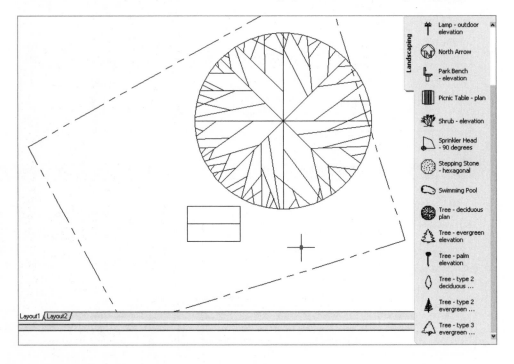

1. Right-click the Tree - Deciduous Plan block on the tool palette, and select Properties as in Figure 3.7.

2. When the Tool Properties dialog box opens, change the scale, the rotation, and the layer onto which the block is inserted. See Figure 3.8 for an example.

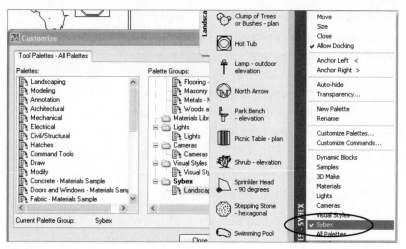

Figure 3.6

Turning off tool-palette groups

Figure 3.7

Opening the Tool Properties window

Figure 3.8

Changing the properties of a tool

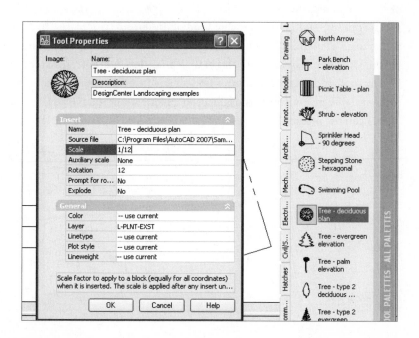

Note that the block definitions aren't stored in the current drawing until they're inserted. They reside in the original drawing. Objects on the tool palettes are completely independent of the current drawing.

Adding Other Tools to a New Tool Palette

Now that you know how to create a tool palette and add it to a new group, let's create a blank palette and add some other kinds of tools to it.

Create a new tool palette by right-clicking a tool palette title and selecting New Palette. Name this one **Drawing**. Notice that the first item on the empty palette is Learn About Customizing Tool Palettes. Selecting this option opens the New Features Workshop.

To create a new tool from any existing object, do the following:

1. Select the object with the left mouse button so it's highlighted.

2. Place the cursor over the highlighted object, and hold down the right mouse button while dragging the object onto the palette.

In Figure 3.9, I've already dragged a polyline onto the tool palette, and I'm in the process of placing an aligned dimension just below the polyline.

For each of these tools, a flyout is created automatically. This flyout gives you access to all the commands related to that object. Even though you used a polyline as an example when creating the drawing tool, if you select the small arrowhead in the lower right corner of the icon and pause, a flyout with tools for lines, arcs, circles, splines, ellipses, rays, and xlines appears. And no matter what kind of dimension you place, the flyout gives you access to all of them: Aligned, Linear, Arc Length, Radius, Jogged, Diameter, Angular, Ordinate, Quick, Baseline, Continue, Quick Leader, and Tolerance (see Figure 3.10).

The toolbar displays the last option you selected from the flyout. I often place the draw and dimension commands on a tool palette more than once. There are two reasons: First, I can use one tool for lines that are to be placed on a specific layer and a different

Figure 3.9

Dragging a tool onto a tool palette

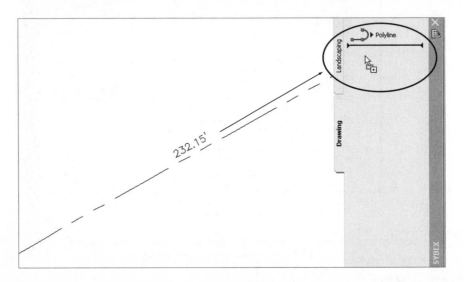

tool for lines on a different layer. Second, I can place all dimensions on a DIM layer but have different dimension commands displayed so I don't have to go through the flyouts each time I want a different one. (See Figure 3.11.)

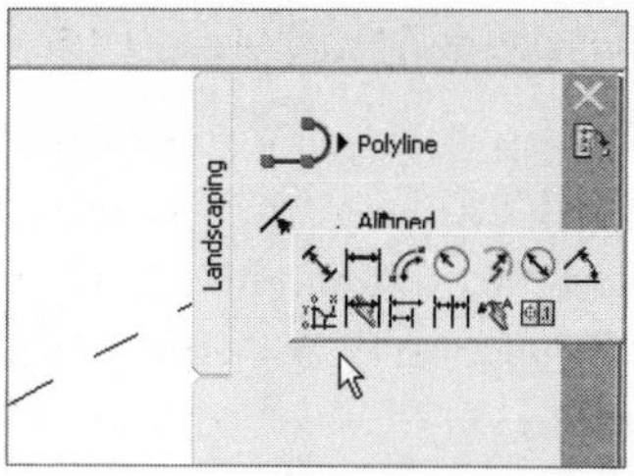

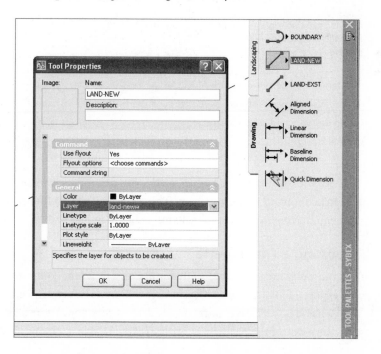

Figure 3.10
Tool palette flyouts

You can also add hatch patterns to a toolbar. You can either drag an existing hatch pattern from the drawing onto the toolbar, as I did with the line and dimension commands, or you can use the file-management pane on the left of the ADC to locate a specific hatch-pattern file. The default file is ACAD.PAT for Imperial drawings and ACADISO.PAT for metric. Because they're both buried in your personal settings under the C:\Documents and Settings folder, it's far easier to place a hatch pattern using the HATCH command and drag it onto the toolbar. Once it's there, right-click the pattern icon, select Properties, and set the angle, layer, and so on.

Prior to the development of the CUI in AutoCAD 2006, you could drag commands directly from the Customize dialog box. That isn't possible as of AutoCAD 2006. If you want a command that's not represented by an object that can be dragged onto a palette, copy (right-click) an example from the sample Command Tools palette that ships with AutoCAD (See Figure 3.12), and paste it (right-click again) onto yours.

Figure 3.11
Displaying different flyout options

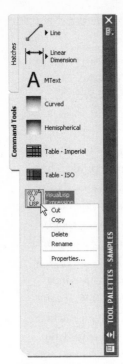

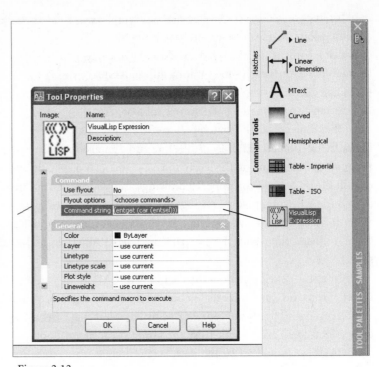

Figure 3.12

Copying existing tools from the sample tool palette

Figure 3.13

Editing the command string

Many tool palettes ship with AutoCAD. As a result, you may not see the Command Tools tab because so many tabs are bunched up at the bottom of the palette. If so, place your cursor on the bunched-up tabs, and left-click. A complete list pops up, and you can select Command Tools.

Once the command is on your palette, you can right-click and edit the properties to add any command string you want. This is particularly useful for running Lisp programs or menu macros from the tool palette, as shown in Figure 3.13.

Exporting a Tool Palette

You can easily export a tool palette for use on a different computer or as a backup. Once you export a tool palette, a different user can then import it. The result is an XLM file, but its extension is .xtp. To export a tool palette, open the Customize dialog box, and right-click the name of the palette you want to export. Give it a name, and save it in the location of your choice. AutoCAD creates a folder with the same name as the tool palette to hold the image files used on the palette.

A different AutoCAD user can't access to this tool palette unless they import it using the same process. The default location of the tool palettes used by AutoCAD is `C:\Documents and Settings\`*`%username%`*`\Application Data\Autodesk\AutoCAD 2007\R17.0` `\enu\Support\ToolPalette` (*%username%* represents the logon name of the current user).

The Customizable User Interface (CUI)

The big customizing change as of AutoCAD 2006 was the creation of CUI files. Users can modify the `ACAD.CUI` by using the CUI command to open the Customize User Interface dialog box. I like this consolidation, but it means that a lot of customizing is no longer consistent from release to release. You don't need to know much about the CUI files themselves, because they aren't meant to be modified directly—so don't try. They are XML files and easily corrupted by editing. The following is taken directly from the beginning of the `ACAD.CUI` file:

```
Warning! Do not edit the contents of this file.
If you attempt to edit this file using an XML editor, you could
 lose customization and migration functionality.
If you need to change information in the customization file, use the
Customize User Interface dialog box in the product.
To access the Customize User Interface dialog box, click the Tools menu >
Customize > Interface, or enter CUI on the command line.
```

There are three kinds of CUI files and some significant differences of opinion over how to best handle them. Autodesk Support makes the following recommendations:

Enterprise CUI file Use this file type for custom company standards that aren't to be modified by individual users.

Partial CUI files Use this file type for third-party menus or custom menus that will be partially loaded.

Main CUI file (ACAD.CUI is the default) Use this file type to allow modification by each user according to their preferences.

> Before you do any customizing, make a backup copy of the ACAD.CUI file, which will be modified indirectly when you use the CUI command in AutoCAD. Don't be fooled by the presence of a file named ACAD.BAK.CUI. Although that file appears when you do any customizing using the CUI command, it's not a copy of the original ACAD.CUI file. It's one CUI modification older than the ACAD.CUI. Make your own backup of the original so you can restore it if things go wrong.

Creating a New Toolbar

The CUI is nice, even for long-time users who have done a lot of customizing in the past. The best thing about the CUI is that most, but not all, customizing is performed using the same techniques, whether you're modifying pull-down menus, toolbars, or any other menu-related item. Here's how to customize the CUI:

1. Open the Customize User Interface dialog box by typing **CUI** or right-clicking a toolbar button and selecting Customize.

2. Select Main CUI File (`acad.cui`) in the top pane. (See Figure 3.14.)

3. Right-click Toolbars in the upper-left pane, and select New → Toolbar from the menu.

4. Name your toolbar—use **Sybex** for this example.

5. Select All Commands in the Command List pane, as shown in Figure 3.15. Note that you can list commands in the following groups:

   • All commands available in AutoCAD

   • Only Express Tool Commands

   • Only control elements (windows that control things like plot scale, layer names, and so on)

   • Only commands associated with a specific category of pull-down menu

Legacy commands are older versions that no longer appear on a pull-down menu.

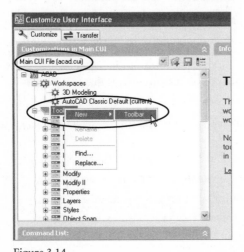

Figure 3.14

Creating a new toolbar in the CUI

Figure 3.15

Selecting commands to add to a toolbar

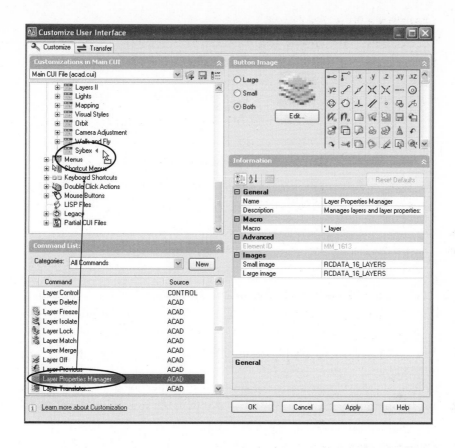

Figure 3.16

Dragging a command to a blank toolbar

6. Drag any command from the list onto your toolbar. A toolbar button for that command is created. (See Figure 3.16.)

   Most of AutoCAD's existing commands have a toolbar button icon already associated with them. If the command you add has a toolbar button image already, that icon is displayed in the Button Image pane. If not, the image in the pane is blank. You'll create a custom toolbar button later so you'll know how to handle a blank button.

7. The toolbar isn't actually created until you click either the Apply or the OK button at the bottom of the Customize User Interface dialog box.

The completed toolbar, shown in Figure 3.17, includes some commands, an express tool, and two control windows. Here's a complete list:

- Layer Properties Manager
- Layer control window
- Layer previous

- A separator
- Viewport Scale control window
- A custom text-placement command
- Match Properties
- Change Space
- Change Text Case
- Quick Dimension
- Dimension Style control window
- Dimension Style update
- Workspace control window
- Workspace Settings
- Flyout named Dims

Because this toolbar contains all the tools I want on a toolbar, I can turn off all the toolbars I don't need and get more drawing space. It's like getting a larger monitor.

Maybe you want to reorganize your toolbar buttons. You do that in the listing in the CUI shown in Figure 3.18, not on the toolbar itself. To rearrange any of the elements, just drag and drop them to new locations.

You can also edit the toolbar or any element of the toolbar by right-clicking the element you want to edit. Using the menu that pops up, you can do any of the following:

- Delete the toolbar or a tool on the toolbar.
- Rename the toolbar.
- Add a separation line by selecting Insert Separator (this toolbar includes three).
- Add a new toolbar.
- Add a flyout button, which is actually a toolbar attached to a single button.

Figure 3.17

Custom toolbar

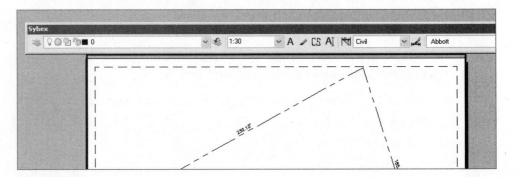

Writing a Custom Toolbar Button Macro

Although it's possible to add an empty button to a toolbar, if you want it to be useful, it must be based on a command. If the command doesn't exist, you have to define it yourself. So, let's start by creating a new command.

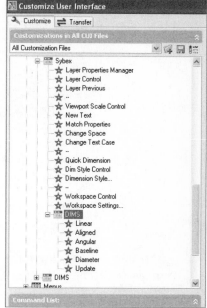

The purpose of this particular command is to create text that's always based on the romans.shx font and always placed on the correct layer, at a height of 0.125 for use in a layout. This is an example of how you can use menu macros to enforce office standards by making those standards easy to follow. When the command is complete, the original layer is made current. You just select the location of the text and type.

Use the following steps to create a new command:

1. Click the New button in the Command List pane.

2. In the Properties pane, change the name of the button from Command1 to something more descriptive, such as **NewText**.

3. Change the macro, which is a small program that creates your new command. To do so, open the Long String Editor shown in Figure 3.19 by clicking the ellipses button (…) at the end of the Macro pane. The ellipses button won't appear until you move your cursor to the end of the pane, and once the Long String Editor opens, the ellipses button is no longer visible.

Figure 3.18

CUI panel for the custom toolbar in Figure 3.17

You can create this command using AutoLISP instead of the language of menu macros. Doing so allows much greater control. For example, you can write it so that the text scales automatically to match the plot scale of the current viewport. For an example of the AutoLISP code required to scale text, see Chapter 9, "AutoLISP by Example—Getting Better."

A tooltip can be displayed for your command, but only if you add something meaningful to the Description window.

The new line should read as follows:

```
^C^C-style;romans;romans.shx;0;1;0;;;;-layer;m;text;;dtext;\0.125;0;layerp
```

The purpose of each element in this macro is identified in Table 3.1.

Figure 3.19

Creating a new menu macro

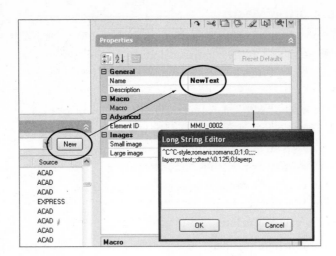

	MACRO ELEMENT	PURPOSE
Table 3.1	^C^C	In menu language, means ESC, ESC. Clicking the button cancels any active command before the command continues. If you're conservative, you can add a third ^C. That used to be necessary if you were editing a polyline vertex using PEDIT, but it no longer is.
Description of Elements of the Menu Macro	-style	Activates the STYLE command. The negative sign used as a prefix is required to prevent a dialog box from opening. If you aren't familiar with this, try typing it that way at the command prompt. Instead of a dialog box, you can create a text style directly. This technique is helpful in creating and troubleshooting menu macros, scripts, and AutoLISP programs.
	;	The equivalent of the Enter key. Put a semicolon in a menu anywhere you would press the Enter key if using the command line. For other files you'll use, the semicolon has a different meaning, so be prepared. The next 12 entries are responses to the STYLE command.
	romans;	Names the new text style. It's ignored if the style already exists.
	romans.shx;	Specifies the use of the romans.shx font for this text style.
	0;1;0;;;	Defines a text height of 0, width factor of 1, angle of 0, and format: not vertical, not backward, not upside down.
	;	Exits the STYLE command. This semicolon is often overlooked when users write macros.
	-layer;	Command-line version of the LAYER command. The next 4 entries are responses to this command, followed by a final semicolon to exit the LAYER command.
	m;text;;	Makes a new layer named text and makes it current. If the layer exists, the command is ignored.
	dtext;	Activates the DTEXT command.
	\	Pauses for user input, in a menu macro—in this case, the start point of text.
	0.125;0;	Sets the text height at 0.125 with a rotation angle of 0. This can be changed, or you can use a pause to let the user set a specific height.
	layerp	Issues the LAYERP (layer previous) command to restore the layer that was current at the time the command started. No final semicolon is needed because this command has no options like the LAYER and STYLE commands.

TOOLBAR BUTTON ICONS

To create a new tool-button icon, you must first select any existing icon and click the Edit button to change it. There's no blank button—that threw me at first, and it still seems odd. Clear the button you've selected, and use the rudimentary drawing tools to create a new one. Save the result. You'll find your new button at the bottom of the Button Image pane.

I don't know who creates all the button icons used in Windows programs, but they're 16-bit geniuses. I've never created anything nearly as nice as any predefined button, but I understand that entire websites are devoted to this art—even software for designing button icons.

By the way: When you take the trouble to create a new icon for a toolbar button, use it for both large and small icons. Select the Both radio button in the Button Image pane of the CUI.

Once you've created a new toolbar button, you must try it to see if it does what you want it to. It probably won't the first time, but don't get discouraged. Customizing requires troubleshooting. If your button doesn't work, you probably left out a semicolon.

Editing Pull-Down Menus

At first blush, it may be hard to imagine why you'd want to add anything to the pull-down menu structure. It seems pretty complete, after all. However, if you use the pull-down menus, you may find something missing, or, more likely, you may want to simplify or rearrange the many existing items. So you can see how to edit the pull-down menu, let's add one overlooked command to the File pull-down: the SAVE command.

I know it looks as if the SAVE command is already there. It's not the same SAVE command you get at the command line, however; it's actually the QSAVE command. But I like the command-line version, because it does something I wish all Windows software did: It lets you save a backup file to a different location, or with a different name, without changing the *default* path or filename. That's how the SAVE command differs from the SAVEAS command in AutoCAD.

Here is where the CUI starts to look really good, because adding a command to the pull-down menus is almost exactly like adding a new button to a toolbar. First, to avoid confusion, change the name of the existing Save command on the File pull-down menu to Qsave, as shown in Figure 3.20. To do so, select the command, and make your changes in the Properties pane of the CUI. (Notice that the existing macro is ^C^C_qsave.)

Now you can create the new version of the Save command and drag it onto the File pull-down menu. Follow these steps, and look at Figure 3.21 as an example:

1. Select the New button in the Command List pane.

2. Move to Properties, and change the command name and description.

Figure 3.20

**Changing the name
of the Save com-
mand to Qsave**

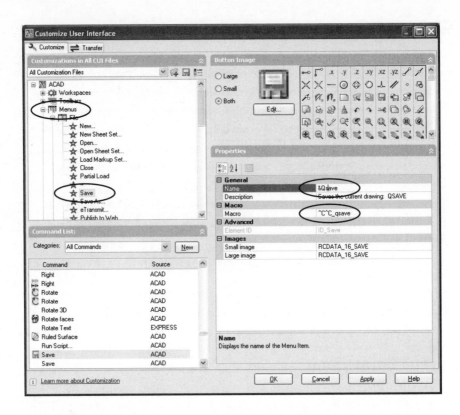

The ampersand (&) is used in a menu name to make the following character a quick-key. If
you hold down the Alt key while the File menu is displayed, typing the letter S selects this
command because it's preceded by the ampersand.

3. Type _save after the ^C^C in the Macro field.

The underscore in front of this and other menu commands forces AutoCAD to use the English-
language version of the SAVE command, even if the menu is being used with a version of
AutoCAD in another language. Sometimes a period is used in front of a command name so
the native version of the command is used even if it has been undefined using the UNDEFINE
command. The only reason to undefine a command is so you can redefine it as something
else—normally, using an AutoLISP program. Although you can use both a period and
an underscore, neither precaution is likely to be necessary. The default menu uses only an
underscore.

4. Drag the new command up to the File menu, and drop it in place.

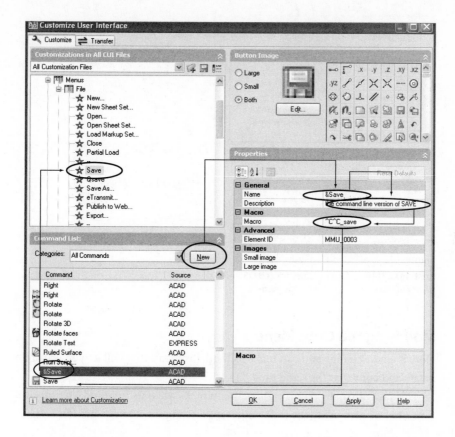

Figure 3.21

Adding the command-line version of SAVE to a pull-down menu

Modifying a Cursor Menu

Just so you can see the possibilities, let's modify the OSNAP cursor menu—the one shown in Figure 3.22, which pops up when you hold down the Shift key and press the right button on your mouse (or the middle button if MBUTTONPAN is set to 0). If you've ever wished this menu were shorter or organized differently, here is your chance. The OSNAP menu is known as a *shortcut menu* in the AutoCAD 2006 CUI. The process of editing the shortcut menu is the same as that to edit the toolbar menu:

- To add options, drag and drop them from the Command List: pane. Note the addition of the QuickCalc command in Figure 3.23.

- To change the order, drag the existing osnaps around. Note that Endpoint is now at the top.

- To eliminate some osnaps, right-click them and select Delete. Note that the Point Filters have been removed. Could this be any easier?

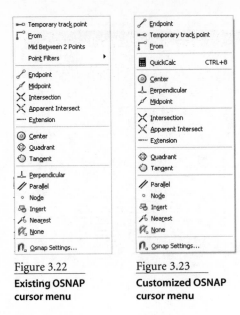

Figure 3.22

Existing OSNAP cursor menu

Figure 3.23

Customized OSNAP cursor menu

Modifying the Grips Menu

Here is a nice change you can make to the grips menu that will let you grip an object to rotate and copy it at the same time.

This task normally requires three menu picks when using standard grips. Let's get it down to one pick using the following steps (see Figure 3.24 as a guide):

1. Create a new command.

2. Give it the name **CopyRotate** for this example.

3. Add a description, if desired.

4. Delete the ^C^C (you don't want to cancel the grip mode, because you're trying to use it).

5. Add the following line to the Macro field: _rotate;_copy;_base; (you could eliminate the underscore in front of each command. They are used to internationalize the new command).

6. Drag the command onto the Grips menu. The result is shown in Figure 3.25.

If you use grips, begin noticing where you make more than one menu pick, and consider creating other combination commands for those actions.

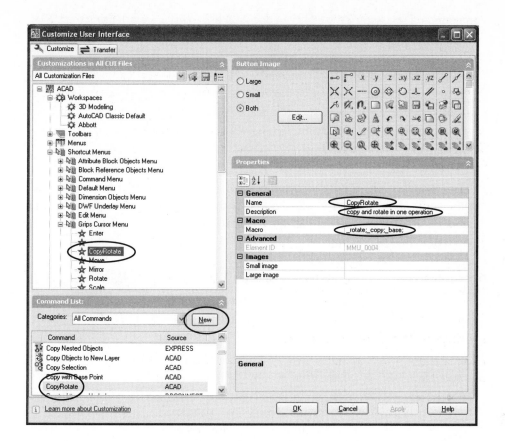

Figure 3.24

**Adding a command
to the Grips menu**

Assigning Keyboard Shortcuts

I don't think I'm the only AutoCAD user who frequently presses the F1 key
when I intend to press Esc, particularly on my laptop. Well, not only can
you redefine the F1 key, you can redefine many other keys on the keyboard
and have them do something immediately when they're pressed. The function keys are the best candidates for customizing; if you don't use the
default settings, why not redefine them? Because I don't use the F1 key to
get help in AutoCAD or any other Windows program, I define it as a cancel
key in AutoCAD. Because I often snap to a point halfway between the endpoints of two lines, I assign the MEE function of the CAL command to the
F4 key (this forces a running osnap of endpoint, where M2P would use
the current setting for running object snaps). I often need to use a paint

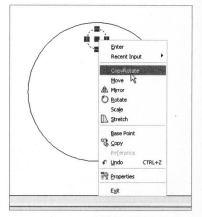

Figure 3.25

**Grips menu with the
new CopyRotate
command**

program, so I've assigned the F8 key to open it. I like to place a mark using the UNDO command, so I've assigned that function to the F9 key.

> To place a mark with the UNDO command, you type **UNDO** and select the Mark option. If, after continuing your editing session in AutoCAD for a while, you decide you want to undo all of your actions since you placed the mark, use the Back option of the UNDO command. If you forgot to place a mark, you can enter an integer instead to UNDO that number of steps. Change your mind again, and the REDO command will cancel all the steps.

You should consider using all the other function keys for something useful as well—your favorite object snaps, undoing multiple steps, performing various zoom commands, flipping from a layout to the Model Space tab, or issuing any commands that are difficult to type or to find on a menu.

> Unfortunately, ^C in AutoCAD isn't the same as Esc in Windows. If F1 is redefined as a cancel command using ^C^C, it does indeed cancel an active command, but it doesn't clear grips or highlighting from a selected object. To do that, add the AutoLISP function (sssetfirst nil) after the ^C^C, as described next.

When you select Keyboard Shortcuts in the top pane, you see a listing of the shortcut keys and their current assignments, as shown in Figure 3.26. There are two kinds of keyboard shortcuts: accelerator keys and temporary overrides.

Before you can assign an action to an accelerator key or combination of keys, that action must first exist as a command. Although two versions of a cancel command are already defined—one with a single cancel represented by ^C, the other with a double cancel represented by ^C^C—this example uses a triple cancel. That will cover any situations in which you must press the Esc key three times to return to an open command prompt from a deeply buried command option. Figure 3.27 shows the sequence for creating a command and assigning it to a shortcut key.

To assign a command to a shortcut key, follow these steps:

1. Define a new Cancel command, just as you defined a command for a new toolbar button in the previous section.

   The macro requires an additional ^C (OK, add two, just to be on the safe side—the ^ is added by pressing Shift+6). After the third ^C, add the small Lisp program (sssetfirst nil), which cancels the current selection set so the highlighting and grips are cleared. I named my version of the cancel command abbott-cancel to differentiate it from the other versions and to place it at the top of the list.

Figure 3.26

Existing keyboard shortcuts

Figure 3.27

Assigning a command to a keyboard shortcut

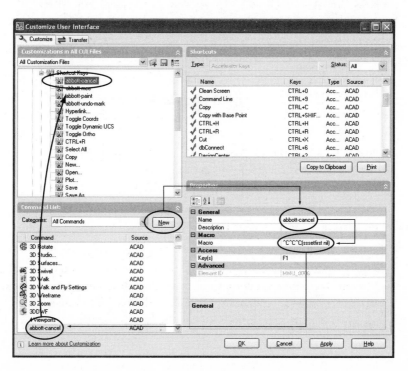

2. Open the Shortcut Keys menu, and drag the abbott-cancel command onto it. Once you've done this, a Key(s) field appears below the Macro field in the Properties pane. At the right of the field is a button with an ellipses (...). It will disappear when you click it to open the Shortcut Keys dialog box, shown in Figure 3.28.

3. Click in the field titled Press New Shortcut Key in the Shortcut Keys dialog box, and then press the F1 key.

In AutoCAD 2006, you must click the Assign button before exiting the Shortcut Keys dialog box, or the key won't be assigned!

You now have a new shortcut key.

The fours keys I've assigned are shown in Figure 3.29; they use the macros listed in Table 3.2. Any command name can be preceded with an underscore to internationalize it, and/or you can add a period to let the command be used on a system where the native command has been undefined.

Figure 3.28

The Shortcut Keys dialog box

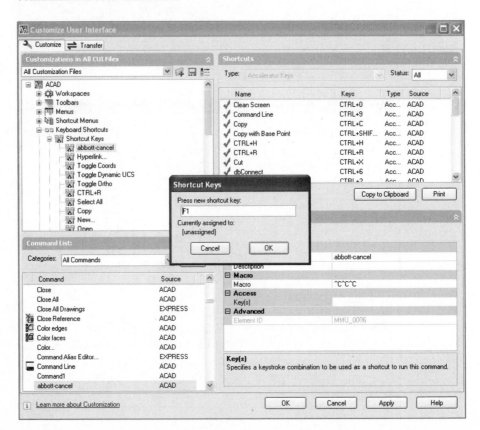

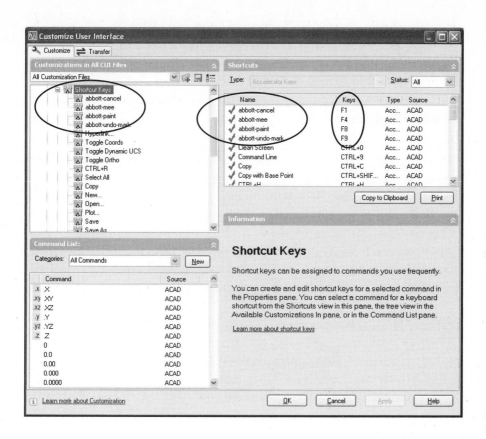

Figure 3.29

New shortcut keys

NAME	KEY	FUNCTION	MACRO
abbott-cancel	F1	Cancel, and clear selection set	`^C^C^C(sssetfirst nil)`
abbott-mee	F4	Snap midway between two endpoints transparently—no ^C	`'cal;mee;`
abbott-paint	F8	Open Paint Shop Pro	`^C^Cstart;psp;`
abbott-undo-mark	F9	Place UNDO mark	`^C^CUndo;m;`

Table 3.2

New Macros Assigned to Short-cut Keys

Linetypes (All Releases)

Linetypes are one of the few areas of customization not controlled by the CUI. They're defined in an external file named either ACAD.LIN for Imperial units or ACADISO.LIN for metric units. Both files are located in the Support folder of AutoCAD located in the user's Documents and Settings folder. Basic linetypes consist of dashes, dots, and spaces. Complex linetypes include text or shapes.

In Chapter 1, "AutoCAD Productivity," I describe an alternative method for creating a linetype—or at least what looks like a linetype—by placing blocks along a polyline with the MEASURE command.

Creating Basic Linetypes

Linetypes come in two flavors in AutoCAD: complex and basic. Most people never have any reason to create a basic linetype, but I have made several, including dotted linetypes that can be used to create grid paper at 4, 5, 8, or 10 dots per inch; and a hidden linetype that starts with a gap. Let's look at the beginning of the ACAD.LIN file and see how a linetype is defined, and then I'll illustrate several possibilities for customizing.

You've seen this trick earlier in the book, but to open this file quickly, type the following AutoLISP code at the command line, including the parentheses: **(startapp "notepad" (findfile "acad.lin"))**. Back up the original before modifying it.

The beginning of the ACAD.LIN file looks like this:

```
;;
;;  AutoCAD Linetype Definition file
;;  Version 3.0
;;  Copyright (C) 1991-2006 by Autodesk, Inc.  All Rights Reserved.
;;
;;  Note: in order to ease migration of this file when upgrading
;;  to a future version of AutoCAD, it is recommended that you add
;;  your customizations to the User Defined Linetypes section at the
;;  end of this file.
;;
*BORDER,Border __ __ . __ __ . __ __ . __ __ . __ __ .
A,.5,-.25,.5,-.25,0,-.25
*BORDER2,Border (.5x) __.__.__.__.__.__.__.__.__.__.
A,.25,-.125,.25,-.125,0,-.125
*BORDERX2,Border (2x) ____ ____ . ____ ____ . ____
A,1.0,-.5,1.0,-.5,0,-.5

*CENTER,Center ____ _ ____ _ ____ _ ____ _ ____ _ ____
A,1.25,-.25,.25,-.25
*CENTER2,Center (.5x) __ _ __ _ __ _ __ _ __ _ __
A,.75,-.125,.125,-.125
*CENTERX2,Center (2x) _____ __ _____ __ ____
A,2.5,-.5,.5,-.5
```

Each linetype definition requires two lines of text: a description line and a definition line. The description line has two fields separated by a comma. The first field gives the linetype a name, and the second field contains the description you see when you load the linetype. The definition line has multiple fields separated by commas; it always starts with the letter *A*, which stands for *aligned*.

> In theory, it's possible to use a code other than A in this field and change the way a linetype starts. I've never been able to make this function work, so perhaps it's a legacy function.

The other fields in the definition line define the linetype as containing a dot, a space, or a line segment. Once you've defined the repeating pattern of the linetype, there are no more fields. A linetype can't start with a space. If you want a space at the beginning of a linetype, start with a dot, then the space, and then the line segment. See Table 3.3 for a description of each field.

I've added two new linetypes at the end of this file. One is a dotted line with a dot spacing of 0.1 to use for making grid paper. The other is a hidden line that has a gap at the beginning for use in special situations (see Chapter 4, "Applying Graphics Standards"). Because of the way linetypes are generated, the first gap is larger than those that follow, and a dot will be at both ends of the line. Because this linetype is used to represent a feature that starts at a visible line, the dot won't show:

VALUE	FUNCTION
0	Represents a dot
-value	Represents a space the length of the value given
+value	Represents a line segment the length of the value given

Table 3.3

Function of Fields in a Linetype Definition

```
;;  User Defined Linetypes
;;
;;  Add any linetypes that you define to this section of
;;  the file to ensure that they migrate properly when
;;  upgrading to a future AutoCAD version.  If duplicate
;;  linetype definitions are found in this file, items
;;  in the User Defined Linetypes section take precedence
;;  over definitions that appear earlier in the file.
;;
*Grid01, 0.1 dot spacing for grid paper . . . . . . . . . . . . . .
A,0,-0.1
*Hidden-gap, specialty hidden line .  --.  --.  --.  --.  --.  --.
A,0,-0.125,0.25
```

Working with Complex Linetypes

There are two kinds of complex linetypes: those that include some text, like `"Hot Water"`; and those that include a shape, like `Batting`. This section will cover two different techniques for creating linetypes: The first modifies the `ACAD.lin` or `ACADISO.lin` file, and the second uses two Express Tools. I like the first technique for complex linetypes containing text and the second for complex linetypes using shapes.

Modifying the *ACAD.LIN* and *ACADISO.LIN* Files

If you're in an Imperial drawing with MEASUREMENT set to 0, the `ACAD.LIN` file is used to load linetypes. If you're in a metric drawing with MEASUREMENT set to 1, the `ACADISO.LIN` file is used. Both files are in the `\support` directory for the user (`C:\documents and settings\...`). Open the one you plan to use in Notepad, and back up the original.

Scroll down to the complex linetypes section. The first group uses shapes from `LTYPESHP.shx`, which is a compiled shape file that's shipped with AutoCAD. The second group uses text. The quickest way for you to create a text-based linetype is to copy and then modify one that exists. Following is the Hot Water Supply linetype that ships with AutoCAD, followed by a modified version of it for Cold Water Supply. Longer words require different settings for the two gaps, defined here as -.2 and -.2.

```
*HOT_WATER_SUPPLY,Hot water supply ---- HW ---- HW ---- HW ----
A,.5,-.2,["HW",STANDARD,S=.1,R=0.0,X=-0.1,Y=-.05],-.2
*COLD_WATER_SUPPLY,Cold water supply ---- CW ---- CW ---- CW ----
A,.5,-.2,["CW",ROMANS,S=0.1,R=30,X=-0.1,Y=-0.07],-.2
```

Just as in the basic linetype, each complex linetype definition with text has a pair of lines: The first contains the name and the description used to identify the linetype when you load it, and the second contains the code that defines the linetype. The basic parts of the linetype—dots, line segments, and gaps—are defined as described earlier. The only difference is that text is defined within square brackets.

> If you use a text style other than Standard for linetype definitions, make sure your drawings always contain the style you use. Otherwise you'll get a *bad linetype definition* error when you try to load a linetype.

Within the brackets are six fields separated by commas, as illustrated in Table 3.4.

> The final value in the definition (the value –.2 is used here) must create a large enough gap for the text string you define.

FIELD	SAMPLE VALUE	FUNCTION
1	"CW"	The text placed in the linetype. You enter it in quotations.
2	ROMANS	The name of the text style used for the text. The default is Standard, which is why complex linetypes always look so bad. You may want to redefine Standard by basing it on the ROMANS.SHX font. I prefer to use a text style named ROMANS.
3	S=0.1	Controls the text size. In this case, it's 0.1 units, making it a little smaller than the other text on a drawing.
4	R=30	Controls the angle at which the text is placed, in this case 30°.
5	X=-0.1	Controls the offset for the X coordinate start point. Setting it for a negative value that's ½ the gap defined centers the text horizontally.
6	Y=-0.07	Controls the offset for the Y coordinate start point. If the rotation angle used were 0, I'd set this to ½ the text height used. Because I used a rotation angle of 30°, a slightly larger value is required here to have the text centered.

Table 3.4

An Explanation of Linetype Fields

Using Express Tools to Create Complex Linetypes

Creating complex linetypes based on shape files is fairly easy with the Express Tools MKSHAPE (Make Shape) and MKLTYPE (Make Linetype). It's a two-step process: First you use the Make Shape tool to create a shape, and then you use the Make Linetype tool to create a linetype that uses that shape. Let's start with the Make Shape tool:

1. Draw a shape consisting of vectors with no solid or gradient hatch patterns. Use a shape that's about one unit long.

2. Select Express → Tools → Make Shape (see Figure 3.30).

Figure 3.30

Make Shape Express Tool

3. Save the shape file with an appropriate name in a folder that's in AutoCAD's search path. This should be a folder that has been placed at the top of the search path using OPTIONS (I discuss the OPTIONS command in Chapter 2, "Managing Your System").

4. Give a name for the shape when prompted at the AutoCAD command prompt.

5. Identify a resolution. The default value of 128 is normally fine for straight lines.

6. Pick an insertion point that will locate the shape properly when used as a linetype.

7. Select the objects you want to use as a shape. Your shape is saved in the file you specified.

Once you've created a shape, you need to use it to create a linetype:

1. Use the SHAPE command to insert one instance of your new shape using the default height and rotation.

> Because AutoCAD's SHX fonts are actually shapes, you can use text based on one of them with the Make Linetype tool. You may find that easier than editing the ACAD.LIN file.

2. Select Express → Tools → Make Linetype.

3. Create a linetype file in which to place the new linetype definition. Don't select an existing linetype file, such as ACAD.LIN, or it will be overwritten. You can copy the definition into the ACAD.LIN file later, if you choose.

4. Give the linetype a name. It can be the same as the filename, but it doesn't have to be.

5. Give the linetype a description.

6. Pick a starting point and an ending point that have enough room between them for the shape plus some space. (See Figure 3.31.)

7. When prompted, select the shape you inserted, *not* the original objects used to create it.

8. The linetype is created and loaded. If you want to load it into a different drawing, you can select the file it's in from the Linetype Manager dialog box and load it manually.

9. Select it like any other linetype, and assign it to a layer. The results of using a spline on a layer with the new arrow linetype are shown in Figure 3.32.

Figure 3.31

Defining the starting and ending points of the linetype definition

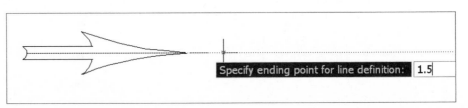

Specify ending point for line definition: 1.5

Figure 3.32
Arrow linetype

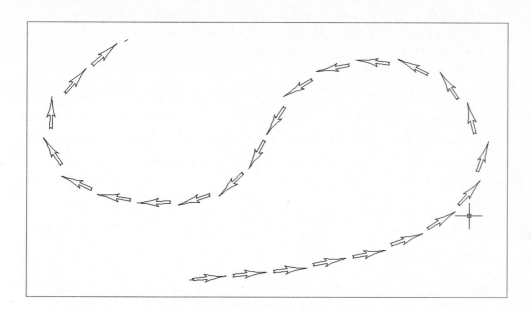

Linetype definitions become part of the drawings database when they're loaded. This presents no problem with the linetypes based on text, as long as the text font you use is a standard AutoCAD font. However, you may have a problem with the shape-based linetypes if you send the drawing file to someone else. Unless the shape file is on their computer and in the AutoCAD search path, the shapes won't display.

I've used an arrow linetype for creating egress plans for public buildings. But because the files use linetypes that may not be readable on someone else's computer, when you need such a linetype, you may want to make a block representing an arrow and then insert it along a polyline using the Block option of the MEASURE command. It looks best if you change its properties to spline-fit the polyline.

Enable Linetype generation for each polyline that is either spline-curved or fit-curved when using complex linetypes., Otherwise the linetype pattern may not display uniformly along its entire length. As an alternative, you could set the variable PLINEGEN to 1, but that may adversely affects the appearance of other lines.

CHAPTER 4

Applying Graphics Standards

Technical-graphics standards are the rules of drafting, developed over many years, that make technical communication more consistent and therefore more reliable. Because AutoCAD doesn't automatically apply proper graphics standards, that job falls to us. And it's not always easy.

Although there is some variation among offices, every discipline has generally accepted universal practices. The most clearly defined standards are those in the mechanical-design industry. Standards for drawings (and other engineering standards) are published by the American Society of Mechanical Engineers (ASME). ASME Y14.5M-1994 is the current standard for dimensioning, but it's due for an update soon. These standards are voluntary, although they're often specified in design contracts between firms.

All other design disciplines in the U.S.—including architectural, civil, surveying, electrical, electronic, piping, and welding—are based fundamentally on the same rules. If you use AutoCAD to design or to document designs, you have an obligation to follow the rules for communicating graphic information. That's especially true if you work in an environment where designs are shared with people from other countries. They probably speak a language other than yours, so you must rely on the common language of technical graphics to efficiently and accurately communicate your design intentions.

The default settings in AutoCAD don't come close to following these standards. The fact that the default settings get used so much, in offices and in books on using AutoCAD, isn't the fault of the software engineers at Autodesk: It's the fault of users who don't apply AutoCAD properly in their chosen discipline. This chapter is my attempt—some might call it a crusade—to rectify the problem.

- Dimensions

- Dimensioning Rules

- Text Styles

- Linetypes and Weights

- Applying Standards

Dimensions

You'll save yourself a lot of time and trouble if you use AutoCAD's associative dimensioning features by creating correct dimension styles. This area of AutoCAD is frequently applied incorrectly, particularly if the default dimension-variable settings are used. In this section you'll be creating several dimension styles that follow standards, work well in most applications, and can form the basis for a default style.

First I'll review some general information about AutoCAD dimensions and several variables that affect them, and then I'll take you step by step through the process of creating each style. You'll create only one dimension style for each discipline. If dimension styles are set to Scale Dimensions To Layout, you usually don't need multiple versions of each style.

> Dimension styles should be made part of the appropriate template files you use to start drawings. Once you've created a dimension style, you can use it in any drawing by using AutoCAD DesignCenter (ADC).

Background

Before getting into the nuts and bolts of setting up specific dimension styles, you may have some questions about dimensions. What kind of entity is a dimension? Why aren't drawing units used for dimensions? Why has the meaning of the term *associative dimension* changed? How standard is the Standard dimension style? How can you make your own arrowhead? I'll answer these questions in this section.

Anonymous Blocks

What is a dimension? It's an *anonymous block*. Anonymous blocks are defined by AutoCAD, not by the user. They aren't listed as block definitions in the Insert and Block Definition dialog boxes; that's what makes them anonymous. They aren't listed, because they have no names—at least, not normal block-definition names. In the drawing's database, dimension blocks have abnormal names: They all begin with an asterisk and the letter *D*, followed by an incrementing value—*D1, for example.

> That asterisk in front of dimension names can be pesky. When I wrote an AutoLISP program to create a drawing file from each block definition in a drawing, I wanted the drawing files to have the same names as the block definitions. Because the asterisk isn't allowed in filenames, I had to filter out anonymous blocks.

Anonymous blocks include both hatch patterns and dimensions, but here we're concerned about dimensions. When you use the Properties palette to look at the properties of a dimension, it's identified as a specific dimension type, such as a Rotated Dimension, an Aligned Dimension, or a 3-Point Angular Dimension, but there's more here than meets the eye. All dimensions, no matter how they're listed in the Properties palette, are actually block references. They don't have the kinds of names that other blocks have, and you won't see them listed in the Insert or Block dialog box, but you can explode them into their component parts: text, lines, and solids. Of course, you shouldn't explode a dimension unless you want to use one of its components for some other purpose. You may want to use the 2D solid used for the arrowhead as a symbol by itself, for example, or generate text that will be placed in a table.

Although exploding a dimension is possible, it's nearly always a bad idea. Once the dimension is exploded, it doesn't update, it can't be selected as a single entity, and it doesn't move with the object it's annotating.

Units

Why aren't drawing units used for dimensions? Because drawing units control the display of numerical information at the command line, in dialog boxes, or in the AutoCAD text window. You may want to use the DIST command to obtain a distance in decimal format, but want dimensions to use Architectural format. I like having the option of using two different systems for two different purposes, but it confuses users sometimes.

Settings in the Drawing Units dialog box determine how AutoCAD displays information in the status bar, the command line, the text window, and certain dialog boxes. Don't make the mistake of thinking these settings have any effect on the appearance of your dimensions; they don't. You set the units used for dimensions in the Primary Units tab of the New Dimension Style or Modify Dimension Style dialog box.

Associativity

If a dimension is *associative*, it's connected with the geometry it represents. Change the geometry, and the dimension changes. Move the geometry, and the dimension moves. But that's only been true since AutoCAD 2002. Before that, dimensions were called associative, but they weren't. At least, they weren't associated with the entities you dimensioned. They were associated with definition points (defpoints), those little dots that are placed at the dimension origins you select. Dimensions seemed associative because if you stretched your geometry, you probably included the defpoints in the crossing window and moved the points as well as the lines, polylines, or arcs you were stretching. As of AutoCAD 2002, dimensions are really associative—move the geometry, and the dimension moves.

The relationship between dimensions and the objects they represent was controlled only by the variable DIMASO before AutoCAD 2002. With DIMASO set to 1, dimensions are blocks. With DIMASO set to 0, dimensions are exploded when inserted. That's why DIMASO should always be set to 1 in all releases of AutoCAD.

DIMASO was superceded, but not replaced, in AutoCAD 2002 by the DIMASSOC variable. Now associativity is controlled by two different variables. If you open an existing drawing done prior to AutoCAD 2002, it doesn't have a DIMASSOC setting, so the setting for DIMASSOC is set to the value used in that drawing for DIMASO.

Unlike DIMASO, which can only be on or off, the DIMASSOC variable has three settings:

- *0*—The same as setting DIMASO to 0. All dimensions are exploded when they're created (a bad idea).

- *1*—The same as setting DIMASO to 1. All dimensions are inserted as block references but aren't associated directly with the objects they represent.

- *2*—No similar setting in DIMASO. All dimensions are inserted as block references, *and* they're associated with the object they're dimensioning.

With DIMASSOC set to 2, if you dimension a circle and move the circle, the dimension moves with it. If you add a dimension in Paper Space, you *usually* get the right value, regardless of the zoom scale of your viewport, and the dimension moves with the object. Leave DIMASSOC set to 2 in new drawings, and set it to 2 on drawings done in prior releases whenever you open one.

Standard Dimension Style

By default, AutoCAD has a dimension style named either Standard (for Imperial units) or ISO-25 (for metric units). Don't be fooled. Neither of these styles meets any standard—don't use them. It's not even a good idea to modify the existing dimension style while retaining either name. Come up with your own name for each dimension style, because there is always a chance that the drawing will be inserted or XRefed into another drawing.

Whenever you try to combine two drawings that use the same name for a dimension style, you have a potential conflict. Unless the styles are identical, one of them will make changes when overwriting the other. The same is true for text and table styles as well. Since most drawings will have a default dimension style that is named Standard, the chances are that you will encounter this conflict if you use the same name. So protect all the work you do by creating a dimension style with a new name. You don't know how a drawing may be used in the future, so your best bet is to avoid using either Standard or ISO-25 as a name at all.

You can delete the Standard style, but don't be surprised when it shows up again if you insert another drawing.

Custom Arrowhead

There aren't many things you can do to make your dimensions look different from those of every other AutoCAD user, but you can create a custom arrowhead. I personally like the traditional open arrowhead that I used when drawing by hand. In AutoCAD, I reproduce that venerable shape with a line segment and two large radius arcs. (See Figure 4.1.) If you're as nostalgic as I am for the arrowheads of yore, do this:

1. On layer 0, draw an arrowhead one unit long and pointing to the right.

2. Define a block with the arrowhead you just drew, using the arrow point as the insertion point.

3. Select User Arrow from the bottom of the First list in the Arrowheads section of the Symbols And Arrows tab of the Modify Dimension Style dialog box.

4. Select your arrowhead block by name. If you want to use your custom arrowhead for leaders, you have to specify that by selecting it from the list of possible arrowheads in the Leader pane of the Symbols and Arrows tab.

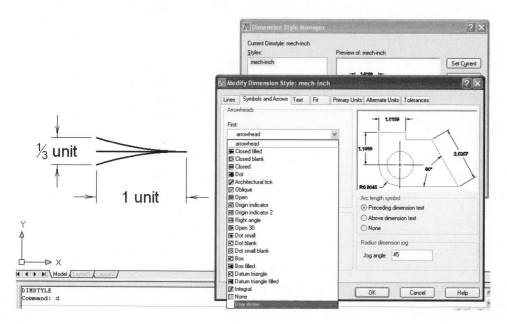

Figure 4.1

Creating a custom arrowhead

Mechanical Dimensions

In the United States, we use three primary kinds of mechanical dimension styles: decimal-inch, U.S. metric, and International Standards Organization (ISO) metric. These styles are defined in a document produced by either the American Society of Mechanical Engineers (ASME) or the ISO. This section includes step-by-step instructions for creating acceptable dimension styles for each of these systems. All recommended changes for each tab are circled in the figure of that tab.

Some of the values that I recommend changing already meet the ASME standard where that standard specifies a range. The default AutoCAD settings in those cases are generally maximum sizes, so I recommend a switch to the minimum sizes to ease the problem of placing dimensions on complex geometry.

DIMVARS

When you make changes to a dimension style using the New Dimension Style or Modify Dimension Style dialog box, you're actually changing AutoCAD system variables. These variables control the appearance of your dimensions. A dimension style is a saved collection of variables.

Each dimension variable starts with the letters *DIM*, and there are now 79 of these variables. DIMCEN, for example, controls both the size and the appearance of center marks; DIMSCALE controls the scaling of dimensions in a floating viewport. Unless you're writing a script or an AutoLISP program that uses or changes dimension variables, you'll seldom have to know their names. If you take the plunge after reading Chapter 7, "Scripts," and Chapters 8 and 9, "Lisp by Example," you can get a list of dimension-variable names in the Help system or type **SETVAR⏎?⏎DIM*⏎** at the command line.

Decimal-Inch

To create an acceptable dimension style for drawings based on decimal-inch units, follow these steps:

1. Start an Imperial drawing.

2. Use the DIMSTYLE command (type the alias **D**) to open the Dimension Style Manager.

3. Rename the Standard style using a name that makes sense to you. (See Figure 4.2.) For this example, I used the name Decimal-Inch.

4. Select the Modiy button and make the changes to each tab, as shown in the following sections.

LINES TAB

The Lines tab contains controls for dimension lines and extension lines. I think the existing settings create dimensions that are too crowded. To allow placement of more dimensions without as much clutter, make the following changes to settings on the Lines tab, as shown in Figure 4.3:

- Dimension Lines → Baseline Spacing: 0.25
- Extension Lines → Extend Beyond Dim Lines: 0.0625 (¹⁄₁₆″)

AutoCAD 2002 and AutoCAD 2004 have a bug that prevents the baseline-spacing value from scaling when dimensions are scaled to a layout. This infuriating glitch was fixed in AutoCAD 2005.

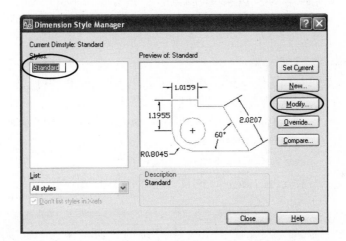

Figure 4.2

Changing name of dimension style

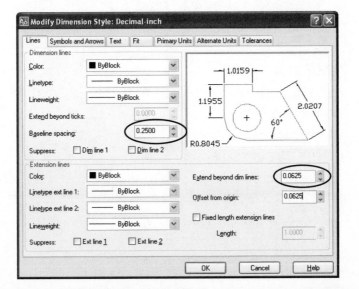

Figure 4.3

Lines tab

SYMBOLS AND ARROWS TAB

The Symbols And Arrows tab controls dimension features that used to be in the Lines And Arrows tab. To control the appearance of arrowheads and center marks, I recommend the changes shown in Figure 4.4:

- Arrowheads → Arrow Size: 0.125
- Center Marks → Line
- Center Marks → Size: 0.0625
- Arc-Length Symbol → Above Dimension Text

Setting the center-mark style to Line allows you to use the DIMCENTER (DCE) command to quickly place proper center marks. This is the equivalent of setting a negative value for the variable DIMCEN. Later, in the section "Child Variations: Radial and Diameter," I'll recommend that you set this value to None for styles used for diameters and radii.

TEXT TAB

The Text tab controls the style, appearance, and position of text. I recommend the following changes, as shown in Figure 4.5:

- Text Appearance → Text Style: romans (or any style name you use for an acceptable font)
- Text Appearance → Text Height: 0.125
- Text Placement → Offset From Dim Line: 0.04

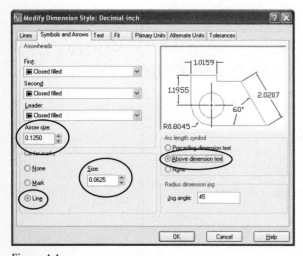

Figure 4.4

Symbols And Arrows tab

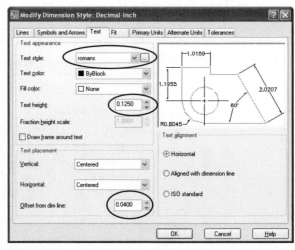

Figure 4.5

Text tab

Set the text style to one that's based on an acceptable font. Only one font that ships with AutoCAD meets all standards of technical graphics: `romans.shx`. Some offices use others, including `arial.ttf`, which I use for illustrations that I plan to put into another document. Whatever font your style is based on, don't name that style Standard. (I use the font name as the style name.)

If you haven't yet created a text style, click the button with the three dots (the ellipses, …) next to the Text Style drop-down list. The Text Style dialog box opens. Create a new style based on the `romans.shx` font with a height of 0, and close the dialog box. Now, select your new style from the drop-down list.

> The height assigned when you create a new text style should always be 0 so that it can be adjusted automatically for plotting. If you ever find that the text height for a dimension is much too small, even though all the other parts of the dimension are fine, check the text style. I'm betting you set the height to a fixed value, not to 0.

A text height of 0.125 meets ASME standards, and changing Offset From Dim Line to 0.04 makes it more likely that a dimension will fit inside the extension lines.

FIT TAB

The Fit tab controls the manner in which AutoCAD places dimensions and text, as well as the important scaling factor used for all dimension features. Set the Fit tab settings to those illustrated in Figure 4.6. Here are the specifics:

- Fit Options → Arrows
- Scale For Dimension Features → Scale Dimensions To Layout

Figure 4.6

Fit tab

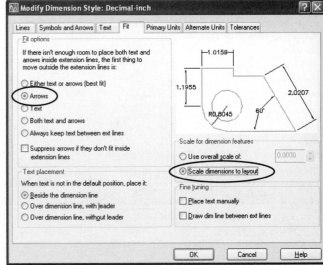

You normally move the dimension arrows outside of extension lines when there isn't room for both text and arrows, so select Arrows in the Fit Options. However, you may encounter a situation where either Both Text And Arrows or Always Keep Text Between Ext Lines works better. If your dimensions don't appear where you want them automatically, try one of those two settings and see if the situation improves.

Select Scale Dimensions To Layout so dimensions are a consistent size when plotting (as discussed in greater detail in Chapter 6, "Plotting"). Selecting Scale Dimensions To Layout requires that you use layouts correctly.

PRIMARY UNITS TAB

The Primary Units tab includes the same kinds of controls found in the Drawing Units dialog box. You don't have to use the same settings in both places. Figure 4.7 demonstrates the settings I recommend on the Primary Units tab:

- Linear Dimensions → Precision: 0.000
- Linear Dimensions → Zero Suppression: Leading (for decimal inch, not for metric)
- Angular Dimensions → Precision: 0.0
- Angular Dimensions → Zero Suppression: Leading

Changes in this tab depend on your application. In the U.S., the number of decimal places used on a mechanical drawing indicates a tolerance as defined in the title block. Don't use too many decimal places, because doing so implies a closer, and much more expensive, tolerance for each dimension. Set the number of decimal places only to what you need—I use three for a general style, and four for mechanical parts where classes of fits or tool-room tolerances are being used. Precision for individual dimensions can be changed to reflect a greater or lesser tolerance.

> You can easily change precision for a particular dimension after it's placed. Select the dimension, right-click, and choose Precision.

ALTERNATE UNITS TAB

The Alternate Units tab was added to AutoCAD at a time when dual dimensions—inches and millimeters—were often used for international customers; however, the current ASME standard is to use either inches or millimeters for dimensions, but not both. In

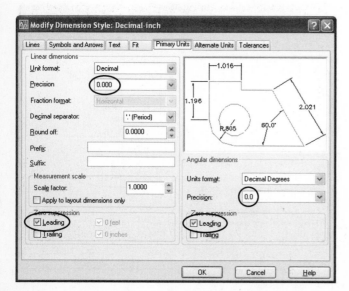

other words, the Alternate Units tab isn't used much these days. In fact, DOD-STD-1476 prohibits dual dimensions on military drawings. If for some reason you must place dual dimensions, you should know about two ways to convert dimensions from inches—hard conversions and soft conversions

A hard conversion is the result of multiplying one value by its exact conversion factor to get the other value. In converting metric to inches, this would mean multiplying all dimensions by 25.4. The result is exact, but it may appear very unusual to those who normally use the alternative units. A value of 3.375″ would be common in the U.S., but its hard conversion to 85.725mm would be unusual to those designing in millimeters. Likewise, a conversion from 1420mm to 55 ²⁹⁄₃₂″ would seem odd to someone who normally uses fractional inches.

A soft conversion is only used when a hard conversion isn't necessary. In a soft conversion one value is close to, but not exactly the same as, the other, but both are common values in each system. Although .125″ may be 3.175mm when a hard conversion is used, a soft conversion of 3mm is close enough for things like text height.

Use the following settings for hard conversions, after checking the Display alternative units box in the upper left corner of the tab:

- Alternate Units → Multiplier For Alt Units: 25.4 (the exact conversion factor between inches and millimeters)

- Alternate Units → Precision: One less than the precision you would normally use for decimal-inches

If you want soft conversions for placing dual dimensions, use these settings:

- Alternate Units → Multiplier For Alt Units: 25.4

- Alternate Units → Precision: 0

Generally, it's easier to read dual-dimensions on parts when one value is displayed over the other, so I also suggest selecting Below Primary Value under Placement.

TOLERANCES TAB

Here are my recommendations:

- Tolerance Format → Method: Limits

- Tolerance Format → Precision: 0.0000

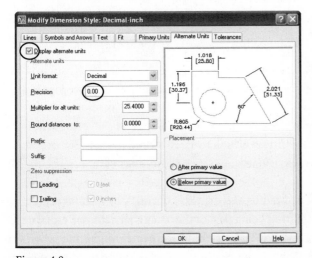

Figure 4.8
Alternative Units Tab

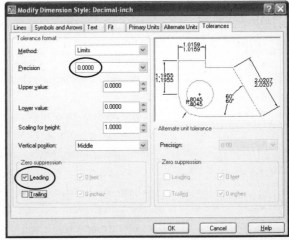

Figure 4.9
Tolerances Tab

If you use tolerances on individual dimensions, try creating a separate dimension style called Decimal-inch-tol for doing those dimensions. I also suggest changing the method to Limits. It takes up less room than the other methods, and most machinists prefer limit tolerances, in my experience.

The reason I'd leave the upper and lower tolerance values at 0 is that they can be changed individually using the Properties palette. This kind of tolerance is generally used for precision fits, so the upper and lower tolerances are different for each dimension. Note the recommendation in Chapter 1, "AutoCAD Productivity," that you create geometry to Maximum Material Condition. If you follow that advice, one of the limits is always zero, depending on the type of feature being dimensioned.

> If you do a lot of tolerance dimensions or apply geometric dimensioning and tolerancing frames, consider using the excellent AutoCAD Mechanical.

CHILD VARIATIONS: RADIAL AND DIAMETER

Once you've created a basic dimension style, you can add variations that apply only to certain kinds of dimensions. These are known as *child styles*; they're associated with a parent style and start with all the same settings as the parent style. These variations let you fine-tune a dimension style.

To add child styles, click the OK button at the bottom of the Modify Dimension Style dialog box, and return to the Dimension Style Manager. Click the New button, and then select Radius Dimensions under Use For, as shown in Figure 4.10. Click Continue, and make the following changes for radius dimensions.

- Symbols And Arrows → Center Marks → None

- Fit → Fit Options → Both Text And Arrows

- Fit → Fine Tuning → Place Text Manually

Now do the same thing for diameter dimensions. When you're done, you have a new style with two child variations that will work for most mechanical dimensions (see Figure 4.11).

> If you prefer to have the dimension line placed inside the arc or circle whenever the dimension text is outside, set Fit to Arrows instead of Both Text And Arrows. This is one of the dimension properties that *cannot* be changed using the Properties palette.

These child variations let you add radius and diameter dimensions without center marks. You prevent a center mark from being part of the block that defines a radial or diameter dimension. If you use DIMCENTER (DCE) to add center marks only when you need them, they have extensions that you can delete without exploding the dimension. In the example shown in Figure 4.12, I added center marks independently and then placed radial and diameter dimensions directly, without any post-placement editing.

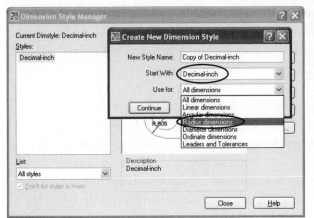

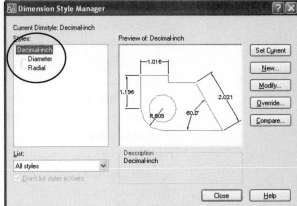

Figure 4.10
Radius variations

Figure 4.11
Child styles

Figure 4.12
Using child styles

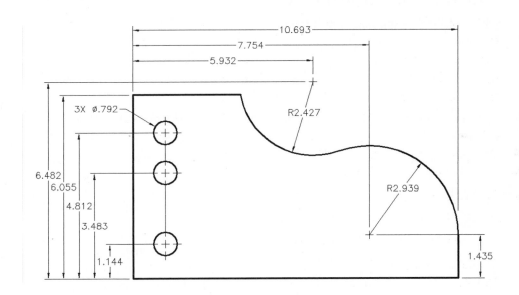

ASME Metric and ISO

The Metric Conversion Act of 1975 committed the United States to convert to the International System of Units (SI, from Le Systeme International d'Unites). Metric units are used widely in manufacturing, but in practice, they're often applied differently in different shops. In a sense, we use two metric systems in the U.S.: an ASME version and an ISO version. What I call the ASME version replaces U.S. customary units with millimeters and retains the horizontal orientation of dimensions. The ISO version uses an aligned orientation and doesn't permit the use of decimal precision to indicate varying tolerances. When you use metric units for ASME standard drawings, dimension orientation usually follows the horizontal format used for U.S. customary units. Some offices change the value of

DIMSCALE to 25.4—the conversion factor from inches to millimeters—when they need to dimension a metric drawing. In my view, it's better practice to spend a little time creating a dimension style that contains dimension sizes in millimeters so you can still set DIMSCALE to 0 for automatic scaling in layouts.

> The U.S. officially adopted the metric system in 1866. U.S. customary units are defined by their metric equivalents. The foot is legally defined to be exactly 0.3048 meter, and the pound is legally defined to equal exactly 453.59237 grams.

For metric drawings under the ASME Y14.5-1994 standard, you can create a Metric style by starting with the Decimal-Inch style described earlier and making the following changes to all size-related values. These are soft conversion values, because hard conversion values would result in values that would be odd in the metric system, like 3.125:

- 0.04 inch is approximately 1mm.
- 0.0625 inch is approximately 1.5mm.
- 0.125 inch is approximately 3mm.
- 0.25 inch is approximately 6mm.
- 0.375 inch is approximately 9mm.

The only other changes are in the Primary Units tab of the Modify Dimension Style dialog box:

1. Set Precision to one decimal place less than you would for a comparable drawing in decimal-inches.
2. *Don't* suppress leading zeros for metric.
3. *Do* suppress trailing zeros for metric.

The standard style used in the ACADISO.dwt template for the ISO system is pretty good, but it requires a font change:

1. Start a metric drawing from scratch.
2. Rename ISO-25 to something logical.
3. Replace the Standard text style with one based on the romans.shx font.

> You'll seldom find the type of chain dimensions created by the DIMCONTINUE command on a mechanical part. Why? Because such dimensioning results in an accumulation of tolerance errors that gets larger with each dimension. It's far more likely that DIMLINEAR will be used to add a base dimension, with DIMBASELINE used to add additional dimensions. For mechanical parts, I usually prefer coordinate dimensioning placed with the Ordinate option of the QDIM command or the DIMORDINATE command.

Architectural Dimensions

Architectural dimensioning practices vary more widely than do mechanical practices, because there's no published standard comparable to the ASME Y14.5 series on technical graphics. However, despite some variation in look and feel from office to office, the basic rules laid out in the ASME standards generally apply. The differences tend to be in the number of lineweights used, the symbols used for sections, and the styles used for dimensioning. My recommendations in this section reflect the kinds of dimensions used by most of the architectural firms I'm familiar with. Generally, we use feet and fractional inches in this country for architectural drawings, with chain (continuous) dimensions. The rest of the world uses millimeters, and some firms are beginning to use ordinate dimensioning for plans, which I think results in fewer measurement errors.

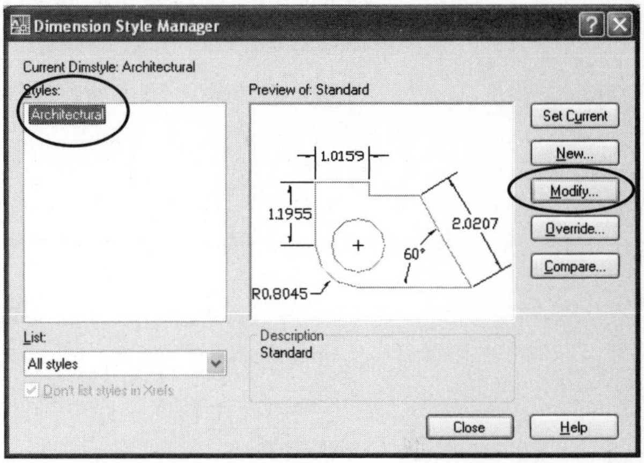

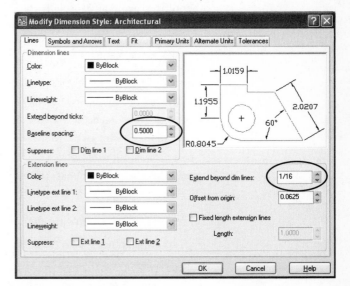

Figure 4.13

Creating an Architectural dimension style

Feet and Inches

Open the Dimension Style Manager, and rename Standard to Architectural. (Don't use the name Standard, of course.) Once the style has been renamed, you can click the Modify button and make the following changes in the Modify Dimension Style dialog box. You may prefer different treatment for arrowheads, dimension lines, extension lines, font, and other settings, but these recommendations have worked well for me. (See Figure 4.13.)

LINES TAB

The spacing of dimension lines and the appearance of extension lines are controlled in the Lines tab. To allow placement of dimensions without as much clutter, I recommend the following changes, as shown in Figure 4.14:

- Dimension Lines → Baseline Spacing: ⅜–½
- Extension Lines → Extend Beyond Dim Lines: ⅟₁₆

Figure 4.14

Lines tab: Architectural

AutoCAD 2002 and AutoCAD 2004 have a bug that prevents the baseline spacing value from scaling when dimensions are scaled to a layout. It was fixed in AutoCAD 2005.

SYMBOLS AND ARROWS TAB

I suggest that you set the values controlled in the Symbols And Arrows tab to the same settings as those for mechanical. I recommend the following changes, as shown in Figure 4.15:

- Arrowheads → Arrow Size: ⅛
- Center Marks → Line
- Center Marks → Size: ¹⁄₁₆
- Arc Length Symbol → Above Dimension Text

Leave arrowheads set to Closed Filled for use with radius or diameter dimensions and set tick marks for linear dimensions as a child style.

TEXT TAB

Fonts with a `.shx` extension are vector-based fonts that come with AutoCAD. Fonts with a `.ttf` extension are Windows system fonts that may or may not be available on any given Windows computer. (See the "Text Styles" section for the solution to that problem.) Therefore, I normally use `romans.shx`, which is an acceptable font for architectural drawings but doesn't look as stylish as most offices like. You may want to use the `cityblueprint.ttf` font, which I find the more readable of the two blueprint fonts (`countryblueprint.ttf` is the other). Most offices have both those fonts on their workstations. If you send drawings to other offices, avoid any specialty third-party fonts that don't come with AutoCAD, or use eTransmit to package the fonts with the drawings when you send them.

As of AutoCAD 2007, AutoCAD finally ships with a hand-lettered looking SHX font named `hand1.shx`. Unfortunately, it's a little *too* hand-lettered looking for my taste. Fifteen years ago, I bought a third-party font named `chisel.shx` to use with R10 that looked better and was much more readable than the CityBlueprint and CountryBlueprint fonts. The SHX fonts have some advantages over TTF fonts, so I'm pleased that `hand1.shx` is included in the shipping version; but could we get one that looks a little nicer? Maybe someday AutoCAD will ship with a nonproportional version of *all* the common fonts.

I recommend the following changes, as shown in Figure 4.16:

- Text Appearance → Text Style: Based on one of the following fonts—`romans.shx`, `cityblueprint.ttf`, or `hand1.shx`
- Text Appearance → Text Height: ⅛
- Text Placement → Offset From Dim Line: ¹⁄₃₂–¹⁄₁₆

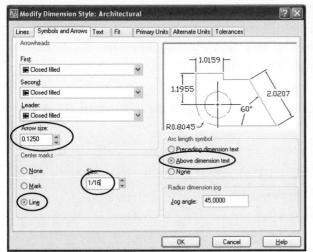

Figure 4.15

Symbols And Arrows tab: Architectural

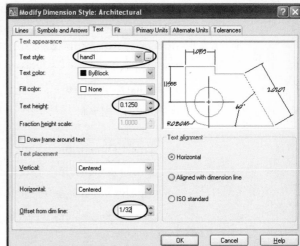

Figure 4.16

Text tab: Architectural

Because the parent style controls only angles, radii, and diameters, leave Text Alignment as Horizontal, and define a child linear style for dimensions that are to be aligned and centered.

FIT TAB

There isn't much to change for the Fit tab in architectural dimensions, but the controls in the Fit tab can cause all kinds of placement problems later. Figure 4.17 shows three settings I always change:

- Fit Options → Arrows
- Text Placement → Over Dimension Line, With Leader
- Scale For Dimension Features → Scale Dimensions To Layout

Figure 4.17

Fit tab: Architectural

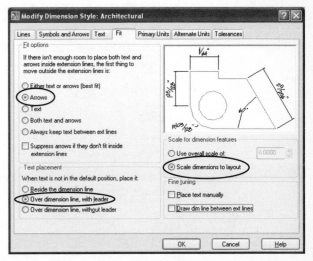

The Fit tab controls the manner in which AutoCAD fits the text and arrows for dimensions into the space available. You normally move the arrows outside of extension lines when there isn't room for both text and arrows, so select Arrows under Fit Options. However, in some situations, either Both Text And Arrows or Always Keep Text Between Extension Lines works better. If your dimensions don't appear where you want them automatically, try one of those two settings and see if the situation improves.

When dimensions are too small to fit between extension lines, I like to have them connected to their proper location with a leader. Select Scale Dimensions To Layout so dimensions are a consistent size when plotting. Selecting Scale Dimensions To Layout requires that you use layouts correctly. See Chapter 6 for information on plotting.

PRIMARY UNITS TAB

The Primary Units tab is where architectural dimensions become architectural. Figure 4.18 shows at least one recommendation that may surprise you:

- Linear Dimensions → Unit Format: Architectural
- Linear Dimensions → Precision: 0′-0 1/256″ (see the following explanation)
- Linear Dimensions → Fraction Format: Diagonal
- Zero Suppression → 0 Feet but not 0 inches

I remind you that the value set in the Drawing Units dialog box isn't used for dimensions. You must set dimension units here. Why the ½₅₆″ precision? I set the precision to the smallest possible value; that way, any drawing errors show up as I add dimensions. If I make no mistakes creating the geometry, I don't ever see a fraction smaller than ¼″ in a dimension.

I find that setting fractions to Diagonal is easiest for me to read, and suppressing 0 feet, but not 0 inches, helps fit text into smaller spaces between extension lines while clarifying that some dimensions really are in whole feet.

> A bug in AutoCAD 2002 prevents any setting for Zero Suppression from being applied. To control suppression in AutoCAD 2002, change DIMZIN to 3 at the command line to display 0 inches and suppress 0 feet. Save the resulting override to the current dimension style. This bug—more of a flea, really—was fixed as of AutoCAD 2004.

Figure 4.18

Primary Units tab: Architectural

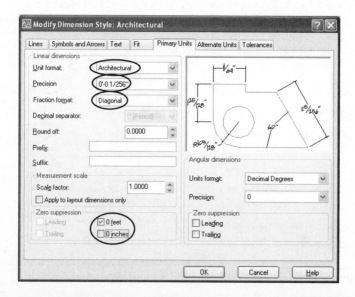

ALTERNATE UNITS AND TOLERANCES TABS

Unless you want to add dual dimensions to a drawing that will be used in another country, there's no reason to change any settings in the Alternate Units tab. Tolerances aren't generally used in architectural drawings, so there is no reason to change the Tolerances tab either.

LINEAR CHILD STYLE

Child variations let you define a single parent style that controls almost all dimension features for most types of dimensions and then customize the appearance of other types. Because I like using horizontal dimensions for radius, angular, and diameter dimensions, I use a child variation to make linear dimensions look right.

To create a child variation, do the following (see Figure 4.19):

1. Select Architectural in the Styles list.

2. Click the New button.

3. Select Linear Dimensions in the Use For drop-down list and select the Continue button.

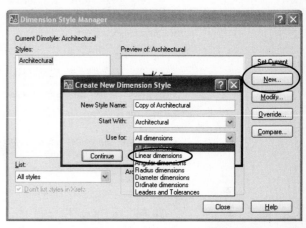

Figure 4.19

Linear child variation

Under the Symbols And Arrows tab, change the following (see Figure 4.20):

- Arrowheads → First: Architectural Tick

- Arrowheads → Second: Architectural Tick

- Arrowheads → Arrow Size: 1⁄16

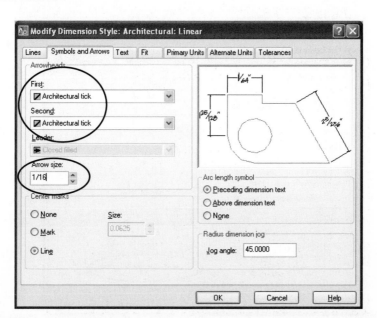

Figure 4.20

Symbols And Arrows tab: Linear

Under the Text tab, change the following (see Figure 4.21):

• Text Placement → Vertical: Above

• Text Alignment → Aligned With Dimension Line

• Under the Fit tab, change the following (see Figure 4.22):

• Fine Tuning → Draw Dim Line Between Ext Lines

When placing linear dimensions in small areas, AutoCAD often leaves out the dimension lines—even though they may fit between extension lines—unless you check Draw Dim Line Between Ext Lines.

Figure 4.21

Text tab: Linear

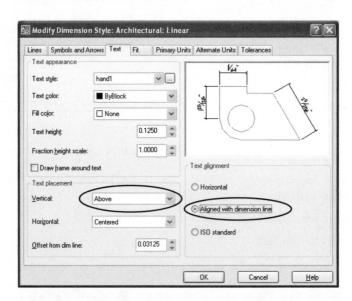

Figure 4.22

Fit tab: Linear

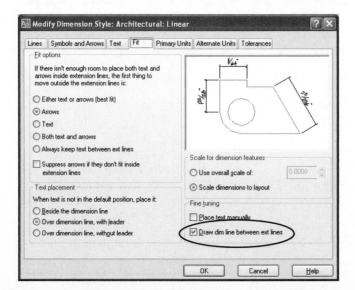

RADIAL AND DIAMETER CHILD STYLES

To set up child variations for radial dimensions, click OK to close the Modify Dimension Style dialog and then do the following:

1. Select Architectural in the Styles list.

2. Select New in the Dimension Style Manager dialog box.

3. Select Radius Dimensions in the Use For drop-down list.

4. Select None for Center Marks on the Symbols And Arrows tab.

5. Check Place Text Manually on the Fit tab.

Repeat these steps to create a child dimension style for diameter dimensions. The result looks like Figure 4.23 when you list dimension styles in the Dimension Style Manager dialog box.

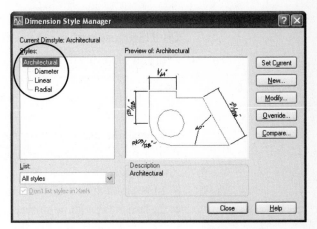

Figure 4.23

Architectural style with child variations

Architectural Metric

To create a metric style for architectural drawings, I recommend the following changes to all size-related values. As with mechanical dimensions, these are soft conversion values, because hard conversions result in values that are odd in a metric drawing:

- ¹⁄₃₂ inch is approximately 1mm.

- ¹⁄₁₆ inch is approximately 1.5mm.

- ⅛ inch is approximately 3mm.

- ¼ inch is approximately 6mm.

- ⅜ inch is approximately 9mm.

- ½ inch is approximately 12mm.

The only other changes are on the Primary Units tab:

- Linear Dimensions → Unit Format: Decimal

- Linear Dimensions → Precision: 0

If you're converting an existing drawing from feet and fractional inches to millimeters, you have two choices. If the drawing has not yet been dimensioned, scale *all* the geometry in the entire drawing by a factor of 25.4, and use the dimension style for architectural metric as shown previously. If the drawing has already been dimensioned using architectural units, leave the geometry as it is, and modify the dimension style by making the following changes *in addition to* the unit format and precision changes recommended earlier: Set Round Off to 2 and Measurement Scale → Scale Factor to 25.4.

Any time you make changes that you intend to apply to an entire drawing—such as scaling a drawing by 25.4 or moving all the geometry to a new location—make sure you've thawed *all* layers that contain geometry.

Civil/Surveying

Civil and surveying drawings generally use dimensions that indicate bearings in degrees, minutes, and seconds relative to either due north or due south. They don't normally use dimension lines or extension lines, but instead align both bearings and distances above or below property lines. Let's make this easier. Property-line bearings can't be added directly as dimensions, because surveying units aren't available for dimension styles. No dimensioning function in AutoCAD places bearings automatically, but the process can be streamlined.

In much of the world, civil and surveying drawings are done in metric, using the meter as the basic unit with up to three decimal places of precision. Angular units on metric civil plans, maps, and nautical charts are generally in degrees, minutes, and seconds.

Decimal Feet

To place dimensions indicating bearing and boundary length, create a new style with the following changes to each tab.

LINES TAB

The Lines tab offers the most significant changes for civil engineering and surveying drawings. Recommended changes are shown in Figure 4.24:

- Dimension Lines → Suppress: Dim Line 1 and Dim Line 2
- Extension Lines → Suppress: Ext Line 1 and Ext Line 2

Figure 4.24

Lines tab

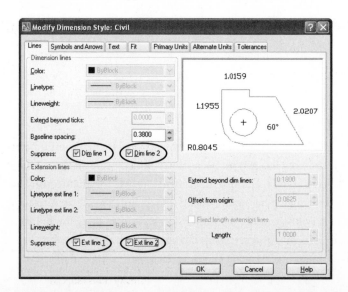

TEXT TAB

The key change in the Text tab is the placement of the text so that it aligns with property lines. Figure 4.25 shows the changes listed here:

- Text Appearance → Text Style: based on `romans.shx` font
- Text Appearance → Text Height: 0.125
- Text Placement → Vertical: Above
- Text Alignment → Aligned With Dimension Line

FIT TAB

The Fit tab has only two recommended changes:

- Fit Options → Always Keep Text Between Ext Lines
- Scale For Dimension Features → Scale Dimensions To Layout

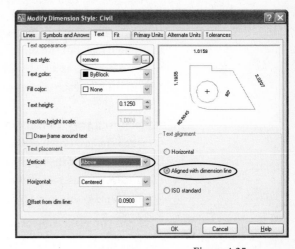

Figure 4.25

Text tab: Civil

The Scale Dimensions To Layout option shown in Figure 4.26 is the important one here. Note that the scale factors you use in floating viewports when you set up a layout are affected by the use of feet as the basic unit. Because the paper is measured in inches and the geometry is measured in feet, the scale factor used for the viewport is ½ the actual plotted scale. This means that a scale of 1:200 for the viewport appears as 1″=200′ in the title block.

PRIMARY UNITS TAB

The Primary Units tab uses the default decimal units because you'll be drawing in decimal feet. The other changes I recommend are shown in Figure 4.27:

- Linear Dimensions → Precision: 0.00
- Linear Dimensions → Suffix: ′

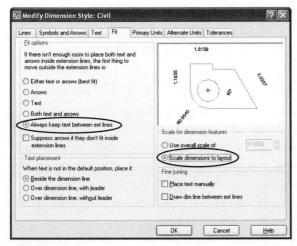

Figure 4.26

Fit tab: Civil

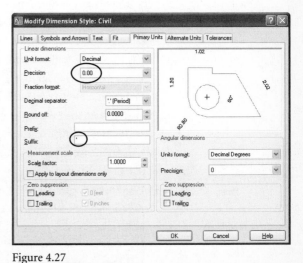

Figure 4.27

Primary Units tab: Civil

Civil and surveying drawings generally use decimal feet, but I occasionally run across someone using engineering units for a civil drawing to make it compatible with architectural drawings that will be used as external references. One user tried adding dimensions in decimal feet, but the values were 12 times too large. I suggested converting inches into feet by placing $\frac{1}{12}$ as a scale factor in the Measurement Scale area of the Primary Units tab. This multiplied each dimension by $\frac{1}{12}$ (0.0833333), converting inch units to feet.

Combining a civil drawing (done in feet) with an architectural drawing (done in inches) can cause a problem. If you insert or externally reference a floor plan into a property drawing, and it's way too big, you probably need to scale it down 1:12. Or, you can scale the property drawing up by 12:1. Use $\frac{1}{12}$ as a scale, not 0.083 as people sometimes do or you will get rounding errors.

When you place dimensions for boundary lines, do the following:

1. Use the DIMALIGNED command (DAL).

2. Select the boundary line.

3. Select a location on the line when prompted for dimension location.

The result is a dimension in decimal feet over the boundary line.

I use this system frequently on nautical charts for course lines. To place the correct angle without having to type values like **N34°15′25″E** all the time, follow these steps:

1. Add distance dimensions using the DIMALIGNED command.

2. Copy each linear dimension below the property line.

NAUTICAL CHARTS? REALLY?

I do a lot of navigating off the coast of Maine, where rocks, tidal currents, shoals, and other hazards abound. Although AutoCAD wasn't designed as a navigation aid, this is a good example of how often software is used in ways the designers didn't intend.

This year, the National Oceanic and Atmospheric Administration (NOAA) made all nautical charts available to the public in raster format. Unfortunately, they neglected to provide an easy means for most people to use them. I converted them to TIF format, placed them in AutoCAD with the External References manager (use the IMAGE command in previous releases of AutoCAD), scaled them using the Reference option of SCALE, clipped them using the IMAGECLIP command, knit them together with the help of DRAWORDER, and created a series of layouts that covers the entire coast of Maine. Using the PUBLISH command, I sent all 24 layouts to my printer, and a mere (unattended) four hours later had the nautical equivalent of an auto-club triptik, which I shared with my colleagues in Flotilla 21 of the Coast Guard Auxiliary.

3. Set Angle Type to Surveyor's Units in the Drawing Units dialog box (see Figure 4.28).

4. Use the DIST command to find the angle of one line.

5. Copy the result from the text window to the clipboard (see Figure 4.29).

6. Edit the dimension, and paste the angle into the text editor (see Figure 4.30).

Meters

I don't think it's unreasonable to assume that eventually, even land will be drawn in metric units. Much of the engineering that goes into civil design is done using metric units, and products used in civil engineering are increasingly being produced in metric units—by necessity, if they're to be sold in any other country. So, I'm presenting a suggested dimension style for civil and surveying drawings done in metric units.

Use the same Dimension Style settings as for decimal-feet, with changes only in the Primary Units tab.

Figure 4.28
Using surveyor's units

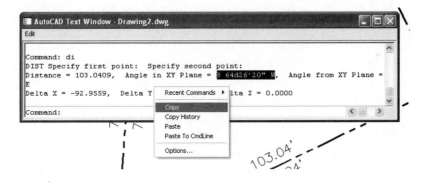

Figure 4.29
Copying the correct bearing

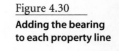

Figure 4.30
Adding the bearing to each property line

The Primary Units tab still uses the default decimal units, but in this case the units are decimal meters. The precision may change to three decimal places because meters are larger than feet, and there is no Linear Dimension suffix:

- Linear Dimensions → Precision: 0.00 or 0.000
- Linear Dimensions → Suffix: None

Dimensioning Rules

Setting up a variety of dimension styles will help you enormously in adding dimensions correctly. However, dimensioning properly is one of the most difficult tasks when documenting design. Despite the apparent promise of automatic dimensioning that came with the QDIM command, there is no magic wand you can wave over a drawing to dimension it.

Dimensioning rules are most significant in mechanical design, because the geometry tends to be more complex than in other disciplines. The placement of a first dimension is often the key to making the others work well. AutoCAD has no variable that controls where a first dimension is placed. You make that decision and then use DIMBASE or DIMCONTINE to work from there.

I recommend that you consider trying ordinate dimensions, whatever your discipline is. They're easier to place, generally more accurate, easier to read, and in many cases easier to use than the more traditional approaches. Ordinate dimensions aren't just for the machine shop. Whenever I design a structure that I plan to build, I use ordinate dimensions, not continuous. I hook my tape (metric, of course), and mark off the location of each opening without ever having to add 4′5″ and 3′9-½″ to see where the next one is.

In this section, I'll discuss mechanical and architectural rules of dimensioning.

Mechanical Dimensioning

The general rules for dimensioning are a great example of how the exception proves the rule, because you'll run into situations where specific rules can't be applied. The rule of thumb is that if you *can* follow the rules, *do* follow the rules:

You'll find further specifics of dimensioning in ASME Y14.5M -1994.

1. True shape A feature should be dimensioned on the view in which it appears in true shape. An exception to this rule exists for the dimensioning of cylindrical objects, which may be dimensioned in their longitudinal view. You must avoid placing dimensions to hidden lines.

2. Tolerance All dimensions must carry a tolerance, either directly on the dimension itself, or in a general note that's part of the title block.

3. Group Dimensions on multiview drawings should be grouped together with related dimensions and placed between views.

4. Spacing A plotted spacing of 9–12mm (.375″–.50″) should be left between an object and the first dimension applied to that object. Subsequent dimensions should be spaced a smaller distance of 6–9mm (.25″–.375″). You can set DIMDLI accordingly for this purpose.

5. Redundant dimensions A feature should be dimensioned in only one location for mechanical drawings. If an overall dimension is given, omit one of the intermediate dimensions, or make it a reference dimension by placing it in parentheses. You may repeat dimensions in architectural drawings.

6. Off object Avoid placing dimensions directly on the object.

7. Crossing lines Avoid crossing dimension lines with any other lines. Extension lines often cross each other or leaders. Unless a line will cross an arrowhead, don't break lines where they do cross other lines.

8. Radius and diameter dimensions Circle sizes are dimensioned with a diameter, and arc sizes are dimensioned with a radius. Even though AutoCAD requests a radius by default when you draw a circle, the dimension generally used for circles is a diameter.

9. Reference dimensions You can use reference dimensions where they clarify a part's size or the location of specific features. Reference dimensions are meant to be approximations and shouldn't be used to replace dimensions that are necessary to manufacture a part. When you use a reference dimension, identify it by enclosing it in parentheses. Do this in AutoCAD by editing the resulting dimension so it looks like this: (<>).

10. Symbols Use symbols rather than words for diameter, depth, counterbore, number of places, and similar features.

Figure 4.31 illustrates a number of common errors in adding dimensions to mechanical parts.

Figure 4.32 illustrates the same part with dimensions added correctly.

Architectural Dimensioning

More variation exists in architectural dimensioning practices from office to office than in mechanical dimensioning, so it's impossible to be specific about its rules. Generally, linear dimensions are aligned and continuous dimensions, which is consistent with both the Construction Standards Institute and the Architectural Graphics Standards format. Three or four levels are normally used, starting from the outside level:

- Overall dimensions farthest from the structure
- Dimensions of external wall offsets or additions
- Dimensions to mid-plane of the interior partitions
- Dimensions to centers of openings in exterior walls

Figure 4.31

**Common dimen-
sioning errors**

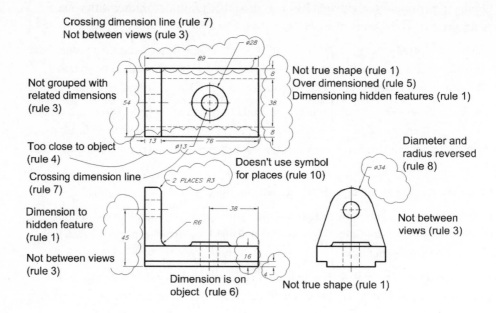

Crossing dimension line (rule 7)
Not between views (rule 3)

ø28

89

Not grouped with
related dimensions
(rule 3)

54

38

Not true shape (rule 1)
Over dimensioned (rule 5)
Dimensioning hidden features (rule 1)

8

8

13   ø13   76

Too close to object
(rule 4)

Crossing dimension line
(rule 7)

Doesn't use symbol
for places (rule 10)

2 PLACES R3

Diameter and
radius reversed
(rule 8)

ø34

Dimension to
hidden feature
(rule 1)

38

45

R6

16

Not between views
(rule 3)

Not between
views (rule 3)

Dimension is on
object (rule 6)

4

Not true shape (rule 1)

Figure 4.32

**Correctly dimen-
sioned part**

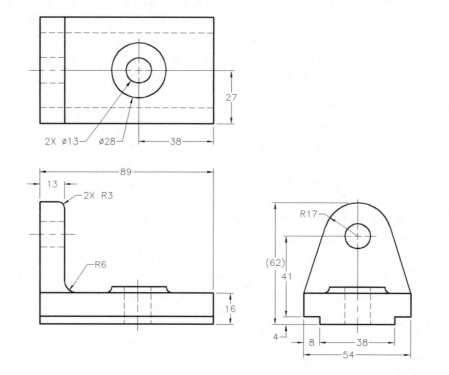

27

2X ø13   ø28   38

89

13   2X R3

R6

16

R17

(62)

41

4

8   38

54

Spacing between dimensions is usually from ⅜″ to ½″. The space between the first dimension and the structure must be large enough to accommodate any symbols, notes, or other annotation necessary, as shown in Figure 4.33.

Text Styles

The single worst thing about AutoCAD is that ugly font: TXT.SHX. There was a time when this font made sense, not from a technical-graphics point of view, but from a computer-resources point of view. It was the original default AutoCAD font for one reason: It has no curved lines. That made it simple to define and simple for AutoCAD to keep track of mathematically. The first computer I used for AutoCAD was an IBM 286. Any amount of text on a drawing dramatically increased regeneration time, especially if that text was romanc.shx, romand.shx, or even romans.shx.

The intent of the ugly font, even then, was not that it would be plotted, but that it would be used as a placeholder for nicer text. You could use it while you were developing the drawing and then redefine it just before plotting. But a funny thing happened on the way to the plotter: Users didn't bother.

Figure 4.33

General architectural dimensioning with hand1.shx **font**

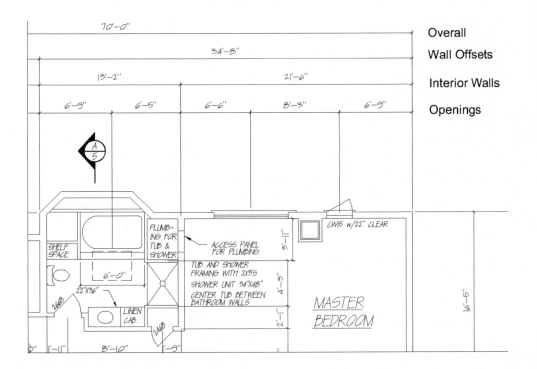

The ugly font started showing up first on drawings and then in many of the books that purported to teach people how to use AutoCAD correctly. Even books that claimed to conform to ASME Y14.5M standards were often filled with illustrations done in AutoCAD using the default font. The more that inexperienced or new users saw it, the more it became a standard.

By default, AutoCAD still uses the `txt.shx` font as its standard text style, and it still doesn't meet any technical-graphics standard anywhere in the world. Normally, I like the fact that AutoCAD maintains legacy behavior, but the legacy of the ugly font is an exception.

In this section, I'll cover two important text-style issues: fonts and letter forms.

Fonts

You have two kinds of fonts at your disposal on which to base a text style: AutoCAD compiled-shape fonts, which have an .shx extension; and Windows TrueType fonts, which have a `.ttf` extension. The shape fonts are provided by Autodesk and are *vector-based* (composed of lines). The TrueType fonts are provided by the Windows operating system and are *raster-based* (composed of pixels), so they take up a little more file space.

Generally, all the AutoCAD SHX fonts are available at any time. If an individual file gets lost, you can replace it by putting it back in your AutoCAD Fonts directory or in another folder in the search path. The TrueType fonts must be loaded by Windows, however, and if any of them aren't installed, you can't just copy a file into the path—you have to load them through Windows.

LOST WINDOWS FONTS

I've encountered a number of situations where Windows fonts either weren't loaded on a computer to begin with or somehow disappeared, leaving AutoCAD users without their favorite TrueType fonts. You can reload fonts from the original Windows CD, but most computer manufacturers no longer ship that CD. You may be able to find the fonts in the appropriate cabs folder, but if not, this is how you can solve the problem:

1. Find another computer that has the TrueType fonts you want.

2. Copy the folder they're in (C:\windows\fonts or C:\winnt\fonts) to a CD or flash drive.

3. Put that CD or flash drive into your computer.

4. Open the fonts folder on your computer (C:\windows\fonts or C:\winnt\fonts).

5. Select Files → Install New Font in that folder.

6. Browse to the CD or flash drive that contains the fonts you want to install.

7. Select the fonts you want, and install them.

The only font shipped with AutoCAD that meets ASME and ISO standards is
`romans.shx`, which is the same font as `simplex.shx`. The one drawback to `romans.shx` is
its lack of a nonproportional version. If you need a nonproportional font, you've got two
choices: `monotxt.shx` (same as `txt.shx`, but each letter gets the same amount of space no
matter how wide it is) or a TrueType font named Monospac821 BT. The TrueType font
is the lesser of two evils, so if you need a nonproportional font, use that. For architectural
or civil drawings, many offices use CountryBlueprint or CityBlueprint..

Letter Form

The ASME standard on lettering, ASME Y14.3M, permits either vertical letters or letters
inclined at an angle up to 30° from vertical. If you use inclined letters, set an oblique angle
of 10–30 degrees when creating your text style.

Letter height can vary, depending on what you're using the text for. I strongly recommend setting a text height of 0 when creating all text styles, so you can create text at any
height, and it will automatically scale for dimensions.

AutoCAD uses two default text heights for Imperial drawings: 0.200 and 0.180. This is
greater than the minimum required by ASME for most text. The default setting of 2.5 for
metric drawings is less than the minimum required. Using the minimum heights specified
in the ASME standard for all text, particularly dimension text, permits you to place the
most information in the drawing and still have it be readable. Recommended text heights
for mechanically produced text are listed in Table 4.1.

USE	DRAWING SIZE	METRIC	INCH
Drawing number, title, and revision letter in title block	Up through 22″ × 17″	3	.12
Drawing number, title, and revision letter in title block	Greater than 22″ × 17″	6	.24
Section and view letters	All	6	.24
Zone characters in border	All	6	.24
Drawing block headings	All	2.5	.10
Dims, tolerances, limits, notes, subtitles for views, tables, revisions, and zone characters in body of drawing	All	3	.12

Table 4.1

**ASME Standard
Text Heights**

Linetypes and Weights

When technical-graphics textbooks discuss the language of drafting, they're referring to
linetypes and their associated lineweights. Probably nothing makes it harder to interpret a
technical drawing than improper application of linetypes.

Every technical person should be able to communicate in three different mediums:
words, numbers, and graphics. If that communication is to make sense, all parties have to

agree on the basic rules of the languages used. If you present a design to me, it should be subject to only one interpretation. That is especially true in a world-based economy where the person creating the drawing and the person interpreting it may be in different parts of the world and speak different languages.

Here is one of the many applications of AutoCAD where you must take control of the output if you're going to communicate effectively. AutoCAD can create lines that are broken into particular linetypes, but it won't place them properly without a lot of help from you. It also has no idea what the lines you're placing represent, so you must decide what lineweight to use to clearly separate the objects you're drawing from the annotation used to describe them. Too many users shirk their responsibilities here, dismissing any complaint with the phrase "That's how AutoCAD does it." It's a poor workman who blames his tools.

Controlling the appearance of hidden lines and especially center lines requires a bit of work, but it's well worth it. This section is designed to show you how.

Hidden Lines

The representation of hidden features is defined in the ASME Y14.2 standard. Some special applications are meant to convey information about the relationship between two features represented by hidden lines, as shown in Figure 4.34. AutoCAD often applies hidden lines properly without the user doing anything special, but sometimes AutoCAD creates hidden lines incorrectly.

The manner in which hidden lines meet or cross other lines is supposed to reflect the manner in which the features they represent are related. Because using hidden lines correctly can help others correctly interpret a drawing, here are some suggestions for working with them.

> Before you tweak hidden lines as suggested below, you must be working within a viewport that has already been scaled for plotting. Otherwise, the length of the segments within linetypes will change when the viewport is scaled.

Figure 4.34 shows the ASME standards for treatment of hidden lines. Each of the numbered locations shows a situation that is discussed below, with my suggestions for managing AutoCAD to get correct results.

1. When a hidden surface intersects a visible feature and stops, the hidden line must terminate at the visible line. AutoCAD does this automatically.

2. When a hidden feature passes either behind or in front of a visible feature but doesn't intersect that feature, the hidden line must either show a gap at the visible line *or* cross through the visible line. The hidden line segment must not terminate at the visible line. AutoCAD may not do this automatically, in which case you must adjust the segment length using the Properties palette.

Figure 4.34

**ASME Y14.2
requirements
for hidden lines**

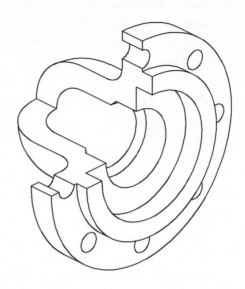

3. When two hidden features terminate at 90°, the hidden lines must close at the corner. AutoCAD does this automatically only if you use two different line segments to represent the corner. If you create this feature with a multisegment polyline, the corner appearance is affected by the setting for the variable PLINEGEN. If PLINEGEN is set to the default value of 0, then linetype generation starts again at each vertex of the polyline, and the corner closes. If PLINEGEN is set to 1, linetype generation is continuous along the length of the entire pline, and a gap may appear at the vertex. You can override PLINEGEN for an individual object by using the Properties palette to control its Lintype generation, as shown in Figure 4.35.

4. When one hidden feature terminates at another hidden feature, the last segment of the hidden line must terminate at the visible line. AutoCAD does this automatically.

5. When multiple features intersect at the same location, the last segment of each hidden line used to represent the features must terminate at the same location. Note also that gaps in parallel hidden lines that are near each other should not line up precisely, but should be somewhat staggered.

Figure 4.35

**Changing PLINEGEN
for a line segment**

6. When a hidden line represents the continuation of a flat surface from a visible line that represents the same feature, there must be a gap between the end of the visible line and the beginning of the hidden line. AutoCAD doesn't do this automatically. You can use the BREAK command to create a gap. If you encounter this situation frequently, create a custom linetype that begins with a gap instead of a segment. See Chapter 3, "Customizing AutoCAD's Interface," for help creating custom linetypes.

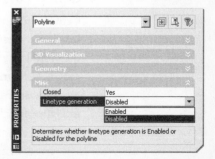

7. When a hidden line crosses a center line, a segment of the hidden line shouldn't intersect a short segment of the center line in such a way that two segments appear to mark a center location. Figure 4.34 demonstrates how you can accomplish this by using two entities: an arc that terminates at the center line; and a straight line that begins with a gap at the center line.

8. When a hidden line represents the continuation of a curved surface from a visible line that represents the same feature, you have to leave a gap between the end of the visible line and the beginning of the hidden line. AutoCAD doesn't do this automatically. You can use the BREAK command to create a gap. If you encounter this situation frequently, create a custom linetype that begins with a gap instead of a segment. See Chapter 3 for help creating custom linetypes.

9. When a hidden feature passes either behind or in front of another hidden feature, but they don't intersect, the hidden lines must either cross with a gap at their intersection *or* cross through each other. Neither hidden line segment should terminate at the other hidden line. AutoCAD may not do this automatically, in which case you have to adjust the segment's length using the Properties palette.

I have a few other suggestions about hidden lines:

• Hidden lines are required only if they help clarify a feature. If hidden features are so numerous that representing all of them would cause confusion, omit them. Hidden lines created from solid models using SOLPROF or SOLDRAW often create this problem; the block that contains them must be exploded and modified.

• If you omit hidden features, start with those farthest from the plane of the view you're creating.

• Adjust linetype scale for objects only *after* you've set up your views in a layout.

• Don't use LTSCALE to adjust linetypes—it's a global variable and therefore affects all entities in the drawing that have a linetype other than Continuous.

• Set PLINEGEN to 1 only if you want linetype breaks to be evenly distributed along a pline, particularly if it's curved or has short segments between vertices.

Center Lines and Center Marks

Center lines and center marks are frequently incorrect on AutoCAD drawings. The problem usually results from using a Center linetype for lines that cross each other. If lines are meant to locate a center point where they cross, they must have a crosshair. If the lines are exactly the same length and cross at their midpoints, AutoCAD often creates a proper center mark. In every other situation, AutoCAD creates unfortunate results like those shown in Figure 4.36.

Each of the dimension styles described previously identifies Line as the style for center marks with sizes that correspond to the extension line gaps: –.0625 for inches and –1.5 for metric. Once you set a proper dimension style, you can use the DIMCENTER (DCE) command to place crosshair center lines on circles or arcs. You'll have six separate lines that can be edited independently without changing the location of the crosshair. (See Figure 4.37.)

Circular Center Lines and Marks

The problem that results from using an AutoCAD Center linetype is even more apparent when applied to circular center lines. Circular center lines are used for patterns like bolt holes; if you want the lines to be accurate, use the ARRAY command.

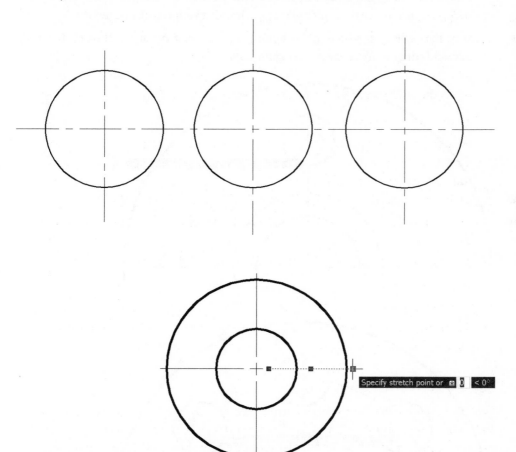

Figure 4.36

Incorrect application of center lines

Figure 3.37

Editing center marks placed with DIMCENTER

Specify stretch point or ▣ 0 < 0°

The crosshairs on circular center lines consist of one arc and one straight-line segment. The size of the crosshair should match the one used for all other center marks on the drawing, so add them only after you've set up a scaled viewport in a layout (see Chapter 6). To create a complete circular center line for representing the locations of boltholes, follow these steps:

1. Draw an arc segment and a straight-line crosshair for one hole by creating two concentric circles whose diameters match the size of the crosshair required, and using the TRIM command, as shown in Figure 4.38. It's a lot easier to determine the correct size if you've added a center mark using the DIMCENTER command, because that mark is scaled automatically for plotting if you followed the recommendations for dimension styles given earlier. Draw two concentric circles using an existing center mark, and then move them into place for trimming your circular center mark.

2. Array the circles that represent the holes, add an arc segment that goes inside the next hole, and trim the arc as shown in Figure 4.39.

Figure 4.38
Circular center mark

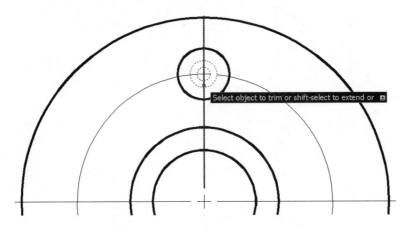

Figure 4.39
Circular center line components

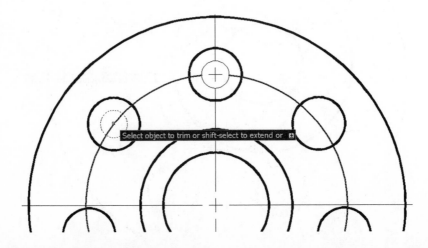

3. Array the group of entities shown in Figure 4.40, which represent the repeatable pattern for the circular center marks as many times as there are holes.

This technique is quicker than it sounds, and it always gives you proper center-line results, as shown in Figure 4.41. If you use circular center lines frequently, see the web site for this book for an AutoLISP program that automates this process and will make your life a lot easier.

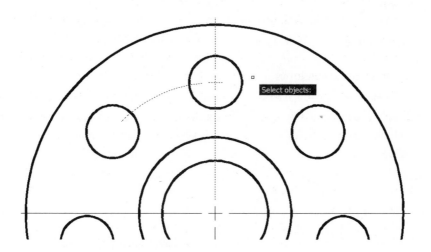

Figure 4.40

Repeatable pattern for circular centerline

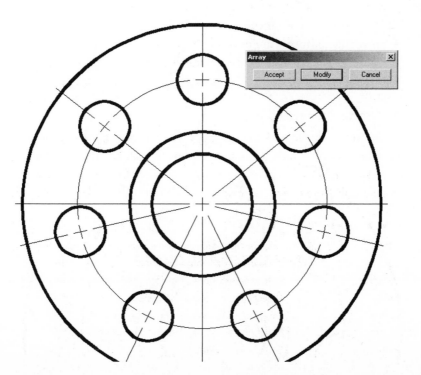

Figure 4.41

Completed circular center lines

Lineweights

Lineweight refers to how wide a line is when it's displayed on the screen or plotted. You can set lineweights as a Layer property, but you won't see them until you turn on Lineweight display, which you can do using the status-bar button labeled LWT. I don't like drawing with lineweights on, but I periodically do a plot preview to see how the whole thing will look. Proper lineweights make a huge difference in understanding what I'm looking at.

The more complex the drawing, the more lineweights matter. This section discusses their application and gives you some advice in applying them.

Mechanical Lineweights

This one is easy. You have thick lines and you have thin lines. If the line represents something you can see, it's thick. Everything else is thin—almost. Line conventions must be consistent with ASME Y14.2M - 1992 (R1998). You have to make a clear distinction between the two weights, with thin lines being approximately half the weight of thick lines. Thick lines can be from 0.4–0.7mm (.016–.028″) when plotted, and thin lines can be from 0.2–0.35mm (.008–.014″) when plotted. Viewing plane, cutting plane, and short break lines are treated as visible; therefore they're thick.

Use your judgment in selecting a lineweight for visible lines that occur close to each other. You may have to reduce the line width of object lines in order to show details. If so, reduce the width of other lines accordingly to maintain the 2:1 ratio between thick lines and thin lines. It's OK for cutting-plane lines to be thicker than object lines if that improves the clarity of your drawing.

Using the correct lineweights can dramatically affect a plotted drawing—for the better. Set the lineweights to BYLAYER using .4 or .5 for thick and .2 or .25 for thin.

Architectural Lineweights

Architectural drawings often use more than two lineweights, depending on office standards. Some offices have two standards: one for manual drawings and one for CAD drawings. Table 4.2 shows a sample lineweight standard for CAD drawing. Standards can vary dramatically from one office to another in this discipline, so this is just an example.

Table 4.2

Sample Architectural Lineweight Standard

LINEWEIGHT	PURPOSE
0.1mm	Thin lines in details, elevations, sections for plotting clarity
0.2mm	Dimension, extension, center, hidden, leader, phantom lines
0.3mm	Text, windows, doors, cabinets, stairs, railing, ramps, existing features
0.4mm	Object lines for mechanical parts
0.5mm	Object lines representing building elements
0.6mm	Elevation, profile, viewing, and cutting-plane lines
0.7mm	Border lines on drawing

Style Tables vs. Color Tables

Lineweights are normally controlled in an AutoCAD drawing by using either named or color-dependent plot-style tables. Most offices that I've worked with use color-based plot styles, but the color of a line doesn't directly control the lineweight used for plotting. Instead, entities are assigned a lineweight by the layer on which they reside. I think this is good practice. For more on plot style tables, see Chapter 6.

Applying Standards

Users who follow standards are far less likely to have their drawings misinterpreted. Figure 4.42 shows the train wreck that results from using the default dimension values, default linetypes, and default lineweights in AutoCAD. It's nearly impossible to decipher the drawing's annotations or to visually pick out the shape of the object.

Figure 4.43 shows the result of using the practices described in this chapter. It's much easier to read. It takes a little setup time, and the center marks require some additional manipulation—but surely this small effort is worth the trouble. After all, the purpose of a drawing is to communicate the intent of the design unambiguously. This is a simple part: the head gasket from a Briggs and Stratton small engine. Complex parts are even harder for someone to interpret if you don't apply these standards.

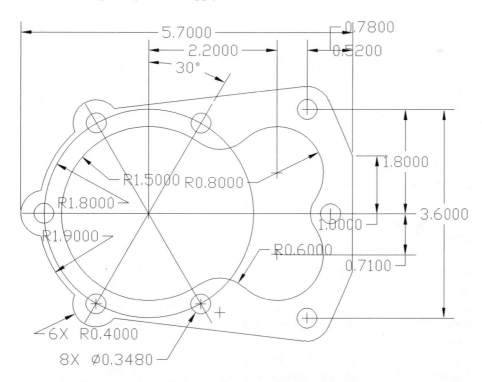

Figure 4.42

Default settings in AutoCAD

Figure 4.43

Applying standards

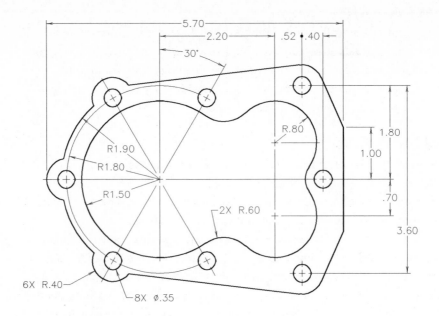

Template Drawings

If you plan to get serious about applying standards, your most important AutoCAD skill will be creating and using template files. Your office should create a series of standard template files as a starting point for every user. Templates don't eliminate the need for checking each drawing—far from it—but they ensure that at the beginning of each project, every drawing has the same basic structure. When coupled with DWS files, tool palettes, custom commands, and old-fashioned checks of drawings by someone other than the drafter/designer, template files go a long way toward establishing and maintaining office standards.

Creating Template Drawings

Create as many template drawings as you need. Begin by creating a folder for your template files and setting it as the path used by AutoCAD for starting new drawings. Select the Files tab of the Options dialog box. Under that tab, search for Template Settings, and click the + sign. You'll see a heading named Drawing Template File Location.

The files are located in a long path under your login name in the `Documents And Settings` folder, a necessary inconvenience designed to conform to the Windows multiuser environment format. This is a lousy place to keep template files that will be used by others in your office. To spare yourself a future migraine, change the location to a common network drive, as shown in Figure 4.44.

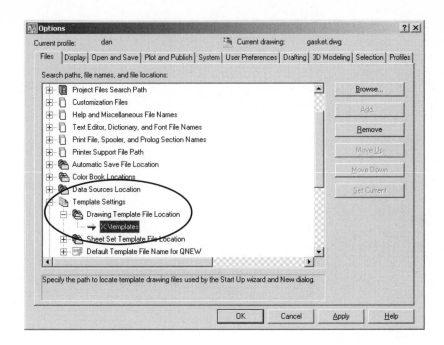

Figure 4.44

Changing the default template file location

If you have an existing drawing that meets, or nearly meets, your office standard, here's the easiest way to create a new template file:

1. Open an existing drawing that meets your office standards.

2. Make sure the drawing uses the type of plot style table that meets your office standard: color-dependent or named.

3. Make as many changes as you can to set up the drawing and delete all entities in the drawing.

4. Save the drawing as a DWT file to the folder you identified as the path in the Options dialog box. That location will open automatically when you select AutoCAD Drawing Template (*.dwt), as shown in Figure 4.5.

> Save a DWG version of each of your template files. That way, you can insert them if you want to quickly add all layer names, dimension styles, text styles, table styles, and block definitions to another drawing.

Once you've saved a DWT file, you can select it when using the NEW command to start a new drawing. The template file location you specified opens automatically, allowing you to select your own template file rather than one of AutoCAD's. You can also direct AutoCAD to use this template when the QNEW command is used, by specifying the template in the Options dialog box (see Figure 4.46).

Figure 4.45

Saving a template file

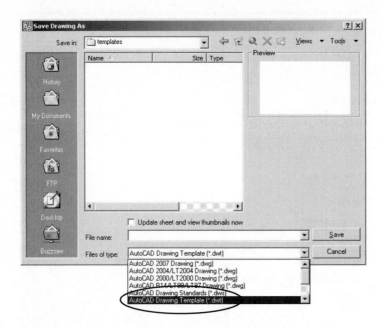

Figure 4.46

Setting the default file for QNEW

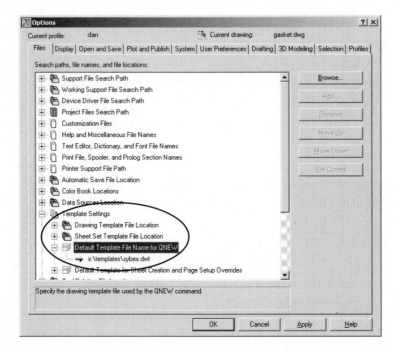

In addition, you can create a custom shortcut on the desktop and edit the target window by adding /t *YOUROWN.DWT* at the end of the line that starts AutoCAD. Once you specify the path and the filename, AutoCAD will start with the specified template whenever you use the shortcut (See Figure 4.47).

Contents of a Template File

Drawing template files should include at least the following settings:

- Layers with the colors, linetypes, and lineweights specified
- Layer states and filters
- Dimension styles
- Appropriate limits
- Appropriate units
- Views and viewports saved with logical names
- Text styles with names other than Standard
- Block definitions for title blocks, borders, and standard symbols
- Layouts for each sheet size used in the office
- Default plot styles and pen styles
- System variable settings that are saved in the drawing

Figure 4.47

Creating a custom shortcut

Recommended Variable Settings

Most variables are now saved in the system registry, not the drawing file. Those variables that are saved in the drawing should be set in your template file. To find out where a particular variable is saved, use the Help system. The help for each variable indicates the location where the setting is changed as well as the default value.

Although system variables aren't the most glamorous aspect of AutoCAD, they can have a profound effect on how the software behaves—or, more to the point, misbehaves. Variables saved in the system registry can't be controlled by a drawing template. The ones that can, with my preferred settings, are listed here. If you wonder what any of these variables controls, check it out in the AutoCAD Help system:

- ATTMODE = 1
- AUPREC = 1
- CELTSCALE = 1
- CMLJUST = 2
- DISPSILH = 1
- DRAWORDERCTL = 3

- PLINEGEN = 0
- PSLTSCALE =1
- PSVPSCALE = 0 for zoom extents, 1 for 1xp, ¼₈ for ¼″=1′, and so on
- REGENMODE = 0 only for very large drawings; REGEN when necessary

continues

continued

- ELEVATION = 0
- FACETRES = 2
- FILLETRAD = 0
- FILLMODE = 1
- HIDETEXT = 1
- INDEXCTL = 3
- INSBASE = 0,0,0
- ISOLINES = 20
- LIMCHECK = 0
- LTSCALE = 1
- MEASUREMENT = 0 for English, 1 for metric
- MIRRTEXT = 0
- OLESTARTUP = 1

- REMEMBERFOLDERS = 0
- SKPOLY = 1
- SORTENTS = 27
- TEXTSIZE = .125
- TEXTSTYLE = Romans
- THICKNESS = 0
- TSTACKALIGN = 1
- UCSICON = 0 for 2D drawings, 3 for 3D drawings
- VISRETAIN = 1
- XEDIT = 0
- XLOADCTL = 1
- ZOOMFACTOR = 100

Dimension Styles

I discussed dimension styles at length earlier in this chapter. Don't forget to make them part of your office templates: They may be the single most important feature you add. In addition to having them in your templates, you can export any dimension style using the DIMEX command included as an Express Tool. Then they can be used in any other drawing—a convenient way to share dimension styles with others without sending a drawing file. And don't forget to add dimension tools to a palette.

Layer Naming

It's important to standardize layer names, colors, and linetypes for all drawings so you can quickly recall them and control them in groups. You can group layer names with wildcards. The most useful wildcards are * and ~. The * wildcard is interpreted as *all* and ~ is interpreted as *all but*.

> In the following statement, all layers except those beginning with the characters *FL1* will be frozen: –LA⏎FREEZE⏎ ~FL1*⏎⏎. To take advantage of selecting names using wildcards, you must group related layers together by giving them names with common fields.

LAYER-NAME WILDCARDS

The AutoCAD Help system identifies the wildcards shown in Table 4.3 that can be used when identifying layer names. See how helpful the Help system is?

CHARACTER	DEFINITION	
#	Matches any numeric digit	Table 4.3
@	Matches any alphabetic character	**Wildcards for Layer Names**
.	Matches any nonalphanumeric character	
*	Matches any string, and can be used anywhere in the search string	
?	Matches any single character; for example, ?BC matches ABC, 3BC, and so on	
~	Matches anything but the pattern; for example, ~*AB*matches all strings that don't contain *AB*	
[]	Matches any one of the characters enclosed; for example, [AB]C matches *AC* and *BC*	
[~]	Matches any character not enclosed; for example, [~AB]C matches *XC* but not *AC*	
[-]	Specifies a range for a single character; for example, [A-G]C matches *AC*, *BC*, and so on to *GC*, but not *HC*	
`	Reads the next character literally; for example, `~AB matches ~*AB* and doesn't interpret the tilde as a wildcard	

> If for some reason a layer name must include one of the characters designated by AutoCAD as a wildcard, precede that character with a reverse quote (`) so AutoCAD interprets it literally, not as a wildcard character. I've never seen a situation where that was done, but you never know.

ARCHITECTURAL LAYER NAMES: COMMERCIAL

Commercial construction projects commonly employ a separate drawing file for each floor or level of a building. When it becomes necessary to compare two or more levels, drawings are externally referenced into a single file. The American Institute of Architects (AIA) has developed layer standards for use in commercial projects. The complete AIA layer standard is lengthy, and you'll have to purchase it if you want a copy for your office. In the meantime, here's my summary of the naming conventions from the AIA publication "CAD Layer Guidelines" (1990, updated 1999).

> Layers created automatically by Architectural Desktop are meant to follow the AIA standards.

Layer names must be composed of up to four fields, each separated by a dash as follows: X-XXXX-XXXX-XXXX. The first field requires a single character, and the other fields require four characters. Not all layer names have all four fields, but where multiple fields are used, each subsequent field modifies the field immediately preceding it. The shortest possible standard layer name is 6 characters; the longest is 16.

For example, the layer name A-WALL-DIMS-NEWW identifies the *discipline*, which in this case is architectural; the *major group*, which in this case is walls; the *minor group*, which in this case is dimensions; and the *status* of the objects being referenced, which in this case is new construction. Users can add minor categories, and the status field is always optional. The following summary shows some of the field names used in each category. Discipline groups are listed in Table 4.4.

	FIELD	PURPOSE
Table 4.4 **Field 1:** **Discipline Group**	A	Architectural
	C	Civil
	E	Electrical
	F	Fire protection
	G	General
	H	Hazardous materials
	I	Interiors
	L	Landscape architecture
	M	Mechanical
	P	Plumbing
	Q	Equipment
	R	Resource
	S	Structural
	T	Telecommunications
	X	Other disciplines
	Z	Contractor/shop drawings

Each discipline group can be modified by a second field that indicates the types of objects placed on that layer. Those four-character fields are shown in Table 4.5.

	FIELD	PURPOSE
Table 4.5 **Field 2: Object** **within Discipline**	ANNO	Annotation
	AREA	Area boundary lines
	CLNG	Ceiling information
	COMM	Communication
	CTRL	Control systems
	DETL	Details
	DOOR	Doors

FIELD	PURPOSE
ELEV	Elevations
EQPM	Equipment
FLOR	Floor information
FURN	Furniture
GLAZ	Windows
GRID	Grids
LITE	Light fixtures
MASS	Massing
PKNG	Parking
PLNT	Planting
POWR	Power
PROT	Fire protection
ROOF	Roofs
SECT	Sections
SITE	Site
STRM	Drainage (Storm)
WALL	Walls

A third field further defines the objects identified in Field 2, indicating the types of objects that are placed on those layers as modifiers. Examples are shown in Table 4.6.

FIELD	PURPOSE
DIMS	Dimensions
IDEN	Identification
LEGN	Schedules (legend)
NOTE	Notes
NPLT	Nonplotting
PATT	Pattern
REVS	Revisions
SYMB	Symbols
TTLB	Title blocks

Table 4.6

Field 3: Definition of Objects in Field 2

If you want to add categories, you can. For example, you may want a layer for center lines (CENT); hidden lines (HIDD); phantom lines (PHAN); or lines with specific lineweights, like 0.1 (LW01), 0.5 (LW05), or 01.2 (LW12).

The final field is a status field, indicating whether the objects shown are to be demolished, represent existing structures that won't be demolished, are new structures, and so on. Table 4.7 lists the four-character status codes.

Table 4.7

Field 4: Status

FIELD	PURPOSE
DEMO	Existing to demolish
EXST	Existing to remain
NEWW	New work
FUTR	Future work
TEMP	Temporary work
MOVE	Items to be moved
RELO	Relocated items
NICN	Not in contract
PHS1	Phase number 1
PHS2	Phase number 2

For more information about the AIA layer-naming guidelines, or to purchase the guidelines, see the AIA website: `http://www.AIA.org`.

> One potential drawback of using standard layer names pops up if you combine two drawings—either by inserting one into the other or by binding one as an external reference to the other using an insert bind.—The entities from each drawing that reside on layers of the same name are all on the same layer. To avoid this result, select bind as the type when binding an external reference to a drawing so that layer names for the bound XRef will all be prefixed with the name of the drawing. That will separate the entities from the two drawings onto different layers.

ARCHITECTURAL LAYER NAMES: RESIDENTIAL

You may find the AIA guidelines cumbersome in residential design. When designing or drawing a single-family residence, I prefer to have all floors in one file and use the following layer-naming system. Like the system developed by the AIA, it uses separate fields, but I use three characters in each rather than four. I present it here as an example of how you may construct your own layer-naming standard independent of the AIA standards.

Some layers have single fields, but most are associated with a floor or level. The four standard fields I use to represent levels are FND (foundation), FL1 (first floor), FL2 (second floor), and ROF (roof). I use the second field to represent the linetype or type of object: OBJ (object), HID (hidden lines), ELE (electrical), and so on. This system may not work for you, but it simplifies things for me. Table 4.8 provides some suggested layer-name fields.

LAYER	PURPOSE	
0	Used for defining blocks	**Table 4.8**
BOR	Contains a border for the sheet	**Simplified Layer-Naming Standards for Residential Design**
TTL	Contains general title-block information	
CON	Used for construction lines	
FL1-OBJ	First-floor object lines	
FL1-APP	First-floor appliances	
FL1-CEN	First-floor center lines	
FL1-DIM	First-floor dimensions	
FL1-ELE	First-floor electrical	
FL1-FIR	First-floor fireplace plan	
FL1-FRA	Framing plan for the first floor	
FL1-HAT	First-floor hatch patterns	
FL1-PLU	First-floor plumbing plan	
FL1-TXT	First-floor notes and title-block information	
FL2-OBJ	Second-floor object lines	
FL2-APP	Second-floor appliances	
FL2-CEN	Second-floor center lines	
FL2-DIM	Second-floor dimensions	
FND-OBJ	Foundation object lines	
FND-APP	Foundation appliances	
FND-CEN	Foundation center lines	
FND-DIM	Foundation dimensions	

LAYER NAMES FOR MECHANICAL DESIGN

If an organization has developed layer-naming guidelines for mechanical design, I haven't heard of it. When creating drawings of parts for use in an assembly drawing, I resort to the basic layer names shown in Table 4.9, with as many part-specific names as necessary. The fields identified as PT1, and so on, are given a specific part name.

Layer Colors

At one time, layer colors were always part of office standards—at least, for offices that had standards. That's because the color of an entity used to determine the appearance of the entity when it was plotted. Colors are still specified for layers as part of most office standards, but it may not be necessary for everyone to use the same colors unless you're plotting in color.

	FIELD	PURPOSE
Table 4.9	0	Layer 0: reserved for blocks
Suggested Layer Fields for Mechanical Design	BOR	Border layer
	CEN	Center lines
	CON	Construction lines
	DIM	Dimensions
	HID	Hidden lines
	OBJ	Object lines
	TXT	Text on the drawing
	PT1-CEN	Center lines on part 1
	PT1-CON	Construction lines on part 1
	PT1-DIM	Dimensions on part 1
	PT1-HID	Hidden lines on part 1
	PT1-OBJ	Object lines on part 1
	PT1-TXT	Text on the drawing on part 1
	PT2-CEN	Center lines on part 2
	PT2-CON	Construction lines on part 2
	PT2-DIM	Dimensions on part 2
	PT2-HID	Hidden lines on part 2
	PT2-OBJ	Object lines on part 2
	PT2-TXT	Text on the drawing on part 2
	PT3-CEN	Center lines on part 3
	PT3-CON	Construction lines on part 3
	PT3-DIM	Dimensions on part 3
	PT3-HID	Hidden lines on part 3
	PT3-OBJ	Object lines on part 3
	PT3-TXT	Text on the drawing on part 3

If you plot using the monochrome plot style, the appearance of entities when they're plotted—their lineweight and linetype—is controlled not by color but by the layer each entity is on. Even though many offices use color-dependent plot style tables, a look at the table properties shows that most of the time, those two properties are set to Use Object Linetype or Use Object Lineweight, as shown in Figure 4.48.

When you're assigning colors, take into account the background color you like to use. Because blue doesn't show up well on a black background, and yellow is impossible to read on a white background, you may try something else. A medium gray background works for some people. I've seen some color combinations that I'd find very hard to work with, but to each their own. I recommend that you assign color, linetype, lineweight, and plot style to BYLAYER.

CHAPTER 5

Symbols, Tables, and Fields

It's impossible to imagine AutoCAD without blocks. They've become as fundamental as drawing lines and circles. When external references were introduced, they were like super blocks that could span multiple drawings, and before long most of us found them nearly as essential as blocks. Now that tables have become internal spreadsheets, and fields can be used to place adaptable text, the process of annotating designs is more efficient than ever. These indispensable annotation tools are now commonplace, but there are times when they can still be baffling.

In this chapter, I'll address the fundamentals of blocks, the appropriate use of the WBLOCK command, and the management of external references. I'll make suggestions for managing symbol libraries, provide an overview of the process of attaching attributes to blocks, and demonstrate how to extract data from blocks in a drawing using two different approaches.

- **Blocks**
- **Editing Blocks**
- **Managing Symbol Libraries**
- **Adding and Extracting Attributes**
- **External References**
- **Tables and Fields**

Blocks

If you ever did any board drafting before the advent of computer aided design, you undoubtedly used a number of green plastic templates containing cutouts of standard symbols used in your discipline. Templates made drafting more efficient and more uniform. Blocks are often compared with those handy templates, and in some ways that comparison is apt—but not entirely. Blocks and the other annotation tools in AutoCAD have far more value than those green templates ever did. Using a computer for design is more about creating a geometric database than it is about plotting lines. Once you've inserted a block definition, it carries information that can be extracted from the drawing's database. You can find out how many times a block definition was used, where it was inserted, what scale was used. You can attach attribute information to block references and extract that information as well.

Let's quickly review some fundamentals about blocks that you may have overlooked, and then look at some related commands and functions, particularly the misunderstood WBLOCK command. After that, I'll try to straighten out the visibility-control problem you may have encountered with blocks that include entities from different layers.

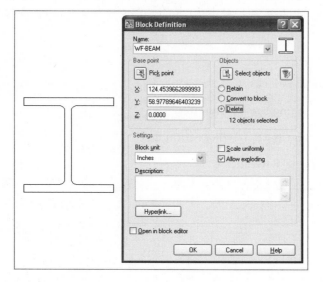

Understanding the Fundamentals

Before I begin the discussion of blocks, I want to run down a list of some important basics. Knowing this information will help you use blocks more effectively:

- A block definition *cannot* be seen in a drawing.
- A block reference *can* be seen in a drawing, but only if
    - The block reference is on a layer that's turned on, and thawed.

- The view on the screen includes the area that contains the block reference.
- You actually selected some entities when defining the block.
- The original layers of the entities used to create the block are turned on and thawed.

Did you know that a block can be defined with *no entities in it*? You can insert it just like any other block, but you won't see anything, because the block consists of…nothing except an insertion point, scale, and rotation angle. This usually happens when a new AutoCAD user tries to insert a block definition using the BLOCK command instead of the INSERT command, accidentally creating a block from nothing. I've known experienced users who create an empty dummy block that they plan to redefine later. If I did that, I'd include at least one entity.

- Blocks can be inserted directly only in the drawing in which they're created.
- AutoCAD DesignCenter allows you to easily bring block definitions from a saved drawing into your current drawing.
- A reference to block definitions from saved drawings can be placed on a tool palette (see Chapter 3).
- Any drawing can be inserted into any other drawing, at which time it becomes a block in that drawing.
- Blocks can be inserted anywhere in 3D space, using coordinates or osnaps, at any scale, even one that's different in each of the X, Y, and Z axes.
- Blocks can be mirrored about any axis when they're inserted by giving a negative scale factor for that axis.
- A block can be inserted as a single entity or broken down into component entities upon insertion. You do this by checking the Explode box in the Insert dialog box or by placing an asterisk (*) before the name of the block when it's inserted from the command line (for example, *block).
- Although a block reference can be broken into component entities using the EXPLODE command, don't do it unless you have a good reason. What would a good reason be? Sometimes you may use a block definition to move a group of entities from one location to another—from the Model Space tab to a layout, for example. In that case, you aren't really defining a symbol, so you explode the result to get the entities back.
- A block reference that has different X, Y, or Z scale factors can't be edited using REFEDIT.

- A block that has been inserted using the MINSERT command can't be exploded in any release. Unless you actually do want to prevent an array of block references from being edited, you're much better off inserting one block and using the ARRAY command to create others.

- Entities within a block that resided on layer 0 when the block was defined take on the visible properties of the layer onto which the block is inserted.

- Entities within a block that resided on a layer other than 0 when the block was defined always retain the properties of their parent layer.

- When exploded, a user-defined block's entities return to the layer on which they were created.

> One of the most popular Express tools is the XPLODE command because it lets you control whether block entities will return to their layer of origin, or be placed on the current layer.

- A *dimension* is an anonymous block. When exploded, its entities are placed on the layer onto which it was inserted. Earlier releases of AutoCAD would place these entities on layer 0.

- A hatch pattern is an anonymous block. When exploded, its entities are placed on the layer onto which it was inserted. Earlier releases of AutoCAD would place these entities on layer 0.

- A block can be redefined after it has been inserted. There are several ways to do this:
  - You can use the Block editor as of AutoCAD 2006.
  - You can use REFEDIT as of AutoCAD 2002.
  - The BLOCK command can be used to define a block with the same name.
  - The block definition can be replaced with a drawing of the same name using the Insert dialog.
  - The block definition can be replaced with any drawing using the -INSERT command and the syntax `oldblock=c:\path\newblock.dwg`.

BLOCK Command

Figure 5.1 shows the current Block Definition dialog box familiar to all AutoCAD users, but there may be a few things you haven't noticed. The top part of the dialog allows you to name a block definition, select a base point (don't forget, or else 0,0,0 will be used as the base point), and select objects. Once the block is defined, you can then control what happens to the entities you selected:

Retain Defines a block from the entities but leaves them in the same state.

Convert To Block Creates a block reference at the same location as the objects you selected, and deletes the objects.

Delete Does what the BLOCK command does at the command prompt—throws the entities away once the block is defined.

Figure 5.1

Block Definition dialog box

The Settings area of the dialog box has two newer options. If you select Scale Uniformly, the block definition can't be scaled independently in the X, Y, and Z axis. If you clear the box labeled Allow Exploding, no one can explode a block reference created with this definition.

The Hyperlink button lets you include a link to a file, layout tab, model tab, or website as part of the block definition. When the block is inserted, it includes that link. To follow it, you hold down the Ctrl key and left mouse button.

If the units identified in the Block unit: pane differ from the units set for the drawing in the Units dialog box, the block will be scaled accordingly when it is inserted. If you define a block with units set to meters, and insert it into a drawing in which units are set to millimeters, the block will be scaled by 1000 when it is inserted.

Related Commands

If you find blocks confusing, it may be because people often use the term *block* to refer to two different concepts: a block definition and a block reference. A *block definition* is the equivalent of a stamp with your name on it that you keep in your desk drawer. It exists, but your name isn't yet stamped on anything. Once you take out the stamp, ink it, and press it onto a sheet of paper, you have the equivalent of a *block reference*.

WBLOCK

WBLOCK isn't a block command; it's a save command. I've fielded countless questions over the years stemming from confusion over this command. I wish it had been named something with the word *save* in the name, but it wasn't. Just keep in mind that you're creating a new drawing file whenever you use this command, and it isn't necessary to use this command to create a file that you intend to use as a symbol in other drawings. You can use any drawing file as a symbol.

There's no WBLOCK entity in AutoCAD. Users who say they made a wblock might as well tell you they made a save. That may make sense in some sports, but not in AutoCAD.

The great utility of the WBLOCK command is the flexibility with which you can create drawing files from part of an existing drawing. Let's say you want to create a separate drawing file using only a portion of an existing drawing file. There's no need to erase objects you don't want in the new drawing—just use the WBLOCK command. There are three ways to use the WBLOCK command to partial-save a drawing (hey, PSAVE might have been a good name). Let's look at each one:

Block The block option converts an existing block definition within a drawing into a separate drawing file. When prompted by the WBLOCK command, type or select an existing block name. The resulting drawing file uses the objects as they existed at the time the block was defined. You can open the DWG file and edit the contents without exploding them, unless the entities used for the block definition were already blocks. You can also insert the resulting DWG file, as you can any DWG file, at which time that file becomes a block in the drawing into which it was inserted.

THE "BLOCK REFERENCES ITSELF" ERROR

A frustrated user once contacted me after he'd meticulously created a single drawing file from each of the blocks he had defined in one drawing that contained all the symbols used by his office. I don't remember how many files he created, but judging from the gritted-teeth sound of his voice, I assume he'd spent a considerable amount of time doing it. When he tried to insert one of the new DWG files, he got the dreaded "Block…references itself" error. When he tried the other files, he got the same error.

This user, like most users who get this error, misunderstood the WBLOCK command:

- He assumed that he *had* to use WBLOCK to create a file for use in other drawings. He didn't.

- He inserted each of his block definitions into the drawing in which they were defined and then used WBLOCK to select that block insertion when he created a new drawing file.

- He gave each drawing file the same name as the block definition he had used.

- He didn't test the first drawing he created to see if he could use it properly, so he didn't know he had a problem until each block definition had been placed into a separate drawing file.

Here's the problem. When you insert any drawing into any other drawing, you get, among other things

- The block definitions in that drawing, with the names you gave them

- A new block definition with the same name as the drawing, consisting of the entities in model space

- Do you see the dilemma? Inserting a drawing file creates a new block with the name of the drawing. If the drawing has the same name as one of the blocks defined *in* that drawing, AutoCAD is being asked to create two entirely different block definitions with the same name. Because it's not possible for a drawing file to have two blocks with the same name, you get the error message "Block…references itself".

If you want to export a block definition to its own drawing file, use the Block option of WBLOCK and select the name of the block. That way, the original entities used to create the block become their own drawing file. When you try to insert that drawing file, you won't get the error message—unless your original block was defined with nested block references, one of which has the same name as your drawing. What are the odds of that happening? Well, the odds are good enough.

Back to my frustrated caller. Relieved to know why he'd gotten the error message, he resigned himself to a long morning redoing all his work…until I told him he didn't have to. He just had to rename his drawing files—different names, no error message. Oh, and he changed the names (this is a promo for rereading Chapter 2) by typing `ren C:\symbols\*.dwg sym*.dwg` at the DOS prompt.

Entire Drawing Selecting this option results in a drawing that has all the entities in the current drawing and everything needed to support those entities. Because unused layers, dimension styles, text styles, and block definitions aren't saved with the drawing, its size is reduced as much as possible.

When using the command-line version of WBLOCK, type *↵ to select all entities in a drawing when prompted for a block name. This is a quick way to reduce drawing size as much as possible, and it can be used in scripts or Lisp programs.

Objects I've seen people erase a lot of entities in a drawing so they can save those that remain as a separate drawing. They then get all the layers, styles, linetypes, and block definitions even if those aren't related to the objects they want to save. WBLOCK creates a drawing file from only those objects you select, and it includes *only* the elements of the drawing necessary to support those objects.

Use any portion of a drawing to create a new drawing file by selecting entities directly and identifying an insertion point. Using the command-line version of WBLOCK, press the Enter key when prompted for a block name. Now entities can be selected in the same way they are for the BLOCK command. When you use the command-line version of WBLOCK, the selected entities are erased. To get them back, use the OOPS command.

Nesting

Nesting is a concept, not a command. It describes the process of using existing block references as entities in a new block definition. There appears to be no limit to how deeply blocks can be nested. I've tried creating an absurd number of nested levels, just to test the theory, and so far I haven't found a limit.

Why would you want to create a block definition from existing insertions of block objects? For starters, you may want to be able to change one aspect of an inserted block but not others. If that aspect is represented by its own block definition, redefining it will change its appearance everywhere it appears, even if used as a nested block in another block definition.

> Before adding attributes to existing block definitions, you may want to insert the desired block without attributes, define the attributes, and then create a nested block from the block reference plus the defined attributes. Now you'll have two versions of that symbol—one with attributes, one without. If you want to change the appearance of the block without affecting the attributes, you can redefine the base block. See the next section for more information on adding attributes to blocks.

BASE

When one drawing is inserted into another drawing, its insertion point is normally 0,0, but you can change that with BASE. The BASE command redefines the insertion point of a drawing from 0,0 to any coordinates you type in or select. If you expect to use a drawing as an inserted symbol in another drawing, it makes sense to be specific about where you want the insertion point.

INSERT

The INSERT command has a useful dialog box, of course. It allows you to view a list of all block definitions, or other DWG files, and select one you want to insert. But you can also use INSERT at the command line by placing a minus sign in front of it when typing: -INSERT. This is helpful in creating AutoLISP programs that insert a drawing into another drawing.

There's another, more unusual use for the command-line version. Typing -INSERT followed by a nonexistent block name gives you a quick indication of the search path AutoCAD is currently using, because it lists all the places it looked for the nonexistent block definition you specified, in order. The first place AutoCAD always looks for a block definition is in the drawing itself. The rest of the list contains the directory where the drawing is currently saved and then the AutoCAD search path specified in OPTIONS. See Figure 5.2.

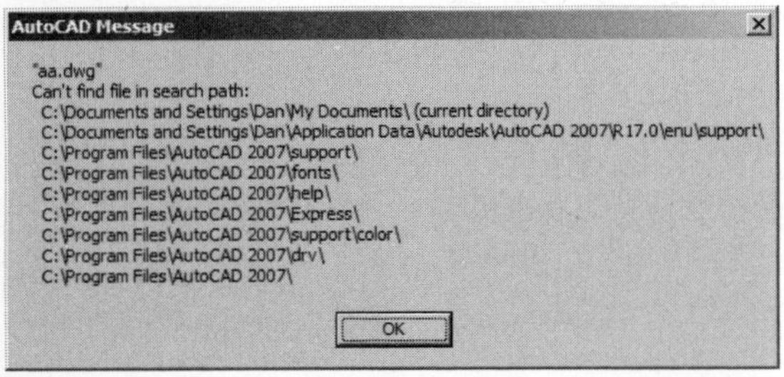

Figure 5.2

Using -INSERT to see the current path

```
AutoCAD Message                                      x
"aa.dwg"
Can't find file in search path:
C:\Documents and Settings\Dan\My Documents\ (current directory)
C:\Documents and Settings\Dan\Application Data\Autodesk\AutoCAD 2007\R17.0\enu\support\
C:\Program Files\AutoCAD 2007\support\
C:\Program Files\AutoCAD 2007\fonts\
C:\Program Files\AutoCAD 2007\help\
C:\Program Files\AutoCAD 2007\Express\
C:\Program Files\AutoCAD 2007\support\color\
C:\Program Files\AutoCAD 2007\drv\
C:\Program Files\AutoCAD 2007\
                    [   OK   ]
```

If you try to insert a drawing using the command-line version of INSERT, you may not get what you expect. If the filename you specify is the same as an existing block definition, the existing definition is used *instead of* the drawing you specify. Unlike the warning you get with the INSERT dialog box, AutoCAD uses the existing definition without asking if you really mean it.

The Block Editor

A brand-new space first appeared in AutoCAD 2006. In addition to Model Space and Paper Space, we now have what I think of as Block Space. Block Space is an editor that makes defining and editing blocks much easier, because you can use all the standard AutoCAD editing and object creation commands, and the odd-colored background never lets you forget which space you're in.

If you can't stand using the block editor, you can still use the standard Block Definition dialog box to create or edit blocks, or the REFEDIT command. Double-clicking a dynamic block won't bring up REFEDIT by default, but you can change that, if you want.

Double-clicking a block can result in different actions, depending on whether the block has included attributes. If it's either a standard block or a dynamic block reference that has attributes, the Enhanced Attribute Editor opens. If it's a block reference without attributes, the block editor opens. Prior to AutoCAD 2006, double-clicking a standard block without attributes opened REFEDIT. You can change any of those double-click behaviors, as of AutoCAD 2007, in the CUI dialog box.

Redefining a Block Using the BLOCK Command

One thing I've always appreciated about Autodesk is that legacy behavior doesn't usually change in new releases of AutoCAD. This reduces, but doesn't eliminate, the surprises that can confront you went upgrading to a new release. Even though there are now two other tools for editing blocks, the old fashioned method still works just fine.

For years you've updated blocks using the BLOCK command. You still can. Just draw a new symbol, use the BLOCK command, and define a new block with the same name as an existing block. It may save time to insert the existing definition, explode it, and then edit the resulting entities. The redefined block immediately updates any block references that have already been inserted into the drawing. This allows you to globally edit even a scaled or MINSERTed block. Redefining a block in this way affects only one drawing file.

REFEDIT

You can still redefine a block or an XRef using REFEDIT, if you prefer, either with the Refedit toolbar, or by typing **REFEDIT** at the command line. The result is the Reference edit dialog box, which displays the block and a tree showing nested blocks. You must select the level you want to edit and then select the objects within that definition that you want to change. Don't close the Refedit toolbar using the X in the upper-right corner; instead, click the third button to discard changes or the last button to save them. If you get a message indicating the objects are "not in the working set," you're still in Refedit: Reopen the toolbar (type **REFEDIT** at the command line), and then select Close Reference or Save Reference Edits.

Updating a Block with a Drawing File

You can also redefine a block by replacing its definition with that of an existing drawing file using the -INSERT command. When you're prompted for the block name, type `oldblock=newblock`. This replaces an existing definition named oldblock with a drawing named `newblock.dwg`. Don't forget to include the path along with the drawing name.

If your old block definition and the new block definition have the same name, you can redefine the existing block using the Insert dialog box. If you try to insert a drawing with the same name as a block that exists in the drawing, you're asked whether you want to redefine the old block. Say yes, and all block references are redefined.

Layer Control

When you create a block definition using entities that reside on layer 0, those entities take on the properties of the layer onto which they're inserted. They also return to layer 0 if the block is exploded. The entities that reside on any other layer always have the properties of that layer, even when inserted onto a different layer. This creates a block whose visibility is controlled by more than one layer: the parent layers and the host layer.

> I use the terms *parent layers* and *host layer* quite a bit in this discussion. By *parent* I mean the layer on which entities reside when you select them to define a block. By *host* I mean the layer onto which you insert a block entity. These aren't official AutoCAD terms, so they're unlikely to be used by others when discussing AutoCAD.

- The parent layer where block entities were located when the block was defined (if not layer 0) control color, linetype, and object visibility. If you freeze or turn off the parent layer, those entities in the block that are on that layer won't be visible. This can be confusing, because it's possible to change the visibility of only *part* of an inserted block object.

- The host layer onto which a block is inserted controls entities in the block as follows:
  - If you freeze the host layer, those entities that reside on the parent layer aren't visible. However, entities on the parent layer aren't affected by turning off the host layer.
  - If you lock the host layer, the block reference can't be erased, copied, moved, rotated, or scaled when the host layer is locked. However, if the block definition is changed, any block inserted onto a locked (or even frozen) layer is also redefined.

Layer 0 is like no other layer, and in my opinion it should be reserved exclusively for entities you place for the purpose of creating a block definition. That way you can leave layer 0 *on* and *thawed* at all times. In pre-2006 versions of AutoCAD, placing dimensions, which are anonymous block definitions whose entities originally reside on layer 0, can be tricky if you have frozen layer 0 and are working in a layout. They won't display until you select their location.

This selective control of the visibility of entities within a block may seem annoying and cause some confusion, but it offers the possibility of a creative unintended consequence. I know of one user who created an elaborate system of nested blocks using entities from various layers so that he could freeze and thaw layers to selectively display the layout of a large mill by location, system, or both. When he combined this with named views and a few menu macros, he had an impressive key system for viewing his drawings.

Dynamic Blocks

Should you use dynamic blocks? Maybe.

Think twice before converting a perfectly usable existing block-library system into dynamic blocks. Doing so will take a lot of time, and other offices with whom you work may still be using a pre–AutoCAD 2006 release and have no way of utilizing the dynamic properties of blocks. Not all block definitions benefit from adding parameters and actions. I recommend the following:

- Continue to use your current block-management system.
- Look for places where a single block definition can replace multiple versions of the same basic symbol.
- If a dynamic version seems useful, create one using the existing block definitions by giving each a separate visibility state.
- Recognize the limitations of using dynamic blocks with earlier releases.

Let's discuss dynamic blocks further in this section.

Getting Started

AutoCAD ships with many dynamic blocks already referenced onto Tool Palettes. You should start by inserting one of them and then double-clicking it to enter the new block editor. All the things you see floating around the block geometry are objects representing parameters or actions. Because they're objects, you can select them and view or change their properties in the same Properties palette as other objects. Figure 5.3 shows a stretch action.

Because it's so new and so different, let's go over the basics of creating these blocks with just enough information to get you experimenting.

Types of Objects: Actions and Parameters

Actions are things that happen and are usually represented by command names; *parameters* are the values that control those actions. In Figure 5.3, the window block can be stretched to change the window's height. The action Stretch is controlled (or constrained, to be more inventor-like) by the Linear parameter window height. To create this image, I added two objects to the window in the block editor: a Linear parameter and an action that's attached to that parameter.

Figure 5.3

Dynamic blocks in the block editor

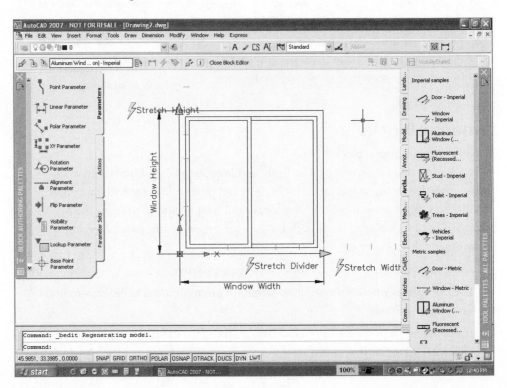

Start With Existing Blocks

Create the entities you want displayed when a block is inserted the same way you've always created blocks: Just draw something. If you have a block, insert it. If not, open the Edit Block Definition dialog box and start drawing. The Help system contains a good overview of the new dynamic-block features, and you can also find some very good papers online at www.autodesk.com.

ROUND-TRIPPING

Like other releases of AutoCAD, AutoCAD 2007 utilizes round-tripping for those situations where you must save an AutoCAD 2007 drawing to an earlier format. Elements that are new in AutoCAD 2007 make it back intact. However, there's one wrinkle with the new dynamic blocks. They have two names: the name you give them, and an anonymous name. The given name refers to the original block definition. The anonymous name is preceded by an asterisk (*) and is randomly assigned (*U9, for example) to each individual variation of the block when it's inserted.

When a drawing containing a dynamic block is opened in a pre–AutoCAD 2006 release, the real name of the block isn't listed in either the Insert or Block dialog box. Although the name is given in the Properties pane or when you use the LIST command, you can't insert a new reference of a dynamic block in an earlier release. A dynamic block reference can, however, be copied, scaled, or exploded. REFEDIT won't work on an anonymous block. Dimensions and hatch patterns are also anonymous blocks and have names beginning with *.

Symbol Libraries

There are a number of strategies for creating and managing symbol libraries. In the distant past, symbols were often added to a tablet menu and picked directly from the tablet with a puck. I occasionally bump into someone who still uses a tablet, but not often. In the not-so-distant past (pre-CUI), an image menu containing slides of blocks was often created and used on the screen as part of a pull-down menu. Creating such an image menu required customization of the ACAD.mns file. AutoCAD's DesignCenter offers a much better alternative. Use it to view and insert blocks from any drawing, including the current drawing if it has been saved.

It is important to have complete symbol libraries that contain blocks that are accurate and easy to use. In this section I'll discuss different strategies for creating and managing your symbol libraries. Which of them you use is up to you.

Creating the Symbols

Block symbols should be created actual size most of the time. In other words, a block that represents a washing machine should be drawn the size of a specific washing machine. A schematic block—like a resistor symbol or a duplex receptacle symbol—should also be drawn full-size, but that means something a little different. Because the same symbol is used to represent objects whose actual size differs, draw the schematic the size you want it to measure when it is *plotted*. If, for example, you want a duplex receptacle symbol to be .25″ when plotted, define the block using objects that are .25″. When you reference the block on a floor plan, scale it to the reciprocal of the plot scale used. It will be the correct size when plotted.

It's tempting to use symbols created by someone else. If they work for you, fine, but I think you're generally better off making your own symbols, unless they're from a manufacturer's site and represent a specific model. Even then, manufacturer's symbols often have too much detail to plot correctly. I've seen people grab a generic stove symbol from DesignCenter only to discover later that the size didn't match the real stove being used.

Sometimes it makes sense to use what is known as *unit sizing*, but a lot of users overdo it. Unit sizing involves defining each block to measure 1 unit × 1 unit. When inserted, the block is scaled in the X, Y, and Z axes to its actual size. In theory, this allows you to use a single block definition for, say, many different sizes of refrigerators. Some symbols lend themselves to unit sizing—a simple door symbol, for example—but most don't, because elements within the symbol get distorted when the scales are different for the different axes.

Here's one of the few uses I have for AutoCAD's SNAP and GRID commands. When I use a snap, I always set a grid that's twice as large. It's a lot easier on the eyes. For schematic symbols, I set a logical snap increment like 0.1 to draw each symbol, making sure insertion points land on a snap. Once I've drawn all the symbols for a schematic diagram using the logical snap increment, I set the same snap increment when I draw a schematic diagram that uses the symbols. I plug them into a grid and connect them with lines that end exactly where I want them—a little like using Lego building blocks. See Figure 5.4.

Once you've defined standard blocks, place references to them on a tool palette as described in Chapter 3. You may want to create a reference drawing by inserting block references into a grid and adding a dot (DONUT) at each insertion point. Include the name of the block, and print the drawing. Now it can be used as a reference in a CAD standards binder. Although it's useful to mark an insertion point with a dot, don't make the dot a part of the block definition. Figure 5.5 shows a partial example of an American Society of Mechanical Engineers (ASME) symbol library.

Figure 5.4

Setting a snap/grid to create schematic symbols

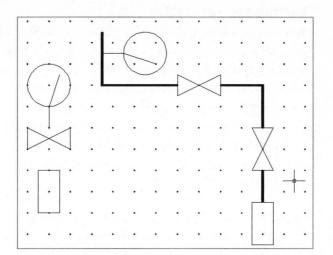

Figure 5.5

Plotted reference sheet for symbols

BLK	ASME SYMBOLS CONTINUED	
A30	COUNTERBORE/SPOTFACE	⌴
A31	COUNTERSINK	⌵
A32	DEPTH/DEEP	▼
A33	SQUARE (SHAPE)	⬜
A34	DIMENSION NOT TO SCALE	15
A35	NUMBER OF TIMES/PLACES	8X
A36	ARC LENGTH	⌒105
A37	RADIUS	R
A38	SPHERICAL RADIUS	SR
A39	SPHERICAL DIAMETER	SØ

Strategies for Managing Symbol Libraries

I've encountered three different strategies for managing symbol libraries. Any of them can be used effectively, and some users will combine them, particularly if they work with a number of different clients or contractors and use symbols provided by them.

- Create a drawing file for each symbol.
- Include all symbols in each template file used.
- Group related blocks into separate library drawings.

I prefer the last option, partly because of how easily the related symbols can be placed on a tool palette, but you should use whatever system makes the most sense to you.

One Symbol per Drawing File

When creating a drawing file for each symbol, you don't use the BLOCK command. Instead, you create a drawing file, place the insertion point of your objects at 0,0, and store each symbol in a subdirectory as a separate drawing file. When you need it, insert the drawing from that directory into any drawing. Once a drawing has been inserted, it becomes a block within the host drawing. Because you only insert symbols that you use, this method results in a host drawing with no unused block definitions.

Many offices use this system, particularly for standard details that are used in a lot of projects, but it does have a drawback: Storing all those drawing files takes a lot more space on the drive. Any individual drawing file requires a minimum amount of hard drive space, so 12 blocks stored as individual files take up more space than one drawing containing the same 12 block definitions. Because of this, and because DesignCenter and Tool Palettes make block management much easier when a single DWG file contains a library of symbols, I don't usually recommend this practice.

All Symbols in Template Drawings

Another method for managing symbols libraries is to place all block definitions in your template drawings. When you start a new drawing, begin with the template drawing, and you have all your standard blocks in the drawing you're working on.

The drawback to this method is that your drawing files become much larger and must be purged when you're done if you want to reduce their size. If you don't purge all the unused block definitions, every drawing you produce will be larger than it needs to be. I recommend this practice only for those block definitions that are used in every drawing, such as title blocks and borders.

Related Blocks Grouped into Library Drawings

My recommended method for maintaining symbols libraries involves creating blocks grouped into library drawings. This is the practice that I find is most common. Place all related block definitions in separate drawings that contain *only* block definitions. If you use a large number of symbols, break them into categories and create a DWG file for each category. You can then use DesignCenter to create a tool palette that contains all the block definitions from each symbol-library drawing or to load individual blocks from the symbol drawing into your current drawing as shown in Figure 5.6.

If you want to bring all block definitions from one drawing into another, insert the entire drawing and press the Esc key when prompted for an insertion point. All the block definitions (and all other user-defined elements) become part of the drawing. This can result in a lot of unused block definitions, layers, dimension styles, text styles, and so on. If so, you can use the PURGE command to eliminate the unused objects.

There's another serious drawback to this method. If you have a naming conflict between any element of the host drawing and the drawing being inserted, the host drawing wins.

This causes a problem if you use the same name for different block definitions in the two drawings. Your changes are discarded if the host drawing contains different definitions. For that reason, I don't recommend inserting a drawing to get the block definitions. DesignCenter is a more efficient method, and you can see what the blocks look like before you insert them.

> If you have block definitions in a drawing that was created with an early release of AutoCAD, the blocks may not all display in DesignCenter. Icons representing blocks weren't added to drawing files before DesignCenter appeared. Even if you've edited the drawing in a release that contains DesignCenter, block icons appear only for blocks defined in the newer release (see Figure 5.7). To create icons, open the old drawing, and run the BLOCKICON command. Select all blocks by accepting the default when prompted to Enter block names <*>.

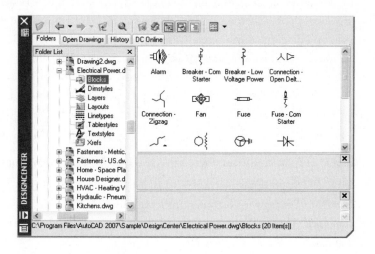

Figure 5.6

Displaying block definitions in DesignCenter

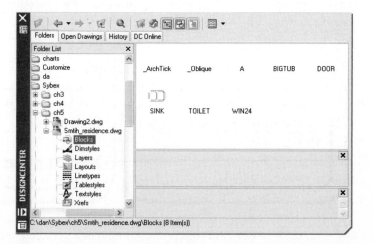

Figure 5.7

Missing block icons in DesignCenter

Assigning and Extracting Attributes

When defining a block, you can include attributes. *Attributes* are text-based information categories that are carried with the block definition. You provide the value for the attribute when the block is inserted. This information can be any property of the block that can be given a value consisting of a text string or number. For example, a single symbol for a tree can include attributes indicating the species, size, cost, age, supplier, and so on for that particular tree.

> Attribute definitions are meaningful only if they're used as part of a block definition. By themselves, they have no utility—at least none that I've come across.

One of the most common blocks to create with attributes is a standard title block. Any information that changes from drawing to drawing should be added as an attribute. When you insert the block, you can provide the values for attributes like project, sheet number, scale, and date. In addition to attributes, you can add fields to title blocks describing information like the filename or path, as shown in Figure 5.8.

Figure 5.8 shows two views of a title block. The left view displays the entities used to define the block; the right view displays an insertion of the block definition. The entities used to create the block include attribute definitions with the following tags:

PROJECT The tag for the project name. It's a visible attribute, as are all the others shown here.

SHEET The tag for the number of this sheet. If this drawing was part of a sheet set, this value could be displayed as a Field.

SHTOTAL The tag for the total number of sheets. Notice that it overlaps the border of the title block. That's OK, because the attribute tag is replaced with a value that has fewer characters, as shown on the right.

DATE The tag for the date. It's possible to use a field for this value, if the date is either the date the drawing is plotted or the date the drawing was created. In this case, the value must be provided by the user, because it represents a completion date.

Figure 5.8
Title block with attributes

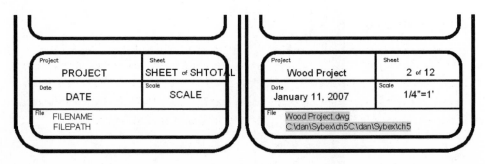

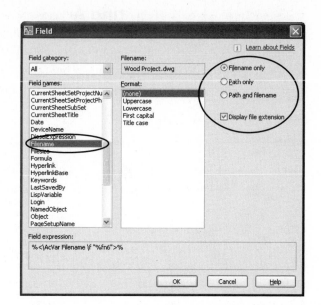

Figure 5.9

Changing properties of a field

SCALE The tag for the scale used to set up the main floating viewport on this sheet. The value must be entered by the user.

FILENAME The tag for the name of the current file. Its default value is a field that's used as an attribute. Because it's a field, its value changes if the default drawing name is changed. Fields are displayed with a mask when inserted into a drawing, as shown on the right. The mask won't plot. It's there for your reference.

> If you use the SAVEAS command with a different filename or path, you redefine the default values. The new values will be displayed by the Filename field.

FILEPATH The tag for the location of the drawing file. It's the same field as used for FILENAME, but with different properties, as shown in Figure 5.9.

Defining Attributes

Attributes can be defined to either appear as part of the drawing or be invisible. Either way, the information attached to a block can be extracted from the drawing into a file for use in another application, generally a database program like Access. The file into which you extract the attribute values can be an ASCII text file or an MDB file (Microsoft Database file). Attributes can also be extracted directly into an AutoCAD table.

The commands listed in Table 5.1 are used to create and modify attributes (consider making aliases for them in your ACAD.pgp file). Those commands that begin with the letter *E* (for *extended*) are used to manage and extract block attributes manually. Those that begin with the letter *A* can be used manually but can also be used in scripts and Lisp routines when you're automating procedures that involve attributes.

Table 5.1

Creating and Modifying Attributes

COMMAND	MEANING	PURPOSE
ATTDEF	Attribute definition	Dialog box for defining attributes for use in a block definition.
-ATTDEF	Attribute definition	Command-line version of ATTDEF.
ATTDIA	Attribute dialog	Variable that determines whether a dialog box or the command line is used to complete attribute information when inserting a block.
ATTDISP	Attribute display	Controls the display of attributes. ON displays all attributes, even invisible ones. OFF hides all attributes, even visible ones. Normal displays them as defined.
ATTEDIT	Attribute edit	A dialog box to be used to edit attributes one block at a time.
-ATTEDIT	Attribute edit	Command-line editor used to modify attributes after a block is created. -ATTEDIT can be used to edit blocks globally, rather than one at a time.
ATTREDEF	Attribute redefinition	Redefines a block and updates associated attributes. Use this command if you have to add or remove attribute definitions in an existing block definition. Don't use the block editor, the BLOCK command, or REFEDIT for that purpose.
ATTSYNC	Attribute synchronize	Updates all instances of a specified block with the current attributes. Use this command if you redefine a block containing attributes and want the changes to any attributes to be reflected in entities that have already been inserted.
ATTREQ	Attribute request	Used to control whether you're prompted for a value when inserting a block that contains attributes. If it's set to 0, any block containing attributes is inserted with the defaults as set when the attributes were defined. Set this variable to 1 to allow prompts.
ATTEXT	Attribute extraction	Dialog box for extracting attribute values into a text file.
-ATTEXT	Attribute extraction	Command-line version of ATTEXT.
BATTMAN	Block Attribute Manager	Allows you to manage existing attributes after they're defined.
EATTEDIT	Extended Attribute Editor	Wizard used to edit attributes as of AutoCAD 2002.
EATTEXT	Extended Attribute Extraction	Wizard used to extract attributes as of AutoCAD 2002.

Adding Attributes to Blocks

Attribute definitions are AutoCAD entities; they can be selected and used to create blocks, either by themselves or in combination with other entities. Usually they're used to annotate graphic symbols or complete title blocks, so they're generally used with other entities. Follow these steps to use them in blocks that also contain geometric entities (See Figure 5.10):

1. Create a symbol to which you'll attach attributes. For this example, use a couple of tree symbols as shown in Figure 5.11.

2. After drawing the symbol, turn it into a block *without* attributes and insert a reference into the drawing.

> Many users create a single block that consists of entities—lines, for instance—as well as the attribute definition. You can do that, but in this example I'm creating two versions of the same block definition—with and without attributes. The one without attributes is nested inside the other one. It's much easier to update the geometry of block references defined this way without affecting their attributes.

3. Add attributes with ATTDEF, and place them in the proper locations with the desired text style and height and the mode you want.

> It's easier to edit existing attributes than to add new ones to existing block definitions. Before defining a block, create any attributes you think you may ever need.

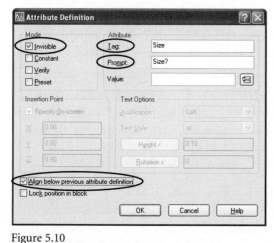

Figure 5.10
Attribute Definition dialog box

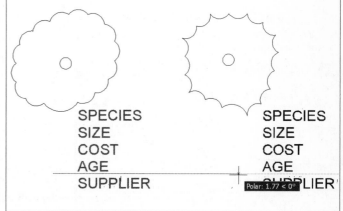

Figure 5.11
Copying attribute definitions

4. Make a new, nested block definition by selecting the inserted block and then the attributes. The new block must have a different name than the nested version, of course. You may want to add *ATT* as either a suffix or a prefix to the original block name. Use a prefix if you want all the attributed blocks to be listed together. Use a suffix if you want the two blocks to be listed together. For example, a symbol for a deciduous tree could be named *deciduous* with its attributed version named either *att-deciduous* or *deciduous-att*, as shown in Figure 5.12.

> When defining a block, if you use any method other than a single pick to select attributes, the order in which the prompts are given or listed is based on the order in which the attributes were defined, starting with the most recent. If you want to have prompts listed in a different order, select them in that order. If you want to change the order after the block has been defined, you can do that using the BATTMAN command.

Attribute Modes

When you're defining attributes, you have the option of setting their mode to Invisible, Constant, Verify, or Preset. The modes affect attributes in the following way:

Invisible Sometimes attributes are used to create text that's part of a drawing; the values entered into a title block are a good example. Such values must be set to the Visible mode. Other times, attributes are used to store information in the drawing that's not part of the drawing itself. Using attributes for storing costs, or model numbers of parts may fit into that category. In that case, values must be set to the Invisible mode. No matter what mode is selected when attributes are first defined, they can all be made to display or not display using the ATTDISP variable.

Constant If the value of a specific attribute will never change from the default, you can use this mode. An attribute value in this mode *cannot* be edited with DDATTE or ATTEDIT.

Figure 5.12

Block naming recommendation

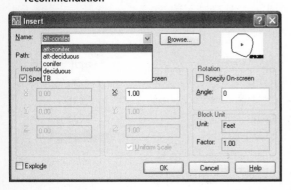

Although I normally recommend against using Constant, because Preset allows you to make future changes, there's one situation where using this mode is useful. If you want a value that never changes but can still be extracted from the drawing using ATTEXT or EATTEXT, make it a constant attribute.

Verify When a block containing attributes is inserted into a drawing, the operator may be prompted for the value of the attribute, depending on the setting of ATTREQ andATTDIA.

If you enable verification, the operator will be asked to verify each of the values given after they have been typed in. Although this may increase accuracy, it also takes time. I recommend against it except for values that are critical and prone to mistake, like part numbers.

Preset If the value of a specific attribute is nearly always the same, this setting can be used to automatically use the default when the block is inserted. It's still possible to edit a preset attribute value using the EATTEDIT, -ATTEDIT or ATTEDIT command.

Attribute Definitions

You have several options when defining attributes. The options include:

Tag You can use any character that can be typed at the keyboard to name a tag for an attribute definition, as long as it has no spaces. Try to create tags that are short and descriptive.

Prompt You can place anything you want in the prompt window, including spaces. However, I recommend that your prompt consist of the tag name you used followed by a question mark. The Edit Attributes dialog displays the prompt but not the tag. If the prompt is always the same as the tag, you always know the tag name even when only the prompt is listed.

Value This is where you can place a default value. You can also set Attribute Mode to Preset so this value is used automatically. If you need to change it, you can use one of the editing commands.

You can also use this as a place to reinforce the format in which you want information to be placed. You may place a dummy date here, for example, so users remember what date format to use. Just make sure you change it to the correct date when you insert the block.

Insertion Point Click OK to pick a point for the location, or select Align Below Previous Attribute Definition to locate the attributes. The attribute tags show up at that location.

> If your attribute definition doesn't show up where you expect, it may be at the default location of 0,0,0. If so, you forgot to pick a location.

When you insert the block, the Edit Attributes dialog appears, allowing you to fill in the values you want. If it doesn't appear, you may have ATTDIA turned off, in which case you'll be prompted at the command line. If you get no dialog box and no command-line prompt, you may have ATTREQ turned off. The Edit Attributes dialog in Figure 5.13 shows the tag Species with the value Quercus rubra.

Whether the values you place are visible on the screen depends on whether you defined attributes that are invisible. Most attributes for things like species, size, and cost are

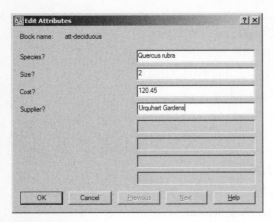

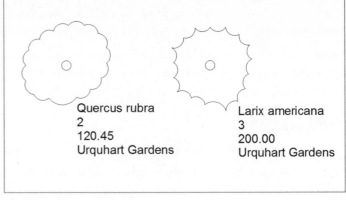

Figure 5.13

Edit Attributes dialog

Figure 5.14

Displaying invisible attributes

invisible—you want the information, but you don't want it shown on the drawing. One exception is a title block. When you create your title block, the attributes should be visible; otherwise, you won't be able to read them in the drawing. If you want to see and/or plot invisible attributes, you can set the variable ATTDISP to ON, as in Figure 5.14.

> Although the order in which prompts are displayed is affected by the order in which you select attribute definitions when defining a block, the *locations* of the attribute values is based only on the location of attribute definitions at the time the block was defined.

Extracting Attribute Values

Attribute values can be useful even if they are only used to display information in a drawing, but they are most powerful when you use them to attach information about each block reference. Most of that information will be invisible, so you have to be able to extract it from the drawing in order to use it. That process can be done in one of two ways. I'll go through both. One is easier when used manually, the other useful for extracting attribute values using an AutoLISP program.

There are two methods for extracting attribute information: EATTEXT and ATTEXT.

The EATTEXT command displays the Attribute Extraction Wizard. It's easy to use, and with it you can extract attribute data from a group of selected block entities, either from the current drawing or from any saved drawing or set of drawings that have been referenced into a sheet set. (See Figure 5.15.)

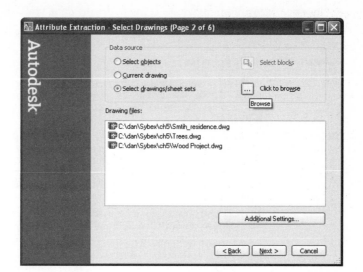

Figure 5.15

**Attribute
Extraction Wizard**

FIELDS AND RECORDS

A number of database programs, including Microsoft's Access, store data using a variety of file formats. Database management can be complex, with myriad means of organizing and retrieving data. When you're dealing with attributes, you don't need to be too concerned about the science of database management, or even with DBCONNECT, AutoCAD's own internal means of connecting to external databases. But you should know two key terms: *fields* and *records*.

Databases are composed of records, within which related data is kept in fields. If you have an address book, you have a database with records and fields. Each person in your address book is represented by one record. For each of those records, you may have several pieces of data: first name, last name, street address, town, state, zip code, phone number, e-mail address, and favorite color. Those pieces of data are values stored in fields.

When you're extracting attributes from an AutoCAD drawing, a single block is a single record. If the same block definition has been used to create 100 block references, each of the 100 referencesis a record. The attribute tags associated with those blocks are the names of the fields used to represent the records. In the example with trees, each of the tree blocks is a record with the five fields: species, size, cost, age, and supplier. When you extract attributes from a group of block references, you're creating a database consisting of records and fields, just like your address book.

Once you identify where you're going to get the data, you can extract it into one of several different formats, as shown in Table 5.2

FORMAT	DESCRIPTION
Table	A table is an AutoCAD object that contains rows and columns of cells. It wasn't until AutoCAD 2006 that attribute values could be extracted into a table, but that feature has become a favorite for this process. Tables are the only internal format for attribute extraction.
CSV	The Comma Separated Value format is also known as the comma-delimited format. It's an ASCII text file with each field within a record separated by a comma. Because this is a common means of delimiting (separating) data, it's a good idea not to include a comma as part of the value you assign to an attribute. It's also common for values in CSV format to be differentiated by placing character values in single quotation marks while leaving numerical values unquoted.
MDB	The Microsoft DataBase format is used by Microsoft Access for its database files. You'll see how to use Access with data from an AutoCAD drawing later in this section.
XLS	Excel Spreadsheet format is used by Microsoft Excel for its spreadsheet files. Although there's some similarity between a database and a spreadsheet, they're very different. However, it's possible to extract attribute values from AutoCAD directly into the cells of a spreadsheet. It's also fairly easy to convert an MDB file into an XLS file and vice versa.
TXT	This is a plain ASCII text file with one record per line and the fields within records separated by spaces. This type of file can be imported into an AutoCAD drawing, but it's hard to line up the columns using an acceptable font. All but a couple of AutoCAD's font options are proportionally spaced, so any time you try to use a TXT file with columns of data, you get wavy columns.

The other method for extracting attributes, the ATTEXT command or its command-line equivalent, predates the EATTEXT wizard and is much more involved. I still consider it useful, though, because it can be used with a script or an AutoLISP program to automate the extraction of attributes from multiple drawings. (See Chapter 8.) ATTEXT involves a number of steps.

Before extracting attribute information from a drawing, you have to create a template file to tell the software how the information should be extracted. This template file must be an ASCII file. It can be created in any word processor, but because you must save the file in ASCII format, I recommend using Notepad. EDIT is a DOS alternative that's run from the system command prompt, but its only advantage over Notepad used to be its line counter. (EDIT was the replacement for the dreadful EDLIN text editor. If you remember using that, you can definitely claim the title of "computer old-timer.") If you're using the XP version of NOTEPAD, the View pull-down menu gives you the option of viewing a line counter. There are also other text editors that you can find as shareware or buy. You can even use VLISP, if you find it helpful.

Don't leave any blank spaces or blank lines in this template file. When you try to extract attribute values, if you get the error message "invalid field specification" when you extract the data, you may have a blank line at the end of the file. Remove any extra lines by moving your cursor to the end of the file and using the Backspace key to delete them. Don't use the cursor keys, because the blank lines will still be there. The cursor should end up at the beginning of the blank line that immediately follows your text. Before saving the template file, use the Down Arrow to move your cursor to the end of the file. If the cursor doesn't stop directly below the last line, remove the blank lines, and check each line to make sure you have no spaces at the end of any individual line.

In the template file shown, the first two lines represent attributes that all block references have; they aren't tags that you can create. All blocks have a block name, layer name, a linetype, the coordinates of its insertion point, and other information. If a block includes at least one custom attribute, you can also extract the general attributes. If you use the EATTEXT wizard, you can extract general data from any block, regardless of whether it has any user-defined tags.

The BLANK1 tag creates a space between a right-justified numerical field and a left-justified character field, not because it's named BLANK, but because no values are assigned to that tag. Any false tag name can be used to create spaces, but only once. This file must have a .txt extension and be an ASCII text file. The file appears as shown in Figure 5.16 if you highlight the entire file to make sure it has no blank lines.

An explanation of the file is shown in Table 5.3.

This template file list provides six rows of information in an extracted file: the block name, layer, species, size, cost, and supplier. The second column in the template file specifies the kind of data (characters or numbers), the field width (008 = 8 characters), and numerical precision (002 = 2 decimal places). All character-based fields have a precision of 000.

Once you've created a template file, open the drawing that contains attributes and use ATTEXT or EATTEXT to extract them. You can specify a filename for the extracted data, or let AutoCAD use the drawing name. In this case the result of extracting block information from two tree symbols using this template file is another text file like the following.

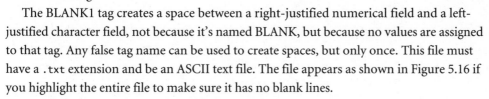

Figure 5.16

Extraction template file

TAGS	FORMAT	EXPLANATION
BL:NAME	C014000	BL: means BLOCK. This extracts the block name.
BL:LAYER	C008000	This extracts the layer on which the block resides.
SPECIES	C012000	This is a Character field, because it includes letters.
SIZE	C008000	This is a Character field in case *ft* is used in an attribute.
COST	N007002	This is a Numerical field. It's right justified so no $ characters appear in attributes.
BLANK1	C004000	This is a space between fields—any nontag word is OK.
SUPPLIER	C014000	This is a Character field because it includes letters.

Table 5.3

Trees_
template.txt

What appears in bold is part of the text file created by AutoCAD. The first example is comma delimited:

```
'att-deciduous','trees','Quercus rubra','2', 120.45,'','Urquhart Gardens'
'att-conifer','trees','Larix americana','3', 200.00,'',' Urquhart Gardens '
```

The second example is space delimited:

```
att-deciduous   trees   Quercus rubra    2     120.45    Urquhart Gardens
att-conifer     trees   Larix americana  3     200.00    Urquhart Gardens
```

Once the information is extracted into a text file, you can insert it into the drawing as text or import it into a database program like Microsoft Access so you can organize the information in any way that's useful. When you use the ATTEXT command, you must decide how the information identified in the template will be listed in the extraction file. The choices are comma delimited (CDF), space delimited (SDF), and Drawing Exchange Format (DXX). DXX is a partial DXF file, containing only block and attribute information. The .dxx extension is used to differentiate the file from a standard DXF file. It has no value to most users. Use SDF for information you want to be able to read or import into AutoCAD. Use CDF if you plan to use the data in a database application. See Figure 5.17.

XRefs: External References

An *XRef* is a drawing that's externally referenced. The process of attaching an XRef is similar to using the INSERT command to bring another drawing into a host drawing, but the result is much more powerful. XRefs allow you to use a single drawing file as a reference in multiple drawings so that the most current version of the XRef is always displayed.

Figure 5.17

Attribute extraction

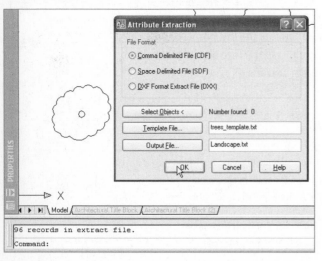

XRefs also let you make a single master drawing from many smaller drawings, even if different designers are working on each of the smaller drawings. XRefs must be managed carefully. They work best in a network environment with clear standards on filenames, locations, and base points for the geometry created in the drawing. In other words, they work best in an office with a good CAD manager.

When you attach an existing drawing file to a host drawing, the external reference doesn't become a part of the new drawing unless you decide to bind it. Instead, AutoCAD stores the location and name of the referenced drawing in the host drawing.

Whenever the new drawing is opened, AutoCAD locates the XRef and displays it. If the XRef has been changed since the last time the new drawing was edited, the changes are automatically reflected in the new drawing. XRefs can also be nested, just like blocks.

Using external references permits several different designers to work on components or subassemblies of a large drawing project. A master drawing of an entire assembly may consist of several XRefs, one for each subassembly. Whenever the master drawing is loaded into AutoCAD, the latest version of each subassembly is loaded as well. When all revisions are complete, XRefs can be bound to the master drawing and become a single drawing file. In most cases, XRefs are maintained and the individual drawings are never bound to the drawing.

Figure 5.18

AutoCAD 2007 External References palette

Attaching an XRef

To attach an XRef, issue the XREF command. If you use an release earlier than AutoCAD 2007, you get the External Reference dialog. In AutoCAD 2007, you get a palette that combines the XREF, IMAGE, and DWFIN commands and that lets you manage all three kinds of externally referenced files. All the functions of the pre–AutoCAD 2007 dialog box are available through the palette—you just may have to right-click a filename to find them.

Let's start by attaching an XRef. Pre–AutoCAD 2007 brings up a dialog box that contains an Attach DWG button. Click it to attach a drawing, image, or DWF file. In AutoCAD 2007, click the Attach icon as shown in Figure 5.18. In both pre-AutoCAD 2007 and AutoCAD 2007, you get the same dialog box (see Figure 5.19) in which to select and control the external reference.

> You can bypass the External References palette with the XATTACH command.

Once you select the drawing you want to reference, the External Reference dialog box shown in Figure 5.19 is displayed. The bottom portion gives you the same options that the INSERT command gives for inserting blocks. The top portion, however, gives you several choices specific to external references.

You have an important choice to make for Reference Type: Attachment or Overlay. If you select Attachment, your XRef will be visible in the current drawing and in any drawings to which the current drawing is attached as an XRef. If the current host drawing is attached to another drawing, any attachment-type XRefs will become nested

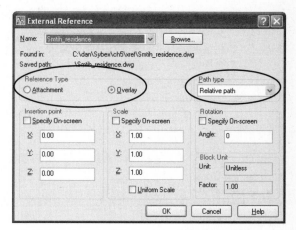

Figure 5.19

External Reference dialog box

XRefs and will always be displayed. That may not be desirable if the nesting gets deep enough that the detail in this drawing won't be readable.

If you select Overlay, the drawing you're referencing will be visible only in the current drawing. If the current drawing becomes an XRef in another drawing, overlay XRefs contains won't display.

You also have the option of selecting Full Path, Relative Path, or No Path. If Full Path is selected, the absolute path, including the drive letter and each folder in the path, is used to locate the drawing when it's needed. If it's not found in the full path, AutoCAD looks in the current folder. If AutoCAD doesn't find the XRef in the current folder, it looks in the default path locations. If it can't find the drawing, a text string identifying the XRef is displayed at its insertion point instead.

If you select the No Path option, no path is saved, and the XRef is found *only* if it's in the same folder as the host drawing. That's not a bad idea, especially when you're transmitting drawings and their XRefs to another user. However, it gets cumbersome with large projects that have multiple XRefs.

The Relative Path option was added in AutoCAD 2005. It's useful when you need to copy an entire folder structure and transmit it to someone else, where it may be placed on a drive with a different drive letter. This method stores the path of the XRef relative to the location of the host drawing file into which it's inserted. There are two requirements for using the Relative Path option: You have to save the host drawing before attaching an external reference file, and the XRef must reside on the *same* drive as the host drawing.

The conventions for displaying a relative folder path are shown in Table 5.4.

When there are more folder levels, another ..\ is added for each. For example, if a host drawing named HOST.DWG is saved in the folder C:\dan\da\dwg\ and has four XRefs, their relative paths are displayed as in Table 5.5.

The AutoCAD 2007 External References palette displays these XRefs as shown in Figure 5.20.

Table 5.4	PATH DESIGNATION	EXPLANATION
Relative Path Designations	.\path	From the folder of the host drawing, follow the specified path.
	..\path	From the folder of the host drawing, move up one folder level and follow the specified path.
	..\..\path	From the folder of the host drawing, move up two folder levels and follow the specified path.

Table 5.5	XREF NAME	ACTUAL FULL PATH	RELATIVE PATH DESIGNATION
Sample Use of Relative Path Designations	XRef1.dwg	C:\	..\..\..\XRef1.dwg
	XRef2.dwg	C:\external	..\..\..\external\XRef2.dwg
	XRef3.dwg	C:\dan\da\dwg	.\XRef3.dwg
	XRef4.dwg	C:\dan\da\dwg\external	.\external\XRef4.dwg

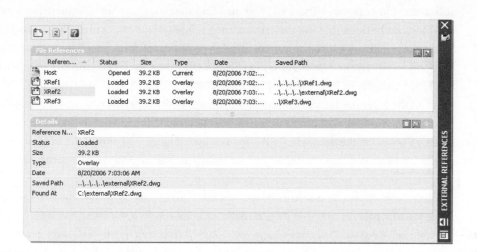

Figure 5.20

Relative path designation

Managing XRefs

Once you've loaded your external references, you manage them using the same palette (in AutoCAD 2007) or dialog box. You can detach them, reload them to get the most current version, unload them, change their path, change their type, or bind them to the drawing permanently.

The Bind option gives you two choices: Bind or Insert. This is also an important decision. Binding an XRef turns it into a block, as though you had used the INSERT command instead of attaching the drawing as an XRef. The choice between Bind and Insert determines how the names for layers, blocks, dimstyles, and so on are treated. Let's look at how those names are treated in XRefs before they're bound.

XRef Layer, Block, and Dimstyle Names

When an XRef is attached to a drawing, AutoCAD differentiates the layers, blocks, and dimension styles in the XRef from those in the host drawing. To distinguish XRef elements from the host-drawing elements, their names include the XRef drawing name as a prefix. A layer with the name Cen in an externally referenced drawing named `Smith_residence.dwg` is displayed in the host drawing as Smith_residence|Cen.

When you bind an XRef, the names of objects in the XRef change, but how they change depends on which Bind option you selected. This gets a little confusing, because choosing to bind a drawing requires a choice between two options, one of which is also name Bind. So you can have a Bind-type bind, or an Insert-type bind. With a Bind-type bind, the layer name Cen in the drawing `Smith_residence.dwg` becomes Smith_residence0cen. With an Insert-type bind, the layer is named Cen, as though the drawing was placed using the INSERT command.

Use the Bind option. Otherwise, you may find that your text styles, dimension styles, and block definitions that use the same name as their counterparts in the host drawing have been redefined. Once you use the Bind-type option of Bind, you'll have some fairly long and cumbersome names for layers, block definitions, text style, and so on. You can quickly rename them by using the RENAME command and applying a wildcard (*) to select all the XRef names. For example, if the names of these elements are prefixed with Smith_residence0, you can type **Smith_residence0*** for the old name and a new prefix followed by the wildcard—**SR***, for example. Figure 5.21 shows the original bind names, and Figure 5.22 shows the result of using the wildcard to rename them.

> Layer 0 and the Defpoints layer behave differently in XRefs than other layers do. They are not identified separately with their drawing name as a prefix. When bound to a host drawing, all entities on the 0 and Defpoints layer in each XRef will be placed on the same layer. For this reason you should avoid placing any entities on either the 0 or Defpoints layer if you intend to use the drawing as an XRef.

VISRETAIN

When you first attach an XRef, the layer visibility of the XRef is determined by its visibility at the time the XRef was last saved. However, you can alter the visibility of XRef layers from within the host drawing to control the display of the referenced drawing. VISRETAIN controls layer visibility the next time you open the host drawing. Will the host drawing display the layers as they appeared when the XRef was saved or when the host drawing was saved?

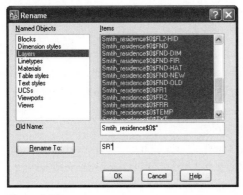

Figure 5.21
Bind-type bind layer names

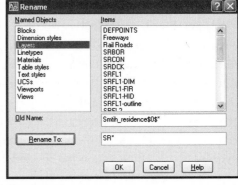

Figure 5.22
Use of a wildcard to rename layers

If VISRETAIN is set to 0, changes to layer visibility in the host drawing are temporary, and XRef layer visibility reverts to the XRef drawing when the host drawing is reopened. If VISRETAIN is set to 1 (the default), layer settings are saved with the host drawing and persist from session to session. Normally, you should leave this setting at 1.

XCLIP

When a large XRef is brought into a host drawing, it often contains far more geometry than the drawing requires. To prevent unwanted geometry from being displayed, you can use the XCLIP command to clip an external reference into either a rectangle or a polygon. If you want the frame of the clipped area to show, set the XCLIPFRAME system variable to 1; if you don't want it to show, set this variable to 0.

> XCLIP also clips block references.

Layer and Spatial Indexing

When a drawing contains many external references or a very large external reference, performance during editing slows down. To reduce the amount of computer resources necessary to manage the host drawing, two indexes can be saved with a host drawing and used during demand loading of external references. These indexes keep track of which XRef-dependent layers are currently thawed and how much of an XRef is being displayed as a result of the XCLIP command. These indexes are added to the database of the host drawing, making it slightly larger, but the performance gain in not loading all layers and all geometry (spatial indexing controls the appearance of geometry) generally makes up for that slightly larger file size.

The INDEXCTL variable controls whether indexes are saved with a host drawing. Its settings are shown in Table 5.6.

Table 5.6
INDEXCTL Settings

INDEXCTL SETTING	DESCRIPTION
0	No indexes are created. The entire external reference loads with the host drawing.
1	A layer index is created. Only thawed layers load with the host drawing.
2	A spatial index is created. Only geometry displayed within an XCLIP is loaded with the host drawing.
3	Layer and spatial indexes are created. Thawed layers and XCLIP geometry are loaded.

You don't need to remember this variable when working with host drawings. All this can be controlled in the SAVEAS dialog box by selecting Tools and then Options. The resulting dialog box allows you to select an index option.

Once you've created and saved an index with your host drawing, you have to enable demand-loading before you gain any performance from setting INDEXCTL. To enable demand loading, either use the variable XLOADCTL or use the Open And Save tab of the Options dialog box, shown in Figure 5.23. Demand Load Xrefs → Enabled With Copy is generally the fastest method when you're working on a network. Only the layers and area specified by INDEXCTL are loaded when a drawing is opened that contains XRefs and the referenced drawings aren't locked.

REFEDIT and XEDIT

Although it can be used to edit blocks, the intended application of the REFEDIT command is to edit external references from within a host drawing. This is a potentially *very* dangerous command, because any changes you make while using it can be saved to the original external reference. Because double-clicking an XRef opens the block editor, it's possible to edit an XRef without noticing it. If you want to prevent the use of REFEDIT on a particular external reference, open that reference drawing and set XEDIT to 0 before saving it. Now you'll have to open the drawing before making changes—a safer method for editing reference drawings, in my opinion.

Figure 5.23

Setting demand-loading and index control

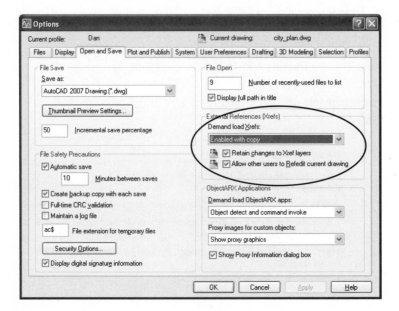

To open an attached XRef quickly, use the XOPEN command. Or, in AutoCAD 2007, select the XRef in the palette, right-click, and select Open.

Fields and Tables

Fields and tables work together to add significant functionality. They first showed up in AutoCAD 2005 and represented two of the most significant additions to that release. Fields pretty much replaced the Express Tool RTEXT for me, making it much easier to add automatically updated information to drawings—mostly because you don't have to understand diesel expressions to use Fields. Tables finally made it possible to do something that had always been clunky in AutoCAD—organize text-based entities as part of a drawing.

Fields

Fields are potentially useful and powerful tools. They can be variable, in the sense that values in fields can be made to change automatically. A date field, for example, always contains the current date (although a REGEN may be necessary to match the display to the value). A system-variable field always contains the current setting of that variable. You can customize fields using the following drawing properties and diesel expressions:

- You can create drawing properties (title, author, comments, keywords, or custom) from the File pull-down menu. Once you've defined custom properties, they're listed by the names you gave them in the list of possible fields. Change the properties, and they change in the field location (either in a table or anywhere else). (See Figure 5.24.)

- Diesel expressions can also be used in fields. However, spreadsheet-like equations were added to tables in AutoCAD 2006, and so many existing fields are specified that it's unlikely you'll need to use diesel. But, who knows what you may find to do with it?

Many of the fields are obvious: date of creation, which doesn't change; date, which does change; time; and so on; but some are more subtle. The listed fields when you right-click

Figure 5.24
Drawing properties as fields

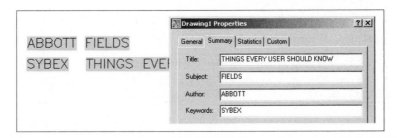

in MTEXT and select Insert Field include the following, plus any custom-drawing properties you create. The asterisk is used here as a wildcard. Wherever it appears, the category has multiple fields that are related.

Author (DWG property)	LastSavedBy
BlockPlaceholder	LispVariable
Comments (DWG property)	Login
CreateDate	NamedObject
CurrentSheet*	Object
Date	PageSetupName
DeviceName	PaperSize
Diesel Expression	Plot*
Filename	SaveDate
Filesize	Sheet*
Formula	Subject(DWG property)
Hyperlink*	SystemVariable
Keywords (DWG property)	Title (DWG property)

Don't overlook the SystemVariable field, which gives you access to 400 or so variables. The Filename field gives both the default path and name of the current drawing. For just the filename without the path, place the variable DWGNAME as a SystemVariable field. For a list of all system variables, type **SETVAR**↵ **?**↵↵ at the AutoCAD command prompt, or use the Help system.

Tables

Creating tables was never easy in AutoCAD, although you've been able to import Access and Excel files as OLE objects since Release 14. Finally it's possible to create and edit tables that retain their format and contain actual data—either text data or fields. Fields are the most interesting of the data types—particularly in AutoCAD 2006, which allows equations to be entered into cells in the table. And if you decide to use a table in some other application, it can be easily exported to a comma-delimited text file that can be read by database and spreadsheet software.

Before I get into specifics about using the calculation functions of tables, here are a few general recommendations:

- Create a table style (click the ellipses button in the Insert Table dialog box) that uses a proper font, with text heights that meet standards, and give it a name other than Standard.

- To enter a field into a table cell, double-click in the cell to open the MTEXT editor. Now, right-click to bring up the MTEXT menu, and select Insert Field.

- To edit a table cell, double-click its contents.

- To edit a table (column sizes, and so on), select the table, right-click to bring up the context-sensitive menu for tables, and select Properties. Now you can use the Properties palette to change the table's structure.

- Each cell in a table has a designation that consists of both a letter and a number.

AutoCAD 2006 gave tables a big boost by adding the ability to place formulas in individual cells that can reference other cells, just like in a spreadsheet. The columns in a table are identified alphabetically, the rows numerically. However, the letters and numbers used to identify each cell aren't displayed. You have to know how the table is structured to figure out how any given cell is named. It's a bit of a mystery but easily solved. Every row, even one that consists of merged cells, must be counted. The same is true for columns. If you have used an application like Microsoft Excel, this format will be familiar.

> AutoCAD always includes sample files that demonstrate various features, particularly when those features are new. The drawing used for Figure 5.25 is one example. For a default installation, the sample files are found in C:\Program Files\AutoCAD 2007\Sample. This folder contains some great stuff that can help you understand how some of these features work. You may find that the sample files weren't installed. If so, it's worth adding them using the installation wizard on the original CDs.

Figure 5.25 shows a table entity. It appears in Blocks and Tables - Imperial.dwg, one of the sample drawings that ship with AutoCAD 2007, so you can open it and see how tables and fields can be used. Each of the highlighted text blocks in the last column (Column I) is a field. In each of these cases, they're fields representing formulas. If you select and right-click one and open it for editing, the Field dialog box opens, as shown.

The formula for cell I3 is shown in the window of the dialog box as G3*H3. This multiplies the value in cell G3 (3) times the value in cell H3 (169.00), for a total cost. The total cost (507.00) is displayed as a field. You can tell it's a field because it's highlighted in the AutoCAD display but the highlighting won't plot.

> Fields don't have to be highlighted. You can turn off field highlighting by setting the system variable FIELDDISPLAY to 0 instead of the default value of 1.

You can apply any of the standard math functions (tan, sin, sqrt) from the CAL command to any cell by using a formula like sin(H3). You can also group expressions that

Figure 5.25

**Formulas in
table cells**

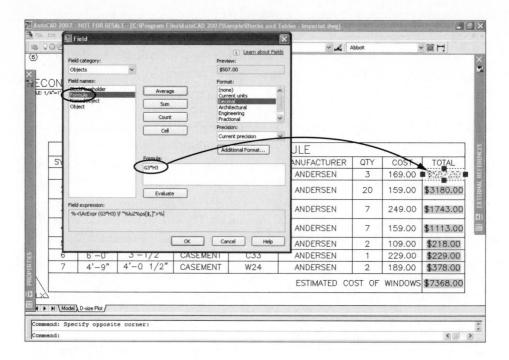

include division, multiplication, subtraction, and addition in the same way you can with a spreadsheet: (g3*h3)/2+(h5*h7)/3, for example.

The last cell, I10, contains the formula Sum(i3:i9), which adds all the values starting with cell I3 and going through cell I9. If you look at the dialog box again, you'll see buttons for Average, Sum, Count, and Cell. These formulas can be applied across multiple cells within a single table or applied to individual cells in *other* tables:

Cell In case you missed the significance of the italics, let me emphasize something: You can place the value of a cell into one table from a different table. To do that, you click the Cell button shown in Figure 5.26 and then select an individual cell in any existing table. That's pretty nifty. The resulting formula has the following format: Table(2124374504).I9+I10. The value (2124374504) is an internally assigned name for the individual table. It isn't assigned by the user.

Average This button prompts you to select a range of contiguous cells, whose values are then added together and divided by the number of cells selected. The formula looks like this: Average(G2:G9).

Sum This button prompts you to select a range of contiguous cells, whose values are then added together. The result is a formula that looks like this: Sum(H3:H9).

Count This button prompts you to select a range of contiguous cells, and the total number of cells selected is shown. The formula looks like this: Count(G3:G9).

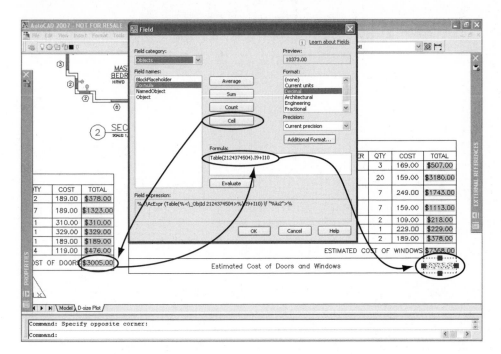

Figure 5.26

Referencing a cell in another table

CHAPTER 6

Plotting

Remember the AutoCAD days of yore? It took days to set up a plotter and hours to plot out a complex drawing. Pens ran out of ink minutes before the end of a job. Plotters seemed to think for themselves when determining the location of the end of a sheet.

Happily, those days are gone. Plotting these days causes far fewer headaches, and in more and more cases you can skip the process altogether. Many designs from AutoCAD exist to communicate directly with a machine that makes parts—from microchips to logs for log homes. As a result, more and more users are distributing only electronic versions of their drawings, often as DWF or PDF files, and using them effectively without ever touching a sheet of paper. We'll always need to lay out our designs—for presentation purposes, at the very least—even if the drawings themselves aren't destined for paper use.

Although Paper Space had been around for several releases, layouts first showed up in AutoCAD 2000. They're the best thing since sliced bread, and you should use them. Well, *I* think you should use them, but I know some companies still plot directly from Model Space. In this chapter, I'll discuss some common elements that apply to plotting from either Model Space or from a layout in Paper Space, and I'll even give you some advice on Model Space plotting. But the bulk of this chapter is devoted to creating output from layouts in Paper Space—plotted sheets and raster images.

- ■ **Model Space, Paper Space, and Layouts**
- ■ **What to Put Where**
- ■ **Plotting a Layout**
- ■ **AutoCAD Graphics in Other Applications**

Model Space, Paper Space, and Layouts

Years ago, Model Space was a lot like plotting by hand. We did everything on a single sheet of paper. We created our geometry, inserted a border at a scale that made sense for plotting, calculated the correct text height, set a proper DIMSCALE, and plotted our drawing. Then came Paper Space, which allowed us to separate the design process from the plotting process. Now, we design in Model Space and plot from a layout in Paper Space. Life is simple.

Life is simple, that is, for those of us who made the switch from plotting in Model Space to plotting in Paper Space. If you didn't make the switch—or you just prefer a more complicated life—then I feel duty-bound to warn you of the severe limitations of plotting from Model Space. Here we go:

- You can't plot more than one view of a 3D object on a single sheet.

- You can't plot a detail at a different scale without copying it and making it larger.

- You have to move your geometry if you decide to plot on a different sheet size or at a different scale.

- You have some calculating to do when you set a text height, a dimension scale, a hatch scale, a block scale, or a linetype scale, all of which have to be changed if the plot scale changes.

The advantages of plotting from layouts in Paper Space, on the other hand, are huge. However, whether you're plotting from Model Space (see the sidebar "Lost in Paper Space") or from a layout in Paper Space, two practices are common to both: geometry creation and block design.

LOST IN PAPER SPACE

Six or seven years ago, I did my first "Lost in Paper Space" workshop at Autodesk University. I've done the same workshop, with minor changes, every year since. And every year I dutifully give the workshop a new name, to suggest that I won't be presenting the workshop again. Three years ago, the title was "Lost in Paper Space One Last Time." But I was asked to present it again the next year, and the year after that. Demand peaked at 400 participants the second time I offered it and was down to 200 the last time, but it's clear to me that even after all these years, some users are still confused by plotting.

Before AutoCAD 2000, I wrote a workshop handout called "Paper Space in 60 Easy Steps." I wasn't kidding. Things got a lot easier when layouts appeared, so later in this chapter you'll find *three* steps for plotting a layout. OK, I take liberties with what constitutes a single step, but it sure isn't 60 steps anymore. If you're still confused by the process, this chapter's for you.

Geometry Creation

No matter how you plot a drawing, the geometry should be created at its actual size. If you're drawing a machine part that's 12 inches long, you draw it 12 inches long in Auto-CAD. If you're doing a civil plot plan with a boundary line that represents 2,500 feet, you draw it 2,500 feet in AutoCAD. If you're designing microchip architecture with traces that are .01mm long, you draw them .01mm long.

In the late 1980s, AutoCAD shipped with a sample drawing named `solar.dwg`. It was an eye-opener back then because it was drawn full size. I remember wondering how that was possible, but of course it is. Large numbers are simple enough in AutoCAD. That's what scientific units are for. Once I understood that the solar system, including Pluto, could be drawn full size I realized that anything could be. And should be. Scaling is for layouts.

Block Design

Whether you're plotting from Model Space or Paper Space, define your blocks full size. Symbols representing real-world objects that have a fixed size should be the actual size of the objects. Symbols that represent a range of possible sizes in the real world should be created at the size you want them to plot onto a sheet. These are symbols like a valve in a piping drawing, a resistor on an electrical schematic, or a duplex outlet on a floor plan that are always the same size no matter how large the actual object they represent. Blocks that are used for annotation on a drawing sheet, like borders, title blocks, and section callouts, should be drawn at the size they will be when plotted onto a sheet. You need only one of those for each sheet size. When you plot from a layout, you plot at a scale of 1:1 because a layout represents a full-size sheet of paper—and you're plotting the sheet, not the geometry. You insert the border and the title block at a scale factor of 1.

See Table 6.1 for some examples.

Definitions

Now that we've got the basics covered, let's move on to the questions I hear most often. What is the difference between Model Space and Paper Space? What does TILEMODE do? How do layouts fit in, and why does it seem as though there are two different places called Model Space? Let's begin sorting it out by defining our terms.

TYPE OF BLOCK	SIZE TO DRAW	DESCRIPTION
Bathtub	60″×30″	Actual size in a house.
50mm fastener	50mm long	Actual size in an assembly.
Resistor symbol	6mm	Actual size on paper for use as a schematic. Resistors vary in size.
B-size border	16″×10″	Actual size on the paper. You need only one if you plot from a layout.
Duplex receptacle symbol	6mm or .25″	Actual size on a sheet of paper. Scale it when it's inserted onto a floor plan.

Table 6.1

Examples of Sizes for Block Definitions

MODEL SPACE PLOTTING

OK, I don't recommend this, but because there are users who still do it, here is how I would approach plotting from Model Space. You can go ahead and create your full-size geometry, but you'll have to manage some variables. The plot scale you use is critical when you place text, dimensions, or hatch patterns, and for making your linetypes look right. Use the reciprocal of the intended plot scale to determine proper text height, the setting for CELTSCALE (or possibly LTSCALE), the hatch scale you use, the scale to use for inserting title blocks, and the setting for the DIMSCALE variable. If you want to plot an AutoCAD drawing at half its actual size, you use a scale of two for all these variables. That way, their actual size is twice as large before plotting, so they end up the proper size when you plot them. Two is the reciprocal of ½.

In mechanical drafting, 1:1, 1:2, 1:4, and 1:10 are common plot scales, so the variables I just listed are set to 1, 2, 4, or 10 for each of those scales. In architectural drafting, ¼″=1′ is a typical scale factor. Because 1 foot is 48 times larger than ¼″, you would use a scale factor of 48 for all of those variables. If you plot from Model Space and your text, dimensions, or linetypes don't show up correctly, you've probably set these variables incorrectly.

Draw your title block and border the actual size you want them to plot, and insert them at the reciprocal of your intended plot scale. That shows you whether you can fit all the geometry onto a sheet at that scale. If everything fits inside the scaled border, it will plot onto the sheet size you intended. Do this before adding any text, dimensions, or hatch patterns so you know for sure what plot scale will work for that drawing. If you have to increase your border 10× to fit around your drawing, you'll have to plot the drawing at a scale of 1:10 to fit on the paper. If you want to be able to read it on the sheet, your text must be placed on the drawing 10× larger than its plotted size.

Model Space

Look at your Model Space tab on the status bar at the bottom of the AutoCAD screen. Whenever you start a new drawing, the Model Space tab is active. While you're in the Model Space tab, the User Coordinate System (UCS) icon (which can be turned off and on with the UCSICON variable) is displayed. It shows the current X-axis and Y-axis (and the Z axis if you're using the 3D Modeling space in AutoCAD 2007) represented by arrows at a right angle to each other. Model Space is where you create all the geometry that represents a 2D or 3D model. You start AutoCAD, and you start designing—simple.

When you're in Model Space, you can use the VPORTS command to create separate viewports, but you're limited in how those viewports can be laid out. No matter how many viewports you create, they must completely fill the drawing editor, be rectangular, and not overlap, and they can't have any gaps between them. It's like having multiple monitors that you can use to view your drawing in many different ways but that you can't move around.

For some users, the confusion comes when they switch to a Layout tab. It turns out that Model Space lurks there as well. When a layout contains viewports, each one can provide a window to Model Space. Make a viewport active, and you can reach through that window into Model Space. So it's not that there are two Model Spaces, it's that there are two ways to access Model Space—either by selecting its tab, or by making a floating viewport active in a layout.

TILEMODE

The TILEMODE system variable switches between the Model Space tab and a Layout tab. Although it's an important variable if you're writing AutoLISP programs that manage layouts, you don't ever have to deal with it directly when using AutoCAD. The TILEMODE setting changes automatically when you select any Layout tab or the Model tab. A setting of 0 turns off TILEMODE, making a layout active, and a setting of 1 turns it on, making the Model Space tab active. The viewports in Model Space (see Figure 6.1) are always placed together like tiles, whereas floating viewports in a layout can be separated, overlapped, and irregularly shaped. They don't have to be tiled together. That's why the variable is named TILEMODE. If it's turned on, viewports must be tiled together, which only happens in the Model Space tab. When it's off, viewports don't have to be tiled together, which can only happen in a layout.

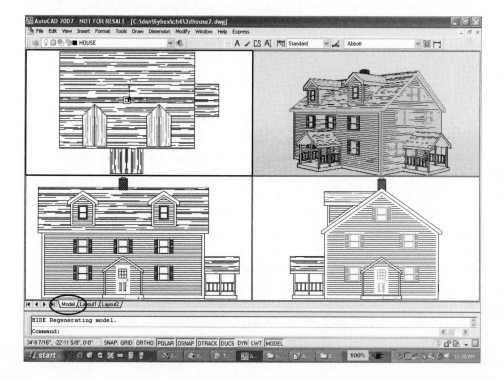

Figure 6.1

Viewports in Model Space

If you haven't ever used viewports in Model Space, you may want to try them. They're critical to me for producing 3D models, because they allow me to view a model from a variety of positions, making it much easier to edit the model. Even with 2D geometry, you can draw from one viewport to another, making it easier to connect two widely separated areas.

Viewports and Floating Viewports?

The term *viewports* can confuse people because it has two different meanings. A *viewport* in the Model Space tab isn't an entity that you can grab or modify. It's a fixed display area. You can turn it off and on, but that's it. A *viewport* in a layout is sometimes called a *floating viewport*, because it's an entity that you can grab and modify. It's similar to entities like polylines and circles in that it can be moved, erased, and stretched. But there are limits—it can't be rotated, for example, at least not with the results you may want.

While you're in a layout, you can switch to Model Space within a floating viewport and stay in the layout. You don't have to change to the Model Space tab to work on objects in Model Space. There are some advantages to working in Model Space through a floating viewport. The most important is that when you add dimensions through a floating viewport, they're scaled automatically to match the plot scale of the viewport.

> Many trainers have tried to come up with a single, crystal-clear explanation of floating viewports. One trainer I know refers to them as "floating Model Spaces." Another calls them "holes in the paper that you can look through to see your model." I use the term *floating viewports* throughout this chapter, but if either of those images works better for you, keep it in mind.

Paper Space

Except for the Model Space tab, every tab at the bottom of the AutoCAD window is a layout. There is no practical limit to how many layouts you can have in a drawing, and every one of them is in Paper Space. Paper Space is so called because each layout represents a sheet of paper on which you organize or "lay out" the views you want to plot. Those views are contained in floating viewports that can display any part of your geometry at any scale. Each floating viewport can display layers in different states than other viewports, and floating viewports can be any shape.

> If your Model Space and Layout tabs disappear, and you're working with AutoCAD 2007, you may have accidentally hidden them. If so, three new icons will appear in the status bar: one representing Model Space, one representing the current layout, and one with two small triangles. To turn tabs back on, right-click any of those icons and select Display Layout And Model Tabs. Oh, and if you do want to hide them, right-click any of these tabs—there's the culprit, in the right-click menu.

A layout is like a paste-up area that allows you to arrange multiple views of the objects you create in Model Space. It's like taping a large sheet of paper to a drafting table and then pasting smaller sheets of paper, each containing different images, on the larger sheet. When the smaller sheets are in place, you can draw on the larger sheet—a title block, perhaps—and add any necessary text or lines. If you don't like the location of some of the smaller sheets, you can move them around. If you don't want to see one of them anymore, you can remove it.

In a layout, the floating viewports are equivalent to those smaller pasted-down sheets. They can contain views of anything that's in Model Space, and you can move them around, make them larger, change what they display, change the scale at which they display, and end up with a beautifully laid out sheet that can be plotted onto an actual sheet of paper at a scale of 1:1. Figure 6.2 shows a layout with multiple views of the same geometry, in this case a residential floor plan. Note the clues that you're in a layout, and not in Model Space:

- The UCS icon changes to a triangle.

- A white sheet of paper is displayed floating above a gray background.

- The last button on the status bar at the bottom of the screen displays the word *PAPER*.

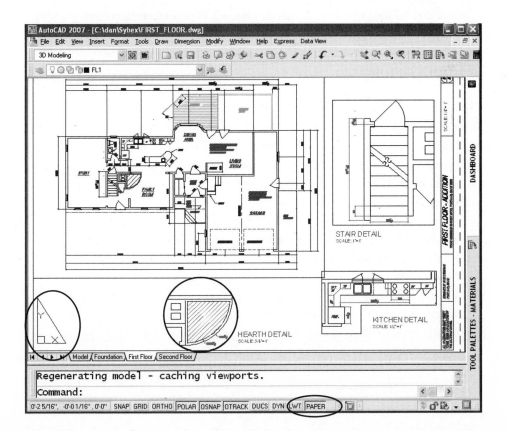

Figure 6.2

Layout with multiple floating viewports

As you can see, each of the details is at a different scale from the ¼″=1′ scale used for the main viewport, and each is a different shape. I'll go through the steps you follow to set up a sheet like this later in the chapter. By default, a single viewport is created whenever you select a Layout tab for the first time. You can add more viewports with the MVIEW (MV) or VPORTS command, which can also be found on the Viewports toolbar.

Drawbacks of Using Paper Space

In a few situations, plotting from layouts in Paper Space may cause you problems. Before I go into all the reasons in favor of using layouts, let's look at two *possible* drawbacks.

It's One More Thing to Learn

Although Paper Space follows a clear logic, it isn't always intuitive, and some complexity is involved. That complexity gives you control over plotting, so it's a good thing. However, it isn't a good idea for an office to suddenly start plotting from layouts and hope that everyone figures it out. If you're a CAD manager hoping to make the switch while maintaining consistency, you should develop office standards and provide training to ensure that everybody knows the ropes. This is one case where a little knowledge can be a dangerous thing—dangerous to your stress level, at least.

If you aren't currently using layouts for plotting, then you aren't likely to be able to convert your Model Space plotting strategy. You need to make some settings changes, as noted later. You may also need to change the order in which you do certain things to take advantage of the power here.

Objects in Paper Space and Model Space Are Separate

You can't select objects in both Model Space and Paper Space at the same time. In fact, you can't select a Model Space entity while Paper Space is active—you must make a floating viewport active to do that, and once a floating viewport is active, you can't select objects that are in Paper Space. Most of the time, that's a good thing, but once in a while it can get in the way.

This doesn't mean you can't use objects in Model Space from Paper Space. Object snaps work on Model Space objects even with Paper Space active. Dimensions placed in Paper Space are even indirectly associated with entities in Model Space if you snap to or select Model Space objects for dimensions. Let's look at several situations where this lack of connection may be a problem.

CREATING BLOCKS

Let's say you want to define a block using objects from both Model Space and Paper Space. To define a block, everything you want to include in the block definition must be in the same space. If you have objects in both spaces that you want to include in a single block definition, do this:

1. Move the entities from Paper Space into Model Space using the CHSPACE command.

2. Define the block.

3. Move the entities back where they came from.

The CHSPACE command appeared in AutoCAD 2007. Before that, it was an Express Tool. If Express Tools aren't installed, you should install them, because CHSPACE is nearly essential in dealing with Paper Space and Model Space. Note that before AutoCAD 2007, some Architectural Desktop (ADT) entities couldn't be relocated using CHSPACE.

> If you use a release prior to AutoCAD 2007, and you don't have Express Tools loaded, you can still move or copy entities from one space to another by using the Windows clipboard. Select the entities, right-click, and pick either Copy With Base Point or Cut from the menu. Change to the space where you want the entities, open the Edit menu and pick Paste As Block, and select a location. If you paste the entities as a block, a block is defined with a name assigned by AutoCAD. If you copy objects from Paper Space into a floating viewport that has a plot scale other than 1:1, you must scale the entities; the same is true if you go from Model Space to Paper Space. Once you're done locating the entities, you may want to explode the results.

USING WBLOCK TO CREATE A DRAWING BY SELECTING ENTITIES

If you want a single drawing with just the Sheet 1 layout shown in Figure 6.3, you can't select the objects in both places. Note that Paper Space entities are selected, including the floating viewport, but not the Model Space entities displayed in that viewport. This isn't a major drawback, because you can use the WBLOCK command to create a new drawing file from those selected Model Space entities and then add the original layout to the new drawing.

> If the entities shown in the floating viewport are the only entities in the drawing, the problem is easier to solve. Use the Entire Drawing option of the WBLOCK command while the Sheet 1 layout is active.

Follow these steps to do that:

1. Save your current drawing.

2. Use WBLOCK to create a new drawing by selecting the entities in the active floating viewport, as shown in Figure 6.4. Make sure the Retain radio button is selected in the Write Block dialog box so you don't erase the entities you select.

3. Open the resulting drawing.

Figure 6.3

**Results of using the
All selection option
in a layout**

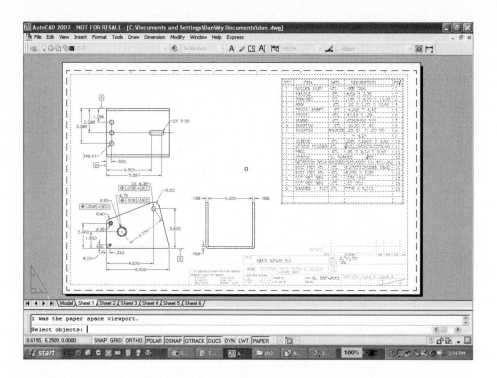

Figure 6.4

**Creating a new
drawing with
WBLOCK**

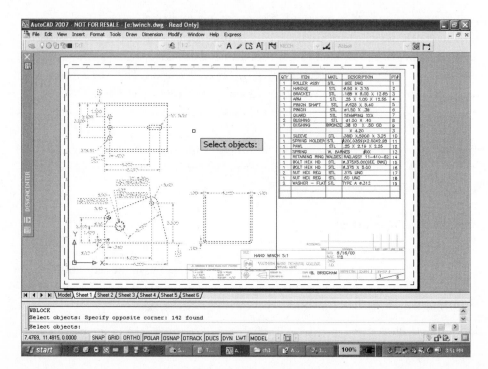

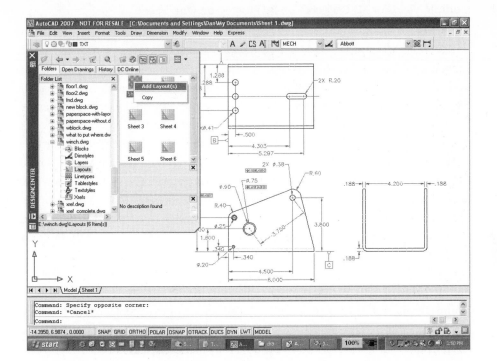

Figure 6.5

**Using ADC to define
a new layout**

4. Open AutoCAD DesignCenter (ADC), and browse to the original drawing as shown in Figure 6.5.

   It looks like the Sheet 1 layout was saved with the Model Space entities. Don't be fooled! The only thing saved was the page setup.

5. To get the entities, including the floating viewports, right-click the layout you want and select Add Layout(s), as shown in Figure 6.5. You get the page setup, the viewports, and all entities in the layout.

> Here's another way to copy layouts. Right-click a Layout tab in the new drawing, and select From Template from the menu. Change the Files Of Type option from the default Drawing Template (*.dwt) to Drawing (*.dwg), and locate the original drawing file. Finally, select the layout from that drawing.

Advantages of Using Paper Space

Enough about drawbacks. As you can see, there aren't many, and there are ways to work around them. Let's look at the *advantages* of using Paper Space, which are considerable. The most significant is that using layouts for plotting makes it far more likely that office standards will be applied consistently. The process of document layout and plotting is also much more efficient and logical when using Paper Space. Here's why.

Multiple Views of 3D Objects Can Be Plotted on One Sheet

Paper Space is essential for any office creating 3D geometry with AutoCAD. I started working with 3D models long before Paper Space was added to AutoCAD. This process had many limitations in early versions, but one of the most frustrating was not being able to create standard orthographic views from the models—at least, not easily. Either you carefully plotted the object several times on the same sheet with the views in different places, or you copied the model two or three times and rotated it into the various positions needed for the multiple views, thus dramatically increasing an already large file size.

Paper Space addresses that problem by allowing the user to place any view of a model— front, top, side, isometric, and so on—on one sheet of paper. The standard views can even be automated using the MVSETUP command. You can then use SOLPROF to create projected 2D drawings of each view. It's quick and it's easy. Or, use the SOLVIEW command to create views individually, including auxiliary views, and then use SOLDRAW to create the drawings.

Multiple Details Can Be Presented at Different Scales

Plotting details at different scales without Paper Space creates a problem. If the details are part of something you've already drawn, you have to copy the geometry to a different location and then scale it up to the proper size. Even if the details are drawn separately, you have to decide after creating them how much larger they should be so you can ultimately plot to a standard scale and label the details correctly. Once the details are scaled up, you have to change the dimensions so they give the correct values, because a DIMLFAC of 1 (the default) gives results that are too large. With geometry that's scaled two times larger than actual size, you have to set DIMLFAC to .5 and then remember to set it back or to change to a different dimension style. There's too much to go wrong.

WMFOUT

I can think of one other instance in which you may want to select entities in both Model Space and Paper Space at the same time. A company that makes wooden molding asked me about creating WMF files from layouts so they could be used to develop posters of the company's products. The company specifically wanted WMF files, so no plotting option I knew of would do what was wanted. The problem with AutoCAD's WMFOUT command is that you have to select all the entities you want included in the file.

The company had a lot of layouts it wanted to use to create WMF files, so the process of using CHSPACE wasn't appealing—too much work. I helped the company write an AutoLISP program that scaled and moved all the entities in the layout from Paper Space into the Model Space viewport, changed the color of all the lines to black, created a WMF file using the WMFOUT command, and then undid the whole thing back to where it started. Consider this a small advertisement for the two AutoLISP chapters later in the book.

With Paper Space, you can add any detail of an existing full-size object to the layout sheet as a view, and the view can be scaled instead of the geometry. You don't need to copy or redraw a detail, so when you make a change, it's reflected in both the view of the whole object and the detail. Even if you have to draw a detail in a separate location—a section elevation detail on a foundation plan, for example—you can still draw it actual size and then scale just the view to whatever scale you desire. As a result, there's seldom a reason to scale the geometry. It's far less likely that you'll find dimensions on a drawing that give the wrong values.

> To scale a floating viewport for plotting, use the Scale control window on the viewports tool-bar. Or, use the XP option of the ZOOM command. To scale a viewport for plotting at a 1:10 scale, type **.1XP** after issuing the ZOOM command.

Fewer Variables to Be Calculated

When plotting from Model Space, you have to calculate certain values to get the desired results. You must decide at what scale you plan to plot the drawing and then use the recip-rocal of that scale factor to identify appropriate text heights, linetype scales, dimension scales, hatch-pattern scales, and block-insertion scales. If you have details, you need to determine an appropriate linear scale factor for dimension values (DIMLFAC).

With layouts, much of that work is eliminated or simplified:

- Text, if placed in Paper Space, can be created at the actual size you want on the plotted sheet.
- Text and blocks placed in Model Space can be scaled using the SPACETRANS command. Create an alias for this useful command, or you'll get tired of making typos. Both the alias and the command can be used transparently.
- Dimension style settings, like text height and arrow size, can be set to actual plotted size.
- You don't need separate dimension styles for each plot scale.
- LTSCALE and PSLTSCALE can be set to 1, and the linetypes can be scaled automatically in the layouts.
- Title blocks and borders can be inserted into Paper Space at actual size.
- Hatch patterns in a floating viewport can be scaled automatically.
- MTEXT, when placed with a leader, can scale automatically.
- CHSPACE can take care of any problems of misplacing entities and automatically scales objects when moving them from Paper Space to Model Space.

TYPING CLUNKY COMMANDS

Although most commands are intuitive, some are hard to type or difficult to remember. AutoCAD has a couple of aids for those situations that you may not have noticed.

Arrow keys If you press the Down and Up Arrows on your keyboard, you can cycle through the text you typed at the command line. When you get to the text you want, press ↵ as though you just typed it, or use the Left and Right Arrow keys to position the cursor anywhere on the line to correct any typos. I find this especially helpful when I want to repeat a long command name or a line of AutoLISP code. If you have dynamic input turned on, you can right-click and select Recent Input to get the same listing.

Tab key If you can't quite remember the name of a command or variable, but you know it starts with DYN, for example, type the first few letters you know and then start pressing the Tab key on your keyboard. All the system variables and commands beginning with those letters scroll past until you find the one you want—DYNPICOORDS, for example.

Plotting Is Much More Consistent

Offices that plot from layouts get more consistent results from the many different users who plot drawings. Template drawings can include preinserted title blocks and borders with all text at actual size. Various layouts can be set up in the template drawing for each sheet size and plotter in the office, allowing a change in plotting with a simple selection of a Layout tab. Layers for both detail and full-size dimensions and hatch patterns can be created and displayed selectively in different viewports.

Layouts Can Be Changed Without Changing the Location of Geometry

Because reorganizing the floating viewports in a layout requires only that they be moved, there's no reason to relocate geometry to change the way a drawing plots. You can eliminate the danger of changing critical information by moving objects. If two views on the sheet are too close together, you can move them without changing the coordinates being used for station points or as origins for baseline dimensions. You can even rotate views, using the DVIEW or PLAN command, without changing the geometry or the UCS.

Moving geometry once it's located can cause all kinds of problems. If you need to relocate the geometry you've created, don't forget to thaw, unlock, and turn on all the layers that may have entities that should be included. If you've placed ordinate dimensions, you may get incorrect values when you update.

Multiple Layouts Can Be Included Within a Single Drawing File

Most offices have more than one plotter, each of which uses more than one sheet size. With the layouts available in AutoCAD, a single file can have a different layout for plotting to different sheet sizes, or have layouts of entirely different views of the same object. A complete set of drawings can be contained in a single file, eliminating the possibility of drawing files getting separated. Sheet sets, new in AutoCAD 2005, can be created from individual Layout tabs across multiple drawings to give you even more flexibility.

Views Can Display Different Layers on a Single Sheet

In residential architectural drawings, it's common practice to place geometry representing the different floors in the same location so that features can be lined up properly. You do this by either placing all the floors in one drawing file or using individual drawings as external references. The layers containing those different floors can be frozen when you don't want them to be displayed.

Using VPLAYER or the Current VP Freeze property in the Layer dialog box, you can have a single file with a layout for the foundation, first floor, second floor, roof-framing plan, and so on, and display each floor in its own layout. Each of the layouts can be consistently laid out with the same border and title block.

Plotting Information Is Stored in the Drawing

Layouts use page setups based on specific plotters and specific sheet sizes. As long as the plotter-configuration files and plot-style tables exist and are in the path, you can always plot the drawing, because information about the plotter, the particular line characteristics, and the particular sheet sizes stays with the drawing. If you've ever used early releases of AutoCAD, you know why this is a huge bonus.

The Display of Objects Can Be Clipped

A user can create a viewport of any shape with the MVIEW command. If a viewport already exists, it can be reshaped using the VPCLIP command. This permits you to be selective about what objects in a drawing will plot. If an object happens to be an XRef or a block reference, that object can also be clipped with the XCLIP command. VPLAYER allows you to be selective about which layers are displayed. Combining XCLIP, VPLAYER, and VPCLIP gives the user nearly unlimited flexibility in presenting geometry and in making plotting changes. You can even use conventional breaks on long objects without breaking the objects.

Layouts Can Be Copied Within and Between Drawings

Once you've created a layout that works well in one drawing, you can duplicate it within the current drawing, or within any other drawing, using ADC or the right-click menu of a

Figure 6.6

Copying a layout

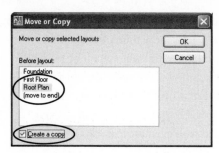

layout. The right-click process isn't as obvious as it should be. To make a copy of an existing layout, right-click its tab, and select Move Or Copy. The dialog box that opens is used for both moving and copying the layout. To copy it, check Create A Copy as shown in Figure 6.6. To select a location, pick the name of an existing layout or (Move To End).

Preparing a Drawing for Plotting

Few things are more frustrating than plotting out a drawing only to discover that the final product is missing an essential feature. Here are some steps you should take to prepare a drawing to be plotted from a layout. Make these changes part of your template drawings:

1. *Title blocks.* Define a block containing full-size borders and title blocks for each sheet size you use in your office. If you use the same sheet size with more than one plotter, make sure your full-size border fits all plotters, because some plotters require a larger paper-gripper margin than others. I recommend adding attributes to title blocks. You don't have to have multiple border blocks for different plot scales, because you'll almost always plot from Paper Space at a 1:1 scale.

   If you use a separate DWG file as a title block and use either INSERT or XREF to bring it into the drawing, make sure all the geometry in that drawing is in Model Space. You can't insert or externally reference entities from a drawing if they're in Paper Space.

2. *Text style.* Create an appropriate text style (using a name other than Standard) with the height set to 0 so it can be used for dimensions and for text at different sizes. The text height for dimensions should be set in your dimension styles at the height you want it to plot. It will automatically scale properly if you follow the advice in step 3.

3. *Dimension style.* Create your dimension styles (again, using a name other than Standard) with the DIMSCALE set to 0. You can do this through the Dimension Style Manager by clicking the Modify button and then going to the Fit tab and selecting the Scale Dimensions To Layout radio button. Don't forget to create child styles for types of dimensions that require different properties from your parent style. I always create a child style for radius and diameter dimensions, and sometimes for linear dimensions, angles, and leaders. See Chapter 4, "Applying Graphics Standards," for detailed instruction on creating dimension styles.

4. *Linetypes.* Set LTSCALE and CELTSCALE to 1 so that linetypes are scaled with the same line-segment length with which they were created. This results in linetypes that may not appear correctly in Model Space. Don't worry; they'll look fine in the layout if you make sure PSLTSCALE is also set to 1. Figure 6.7 shows what hidden lines look

like in Model Space. Figure 6.8 shows the same geometry as it's displayed in a floating viewport in a layout. With PSLTSCALE set to 1, linetypes are scaled so they have the same appearance when plotted, no matter what scale is used in a floating viewport. You can also set PSLTSCLAE by checking the Use Paper Space Units For Scaling option in the Details area of the Linetype Manager dialog box.

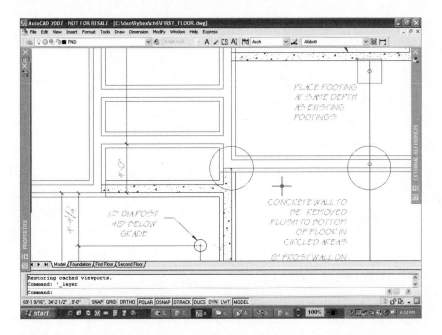

Figure 6.7
PSLTSCALE = 1
Model Space display

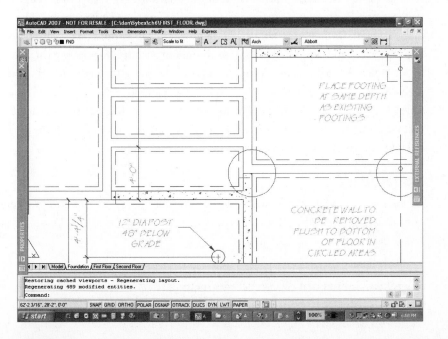

Figure 6.8
PSLTSCALE = 1
layout display

5. *Layers.* You should create a few specialized layers in addition to your typical layers. You should have a special layer just for detail dimensions and hatch patterns if you have multiple details with features that show in more than one floating viewport. Your floating viewports should be on their own nonplot layer. Don't place then on the Defpoints layer. If you do, you won't be able to select them if layer 0 happens to be frozen.

   Create separate layers for the following entities.

   • General dimensions

   • Detail dimensions

   • General hatch patterns

   • Detail hatch patterns

   • Floating viewports (make this a non-plot layer)

6. *Preset layouts.* Set up a layout for each sheet size you use in your office or for the specific layouts you're most likely to use. If your office uses consistent layouts that have floating viewports with the same scales for most drawings, your template drawing should include those. You can even have borders and title blocks preinserted.

What to Put Where

Let's begin again, as simply as possible, with two lists—one for Model Space, one for Paper Space—and my advice for what should go into each space. You may have good reasons to vary from the following recommendations, but they work well for most applications. Some of my recommendations here may be controversial. There is some disagreement, for instance, about whether dimensions should be in Model Space or in Paper Space. I'm going to make a case in the next section for having them end up in Model Space. I recommend adding them to Model Space through a floating viewport, but if you forget and place them in Paper Space, you can move them to Model Space using the CHSPACE command. Some people do that on purpose. Make sure the display is locked in that viewport before you place your dimensions. These recommendations are illustrated in Figure 6.9. Now, to the lists.

Model Space

As you know, Model Space is where you do your designing, as opposed to where you lay out a drawing sheet. The following types of entities should be created in, or at least end up in, Model Space:

• 3D models

• All visible lines that describe 2D geometry

• All hidden lines

Figure 6.9

What to put where

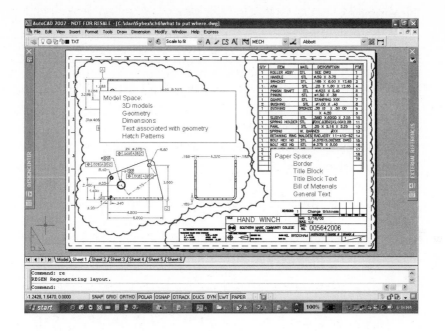

- All annotation lines that locate features
  - Center lines
  - Phantom lines
  - Symmetry lines
- Dimensions
- Hatch patterns
- Text that's associated directly with the geometry, including any text attached to a leader, or text that would be meaningless if it was separated from the geometry.

Paper Space

Once you're ready to annotate and present your design, you need to create a layout in Paper Space. That layout should contain the following kinds of objects:

- Sheet border
- Title block
- Title block text
- Bill of materials
- Viewports at specified plot scales
- Titles of views
- Text used for general annotation (any text that would not be affected if it was moved away from the geometry)

Dimensions

As I mentioned earlier, some users disagree with me when it comes to placing dimensions in Model Space. With the addition of the DIMASSOC variable, dimensions can now be placed in Paper Space and be indirectly associated with the entities in Model Space that they represent. Even though they're in a different space, they usually move when the geometry moves, they usually display the correct dimension, and they usually stay that way. But *usually* doesn't mean *always*—and that's the problem. You shouldn't have to worry about dimensions misbehaving some day down the road because the connection between Model Space and Paper Space isn't perfect. This is especially true when you're dimensioning complex geometry.

Whether or not you agree, if your office standard is to put dimensions in Paper Space, you have to be consistent about it. But for what it's worth, here are the reasons I come down on the side of Model Space in this discussion. (Remember, you can always move dimensions between spaces now that CHSPACE is an actual command.)

WHY DO SOME PEOPLE PUT DIMENSIONS IN PAPER SPACE?

I can think of four reasons to put dimensions in Paper Space rather than Model Space. In two cases, it represents a work-around for bugs in some releases of the software. In the other two, placing dimensions in Paper Space is an office preference that has nothing to do with bugs.

DIMDLI For several releases prior to AutoCAD 2006, the one variable that wouldn't adjust automatically in a floating viewport was DIMDLI (dimension line increment). Anyone using baseline dimensions had to place them using the DIMLINEAR command rather than DIMBASE. To avoid that, users placed dimensions in Paper Space and then moved them into Model Space using the CHSPACE Express Tool (now a command in AutoCAD 2007).

AutoCAD Mechanical The Mechanical version of AutoCAD 2006 had a bug that prevented proper scaling of dimensions in a floating viewport. The same work-around could be used—place dimensions in Paper Space and then move them with CHSPACE. It didn't affect AutoCAD, only AutoCAD Mechanical.

Separating geometry from annotation Some offices find it easier to work with geometry if all the annotation is separated and then relegated to Paper Space, particularly when dimensioning 3D models.

Automatic scaling If you place dimensions in Paper Space, you don't have to worry about text heights, arrow size, and so on, because the layout is plotted at 1:1. You can achieve this same effect by setting DIMSCALE to 0 so that dimensions scale to a layout.

Can't use entities in XRefs and blocks If you place one drawing in another as either an inserted block or an external reference, you get only the objects in Model Space. Dimensions placed in Paper Space aren't part of the reference.

QDIM won't work I'm a big fan of the QDIM command, but it can't be used to place dimensions in Paper Space. Because QDIM requires you to select the objects themselves, rather than snap to locations on the objects, it can currently be used only in Model Space—either through a floating viewport or in the Model Space tab. QDIM provides an enormous advantage, particularly when creating ordinate dimensions, but I also use it for placing continuous dimensions on floor plans.

> If you want dimensions in Paper Space, you can use QDIM to place dimensions in Model Space; then, use CHSPACE to move them into Paper Space.

Associativity sometimes breaks If you place dimensions in Paper Space and later move the objects in Model Space, the dimensions may not move with them. I know they're supposed to be associated, but that connection sometimes breaks down.

> This is what the DIMREASSOCIATE command is for. You can use it to reestablish a connection between a dimension and the entity it represents.

Dimensions can be too associative If you move entities outside the limits of a floating viewport, their dimensions in Paper Space may move well off the sheet of paper to retain their associative relationship, even though the objects they dimension aren't displayed.

Dimensions don't copy with entities If you want to copy an entity with its dimensions, you can't select the dimensions if they're in Paper Space.

Leaders get corrupted Leaders can pose problems if you place them in Paper Space. Generally, a leader is in a specific location in reference to an object. If you move the object (or objects) the leader refers to, you should also move the leader *and* text. If you place a leader in Paper Space, only the arrowhead moves with its associated object, and then only if you snapped to the object at the time the leader was placed. In Figure 6.10, the leader was placed in Paper Space. When the arc it's attached to was moved, the leader was distorted.

Wrong dimension values are displayed Dimensions placed in Paper Space sometimes display a value that's based on the distance in the layout, not the distance on the model. If the floating viewport has a scale other than 1:1, the value shown is incorrect. Model Space always reflects the actual dimension of the geometry and updates when you edit the geometry.

Can't define detail blocks You can create blocks or use the WBLOCK command to create new drawings that include both geometry and dimensions if they're all in Model Space.

Have to dimension to an entity In order for dimensions in Paper Space to be associated with a Model Space object, you must select the object. If you're dimensioning near the object (to the middle of walls, for example), dimensions may have a Paper Space value and not an actual value, as shown in Figure 6.11.

Most users expect dimensions to be in Model Space Because of the long legacy of placing dimensions in Model Space in earlier releases, people with prior experience are more likely to understand how your drawings are put together.

DIMASSOC may have the wrong setting Before AutoCAD 2002, dimensions were controlled by the variable DIMASO, which had two settings: 0 and 1. If it was set to 0, dimensions were exploded when they were created. If it was set to 1, dimensions were

Figure 6.10

Paper Space leader problem

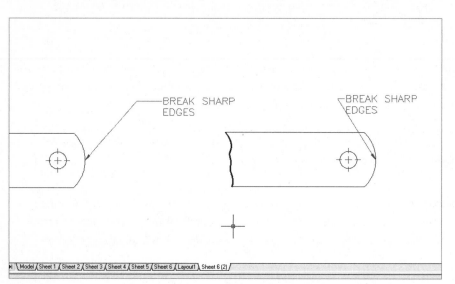

Figure 6.11

Dimensioning to spaces between lines

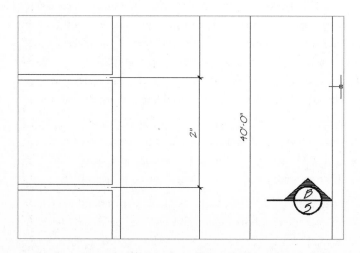

anonymous blocks. If you open a drawing created before AutoCAD 2002, its DIMASO setting is used as the setting for DIMASSOC. However, DIMASSOC has three settings: 0, 1, and 2. If it isn't set to 2, dimensions in Paper Space don't reflect Model Space distances—they reflect Paper Space distances.

If you open a drawing done in an early release of AutoCAD and want to add dimensions in Paper Space, you must remember to set DIMASSOC to 2 after you open it and before you add dimensions.

Scroll wheels cause problems When you zoom or pan in a floating viewport using your mouse's scroll wheel, you may find that Paper Space dimensions float free from the Model Space entities they're supposedly associated with. The DIMREGEN command is designed for this situation. When you use it, things get back together—almost always. However, if you don't notice the problem, the dimensions don't plot in the correct location—a fact you may overlook on a complex drawing.

DIMCENTER doesn't work right A Paper Space center mark applied to a circle in Model Space using DIMCENTER doesn't scale correctly unless the floating viewport plot scale is 1:1. DIMREGEN has no effect on center marks placed this way, so they can't be reconnected to an entity after a pan or zoom of any kind. See Figure 6.12.

A dimension can have an origin in each space It's possible, particularly when you're dimensioning something with some complexity or under time pressure, to snap to a location in Model Space for one dimension origin and to a location in Paper Space for the other. The resulting dimension value is meaningless.

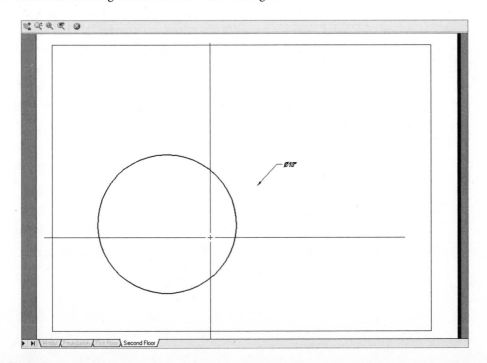

Figure 6.12
Scroll-wheel and center mark problems

3D Dimensions

Some users place dimensions for 2D geometry in Model Space and dimensions for 3D models in Paper Space. Your own decision rests on the kind of 3D dimensioning you're doing. You have two ways to add dimensions to 3D objects: directly to the model itself, or on 2D projections of a 3D model.

Suppose you use a floating viewport to display an isometric view of a model in a layout. If you put the dimensions in Paper Space, they're incorrect because of the foreshortening that happens when a view is isometric. If you add dimensions this way, be prepared to override each value. Place them in Model Space instead, and you get the correct value.

If you project standard orthographic views of a model using SOLPROF or SOLDRAW, you may choose to dimension the views in Paper Space to avoid using multiple layers for dimensions. If so, make sure that DIMASSOC is set to 2. If you're using a release prior to AutoCAD 2002, set DIMLFAC equal to the reciprocal of your intended plot-scale factor.

> Whenever you set the scale of a floating viewport, lock the display immediately. Right-click the viewport, or use the MVIEW command, but do it before you try to place dimensions or hatch patterns, or start any editing.

Hatch Patterns

Hatch patterns really have to be placed in Model Space, so there's no controversy here; but I'd like to make the same recommendation for hatch patterns that I've made for dimensions. Don't place any hatch patterns until you set up your layout and scale and lock your views. Only then will a hatch scale automatically in a floating viewport.

You may have to hatch the same area more than once if it shows up in different viewports at different scales. Note that in Figure 6.13, the two hatch patterns shown have the same boundary. Even though their floating viewports use different scales, the hatch-pattern spacing is the same because each pattern was placed separately in its own viewport and scaled automatically so it looks right in that viewport.

Before placing each hatch pattern, do the following:

1. Create a separate hatch layer for each viewport that has a different scale where the hatch pattern will be displayed.

2. Create, scale, and lock each floating viewport.

3. Create the hatch pattern through the floating viewport on its corresponding layer.

4. Check the Relative To Paper Space option in the Hatch And Gradient dialog box.

5. Set the scale to 1 in the Scale window.

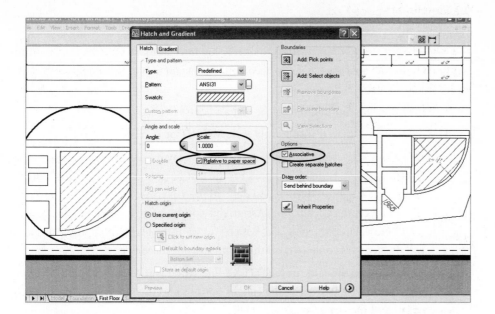

Figure 6.13
Placing hatch patterns in floating viewports

6. Check the Associative box so that hatch patterns update with changes to the boundary.

7. Select the appropriate Hatch Origin and Create Separate Hatches options (added in AutoCAD 2006).

> Note that you can use the Inherit Properties button to select an existing hatch pattern to set the characteristics.

Text

Where you place your text depends on the kind of text you have. My advice is to place text in Paper Space at the size you want it to plot (.125″, 3mm, and so on), if it falls into the following categories:

- A general note
- Title-block information
- Bill of materials information
- Other text that isn't associated directly with the geometry

Put text in Model Space, however, if it falls into one of three categories:

- Associated directly with the geometry
- Attached to a leader
- A note that must have a fixed location (room tags, balloon tags, local notes)

Scaling Model Space Text

Text doesn't do anyone much good if they can't read it. When your drawing is large enough to require a plotting scale less than 1:1, you have to make sure the text that must be placed in Model Space is scaled up accordingly. Several aids are available for creating text at the correct size in Model Space:

- Use the LEADER command to place text and erase the leader.
- Use 'SPACETRANS to transparently scale MTEXT or DTEXT:
  - *DTEXT*—Activate a floating viewport from a layout. Issue DTEXT, and select a starting point. When prompted for the text height (you're prompted *only* if you set the height to 0 when you defined the Text Style), type 'SPACETRANS. (Don't forget the apostrophe. Assign this command to a shortcut key if you use it a lot.) Now, enter the height at which you want the text to plot, and AutoCAD will do a conversion based on the zoom scale of the viewport.
  - *MTEXT*—Do the same as for DTEXT; but when you're prompted for the opposite corner type, **H** to select the Height options and then use the 'SPACETRANS command the same way as for DTEXT.
- Calculate the text height manually based on the plot scale in each viewport. Make a table or poster with the common sizes you use at each plot scale. Hang it up, or put it in a notebook for reference.
- Use CHSPACE. Place text in Paper Space at the size you want it to plot (.10 inch, for example), and then use the CHSPACE command to move the text into Model Space. It's automatically scaled to match the plot scale of that viewport. I repeat: CHSPACE was not a command until AutoCAD 2007. Before that, it was an Express Tool, so it's possible it wasn't loaded on your particular workstation.

> You can use SPACETRANS with schematic blocks and treat them like text when you place them in Model Space. As with text, you can also place schematic blocks in Paper Space and use CHSPACE to move them into Model Space.

Plotting a Layout

In case you're still fuzzy on using layouts in Paper Space to set up and plot drawings, here is a step-by-step explanation, starting with the big picture. If you think of using AutoCAD as a process that involves three stages, it may help you to keep track of what to do when. I'll start you off with a three-step overview and then provide a more detailed version. The steps should be done in sequence, but once you understand this process, you can easily mix things up.

AUTOMATING SCALING

The requirement that text be scaled properly in a floating viewport is so common that I've been asked several times to write an AutoLISP program to automate the process and save people the time of using the aids listed in this chapter. Because no variable controls the scale of a floating viewport, this isn't as straightforward as it could be. Chapter 9, "AutoLISP by Example—Getting Better" includes the code for a the program. It creates a new command that places text that's automatically scaled to plot at the size specified by the variable DIMTXT, no matter what scale the viewport is displaying. It works in the Model Space tab, in any floating viewport, or in Paper Space. It starts by creating an office standard style named Romans. You'll have to modify that style to meet your office standards:

The Big Picture

You can avoid most problems people have with plotting if you just follow this simple sequence when working with AutoCAD.

1. Create your geometry full-size in Model Space with no dimensions or hatches.

2. Set up your layout with a title block and scaled viewports in Paper Space.

3. Add dimensions and hatch patterns, in Model Space, through a Paper Space viewport. Simple, isn't it?

The Detailed Steps

Those are the three big steps, but of course, the devil's in the details. So here are the details; 23 of them.

1. Create appropriate blocks, text styles, dimension styles, and layers as indicated in earlier chapters of this book.

2. Create your geometry in Model Space with *no* dimensions or hatch patterns. Include object lines, hidden lines, phantom lines, and center lines.

3. Switch to Paper Space using the Layout tabs or the LAYOUT command.

4. Set up the page using the Page Setup Manager (right-click the Layout tab). Either create a new page setup or modify the existing one, as shown in Figure 6.14.

5. Select a plotter.

6. Select a plot-style table.

7. Select a paper size.

8. Make sure you're plotting the layout at a 1:1 scale unless you're plotting a metric drawing. AutoCAD automatically plots at a 1:25.4 scale as of AutoCAD 2005 if you're in a metric drawing and the paper size used is measured in inches. In prior releases, you must select the Metric option to get this relationship straight.

Figure 6.14

**Page setup dialog
box**

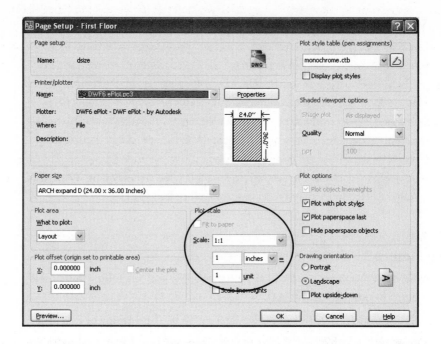

This notion of plotting the sheet 1:1 sometimes causes confusion, but it's logical. You aren't plotting geometry—you're plotting the layout. That layout is the same size as the sheet of paper. If they're the same size, that's a 1:1 plot scale. Each floating viewport may display geometry at any number of scales, but those scales have nothing to do with what you select for a plot scale.

9. If they aren't already part of your template, insert a full-size border and title block so you can see how much area you have to set up your views.

10. Modify the existing floating viewport or create a new one of any desired shape and size, and place it on a Viewports layer. Set the Viewports layer to nonplot, or freeze it before plotting. I like to have the edges of the viewports visible while I'm working so I can modify their properties, but others like to work with a sheet as it will look when plotted.

11. Add other floating viewports for drawing details using the MVIEW command. Place them on the same nonplot Viewports layer. You can move or edit the floating viewports after the fact using any of the standard AutoCAD commands, but try using grip editing.

12. Create an appropriate plot scale for each view using the Viewports toolbar. Select the edge of a floating viewport, and then select a scale. If the Viewports toolbar isn't showing, turn it on. The window on that toolbar is the Scale control window. See Chapter 3, "Customizing AutoCAD's Interface" if you'd like to add the control window to a different toolbar.

> You can set a scale in an active floating viewport using the XP option of the ZOOM command. However, if you inadvertently change the zoom magnification while in that floating viewport, the scale displayed in the Viewports toolbar doesn't immediately update. If that happens, you can lock a viewport with the wrong scale. Avoid this problem by selecting the edge of the viewport to set the scale.

13. Once you have the floating viewport display the way you want it, lock the display so you don't change your plot scale accidentally. Otherwise, your dimensions could all have different sizes. You can lock a viewport in Paper Space by selecting the edge of the viewport and right-clicking. (See Figure 6.15.) You can also lock one or more viewports using the Lock option of the MVIEW command.

Figure 6.15

Setting the viewport scale and locking the display

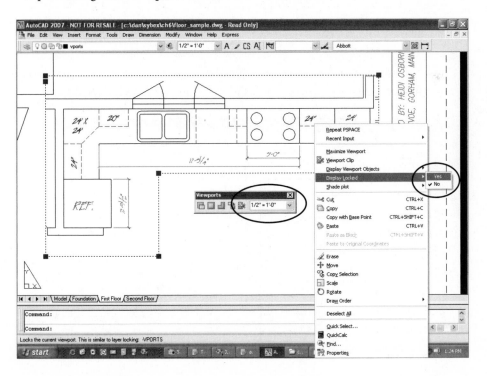

Locking a viewport isn't the same as locking the layer the viewport is on. If its layer is locked, you can't erase or move the viewport, but you can still change its display.

14. Create a dimension layer for each view. When you show two views of the same geometry at different scales, you may end up showing the dimensions intended for one view in another view. The dimensions appear to be different sizes in the floating viewports, because you have them zoomed to a different magnification in each floating viewport. In Figure 6.16, the dimensions in the viewport on the right don't appear in the active viewport on the left because the layer they're on, fl1-dim-det, is frozen in the current layer.

15. Freeze layers by viewport to control their display in each floating viewport:

    - Make the viewport active where you *don't* want the dimensions to show.

    - While this viewport is active, use the Layer Control window in the Object Properties toolbar to select the Freeze Or Thaw In Current Viewport icon. You can do this in the Layer Manager dialog box too, but the Layer Control window is quicker.

The command VPLAYER is even faster. Use it at the command line, in a script, or in a Lisp program.

    - Make a separate dimension layer for detail dimensions, and freeze that layer in the main viewport and any others where you don't want it to be displayed.

Figure 6.16

Freezing layers by viewport

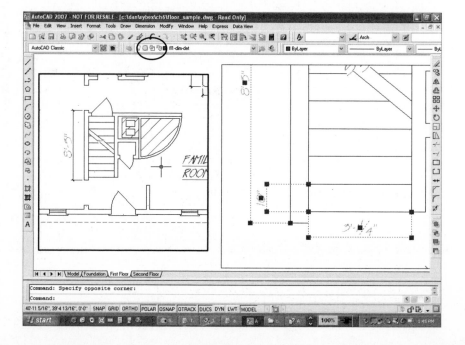

16. Add your dimensions in each viewport. If you set up your dimension style as suggested in Chapter 4, the dimensions are automatically scaled based on the zoom magnification in each viewport. As a result, all heights plot the same in each view.

17. You can add hatch patterns to the same dimension layers or create similar layers just for hatch patterns. Add your hatch patterns in the proper views, scaling them to Paper Space as shown earlier. Remember, this works only if they're added to a floating viewport.

18. Add your notes in Paper Space using full-size text.

19. You can use MVIEW to control how 3D models display or plot. They can be displayed as Wireframe, Hidden, 3D Hidden, 3D Wireframe, Conceptual, Realistic, or Rendered. The options are a little different prior to AutoCAD 2007, but nothing that would confuse you.

20. Place all viewports on a nonplot layer before plotting, unless you want them to plot. The edges of viewports always plot as thin lines. If you want to see them, trace a pline over them.

21. Use VPLAYER or the drop-down list in the Object Properties toolbar if you need to manage the visibility of layers in existing viewports. VPLAYER allows you to control the visibility of multiple viewports using wildcards. Figure 6.17 shows the VPLAYER being used to freeze all layers except those starting with the characters *FL2* in the active floating viewport. Figure 6.18 shows the immediate results.

Figure 6.17
VPLAYER with wildcards

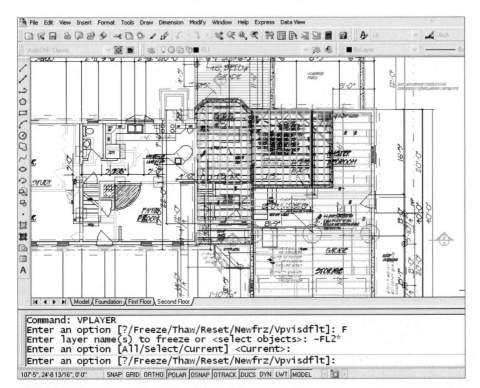

Figure 6.18

VPLAYER results

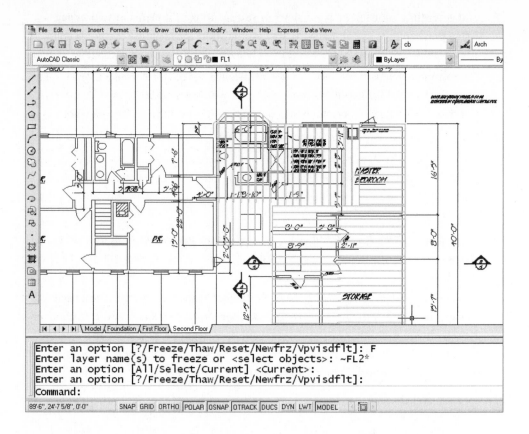

22. Do a plot preview, check that linetypes and lineweights are correct, and send the plot off to the plotter, which you've already set up using appropriate plot-style tables as shown later.

23. To add more layouts, right-click any layout, select New, and go through these steps again.

> Now that you understand layouts, look at the Layout Wizard. Although it can simplify the process of using layouts, it can also complicate your day if you want to change something and don't understand what the wizard has already done. Why didn't I tell you sooner? Hey, it's in the Help system.

Organizing Geometry in Model Space

You can use two general strategies to organize geometry in Model Space. The first is what I call a *true position* strategy. Imagine a building plan created by externally referencing a drawing representing each floor into the same host drawing. The floors are placed in their proper locations on top of each other. This makes it difficult to decipher the drawing in the Model Space tab but lets you check alignments from floor to floor. You then separate the floors by creating a layout for each one and freezing all the layers that aren't part of that XRef in each viewport on that layout. All the layers are thawed globally and then controlled within floating viewports. That strategy is illustrated in Figure 6.19. You can see from the clutter that it would be impossible to work in the model space tab without freezing groups of layers. But you don't have to edit in the model space tab. You eliminate the confusion by creating layouts and then you do your editing in floating viewports in each layout.

I call the second strategy the *warehouse floor* strategy. This time, imagine individual parts that will be combined into an assembly drawing. If you want to create a different sheet of each part, you can think of Model Space as a large warehouse floor. Put anything you want anywhere on the floor. Completely unrelated drawings can be inserted or externally referenced into one drawing and placed on the floor. Or, you can draw all the parts in different locations in Model Space. Then, a floating viewport can be created for each of the areas you used, and you can create as many layouts as you like. That strategy is illustrated in Figure 6.20. Each Layout tab represents a single sheet in a set of drawings of the parts and the final assembly.

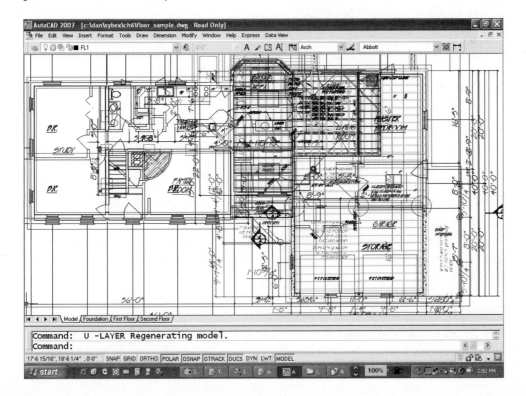

Figure 6.19

The true-position strategy

Figure 6.20

**The warehouse-
floor strategy**

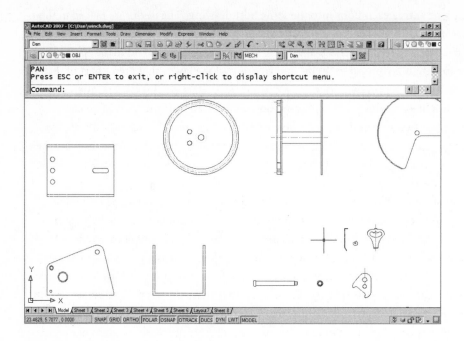

Other Layout Considerations

You may think there's nothing left to say about layouts. Well, there are a few things I haven't covered. Here's a collection of final tips for plotting from layouts that I hope you'll find handy.

Switching Viewports

Sometimes layouts can be too flexible. It's possible to make them any shape and place them in any arrangement, including overlapping each other, but occasionally I run into someone who has created a layout that's completely inside another layout. Once they make the larger viewport active, they can no longer activate the smaller one by clicking in it. See Figure 6.21.

The Ctrl+R key combination cycles through all your floating viewports in a layout. You can also activate a particular viewport with the CVPORT variable, but you must know what number has been assigned each viewport. This option is most likely to be used in a Lisp program.

VPMAX

Viewport Maximize and Viewport Minimize (VPMAX and VPMIN) looked like good features to me when they were introduced. If you double-click the edge of any floating viewport, it fills the screen, and you're working in Model Space. VPMAX honors the layer

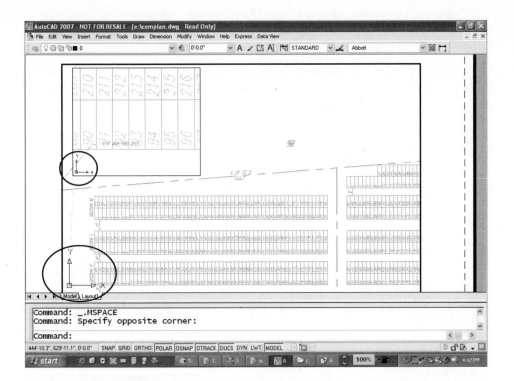

Figure 6.21

Use Ctrl+R to activate a floating viewport enclosed by a larger one

state for that viewport, allows you to edit geometry, and zoom in and out, pan around, and then takes you right back to the scale you started with when you type VPMIN or click the Minimize Viewport button on the status bar.

Well, VPMAX looked good, but it doesn't do the one thing that would make it more useful: Inexplicably, it doesn't honor the scale factor when you place dimensions. Even with DIMSCALE set to 0 and the viewport locked, any dimensions you place using this feature are scaled to the zoom factor *at the time the dimension is placed.* I can't call that a glitch, because it may be a feature, but I hope it changes.

Viewports with Islands

A workshop participant once asked me if there was a way to create a floating viewport with an island. At the time, I hadn't thought about it, but she wanted a blank area within a viewport where she could place text in Paper Space. Wipeouts were Express Tools at the time, and she didn't have them loaded. The results of using the DRAWORDER command couldn't be locked anyway then, so she couldn't guarantee that the text would always be readable, and she didn't want to trim out any of the geometry in the viewport. She just wanted to block it from view. We came up with something that did what she wanted, using the REGION command.

Regions are 2D shapes, but they behave like 3D models with a zero thickness. This isn't the real world, so you can have zero-thickness objects. Regions can be modified like 3D models. They can be combined using the UNION command, and subtracted from each other using the SUBTRACT command, and the results can be extruded into 3D solids that *do* have a thickness. But you can also use regions to create floating viewports, as follows:

1. Draw rectangles, circles, or closed polylines that represent the size, shape, and location of the viewport and the islands.

2. Use the REGION command to turn them all into regions.

3. Use the SUBTRACT command to remove the smaller shapes from the larger one. These become the islands, and you have a single region.

4. Use the MVIEW command or the proper button on the Viewports toolbar to convert the region object into a floating viewport. See Figure 6.22.

There's one thing to watch out for if you use a region with islands to create a floating viewport. You can still snap to objects covered by the islands, even though you can't see them. Any irregular floating viewport has that problem if you pass over the covered part of the viewport.

Figure 6.22

Using a region as a floating viewport

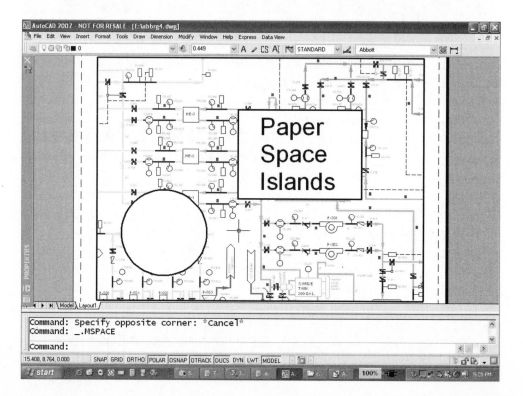

Irregular Viewports

When you select a floating viewport that was created from another object, you're picking two entities: a viewport and the original object. The viewport is rectangular, but part of it is masked by the other entity. If you select the viewport and check its properties, you'll see that you have two objects. You can list the properties of each object independent of the other.

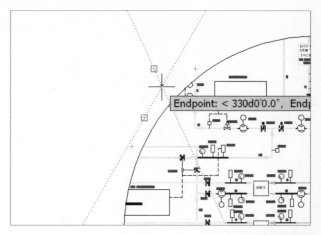

Figure 6.23

Object snaps with irregular viewports

Two possible problems may result:

- If you freeze the layer the viewports are on, the viewports become rectangular.

- If you turn off the layer the viewports are on, the first time you pan or zoom in Paper Space with the middle wheel, it appears as though the Model Space objects stay fixed as the layout moves over them. You may even lose the visibility of your Model Space entities. Use REGEN to get the display back on track.

Conventional Breaks

Traditionally, in mechanical design, if you wanted to show detail on the ends of a long part, you drew just the ends with a conventional break symbol and added the overall length as a broken dimension. There was no reason to draw the entire length, because that required a scale so small that the detail wouldn't show. Now that you're using a CAD system, though, why not draw the whole part and use a layout to create the impression of a conventional break?

Here's how:

1. Draw the long part in the Model Space tab.

2. Create a layout for the sheet size you use.

3. Create a single floating viewport to represent one end of the part, and place it in an appropriate location. Make sure it's on a nonplot layer.

4. Set the proper scale for the viewport, and frame the geometry for one end as shown in Figure 6.24.

5. Copy the viewport by tracking horizontally, and place the copy beside the first with a small gap between them (see Figure 6.25).

6. Activate the second viewport, and pan to the other end of the part, as shown in Figure 6.26.

Figure 6.24

Place the first view-port for a conventional break

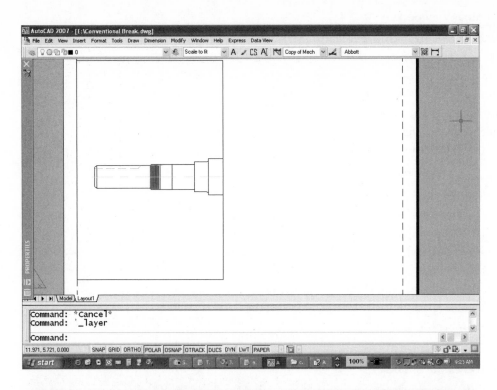

Figure 6.25

Add a second viewport for a conventional break

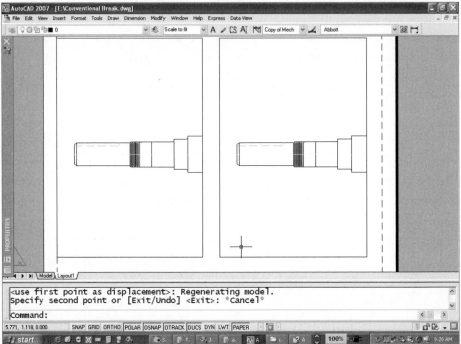

Figure 6.26

Pan the second viewport for a conventional break

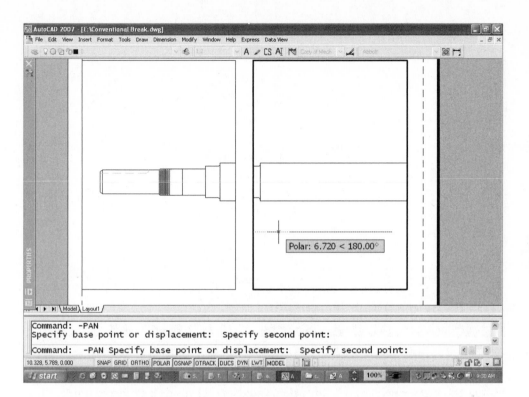

Don't use the scroll wheel or the standard PAN command to set up the second viewport. Use the -PAN command instead. This command-line version isn't free floating; it requires you to select a base point and a displacement point. Do so using tracking, and the two views will line up perfectly at exactly the same scale.

7. Create a block for a conventional break symbol, and make it the right size for a 1 unit diameter shaft. Now you can scale for any size shaft. In this case, the shaft has a diameter of 2.25, and its viewport is scaled at 1:2. So, you add the conventional break symbol at a scale of 1.25 in Paper Space, as shown in Figure 6.27.

Have you ever tried to snap directly to the intersection of a line in Model Space and the edge of a viewport in a layout? You can't do it. But you can accomplish the same thing by acquiring an object snap on the part and tracking to the intersection with the edge of the viewport. You may be surprised how often you'll use this technique.

Figure 6.27

Adding a conventional break

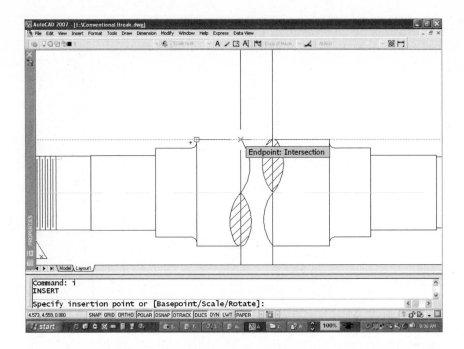

Figure 6.27

Adding a conventional break

8. Add dimensions to the part. To add any dimension that spans the two floating viewports, activate one, start the dimension, and then click inside the other to finish it. If a dimension spans both viewports (as two of them do in Figure 6.28), connect it between the two viewports by drawing a short line segment in Paper Space, and then move the dimension text so it's displayed in one of the viewports.

If you change the overall length of the part, its dimensions update. When plotted, the object appears as in Figure 6.29.

PSVPSCALE

This variable comes in handy for controlling the scale used to display Model Space entities when you create a new floating viewport. Because you probably use one plot scale most of the time, you may as well set PSVPSCALE to that plot scale (actually, to the reciprocal of that plot scale). Table 6.2 shows several examples in different disciplines.

Table 6.2

Sample Settings for PSVPSCALE

PSVPSCALE SETTING	ZOOM FACTOR	ACTUAL PLOT SCALE
0	Extents	Random
1	1 xp	1:1
0.1	.1 xp	1:10
.002	$^{1}/_{500}$ xp	$1'' = 500'$
$^{1}/_{48}$	$^{1}/_{48}$ xp	$^{1}/_{4}'' = 1'$
.0625	$^{1}/_{16}$ xp	$^{3}/_{4}'' = 1'$

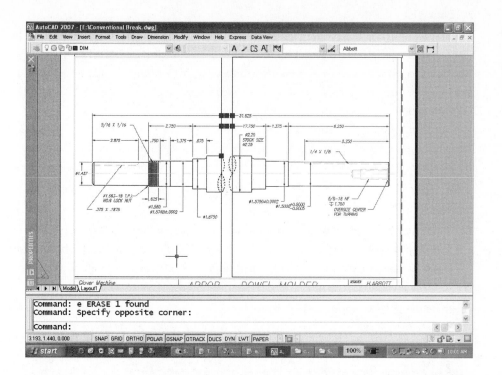

Figure 6.28
Adding dimensions to a part shown with a conventional break

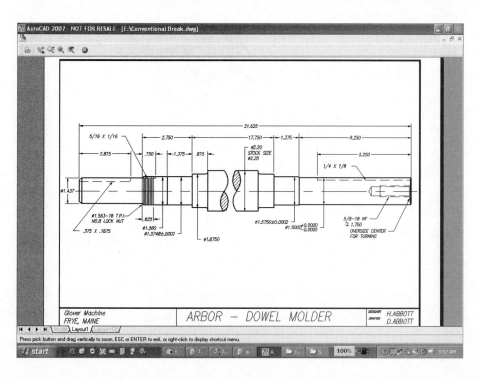

Figure 6.29
Plotted shaft with a conventional break

DVIEW TWist

You may want to rotate a floating viewport sometime, expecting the display of Model Space to rotate as well. That won't happen. However, you can use DVIEW (an often-overlooked command) to rotate a view within a viewport without changing the orientation of the entities. Its purpose is to set up views of 3D models, but now that AutoCAD has camera objects, it isn't used as much as it once was.

A drawing whose orientation is fixed may not fit well on a sheet of paper. Figure 6.30 shows a campus plan with the North arrow showing a north-up orientation. To fit it onto the sheet more efficiently, you may want to rotate the view without rotating the entities.

Here's how you can use DVIEW to do that:

1. Make the viewport active.

2. Determine the angle at which you want the view rotated. Select a line that represents a feature you want to display horizontally, and use DIST to determine its absolute angle from 0 in the X-Y plane. In this case, that angle is 57.00°, so you rotate the view −57° to make it rotate clockwise.

3. Issue the DVIEW command.

Figure 6.30

North-up orientation

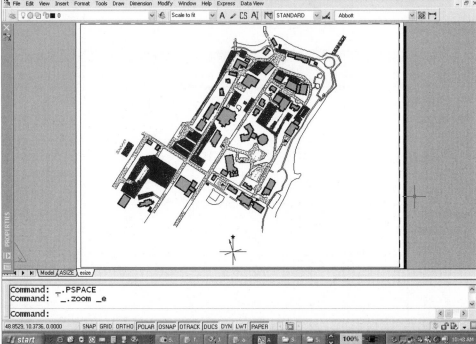

4. Select the objects you want to use to determine the orientation, or press ↵.

5. You're now in DVIEW, which is its own little universe with the following command-line prompt: [CAmera/TArget/Distance/POints/PAn/Zoom/TWist/CLip/Hide/Off/Undo]. I won't go into all of these here. The option you want is TWist.

6. You're prompted to Specify view twist angle <0>. Enter **-57** to twist the view clockwise, unless you've changed the default angle direction.

7. Type **x**↵ to exit DVIEW, and scale the floating viewport. The results are shown in Figure 6.31.

PUBLISH

The PUBLISH command is used to plot multiple sheets from saved drawings, using either the Model Space tab or the Layout tabs in the drawings. It's a replacement for the Batch Plotting utility that shipped with AutoCAD prior to AutoCAD 2004, and it can still use the older BP3 files created for batch plotting. However, you're more likely to use a drawing set description file (DSD) than a BP3 file.

Figure 6.31

Results of using DVIEW TWist

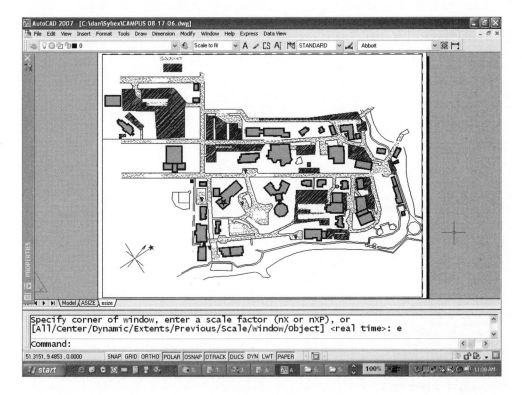

Plotting can be done to either a physical plotter or a DWF file, including what is known as a *multisheet DWF*, using the PUBLISH command. The DWF file is electronic and designed to be shared with others who don't have AutoCAD. The process of using PUBLISH is straightforward for both kinds of output. Here, I'll deal with plotting to a sheet of paper.

> If you're using the PUBLISH command to plot sheets from any open drawings, make sure each layout has a page setup defined and that the drawings have been saved before you use the PUBLISH command.

The Publish dialog box is shown in Figure 6.32. As you can see, it contains a list of sheet names. Those sheet names are composed from the drawing name and the layout name of the sheet, although Model Space sheets can also be shown. I don't recommend plotting the Model Space tab, but it's there. The buttons circled in Figure 6.32 are used to organize the sheets you plan to publish.

The buttons shown are used for the following actions, starting on the left and moving to the right:

- Preview
- Add Sheets
- Remove Sheets
- Move Sheet Up
- Move Sheet Down
- Load Sheet List
- Save Sheet List
- Plot Stamp Settings

Figure 6.32
Publish dialog box

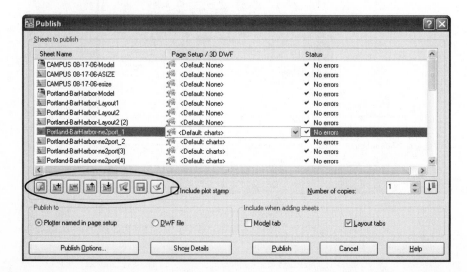

If you haven't activated a Layout tab for a listed sheet, you get the *Layout not initialized* error when you try to select it in the PUBLISH command.

Once you've established a list of sheets, click the Publish button, and they're plotted using the settings in the Page Setup dialog box for that sheet. This happens in the background as of AutoCAD 2005, allowing you to continue working.

If you use the command-line version of the PUBLISH command, plotting isn't done in the background.

If you want to quickly plot all the layouts in a drawing, you can do so without using the Publish dialog box. Right-click any Layout tab, pick the Select All Layouts option, right-click again, and then select Publish Selected Layouts. Plotting is done in the background, although you may find that your computer's performance is affected. In Figure 6.33, I selected all 24 layouts; each one plotted with its page setup with no further input from me.

Sheet Sets

Sheet sets can be composed of layouts from a variety of saved drawings. Once a sheet set is created, you can manage it with the Sheet Set Manager palette. You can also use it as the basis for the PUBLISH command to create a DWF file consisting of the entire sheet set, with an index and a table of contents. This can be helpful in plotting groups of drawings for transmittal to a client.

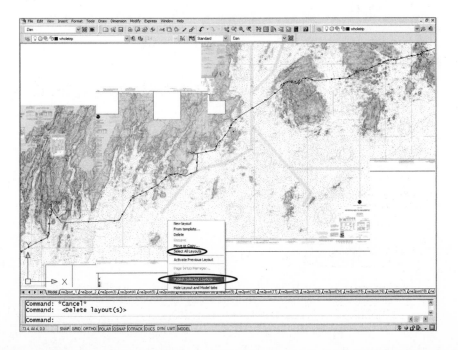

Figure 6.33
**Publishing
all layouts**

You can organize sheet sets as projects and give them tracking numbers, project names, phase-completion data, cross sheet call-outs, and additional custom properties. As with other file-management tools, be careful not to change drawing names or locations within projects once you've identified layouts as part of a sheet set.

> Sheet sets haven't caught on as quickly as I expected, probably because they have so many options. Don't be intimidated. Despite the large number of new commands and the potential complexity associated with this feature, the New Sheet Set Wizard makes sheet sets easy to use.

AutoCAD includes some sample sheet sets, but I don't think you'll find them useful as a starting point. Instead, select Existing Drawings when you create a sheet set. Use the Browse button on the Sheet Set Wizard to display the panel where you can select layouts to add to the set. (See Figure 6.34.) You must save the drawings first.

Sheet Sets aren't that difficult, so jump in and try using them. Once you see how easy it is to get started, you'll want a much more thorough discussion of their complexities: Look at the extensive PDF file on Heidi Hewett's AutoCAD Insider website: `http://heidihewett .blogs.com/`. It's a great site.

Plot-Style Tables

AutoCAD uses plot-style tables to control the appearance of lines when you plot. There are two kinds of tables: color dependent and named. They're saved in files with either a `.ctb` or an `.stb` file extension.

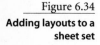

Figure 6.34

Adding layouts to a sheet set

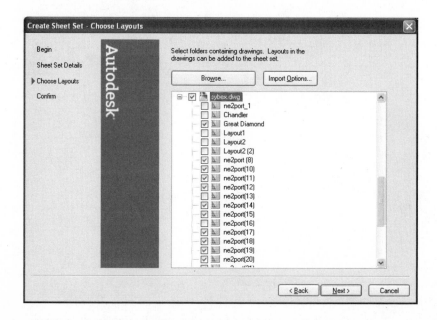

WBLOCK TO THE RESCUE

I've had some drawings that I couldn't get to display in the New Sheet Set Wizard. They had large numbers of layouts or image files, but otherwise nothing appeared wrong with the files. When I used RECOVER or AUDIT, no errors showed up. If this happens to you, try this trick.

Use the WBLOCK command to save a copy of the entire drawing (select "Entire drawing" as the source), and see if the Sheet Set Wizard will display that version. This has worked every time for me, but I don't know why. It's an old trick I've used over the years to solve problems with drawing files that appear to be corrupted, even when the AUDIT or RECOVER commands find no errors in the drawings. I lose any unused blocks and layers, but I can bring those in using ADC without causing the same problem to appear.

Color-Dependent Plot Styles

Each individual drawing can use only one kind of plot-style table. For historical reasons, most offices use color-dependent tables. The color-dependent tables have 255 pens, one for each standard AutoCAD index color. If you're using True Color colors, or one of the Color Books, color tables can't map a plot style to them, so I recommend using only style tables if possible.

Two commands convert a drawing from one type of table to the other:

- CONVERTPSTYLES converts a style-dependent drawing into a color-dependent drawing. It also converts a color-dependent drawing into a style-dependent drawing, but you must first use the CONVERTCTB command.

- CONVERTCTB converts an existing color-dependent table into a style-dependent table. This should be done prior to using CONVERTPSTYLES.

ACAD.STB and ACAD.CTB control color by plotting the same color as on the screen because they're set to Use Object Color by default. If you plot to a monochrome plotter using a style that plots in color, each color plots as a shade of gray. To force plotting with black lines, use the MONOCHROME.STB or MONOCHROME.CTB table.

If you use Pantone or one of the Color Books for any entities in your drawing, they always plot that color even if the plot-style table indicates that they will plot black. Only the standard index colors plot black when you use the monochrome plot-style table.

To open a table for editing, select the plot-style table you want from the Plot dialog box, and click the Edit button that appears beside the window. You can then modify the plot style contained by that table. However, if you've converted an existing drawing from color-dependent to style-dependent after converting a CTB to an STB file, there's a significant limitation on editing the resulting table: You can't add new styles.

Using a Style-Dependent System

If style-dependent tables are used, you can define as many styles as you want for an individual drawing. In most cases, one style is sufficient if you assign lineweights and linetypes ByLayer, because lineweight is the characteristic that's most likely to be controlled by a plot style.

To use a style-dependent system, do the following:

1. Create a template that's based on named plot styles. You have to start a drawing using a template that's already based on a named plot style, such as acad -Named Plot Styles.dwt. If you already have a template, you can convert it into a style-dependent drawing using CONVERTPSTYLES.

2. If you start a drawing without a template, set Use Named Plot Styles as the default in the Plot Style Table Settings dialog box, accessed through the Plot tab of the Options dialog box.

3. Change the default for QNEW in the Files tab of the Options dialog box (as of AutoCAD 2006) to your style-dependent template.

4. Create (or edit) a plot-style table using the Plot Style Manager found in the File pull-down menu. Select Add-A-Plot Style Table Wizard from the folder, and follow the instructions given by the wizard. You can also access the wizard by choosing Tools → Wizards → Add Named Plot Style Table.

Figure 6.35 is a sample taken from the website of the Natural Resources Conservation Services of New York. It's the most extensive collection of plot styles that I've found by searching the web. Any entity or layer that has the highlighted style named As Built applied to it plots in red with a lineweight of .0150″.

Figure 6.35

Plot Style Table Editor

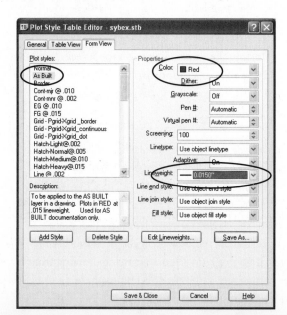

AutoCAD Graphics in Other Applications

Computers use two kinds of graphic images: vector and raster. CAD programs produce vector images. Entities are defined mathematically and can be redisplayed as the magnification of the view changes. No matter how far you zoom in to a vector image, it looks good. AutoCAD DWG and DWF files are vector-based, as is the Windows Metafile (WMF) format.

Raster images are based on pixels. When you zoom in on a raster image, it looks increasingly worse, the higher the magnification, because the pixels are displayed as increasingly large. Because a computer monitor displays images in raster format, even vector-based graphics images don't always look good on the screen. You've noticed, I'm sure, that AutoCAD lines drawn at an angle are displayed with a staircase effect. That's because the rectangular shape of the pixels used for monitors are always displayed in a fixed orientation. Their edges are horizontal and vertical, so lines drawn at an angle appear jagged because you can see the corners of the pixels. Figure 6.36 demonstrates this with two images: a raster image above, and a vector image below.

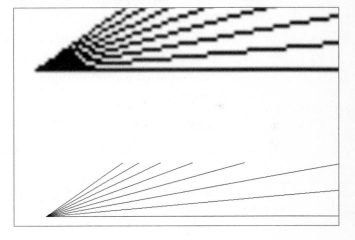

Figure 6.36
Raster and vector images

Let's say you want to illustrate a document created with a word processor, or add a high-quality image to a presentation, or provide an AutoCAD drawing to someone who doesn't have access to AutoCAD. In other words, you want to share an AutoCAD drawing with another application. I do this in one of four ways, depending on the image quality I'm looking for.

- Screen capture
- Plot to a raster file
- WMFOUT
- Plot to a DWF file

Screen Capture

This is the easiest method. You press the Print Screen key on your keyboard, and an image of your screen is stored on the Windows clipboard. You can paste it into many other Windows applications by pressing Ctrl+V or right-clicking and choosing Paste. This is a low-resolution process, but if you want to display the whole screen, it's great. Many of the graphics in this book were created that way. It works best when you want to show a dialog box, or the entire screen including the AutoCAD interface, but AutoCAD entities won't show much detail.

To capture just an active dialog box, use the Alt+Print Screen combination. Unfortunately, this doesn't work with some of AutoCAD's tool palettes, but it works with most of them and is a great way to document a process for other users.

Plot to a Raster File

You can set up a plotter that creates one of several raster-based files. Autodesk added a PDF plotter to AutoCAD 2007. It works great for plotting vector-based entities, but I've had problems using it with drawings that contain images. To use it, select the DWG To PDF.pc3 plotter in the Page Setup dialog box.

If you need a TIFF file, you can add a plotter definition using the following steps, starting with the AutoCAD File pull down menu: Plotter Manager → Add-A-Plotter Wizard → My Computer → Raster File Formats → Plot To File → Assign A Name → Finish.

When you plot with this plotter setup, select the highest possible resolution if you want to use the images for anything critical. The highest listed resolution is 1600×1280 pixels. If you need something higher, create a larger custom paper size. Those pixels are units, so your sheet size will seem huge. You may not even notice the tiny 10×8 viewport in the lower-left corner of the sheet. To determine how that translates into an actual size, divide the numbers by the dots per inch (DPI) required for your application. If you need to print the result at 300dpi, for example, an image that's 1600×1280 pixels will measure 5.3×4.3 inches when it's printed. Double the resolution to 600dpi, and you cut the printed size in half.

WMFOUT

I generally use this system to convert an AutoCAD drawing into the highest-quality image for use by someone who doesn't have AutoCAD and doesn't want to download one of Autodesk's viewers. Because WMF is vector-based, when a WMF file is inserted into Microsoft Word and plotted out, it looks just as good as the original AutoCAD drawing. If you use this method, here are some things to keep in mind.

- Since AutoCAD 2006, the WMFOUT command always adds a white background. Prior to that, the background took on the color used at the time a WMF file was created. Using white lines on a black background is a lousy combination for a graphic that will be printed in a report, a magazine, or a book (although I've seen it done). Change the Uniform background to white in the Options dialog box for releases prior to AutoCAD 2006. I used to have a special WMF profile for that reason.

- WMFOUT isn't a plotting function, so your plot style isn't used. Make sure the entities you're going to select are displayed correctly before using WMFOUT. If you want to use an illustration that has different lineweights, set them, and turn on Lineweight Display. If you're using a 3D model, use the HIDE command before exporting the WMF file as shown in Figure 6.37.

Figure 6.37

AutoCAD entities exported with WMFOUT

You must select entities when using WMFOUT. If you want to include both layout and Model Space entities, you must temporarily move one group to the other space.

To use the WMF file in another Windows application, such as Microsoft Word or PowerPoint, use the pull-down menu in that application, as follows: Insert → Picture → From File → select the WMF file.

You can place it where you want it. Word can be frustrating to work with when adding graphics. Sometimes they seem to fly around on their own or move unexpectedly when you add material. It may help you to control them if you don't allow graphics to overlap in Word.

Plot to a DWF File

This method works great, of course; just select the DWF plotter in the Page Setup dialog box.

Someone without AutoCAD can't view your DWF file without a viewer or other software capable of reading and plotting DWF files. Most people don't have such software, so they have to get it from Autodesk—either by downloading a free version or by purchasing a version now known as Autodesk Design Review (once known as DWF Composer), which has markup, measurement, and other functions that go beyond simple viewing and plotting.

Autodesk hopes this format will become the default vector-based format for viewing CAD files. It hasn't happened yet, but Autodesk is putting a lot of emphasis on DWF in an effort to counter Adobe's efforts to get people to use the PDF format instead. At this point,

DWF is clearly a better format, but most people don't have a means of working with DWF files. In contrast, most people have Adobe Reader.

A summary of the possible viewers is available at www.Autodesk.com (as of August, 2006). Some of these may be free or trial versions, but check the site for more information:

- Autodesk Design Review
- Autodesk DWF Viewer
- DWG TrueView

CHAPTER 7

AutoCAD Scripts

Most users have forgotten AutoCAD Scripts over the past few years, and that's too bad, because scripts are simple—and powerful. I use them every day to manage network computers, set up drawings, and test individual workstations to see how well they run AutoCAD. Scripts are my own personal insurance policy—they prevent those unwelcome surprises that sometimes occur when I'm presenting material on somebody else's computer.

But when it comes to updating drawings, this poor-man's programming tool packs an even bigger punch. I've written scripts that update literally thousands of drawings while I'm busy doing something else. In the last section of this chapter, I'll show you a few examples. Once you've seen them, I guarantee you'll be thinking up a few of your own.

> If you changed the default path for AutoCAD when it was installed, you must use your own path in the code used in this chapter. `C:\Program Files\AutoCAD 2007\acad.exe` is used as the path to the `acad.exe` file throughout.

- ▪ **Characteristics of Scripts**
- ▪ **Writing and Running Scripts**
- ▪ **Updating Thousands of Drawings**

Characteristics of Scripts

Scripts are essentially extremely fast typists. When you have to do one thing the same way every time, scripts can't be beat. They even have one advantage over real programming languages: You can use them in AutoCAD LT.

Let's start with a few characteristics of scripts:

- Scripts are ASCII text files. Use a text editor for best results.
- They consist of things you would normally type at the command prompt, such as:
    - Commands, but not command aliases
    - Command options as you would type them (E or Extents works for the ZOOM command)
    - AutoCAD system variables
    - Lisp code (unless you're using AutoCAD LT)
    - External commands defined in the ACAD.PGP file, but not aliases
    - Commands and functions defined with AutoLISP, ARX, or VBA

- They can be run automatically at AutoCAD startup by using the /b switch.
- They must be saved with an .scr extension.
- They form the basis of a process used to update large numbers of drawings.
- They can load AutoLISP programs.
- They can run AutoLISP programs.
- They can call another script using the SCRIPT command.
- They can open tool palettes but can't make selections from them.
- You can make a script open a file-management dialog box by placing a tilde after the command name, as in SAVE ~.

Scripts also have a few limitations:

- The only possible user input is to pause and restart the script.
- Variables can't be defined directly in a script the way they can in a Lisp program—but if you need to define variables, you can run Lisp code in a script to do it.
- If something goes wrong, a script stops until the user takes some action.

Table 7.1 shows the few special functions used with scripts.

Writing and Running Scripts

If you can type, then you can write script files. The script file is AutoCAD's version of a batch file. It's an ASCII text file with the extension .scr. You can create one in any word processor or text editor, but a text editor is far preferable because word processors add codes that will interfere with the script if you don't save the file in the proper text format.

FUNCTION	PURPOSE
Backspace key	Pauses a script in progress
RESUME	Resumes a paused script when typed at the keyboard
;	Designates that a remark line follows
DELAY	Delays the next step in the script for a specified time period
RSCRIPT	Repeats the entire script when placed at the end of the script file.
Space in a line	The same as pressing ↵ at the AutoCAD command prompt
↵	Also the same as pressing ↵ at the AutoCAD command prompt

Table 7.1

Special Functions Used with Scripts

UPDATING DRAWINGS IN A HURRY

Back in the good old days of R12, an engineer contacted me with an intriguing AutoCAD problem. He had a group of DXF files in which he needed to explode all the polylines. Most of them were nested several levels deep in block definitions, so first he had to explode each of those levels—that meant using the EXPLODE command as many times as there were nested levels—and then he had to explode the polylines.

The drawings had been created on a mainframe CAD system before the company switched to an application that ran on a PC. The company had saved all its files in DXF format and then opened them on the new system (need I mention that it wasn't AutoCAD?). That worked fine, except for one thing: Every polyline was the wrong shape. The company made molded cardboard packaging used for shipping all manner of products, including eggs, so those shapes were critical.

The engineer found that if he opened the drawing in AutoCAD, exploded the polylines, and saved the file in DWG format, he could open the drawing in MicroStation, and the resulting shapes were perfect. Great—except that he had more than 2,500 files, and they all had to be converted. At 10–15 minutes each, he didn't like the tally, so he was looking for a quicker solution.

With the help of AutoCAD scripts, I came up with one. The solution required a Lisp program to do the multilevel exploding, and a batch file was part of my scheme, as well; but the only way I could get that Lisp program to run in multiple drawings was with a script file.

On a Friday night, I sent three files to my engineer friend. On Monday, all his drawings were done. He had escaped nearly 700 hours of tedium. I just looked up the bill in my archive files. It must have taken me some time to develop that system, because the bill, from 1995, is a little higher than I remembered. But I do recall that I got the check in three days.

Windows uses the .scr extension for screen savers. Before AutoCAD 2006, unless you've changed the association, you can't double-click a script file to open it. If you try, Windows assigns it as your screen saver. After a set period of inactivity, you'll get a confusing error message about not being able to run the screen saver. Change the association of the file extension in Windows Explorer (or any Windows file-management dialog box) by using the menu sequence Tools → Folder Options → File Types → New → SCR → Advanced → AutoCAD Script.

A script automatically executes a series of commands that are contained in a text file, as long as it has an .scr extension. You can use it for any number of tasks, such as the following:

- Create a drawing.
- Test a computer.
- Set up layers, text styles, dimension styles, and other things in a drawing.
- Change variable settings that are saved in the drawing.
- Change settings that are saved in the system registry.
- Extract block attributes.
- Make slides, and run a slide show.
- Edit an unlimited number of drawing files while you do something else.

Creating and using a script file requires the following steps:

1. In a text, file, type a list of AutoCAD commands just as you would at the command prompt.. You can place one command on each line or separate commands with spaces. Be careful not to put extra spaces between commands or at the ends of lines. A space in a script has the same effect as pressing the Enter key, as does a new line.

2. Save the file with a filename and the extension .scr. This is critical. Without the .scr extension, AutoCAD won't recognize the text file as a script when you try to run it.

3. Have AutoCAD run the script. Use the SCRIPT (SCR) command, or choose Tools → Run Script.

By default, the SCRIPT command uses a file-management dialog box. If you want to enter options at the command line, first turn off the File dialog box by setting FILEDIA to 0. That way, you can see how the command works. If you run the SCRIPT command *from* a script file, it won't open the dialog box.

A Simple Script File

To get a sense of how a script works, create a text file named `layer.scr` and type the following lines. Be careful not to create extra lines or spaces anywhere in the file. However, enter ↵ twice at the end of the last line. The first ↵ will execute the color option and the second ↵ will exit the LAYER command.

```
LAYER
New
fl1,fl1-dim,fl1-txt
Color
2
fl1
Color
3
fl1-dim
Color
4
fl1-txt
```

If you highlight the entire file in Notepad you can see whether you have any extra spaces or lines. Notice the location of the cursor in the image.

You can also type the script file on one line, with a single space between the commands. The same setup script looks like this:

```
Layer new fl1,fl1-dim,fl1-txt color 2 fl1 color 3 fl1-dim color 4 fl1-txt
```

Save the file (don't forget the `.scr` extension). Run the script in AutoCAD. If everything goes right, three new layer names are created, with their colors set to 2, 3, and 4.

> If you're wondering why the Layer Properties Manager doesn't appear when you run this script file, remember that some commands work differently in a script than they do when typed at the keyboard. A script can't be paused, but a dialog box would cause it to stop. The LAYER command in a script doesn't open the dialog box; it behaves like the version of the LAYER command you get if you type -LAYER.

Drawing Setup

The simple script in the previous section can be expanded to automatically set up limits, units, variables, a text style, and so on. If you use good template files, much of this setup is already be in place, but I can think of a few reasons why a script may be a better choice than a template file:

- An existing drawing's setup may need to be changed after the drawing has been created. By then it's too late to start the drawing with a template file, and you can't insert a DWT file to bring in layers and styles.

- You may be working with drawings from other offices that don't follow your standards. A script can help you fix that.

- Many of AutoCAD's system variables are saved in the system registry, not in the drawing file, so a template can't control them.

- You may have to use a shared computer on which another user has changed some AutoCAD settings. Restoring the defaults or your preferred settings is much easier with a script than manually.

Let's take the script layer.scr and rewrite it with a few additional functions:

```
;Create new layers
LAYER New obj,hid,cen,txt,dim Color 1 hid Color 3 cen
Color 4 txt Color 5 dim L hidden hid L center cen S obj

;Create new text style
STYLE romans romans 0 1 0 N N N
;Reset variable values
APERTURE 5 ATTDIA 1 AUNITS 0 AUPREC 1 BLIPMODE 0
CECOLOR bylayer CELTSCALE 1 CELTYPE bylayer
CMDDIA 1 CMDECHO 1 CURSORSIZE 5 DRAGMODE A ELEVATION 0
EXPERT 0 FACETRES 1 FILEDIA 1 FILLETRAD 0 GRIPCOLOR 5
GRIPHOT 1 GRIPS 1 GRIPSIZE 3 HIGHLIGHT 1 LTSCALE 1
MBUTTONPAN 1 MIRRTEXT 0 OSMODE 4133 PELLIPSE 0 PICKADD 1
PICKAUTO 1 PICKBOX 3 PICKFIRST 1 PICKSTYLE 1 PLINEGEN 1
PSLTSCALE 1 SAVETIME 15 SDI 0 SORTENTS 23 THICKNESS 0
UCSICON off UCS w UCSVP 1
```

The following graphic shows the result of highlighting this file. In this case the cursor is directly below the beginning of the last line. There is no need for a blank line to exit the previous command.

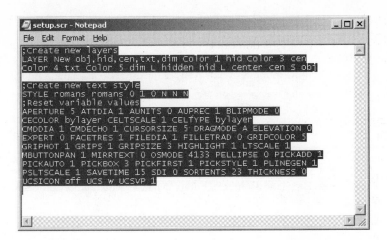

This script sets up layers, an acceptable text style, and set key variables. The purpose of a setup script is to restore standard settings if something goes wrong with AutoCAD and you can't figure out why.

> Make sure there are no extra spaces or lines anywhere in this file. (There's a reason why I'm mentioning this over and over.) Each of them is interpreted as the ↵ and can break your script. ↵ often repeats the last command in AutoCAD; so, if you have problems, check to see what happened just before your script crashed for a clue as to where you may have an extra space or line.

Computer Bench Testing

If you've ever wondered how well AutoCAD will run on a particular workstation, the script function gives you a handy way to find out. You may want to duplicate a colleague's problem with AutoCAD crashing (unless, of course, AutoCAD has never crashed for you). Or, you may want to compare a variety of computers to decide which one to buy.

I wrote the following script because, as the person responsible for all the computers in my department, I'm all too familiar with the Law of Unintended Consequences. Whenever it's time for the college to upgrade or add computers to a lab, I load AutoCAD on each station and then run a version of the following script. You'd be surprised at the amount of variation between systems with similar specs.

SLUGGISH COMPUTERS

I once had a problem with four computers out of a group of 40 identical systems. AutoCAD ran much more slowly on those four than it did on any of the others. I called the vendor's rep, who insisted that the difference was based on the users—either they were working on more complex drawings, or they simply *perceived* their computers to be slower.

I wrote a test script and ran it on all the computers before the rep arrived. When he got there, I pointed out that the times required for 36 of the computers was around 2 minutes, whereas the four "problem" computers required nearly 12 minutes. Convinced, he did some diagnostics and discovered that those four computers all had a cache-memory problem that slowed them down.

Before running this script you *must* start a new Imperial drawing from scratch.

```
TIME R

BOX 0,0 10,10,10 SPHERE 5,5,5 5 SUBTRACT NON 0,0  L

VPOINT 1,-1,1 SLICE L   5,0 5,5 5,5,5 -1,0
3DARRAY L  R 4 4 4 10 10 10
ZOOM ALL HIDE
VPORTS 4
CVPORT 5 UCS X 90 PLAN C
CVPORT 4 UCS W PLAN C
CVPORT 2 UCS X 90 UCS Y 90 PLAN C
TILEMODE 0 ERASE ALL  MVIEW R  F
MSPACE CVPORT 3 SOLPROF ALL  Y Y Y
CVPORT 4 SOLPROF ALL  Y Y Y
CVPORT 5 SOLPROF ALL  Y Y Y
CVPORT 6 SOLPROF ALL  Y Y Y
TIME
```

This script will run properly only if you start a new drawing before executing it.

To make sure you have no spaces at the end of each line, highlight the entire file by dragging the mouse with the left button held down, and make sure it looks like the following image. Note that the cursor is by itself on the last line, which is below TIME. If you have trouble running this script, try turning off running object snaps or setting APERTURE to 3.

What does this script do? Let's take one line at a time; see Table 7.1.

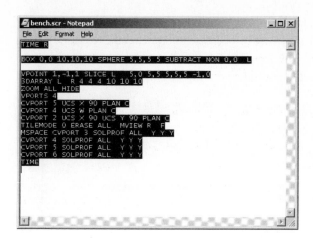

SCRIPT LINE	PURPOSE	
TIME R	Resets the time.	Table 7.1
	A ↵ to exit the TIME command.	benchtest.scr
BOX 0,0 10,10,10 SPHERE 5,5,5 5 SUBTRACT NON 0,0 L	Creates a solid box and a sphere, and subtracts the sphere from the box. The use of NON cancels any running object snaps. Giving a location of 0,0 selects the box. An extra space is a ↵ that cancels the selection prompt. The L selects the last entity (the sphere) as the object to subtract from the box.	
	A ↵ to cancel the selection prompt.	
VPOINT 1,-1,1 SLICE L 5,0 5,5 5,5,5 -1,0	Creates an isometric view, and slices the resulting solid using a plane defined by the coordinates given. Note the 3 spaces after L.	
3DARRAY L R 4 4 4 10 10 10	Creates a rectangular 3D array of the sliced object. The larger the values used for the number of entities, the more entities are created in the array. To decrease the amount of time it takes to run this test, lower the value from 10. To increase the amount of time, increase the value.	
ZOOM ALL HIDE	Displays the entire array, and displays it as hidden.	
VPORTS 4	Sets up four tiled viewports.	
CVPORT 5 UCS X 90 PLAN C	Makes viewport 5 active, and creates a front view.	
CVPORT 4 UCS W PLAN C	Makes viewport 4 active, and creates a top view.	
CVPORT 2 UCS X 90 UCS Y 90 PLAN C	Makes viewport 2 active, and creates a right view.	
TILEMODE 0 ERASE ALL MVIEW R F	Switches to a layout, and creates four views.	
MSPACE CVPORT 3 SOLPROF ALL Y Y Y	Creates a solid profile in viewport 3.	
CVPORT 4 SOLPROF ALL Y Y Y	Creates a solid profile in viewport 4.	
CVPORT 5 SOLPROF ALL Y Y Y	Creates a solid profile in viewport 5.	
CVPORT 6 SOLPROF ALL Y Y Y	Creates a solid profile in viewport 6.	
TIME	Activates the TIME command, and displays the total elapsed time.	
	↵ after TIME.	

I use these particular functions because they have caused me past problems in AutoCAD. You can easily adjust the program to increase or decrease the time it takes to run by changing the number of objects in the 3D array. When I ran this program on my current workstation, I got the following result at the end.

```
AutoCAD Text Window - Drawing8.dwg                                    _□×
Edit
[?/Freeze/Thaw/Reset/Newfrz/Vpvisdflt]:
Command: _.VPLAYER Enter an option [?/Freeze/Thaw/Reset/Newfrz/Vpvisdf
Enter name(s) of new layers frozen in all viewports: PH-119 Enter an op
[?/Freeze/Thaw/Reset/Newfrz/Vpvisdflt]: _T
Enter layer name(s) to thaw: PH-119
Enter an option [All/Select/Current] <Current>: Enter an option
[?/Freeze/Thaw/Reset/Newfrz/Vpvisdflt]:
Command:
64 solids selected.

Command: time

Current time:              Saturday, August 26, 2006  4:25:00:734 PM
Times for this drawing:
  Created:                 Saturday, August 26, 2006  4:24:53:203 PM
  Last updated:            Saturday, August 26, 2006  4:24:53:203 PM
  Total editing time:      0 days 00:00:07:547
  Elapsed timer (on):      0 days 00:00:01:734
  Next automatic save in:  0 days 00:09:58:266

Enter option [Display/ON/OFF/Reset]: |
```

Using Scripts at Drawing Startup

You can automate AutoCAD at startup with switches by using the RUN option or using a startup icon. One of those switches, /b, allows you to name a script that runs each time AutoCAD starts.

You can also start AutoCAD by having it open a named drawing. By combining the two functions, you can have AutoCAD start with a specific drawing and then run a script.

Figure 7.1 shows the Properties window of an AutoCAD desktop icon. In the Target field, I've added the /b switch and the name and path of a script file. The entire line reads like this:

```
"C:\Program Files\AutoCAD 2007\acad.exe" /b R:\setup.scr
```

When you select the icon, AutoCAD starts up and executes the named script, which is on a network drive. I use this script to easily change the setup for plotters and specific variables; I can also send a message to users by adding an Alert box. AutoCAD system variables, such as REMEMBERFOLDERS, can be set directly; you need AutoLISP code to set environmental variables. Here's a sample startup script:

Figure 7.1

Running a script on startup

```
;;No blank lines!
rememberfolders 0
ACADLSPASDOC 1
Savefilepath S:
(if (= 120 (getvar "savetime"))(setvar "savetime" 5))
(setenv "HideSystemPrinters" "1")
(setvar "pickadd" 1)
(setenv "PrinterConfigDir" "r:\\plotters")
(setenv "PrinterStyleSheetDir" "")
(setenv "PrinterDescDir" "r:\\plotters\\pmp files")
(startapp "net start spooler")
(alert "Message text begins after the quote, for display
➡in an AutoCAD Message box.
\n A new line would start after the backslash n and appear here.
\n A third line would appear here. The closing quote and parenthesis
➡ is on the next line.
")
(defun C:AED()(startapp "C:\\Program Files\\Adobe\\
➡Acrobat 6.0\\Reader\\AcroRd32.exe"
➡"r:\\TECHNICAL GRAPHICS STANDARDS_rev8.pdf"))
(princ)
```

Resetting All AutoCAD Variables

Let's say AutoCAD starts misbehaving: You know something's gone awry but can't target the problem. Sometimes the only solution is to reset all variables to their defaults.

If Express Tools are installed on your system, look for a file named defaults.scr in the Express folder under the AutoCAD folder in Program Files. That file is a script you can use to restore all default settings for AutoCAD variables. Unfortunately, it hasn't been updated for the past several releases. The website for this book contains contains an updated version of this file with the default values. It uses Lisp language to reset each variable, primarily because that approach allows more accuracy in values that must be calculated using pi. It also lets you set environmental variables like MAXHATCH that can only be set with AutoLISP.

Figure 7.2

**System Variables
dialog box**

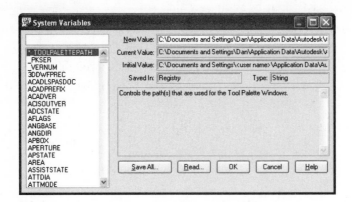

You can use another Express Tool, SYSVDLG (the System Variables editor), to save your current settings and then retrieve them, as shown in Figure 7.2. These won't be the default values if you've changed anything.

Updating Thousands of Drawings

Although I've yet to run into another engineer who needs to explode all the blocks and polylines in a drawing, I've nevertheless created various sets of programs over the years to solve the problem of updating large numbers of drawings. One company wanted to reduce the size of its archived drawings to preserve drive space. Another wanted to extract specific attribute data from all of its drawings and place the data in a text file. Yet another wanted to update the title block in all of its drawings to reflect a company name change. And still another wanted to create a separate drawing file from each block definition in all of the company's symbol-library drawings.

I'll share three of these solutions with you. Each one requires the following three elements:

- A script file
- A batch file
- A Lisp program

Write your programs in such a way that *new* drawing files are created. Don't delete the existing files until you're confident that the program did what you wanted it to. You may even want to mark them as read-only before you try this system.

Batch File

In these solutions, I use a batch file to edit multiple drawings primarily because doing so allows me to use the DOS function FOR. The FOR function lets you specify a directory and filenames using wildcards and have the operating system do something with those files. In this case, I use the batch file to start AutoCAD and open each DWG file in a specified directory. The key line of each batch file is in the following form:

```
FOR %%f in (C:\dwg\*.dwg) do start /wait acad.exe "%%f" /b
➥C:\Sybex\wbout.scr
```

To process drawings in subdirectories, you can add a /r switch to the FOR command in the batch file. Note that the path comes before the replaceable parameter, and the set (in parentheses) includes only the files, designated by a wildcard and file extensions. You can also reference a text file to specify a list of filenames, but this is the system I use. Consult the DOS help system for the FOR command if you want more details:

```
FOR /r C:\Sybex\DWG\ %%f in (*.dwg) do start /wait
➥C:\"Program Files"\"AutoCAD 2007"\acad.exe "%%f" /b
➥C:\Sybex\wbout.scr
```

Script File

In addition to the batch file, I also use a script for these solutions because I can run a script on startup by pointing to it in the batch file. The following line shows the syntax to use at a DOS command prompt in the target window of a desktop icon, or in the Run window reached from the Windows Start button:

```
C:\"Program Files"\"AutoCAD 2007"\acad.exe C:\dwg\house.dwg /b
➥C:\Scripts\startup.scr
```

This line starts AutoCAD (acad.exe), opens a specified drawing (house.dwg), and executes a named script (C:\Scripts\startup.scr) automatically.

AutoLISP File

Like both script files and batch files, an AutoLISP file is a text file, but it's designated by an .lsp extension. Lisp is a programming language, and its tie to AutoCAD makes it possible to do nearly anything to a drawing. Every experienced AutoCAD user should be familiar with it. In this system for updating drawings, AutoLISP generally does the real work.

Learning AutoLISP is beyond the scope of this chapter, but read Chapters 8 and 9, "AutoLISP by Example: Getting Started," and "AutoLISP by Example: Getting Better." For now, I'll provide you with the necessary AutoLISP code for these examples. Go ahead and copy it.

Because AutoLISP functions can be typed at the command line in AutoCAD, AutoLISP code can be placed directly within a script file as long as it is enclosed in parentheses. I use that feature in these solutions only to load an AutoLISP file. Most of the AutoLISP code resides in its own separate file.

For the purpose of these examples, specific folder names and filenames are used. To complete these exercises, create the following folders:

- `C:\Sybex`
- `C:\Sybex\DWG`

Once the folders exist, place some sample drawings in the `C:\Sybex\DWG` folder.

- Include one drawing named `new-border.dwg`, which will be used in the border update example.
- Include a few drawings whose file names start with the characters `D5`.
- Copy some of the symbol drawings from the `C:\Program Files\AutoCAD 2007\Sample\DesignCenter\` folder, and rename them by adding `SYM` at the beginning of each file name.

Putting Them All Together

All these files—batch, script, and Lisp—must work together to accomplish the task of updating a lot of drawings. That makes troubleshooting this system at least three times more difficult than if it used a single file. So, let me make a point about frustration. When you do any kind of programming, the chances are good that when you test it, it won't work. Why? For one thing, it's easy to overlook a little thing, like a ↵ or an option to a command; but the primary reason is that it's difficult to type anything without a typo. Treat this troubleshooting process like a puzzle, and maybe it'll be fun. Honest. Just don't expect perfection the first (or second) time.

Troubleshooting

What if you create these three files and fire up the batch file, and things don't work the first time? Start by looking for the most common typos. Next, look for clues that can help you pinpoint which of the three files may be the culprit, so you can focus your attention in the right place. With that in mind, here's a little troubleshooting advice:

Typos Carefully review each file for typing errors, which may be obvious or subtle:

- 1 and l look a lot alike. What, you think I just typed the same character? Nope, I typed the number one and a lowercase *L*.
- O and 0 can get you, too (in the old days, that zero would have had a dot in the middle).
- 2 and Z can fool you on a bad day.

Batch file Look here if AutoCAD never opens, or if it opens but can't "find the specified drawing file":

- Check to see whether the first line of the batch file worked. If the new folder was created, you know the batch file was named correctly.

- Count quotation marks in the second line. If you don't have an even number, figure out why.

- Quote filenames and folder names that contain spaces. That includes putting quotes around the variable name %%f, but only when it follows the program name acad.exe.

- Sometimes case matters. The variables %%f and %%F aren't the same. Make sure you haven't changed the case in the second reference.

- Make sure you haven't left out a space. Check in front of the /b switch.

Script file Look here if AutoCAD opens a drawing file but goes no further. Press the F2 key to see the entire text history, and look for a line showing that the program stopped working:

- Check the line that loads the AutoLISP file to make sure you used a double backslash to separate folder and filenames.

- Make sure there are no extra spaces within a line or at the ends of lines.

- Make sure any command option is separated from its command name by one space.

- Make sure there are no extra lines at the beginning or end of the file.

AutoLISP file This file will be harder to troubleshoot if you have no experience yet with AutoLISP:

- Be even more careful about spelling errors on words like *defun*, because they won't be as familiar to you as English words.

- Make sure there's no space after the C: in the first line of each AutoLISP program. The C: defines the new function as an AutoCAD command name and should appear as C:WBOUT(), for example.

- Anything between quotes must appear exactly as shown in each example. Don't add any spaces that shouldn't be there.

Use a text editor for programming, not a word processor. Smart quotes and other specialty characters can cause programs to fail even if you've saved the file in text format.

Example 1: Reducing File Size

The first example of a solution for automated updating involves reducing the size of all drawing files within one or more directories to their minimum. I use the WBLOCK command, but you can use the PURGE command instead. This solution was written for an office that wanted to clean up archived drawings, eliminating unused layer names, block definitions, dimension styles, and so on to reduce the amount of space they took up.

The batch file starts AutoCAD, loads the first drawing in the named directory, executes the script file, and waits until AutoCAD finishes with that drawing so it can go on and load the next file in the directory. The script file loads the AutoLISP file, runs the command it defines, and then quits AutoCAD. The AutoLISP file gets the name of the drawing and uses the WBLOCK command to save it with the same name, but in a different directory. Once the script file quits AutoCAD, the whole process returns to the batch file and continues until all the files are processed.

STEP 1: *WBOUT.BAT*

Use a text editor to create the following batch file, and save it as wbout.bat in the folder C:\Sybex. Type the entire FOR statement on one line. When you type it in a text editor, it will appear as a single line, even though it appears on multiple lines here. This batch file has only two lines of text:

```
MD C:\Sybex\DWG\wb
FOR %%f in (C:\Sybex\DWG\*.dwg) DO START /WAIT
➥C:\"Program Files"\"AutoCAD 2007"\acad.exe "%%f" /b
➥C:\Sybex\wbout.scr
```

When you execute this batch file, AutoCAD starts, and opens each drawing. Because of the /b switch, the script file named wbout.scr runs every time AutoCAD starts. When all files with a .dwg extension have been processed (made equal to variable %%f), the program stops.

Table 7.2 shows the purpose of each line.

	LINE IN BATCH FILE	PURPOSE
Table 7.2 wbout.bat	MD C:\Sybex\DWG\wb	This line makes a new folder named wb within the C:\Sybex\DWG folder. The drawing files created in this example are placed in this folder.
	FOR %%f in (C:\Sybex\DWG*.dwg) DO START /WAIT C:\"Program Files"\"AutoCAD 2007"\acad.exe "%%f" /b C:\Sybex\wbout.scr	FOR each filename represented by the replaceable parameter %%f, within the folder named C:\Sybex\DWG, DO the following: START a Windows application, and WAIT for it to finish before continuing on to the next file in the directory.
		The Windows application is the ACAD.EXE program. When it's started, load the drawing whose name is represented by the replaceable parameter %%f, and run the script named wbout.scr, which is located in the C:\Sybex\ folder.

I used the default path for AutoCAD in all of these examples. If you installed AutoCAD in a location other than the default, edit this file so it uses your path. You can omit the path and use only the filename ACAD.EXE unless there is more than one ACAD.EXE file on your computer. This can happen if you have multiple releases of AutoCAD or if you have one or more vertical applications. It's generally better to be explicit in giving a path.

STEP 2: *WBOUT.SCR*

Use a text editor to create the following script file, and save it as wbout.scr in C:\Sybex with wbout.bat. You should have five lines of text, with *no* extra spaces or extra lines anywhere. You must press ↵ at the end of the last line, but only once:

```
(load "C:\\Sybex\\wbout.lsp")
ZOOM All
WBOUT
QUIT
Y
```

When AutoCAD runs this script, an AutoLISP file is loaded that defines WBOUT, a new AutoCAD command. The script runs the WBOUT command and then quits AutoCAD.

Table 7.3 shows the purpose of each line.

LINE IN SCRIPT FILE	PURPOSE
(load "C:\\Sybex\\wbout.lsp")	This line of AutoLISP code loads the wbout.lsp file. Note the \\.
ZOOM All	This is here to make a change in the drawing. Otherwise, AutoCAD won't allow a file to be saved by the WBLOCK command, which is used in the AutoLISP program.
WBOUT	This is the name of the new command defined in wbout.lsp. Placing it here executes that command.
QUIT	The AutoCAD QUIT command closes AutoCAD without saving the drawing file that was opened.
Y	This confirms that AutoCAD should quit without saving. See the following note for an explanation.

Table 7.3

wbout.scr

The QUIT command, when used in a script, results in a different prompt than it does when used in AutoCAD directly. The prompt for the script version is Really want to discard all changes to drawing? <N>, which requires the response **Y** to quit without saving.

STEP 3: *WBOUT.LSP*

Use a text editor to create the following AutoLISP file, and save it as wbout.lsp in the folder C:\Sybex:

```
(defun C:WBOUT(/ dn pa pawbdn)
    (setq dn (getvar "dwgname"))
    (setq pa (getvar "dwgprefix"))
    (setq pawbdn (strcat pa "wb\\" dn))
    (command "WBLOCK" pawbdn "*")
)
```

This program gets the current drawing name, issues the WBLOCK command, selects all entities in the drawing (that's what the * does), and saves the drawing in the new \WB folder with the same filename as the original drawing file.

Table 7.4 shows the purpose of each line.

Table 7.4

[.] wbout.lsp

LINE IN AUTOLISP FILE	PURPOSE
(defun C:WBOUT(/ dn pa pawbdn)	This line defines the new function named WBOUT. The C: makes it an AutoCAD command. Leave a space after the forward slash.
(setq dn (getvar "dwgname"))	This line gets the name of the current drawing and saves it as a variable. Type both quotes.
(setq pa (getvar "dwgprefix"))	This line gets the path of the current drawing and saves it as a variable.
(setq pawbdn (strcat pa "wb\\" dn))	This line creates a new path by adding the folder WB to the existing path where the current drawing is stored.
(command "WBLOCK" pawbdn "*")	This is the line that saves the drawing in the new WB folder using the same drawing name.
)	This line closes the opening parenthesis in the file. Every opening parenthesis must have a closing one.

By using a Lisp program to change the drawing and then save it to a new location, you can get the current location and the current filename, modify them by appending a new folder name, and store them as variables. This can't be done using a script file alone.

STEP 4: RUN THE PROGRAM

Once there are drawing files in the C:\Sybex folder, you can start this process by running the batch file. The batch file gets the whole thing moving, because it selects each drawing file and starts AutoCAD with the proper script. You can run this program from the Run window, a command prompt, Explorer, My Computer, or a desktop shortcut.

For now, use Explorer to find the C:\Sybex folder. Double-click the wbout.bat icon; or select it, right-click, and select Open. See Figure 7.3. If everything goes well, you can sit

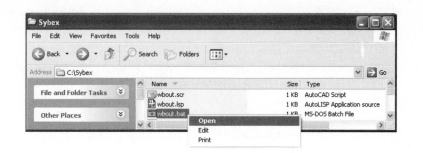

Figure 7.3

Running a batch file

back and watch AutoCAD opening and closing as it modifies each file. When the batch file is completed, the DOS window closes. Look in the C:\Sybex\DWG\WB folder, and see whether your new files are there.

> Don't double-click a batch file if you only want to edit it. To change text, select Edit from the right-click menu. Double-clicking automatically launches the batch file. (You can also launch the batch file by selecting Open from the right-click menu.)

You may have to try this several times. If so, delete the \WB folder before running the batch file a second time. Otherwise, you'll get a prompt asking you if you want to replace the existing drawings as AutoCAD tries to save files with the same name to the \WB folder.

Using this collection of programs—a batch file, a script, and an AutoLISP routine—can greatly reduce the space used for archiving DWG files. However, as with any automated process, there are a number of things to consider, including whether you really want to eliminate all unused layers, block references, text styles, and dimension styles from the drawings.

This kind of programming should be tested carefully on a limited number of test files before you use it. Once you've run this program and are convinced that it did what you wanted, you can delete the old files and place the new files where you want them.

Example 2: Redefining Existing Block Definitions

I devised this second solution for a company that had been purchased and renamed. The company didn't want to send out or plot any existing drawings with the old name in the title block. Over a number of years, the company had inserted the same title block drawing into all of its AutoCAD drawings, and now it wanted to redefine the resulting block reference in all of them. I had one preliminary question: Did the company ever explode its title blocks? It hadn't, which is why this system worked. Except for the logo and company information, the new title block and the old title block were identical, so all it needed to do was replace the definition for the Border block in each drawing.

If you want to try this example, you'll have to create a drawing with entities representing a title block in Model Space and save the drawing with the name new-border.dwg. Place it in the C:\Sybex\DWG folder along with several drawings that have a block reference named border. The new-border.dwg file is used to update the border Block definitions in each drawing.

REPLACING EXISTING FILES

You can make this process replace existing drawings by altering the behavior of wbout.1sp. I don't recommend replacing drawings directly, but if you have a limited amount of drive space, you may not be able to store two copies of each drawing until you're done.

This requires some changes to the AutoLISP program. Before you try this, make sure you really understand what you're doing and are convinced the program works.

Remove the reference to the \wb folder, set EXPERT to 4 in your AutoLISP program, and reset it when the program is finished, as follows:

```
(defun C:WBOUT (/  dn pa padn x)       ;define a new command WBOUT
    (setq x(getvar "expert"))           ;get current expert value
    (setq dn (getvar "dwgname"))        ;get name of current drawing
    (setq pa (getvar "dwgprefix"))      ;get location of current drawing
    (setq padn (strcat pa dn))          ;combine path and name of drawing
    (setvar "expert" 4)                 ;suppress warnings
    (command "wblock" padn "*")         ;replace existing drawing
    (setvar "expert" x)                 ;reset value of expert
)                                       ;closes the first parenthesis
```

It's wise to add an error-trapping function to this new program, to make sure the value for EXPERT is returned to its original setting, no matter what. See Chapter 9.

STEP 1: *TBUPDATE.BAT*

Use a text editor to create the following batch file, and save it as C:\Sybex\tbupdate.bat. Type the entire FOR statement on one line. When you type it in a text editor, it will appear as a single line, even though it appears on multiple lines here. This file has only two lines of text:

```
MD C:\Sybex\DWG\NewBorder
FOR %%f in (C:\Sybex\DWG\d5*.dwg) DO START /WAIT
➥C:\"Program Files"\"AutoCAD 2007"\acad.exe "%%f" /b
➥C:\Sybex\tbupdate.scr
```

Table 7.5 shows the purpose of each line.

LINE IN BATCH FILE	PURPOSE
MD C:\Sybex\DWG\NewBorder	This line makes a new folder named NewBorder in the C:\Sybex\DWG folder. The drawing files created in this example are placed in this folder.
FOR %%f in (C:\Sybex\DWG\d5*.dwg) DO START /WAIT C:\"Program Files"\"AutoCAD 2007"\acad.exe "%%f" /b C:\Sybex\tbupdate.scr	FOR each file name represented by the replaceable parameter %%f, within the folder named C:\Sybex\DWG, DO the following: START a Windows application, and WAIT for it to finish before continuing on to the next file whose name begins with D5 in the directory.
	The Windows application is the ACAD.EXE program. When it's started, load the drawing whose name is represented by the replaceable parameter %%f, and run the script named tbupdate.scr, which is located in the C:\Sybex\ folder.

Table 7.5

tbupdate.bat

This example is more selective about the files being processed than the first example. Only drawings whose names begin with the characters D5 are opened.

STEP 2: *TBUPDATE.SCR*

Use a text editor to create the following script file, and save it as tbupdate.scr in a folder named C:\Sybex. You should have eight lines (one is blank), with *no* extra spaces anywhere. You must press ↵ at the end of the last line, but only once:

```
INSERT border=C:\Sybex\DWG\new-border.dwg
0,0 1 1 0
ERASE L

(load "C:\\Sybex\\tbupdate.lsp")
TBUPDATE
QUIT
Y
```

When AutoCAD runs this script, an AutoLISP file is loaded that defines TBUPDATE, a new AutoCAD command. The script runs the TBUPDATE command and then quits AutoCAD.

Table 7.6 shows the purpose of each line.

STEP 3: *TBUPDATE.LSP*

Use a text editor to create the following AutoLISP file, and save it as tbupdate.lsp in the folder C:\Sybex:

```
(defun C:TBUPDATE(/  dn pa panbdn)
   (setq dn (getvar "dwgname"))
   (setq pa (getvar "dwgprefix"))
   (setq panbdn (strcat pa "NewBorder\\" dn))
   (command "SAVE" panbdn )
)
```

It gets the current drawing name and saves the drawing in the new NewBorder folder with the same filename as the original drawing file. The WBLOCK command isn't used here because it isn't necessary. This system isn't designed to reduce the file sizes.

Table 7.7 shows the purpose of each line.

STEP 4: RUN THE PROGRAM

Double-click the tbupdate.bat icon; or select it, right-click, and choose Open. This one goes by quickly. Look in the C:\Sybex\DWG\NewBorder folder and see whether your new files are there. Open one to see if the block did in fact update.

Table 7.6 tbupdate.scr	LINE IN SCRIPT FILE	PURPOSE
	INSERT border=C:\Sybex\DWG\ new-border.dwg	Using the INSERT command in this manner redefines the existing block reference border using the entities in Model Space in the drawing new-border.dwg.
	0,0 1 1 0	The block reference created from the NEW-BORDER drawing is inserted at 0,0. X and Y scale factors and a rotation angle are required when inserting a block reference. Here, you use scale factors of 1 and a rotation angle of 0.
	ERASE L	This line erases the last object created, which is the block reference just inserted. Why erase it? Because the only reason to insert it is to update the existing block reference. Once that is accomplished, this additional reference isn't needed.
		This blank line is used as a ↵ to exit the Select Objects prompt of the ERASE command.
	(load "C:\\Sybex\\tbupdate.lsp")	This line loads the AutoLISP program that is used to save the drawing file.
	TBUPDATE	This is the name of the new command defined in tbupdate.lsp that saves the resulting updated drawing file. Placing it here executes that command.
	QUIT	The AutoCAD QUIT command closes AutoCAD without saving the drawing file that was opened.
	Y	This confirms that AutoCAD should quit without saving.
		↵ with no spaces.

Table 7.7 tbupdate.lsp	LINE IN AUTOLISP FILE	PURPOSE
	(defun C:TBUPDATE(/ dn pa panbdn)	This line defines the new command TBUPDATE.
	(setq dn (getvar "dwgname"))	This line gets the name of the current drawing file and saves it to a variable named dn.
	(setq pa (getvar "dwgprefix"))	This line gets the path of the current drawing file and saves it to the variable pa.
	(setq panbdn (strcat pa "NewBorder\\" dn))	This line creates a new path by adding NewBorder\\ to the existing path where the drawings are saved.
	(command "SAVE" panbdn)	This line saves the drawing in the NewBorder folder using the same drawing name.
	)	This line closes the opening parenthesis in the file.

Example 3: Creating Drawings from Block Definitions

I wrote this one for an architectural firm that decided to change its system for managing its library of symbols. The company had been using single drawings with related groups of block definitions to store symbol libraries. It decided it would prefer to have a separate drawing file for each of the block definitions used and assigned the task of creating them to a recently hired designer. After doing a few, he called me to see if there was some way to reduce the tedium of manually creating the drawing files.

The purpose of this final example is to automatically open a group of drawings that contain block definitions and create a new drawing file from each of them. It uses the same process as in examples 1 and 2, but with a somewhat more involved AutoLISP program.

STEP 1: *BLOCKOUT.BAT*

Use a text editor to create the following batch file, and save it as `C:\Sybex\blockout.bat`. Type the entire FOR statement on one line. When you type it in a text editor, it will appear as a single line, even though it appears on multiple lines here. Like the earlier examples, this file has only two lines of text. For an explanation for what this file does, see Table 7.8:

```
MD C:\Sybex\DWG\NewBlocks
FOR %%f in (C:\Sybex\DWG\sym*.dwg) DO START /WAIT
➥C:\"Program Files"\"AutoCAD 2007"\acad.exe "%%f" /b
➥C:\Sybex\blockout.scr
```

STEP 2: *BLOCKOUT.SCR*

Use a text editor to create the following script file, and save it as `blockout.scr` in the folder named `C:\Sybex`. You should have four lines with no blank lines anywhere in the file. You must press ↵ at the end of the last line, but only once:

```
(load "C:\\Sybex\\blockout.lsp")
BLOCKOUT
QUIT
Y
```

LINE IN BATCH FILE	PURPOSE
`MD C:\Sybex\DWG\NewBlocks`	This line makes a new folder named `NewBlocks` in the `C:\Sybex\DWG` folder. The drawing files created in this example are placed in this folder.
`FOR %%f in (C:\Sybex\DWG\sym*.dwg) DO START /WAIT C:\"Program Files"\"AutoCAD 2007"\acad.exe "%%f" /b C:\Sybex\blockout.scr`	FOR each filename represented by the replaceable parameter `%%f`, in the folder named `C:\Sybex\DWG`, DO the following: START a Windows application, and WAIT for it to finish before continuing on to the next file whose name begins with Sym in the directory. The Windows application is the `ACAD.EXE` program. When it's started, load the drawing whose name is represented by the replaceable parameter `%%f`, and run the script named `blockout.scr`, which is located in the `C:\Sybex\` folder.

Table 7.8

`tbupdate.bat`

It isn't necessary to do a ZOOM ALL in this example. Once the Block definitions have been extracted using the `blockout.lsp` program, the drawing can be closed.

Table 7.9 shows the purpose of each line.

Table 7.9

blockout.scr

LINE IN SCRIPT FILE	PURPOSE
`(load "C:\\Sybex\\blockout.lsp")`	This line of AutoLISP code loads the `blockout.lsp` file. Note the \\.
`BLOCKOUT`	This is the name of the new command defined in `blockout.lsp`. Placing it here executes that command.
`QUIT`	The AutoCAD QUIT command closes AutoCAD without saving the drawing file that was opened.
`Y`	This confirms that AutoCAD should quit without saving.
	↵ with no spaces.

STEP 3: *BLOCKOUT.LSP*

Use a text editor to create the following AutoLISP file, and save it as `blockout.lsp` in the folder `C:\Sybex`. Table 7.10 shows the purpose of each line:

```
(defun C:BLOCKOUT (/  dn pa sl blkdata blname fullname)
   (setq dn (getvar "dwgname"))
    (setq pa (getvar "dwgprefix"))
    (setq sl (strcat pa "NewBlocks\\"  dn))
    (setq blkdata (tblnext "BLOCK" T))
      (while blkdata
         (setq blname (cdr (assoc 2 blkdata)))
         (setq fullname (strcat sl blname))
         (command "WBLOCK" fullname blname)
         (setq blkdata (tblnext "BLOCK"))
      )
   )
```

STEP 4: RUN THE PROGRAM

Put some DWG files that contain block definitions into the `C:\Sybex\DWG` folder. Then, double-click the `blockout.bat` icon; or select it, right-click, and choose Open. This one is fun because it shows you each drawing file in a preview window as the program creates it from a block definition. Look in the `C:\Sybex\DWG\NewBlocks` folder, and see whether your new files are there. Open one to see if it contains the entities used to define the original block.

LINE IN AUTOLISP FILE	PURPOSE	
`(defun C:BLOCKOUT (/ dn pa s1 blkdata blname fullname)`	This line defines the new command BLOCKOUT.	Table 7.10
`(setq dn (getvar "dwgname"))`	This line gets the name of the current drawing and saves it to the variable dn.	`blockout.lsp`
`(setq pa (getvar "dwgprefix"))`	This line gets the path of the current drawing and saves it to the variable pa.	
`(setq s1 (strcat pa "NewBlocks\\" dn))`	This line adds a new folder name to the path, appends the drawing name to the end of the path, and saves the result to the variable s1.	
`(setq blkdata (tblnext "BLOCK" T))`	This line sets the variable blkdata to the first name in the list of block definitions.	
`(while blkdata`	This line uses the while function to begin the loop through the following steps while blkdata has a value.	
`(setq blname (cdr (assoc 2 blkdata)))`	This line sets blname equal to the name of the next block definition in the list.	
`(setq fullname (strcat s1 blname))`	This line creates a variable fullname from the path and block name set in the variables s1 and blname. The result is a drawing file whose name is a combination of the name of the current drawing file and the name of the block definition.	
`(command "WBLOCK" fullname blname)`	This is the line that does the work. It uses the WBLOCK command to create a drawing file from the block definition and save it to the new location with the new filename.	
`(setq blkdata (tblnext "BLOCK"))`	This sets blkdata equal to the next block definition in the list, which causes the While function to repeat the previous three lines. Once all the block definitions have been used, blkdata is nil, and the WHILE function causes the program to execute the next line.	
`)`	This ends the WHILE function.	
`)`	This ends the program.	

Other Possibilities

In your own company or practice, you'll find many other possibilities for using this updating system. I certainly have. I've used it for lots of different companies, all of whom have specific, even unique, needs. Here's a short list of applications:

- Extract the title block attributes from all drawings.
- Convert layer names to a new standard using the RENAME command.
- Change page setups for all drawings.
- Create WMF files from a group of drawings.
- Batch-plot all the drawings in a folder and subfolders.

Even if you don't have a specific use for this system right now, try it anyway. It's a great way to develop troubleshooting skills with each of these types of files. The more you understand this system, the more likely you are to find a use for it.

CHAPTER 8

AutoLISP by Example: Getting Started

I don't know why more users don't write programs in AutoLISP; perhaps the very notion of programming is too intimidating. And yet nothing has more potential to expand your AutoCAD efficiency than programming new commands. Of all the programming tools out there, AutoLISP is the most accessible to AutoCAD users; but do I really think every user should know how to program in AutoLISP? Yes, I do—and you'll see why as you work through this chapter.

If the prospect of programming leaves you a bit daunted, I've got good news: If you can use AutoCAD, you can program in AutoLISP. To show you how easy it is, let's write a program right now. Just follow these steps:

1. At the AutoCAD command line, type this: **(defun C:OO()(setvar "osmode" 4143))**↵.

2. Clear your osnap settings in the Object Snap tab of the Drafting Settings dialog box.

3. Type **OO**↵ at the command line.

Congratulations, you've just written an AutoLISP program. To see what it did, check the settings for running object snaps again. We'll get back to this program after I give you a little background. When you finish this chapter, you'll be thinking up—and creating— all kinds of useful new AutoLISP functions of your own.

- ▪ **Background**

- ▪ **Writing AutoLISP Programs**

- ▪ **AutoLISP Examples**

- ▪ **Automatic Loading**

Background

AutoLISP is a powerful customizing tool with which you can write useful new AutoCAD commands in minutes. Although other programming languages are often used with AutoCAD (most notably Visual Basic for Applications [VBA] and C++), AutoLISP is an especially good choice for AutoCAD users because it relies heavily on native AutoCAD commands. It may not be the most sophisticated programming language, but what do you care as long as it's easy to use? Every accomplished VBA programmer I know still uses AutoLISP for some AutoCAD-related programming.

The AutoLISP programming language first appeared in AutoCAD R2.18. Its early appearance is one of the reasons AutoCAD is the most widely used CAD program today. The existence of a programming language made it possible for savvy users to dramatically improve AutoCAD by adding new functions. Those functions often became commands in later releases, but even when they didn't, they made AutoCAD much more useful than competing applications. Despite the appearance of other programming languages since its inception, AutoLISP is still the primary means by which users customize AutoCAD.

AutoLISP is a subset of LISP (List Processing), which goes back to the late 1950s. I've often seen LISP referred to as the second-oldest programming language still in use, Fortran being the oldest. In addition to its use in AutoCAD, LISP is still used widely in Artificial Intelligence programming.

Visual LISP (VLISP or VLIDE) appeared in AutoCAD 2000 as a major enhancement to AutoLISP. It adds a development environment with debugging tools and a compiler, as well as a set of new functions, including some known as *reactors*. Although I'll introduce some features of the Visual LISP editor in this book, I can't do it justice here. Once you get the AutoLISP bug, you can learn more about special Visual LISP editing features and the extensive collection of Visual LISP functions by consulting AutoCAD's help system for more information or using your favorite search engine to find Visual LISP references.

> You can access the AutoLISP, Visual LISP, and Drawing Interchange File (DXF) documentation by choosing Help → Additional Resources → Developer Help from the AutoCAD menu.

AutoCAD Commands

Because some commands and many Express tools are written in AutoLISP, most of us use AutoLISP programs on a regular basis without knowing it. The C:\Program Files\AutoCAD 2007\Express directory contains 70 AutoLISP programs, including the following programs that are so useful you might think they're native commands.

- aliasedit.lsp
- aspace.lsp
- attout.lsp

- `break1.lsp`
- `bscale.lsp`
- `burst.lsp`
- `dimassoc.lsp`
- `flatten.lsp`
- `layoutmerge.lsp`
- `lman.lsp`
- `overkill.lsp`
- `saveall.lsp`
- `tcase.lsp`
- `textmask.lsp`
- `txtexp.lsp`

Finding AutoLISP Programs

You can find other AutoLISP programs at countless websites, in books, in magazines, and on the computers of your friends and colleagues. For a great place to start, visit the Autodesk User Group International website at www.AUGI.com. Other sites come and go, so I won't list them here, but a web search will turn up millions of AutoLISP programs on hundreds of thousands of sites. Many of them are free, because AutoLISP programmers are generous with their work. (Remember this when you become good enough to create useful programs.) Check the copyright information of any program you find, and always follow the author's requirements. After all, an AutoLISP program is the intellectual property of its author.

AutoLISP programs range from simple to complex, and they require a thorough knowledge of AutoCAD commands. Because you already know the AutoCAD command structure, you're ready to start programming in AutoLISP.

Writing AutoLISP Programs

I call this chapter "AutoLISP by Example" because I use code examples to demonstrate key features of programming. This chapter isn't for experienced programmers; it's for AutoCAD users. When I first decided to try AutoLISP, the reference I consulted began with a discussion about atoms, lists, Lambda expressions, cons, and Mapcar, with one-line examples that were out of context and meant nothing to me. I had a specific goal: to write a command that would automatically insert one drawing into another. I didn't solve my problem until I looked at actual programs to see how they worked. With that experience in mind, I'm going to give you sample programs and explain how they work. All you have to do is type them in correctly, try them, and read the explanations. It's that simple.

MY FIRST AUTOLISP PROGRAM

I taught introductory AutoCAD for the first time in 1989. At the outset, I knew I'd have to evaluate student work electronically to check their geometry for accuracy, so every week I loaded each student's drawing, used the DIST command and ID to check the dimensions and locations, zoomed in on the most likely problem areas, and otherwise attempted to be diligent about giving useful and timely feedback. But with 60 students submitting drawings once a week, grading took forever. Then I had a brainstorm—the one you probably had as soon as you started reading this sidebar. Why not insert my drawing directly on top of theirs, on a grade layer with a dashed linetype in a color students didn't use? That way I could eliminate a bunch of steps.

That helped, but not enough. I decided to automate the whole process, which meant I had to learn AutoLISP in a hurry. It seemed easy enough to use DEFUN to create a new command, and to run AutoCAD commands from an AutoLISP program. But I couldn't get my program to work. After hours of frustration, I opened all the AutoLISP programs I could find to see if any of them dealt with drawing files. And I discovered something puzzling: Whenever a program made a reference to a filename, it used a *double* backslash to separate folders and files in a path. Is that why I couldn't insert a drawing? Could it be that simple?

In a word: yes. I was hooked! Grading for three introductory classes became a breeze as I added more features to the grading commands. Students got their work back quickly, affording me more time for the real work of teaching. That's the true appeal of AutoLISP to me—a more interesting work life.

Program Structure

I want you to get started writing programs, but to avoid some common pitfalls, you should understand something about the structure of AutoLISP programs. These rules for program structure apply to all AutoLISP programs. They have the same importance to programming that the rules for sentence structure have to writing:

- Every program contains one or more AutoLISP functions, such as DEFUN, GETPOINT, +, and -.

- Each function name is preceded by an opening parenthesis.

- Every opening parenthesis must have a balancing closing parenthesis somewhere.

- Spaces or quotation marks are used to separate components within parentheses.

- Functions are followed by arguments to the function, if they're necessary.

Let's take a computational function as an example. Because the division function in AutoLISP is represented by the forward slash, the syntax for dividing two numbers is as follows: (/ 4.0 2).

An open parenthesis is followed by the function / which is followed by at least one space, which is followed by at least two arguments separated by spaces—the numerator 4.0 and the divisor 2—followed by a closing parenthesis. This function would be translated into English as "divide 4.0 by 2." Other functions, such as (* 4.0 2), (+ 4.0 2), and (- 4.0 2) are formatted the same way. This isn't the same structure you may expect from having studied math, so don't try using (2 + 2). It won't work, because the first element after the parenthesis is an integer, not a function.

Entering Programs in AutoCAD

You can do all the programming you want in your mind, but until you enter your programs into AutoCAD they won't do anything. Unfortunately, there is no way to dump the contents of your head directly into AutoCAD, so you have to do some typing. There are three ways to get AutoCAD to use an AutoLISP program:

- Type it at the command line.
- Load a text file that contains AutoLISP code.
- Use the load function of the Visual LISP editor.

Typing at the command line is generally used only for testing short lines of code. However, I often write a very short program this way when I need to do something that's so specific to the current drawing that there's no reason to save it. I did that recently to create polyline circles. I didn't think I'd need to do it again, so I just wrote a program at the command line. When I exited AutoCAD, the program ceased to exist.

UPPERCASE OR LOWERCASE?

There are only a few places where case matters in AutoLISP.

- When you place a control character, such as the new-line character, in a prompt or other quoted string, it must be in lowercase, as in "\nSelect point: ".

- When you indicate during a file-opening procedure how you want to treat the file (read, write, or append) the letters for that must also be lowercase, as in (open "c:\\file.dwg" "r").

Otherwise, it's your call whether to use uppercase or lowercase. Just be consistent, so you won't confuse yourself later.

Let's get the command-line procedure out of the way first.

Command-Line Entry

Go back to the program introduced in the introduction to this chapter. To enter that AutoLISP program at the command line, you did this:

1. You typed **(defun C:OO()(setvar "osmode" 4143))** ↵ at the command line. If you made no errors, **"C:OO"** appeared on the command line.

2. To test the program, you cleared your existing running osnaps.

3. To use the new command you created, you typed **OO** at the command line. You should have seen **"4143"** returned.

4. When you checked again, you should have had the following object snap settings: End, Mid, Cen, Nod, Int, Ext.

You just defined a new AutoCAD command with the name OO. When you type it, the setting for OSMODE, which controls your object snap settings, is changed to 4143. That happens to be the value of my standard running osnaps. I like this little command, because I often change to a single running object snap for a series of actions. When I want my old settings back, typing **OO** is much quicker than opening the Drafting Settings dialog box.

> AutoCAD uses system variables (sometimes referred to as *setvars*) to control many aspects of the program. All of AutoCAD's system variables (there are nearly 550 of them in AutoCAD 2007) can be read from AutoLISP using the GETVAR function, and many of them can be changed using the SETVAR function. OSMODE is such a setvar, for example. The more familiar you are with system variables, the more effectively you can use AutoLISP. You can view all setvars by typing **setvar** ↵**?** ↵* at the command prompt or looking at the alphabetically organized list in the Help system.

There's one problem. This nifty new command is stored in RAM, so it won't be available if you open another drawing, and it will disappear if you close the current drawing. If you want to use it again, you have to save it.

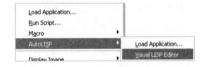

Creating and Saving AutoLISP Text Files

To create reusable programs, you must save them in a text file with an .1sp extension. Like the acad.pgp file, AutoLISP files are American Standard Code for Information Interchange (ASCII) text files and can be created in Notepad or any other text editor. However, I far prefer AutoCAD's Visual LISP text editor, which you can start from the command line by typing **VLISP** or by selecting it from Tools → AutoLISP → Visual LISP Editor.

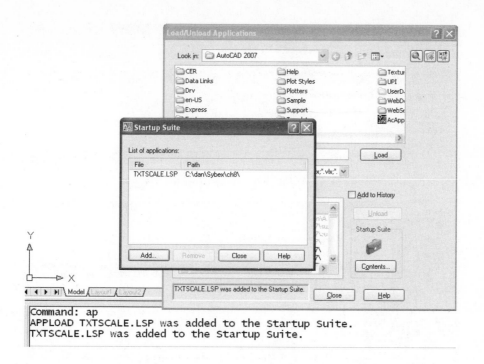

Figure 8.1

**Load/Unload Appli-
cations Startup Suite**

Once you've saved an AutoLISP file, you can load it using the APPLOAD (AP) command in AutoCAD. If you want it loaded every time you start AutoCAD, put the file in the Startup Suite of the Load/Unload Applications dialog box shown in Figure 8.1.

The Visual LISP Editor

Visual LISP has a couple of quirks. You can start Visual LISP by typing **VLISP** at the command line, but VLISP is actually an alias for Visual LISP Integrated Development Environment (VLIDE). It differs significantly from programs like Notepad. Because it's integrated into AutoCAD itself, it won't run on its own and must be started from an active AutoCAD drawing. While you're using it, it interacts with the AutoCAD drawing, so you should have an empty or dummy drawing open, not one that matters to you.

Unlike Notepad, the Visual LISP editor uses more than one window while you're editing a file:

- The text editor in which you type your program (more than one can be open)
- The Visual LISP Console, where you can type variable names or try small pieces of code
- The Trace window, which can be used while debugging
- The Build Output window, which shows the results of using the Check Edit Window button to check the program, including warnings and error messages

Figure 8.2

Four windows of the Visual LISP editor

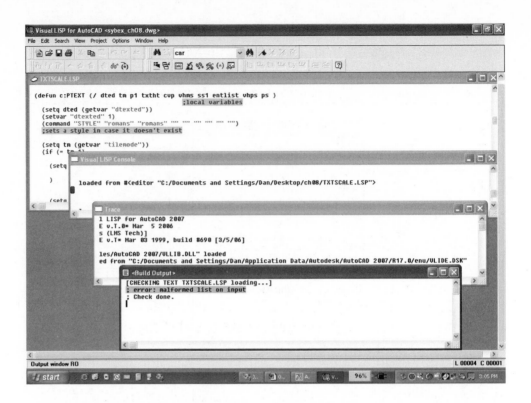

The four different windows are shown in Figure 8.2. Note that in the lower-right corner of the Visual LISP editor window is a report of both the line you're on and the character within that line (L00004 C 00001 in the illustration).

Although this illustration shows the four windows that can be open, they don't normally appear in this form. They may be minimized, placed on top of each other, or otherwise arranged. To keep them straight, notice that the three bottom windows have names that don't change: Visual LISP Console, Trace, and Build Output. You can minimize the Trace window and the Build Output window until you need them. The Visual LISP Console can be used for testing, but be careful—it's *not* where you type your program. That happens in the text editor, which in the illustration is the top window with the name TXTSCALE.LSP.

The text used in the text editor is displayed using different colors. The default colors are described in Table 8.1.

One more thing before you try your next AutoLISP text program. The tools I think you'll use most often are illustrated in Figure 8.3 on the Visual LISP toolbar. The Load Active Edit Window, Check Edit Window, and Format Edit Window tools apply to the

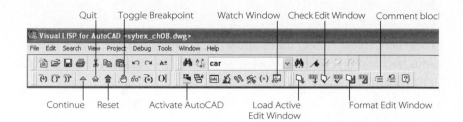

Figure 8.3

Selected toolbar buttons from the Visual LISP editor

COLOR	USED FOR
Blue	AutoLISP functions like /, DEFUN, and SETQ
Magenta	Strings, which are always between quotation marks
Black	User-created items, such as program variables and function names
Green	Integer values
Teal	Real numbers, which must have a decimal point
Maroon on gray	Comments, which are preceded by a semicolon

Table 8.1

Colors Used in the Visual LISP Text Editor

entire file, but each of these buttons has a tool button to its right. These buttons have the same functions but apply only to text you've selected. They're helpful when you're testing only a portion of the file.

Continue Continues running a program that you're testing after it stops at a break point.

Quit Stops the process when you're testing your program by executing it in a controlled fashion.

Reset Resets a program during testing. Use it when the replacement Visual LISP cursor—which looks like two parentheses—shows up when you're debugging a program.

You'll also see this button if you switch from AutoCAD to the Visual LISP editor while a command is still active. The Reset button won't be available then. You have to go back to Auto-CAD and exit the command.

Toggle Breakpoint Stops (breaks) the program at the cursor location as it runs so you can check for errors. A breakpoint is denoted by a red parenthesis.

Activate AutoCAD Switches from the Visual LISP editor to the AutoCAD drawing editor.

Watch Window Opens a window in which you can keep track of the value of your program variables, even local program variables, while debugging your program.

Load Active Edit Window Loads every line of code in the edit window—unless there are errors. The button to its right loads only text in the window that's been selected.

Check Edit Window Checks the structure (balanced parentheses, proper number of arguments, and so on) of the entire contents of the window. The results are displayed in the Build Output window. If an error is detected, place your cursor on the highlighted area in the Build Output window, and double-click to find the error in your program. The button to its right checks only highlighted text in the window.

Format Edit Window Formats the text in the entire window using rules that you can modify if you choose. Formatting doesn't affect how the code runs; it only affects how it looks. Until you have some experience writing AutoLISP programs, you should probably use the default settings. Like the two prior buttons, this one has a version to its right that you can use to format only highlighted text.

Comment Block Adds semicolons in front of the highlighted lines of text so AutoLISP won't try to execute them as part of the program. This is how you annotate your code.

I'll return to some of these tools in the debugging section.

AutoLISP Examples

Throughout this chapter, I'll use a number of programs to illustrate specific AutoLISP concepts. Neither this chapter nor the next is meant to cover all AutoLISP functions. In particular, I've omitted all discussion of the newer vl- prefixed functions. After you've digested the material in the next two chapters, I hope you'll develop programming skills that go well beyond what I'm covering here. In that process, don't overlook the Help system in the Visual LISP editor. It should be your first stop for answers to syntax questions about any particular function.

> You'll notice that many of the AutoCAD commands used in the programs in this chapter have a period and an underscore in front of their names. The period instructs AutoCAD to use the named command even if you've undefined it. The underscore tells AutoCAD to use the command, even if your version of AutoCAD is a non–English language version. Neither is necessary, but adding both is prudent.

At the beginning of this chapter, I showed you a simple AutoLISP program. Let's try another, so you can see how easy it is to define a new AutoCAD command. The two AutoLISP functions you need are DEFUN and COMMAND. But first, you need a problem whose solution requires a new command.

ZX Command

When you double-click the scroll wheel on your mouse, AutoCAD ZOOMs to the extents of your drawing, but that often puts entities too close to the edge of the screen. So, you roll the scroll wheel to zoom out just a little, but the screen zooms out too far. If only there were a command that would zoom to 95 percent of the extents, no matter what the current zoom magnification. Why not create one?

First, you have to identify the steps for performing the task manually. Then you can write an AutoLISP program that will execute the steps automatically.

To do a 95 percent zoom at the keyboard, you would have to go through the following steps:

1. Type **ZOOM**↵.

2. Type **E** for Extents and ↵.

3. Type **ZOOM** again, or ↵ to repeat the last command.

4. Type **.95X**↵.

The solution here is to combine all four steps into a single new AutoCAD command named ZX. To create the program, use the following steps:

1. Start AutoCAD.

2. Start the Visual LISP environment by typing **VLISP** or **VLIDE**, or by choosing Tools → AutoLISP → Visual LISP Editor.

3. Start a new file using the New File option of the File pull-down menu in the Visual LISP editor.

4. Add the following three lines to your new file:

```
(defun C:ZX ()
  (command "._ZOOM" "E" "._ZOOM" ".95x")
)
```

5. Pick the Load Active Edit Window button as shown in Figure 8.3.

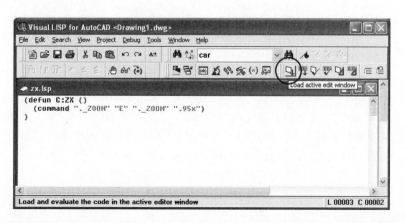

Figure 8.4

ZX program in the Visual LISP editor

6. Switch back to AutoCAD, and draw some objects.

7. Type **ZX** at the command line.

That's it. These three lines compose an entire AutoLISP program, which creates a new command named ZX that can be typed at the command line like any other command. By duplicating this basic format, you can create hundreds of other new commands. Make sure you review and understand the following explanations for each line:

(defun C:ZX () This line begins with an opening parenthesis, indicating to AutoCAD that an AutoLISP function will follow. You must enclose all elements in parentheses, and you must have a closing parenthesis for every opening parenthesis. Notice that this line has two opening, but only one closing, parenthesis. The second closing parenthesis appears at the end of the program on line 3, all by itself.

An AUTOLISP expression name must appear first after an opening parenthesis. The word DEFUN is an AutoLISP expression, which stands for *define function*. It's blue when you type it in the Visual LISP editor.

The C:ZX means that the AutoLISP function you're defining will operate as if it were an AutoCAD command. This code is black when typed in the Visual LISP editor. The C: means *new AutoCAD command*. ZX is the name of the new AutoCAD command you're creating, which can be called like any native command—typed, assigned to a toolbar button, assigned to a key, added to a cursor menu, or assigned to a mouse button. You can name your new command nearly anything you want except an existing command name. Well, you *could* use an existing command name if you undefined the command first, but let's avoid using existing commands or aliases for now. ZX makes sense to me—your command names should make sense to you.

The two parentheses () at the end of the line are empty for this program, but they must be there. In other programs, they may contain arguments or user-defined local program variables—more on that later.

> One confusing aspect of AutoLISP is the C: that appears before a new function name that will act as an AutoCAD command. People automatically think "hard drive." Get that thought out of your head. The C: stands for AutoCAD command.

(command "._ZOOM" "E" "._ZOOM" ".95x") Once again, you start with an open parenthesis, so the first thing to appear must be the AutoLISP function. The COMMAND AutoLISP function allows you to use any native AutoCAD command within a new AutoLISP program. Use a command here, *not* an alias. "ZOOM" will work, but "Z" won't. Placing the dot and the underscore before the command name is optional.

This line of the code controls what happens on the screen when you use the ZX command. It issues the AutoCAD ZOOM command, followed by the E option. Then, it issues the ZOOM command again, followed by the scale option .95x. The entire line must be enclosed in parentheses. Anything you would normally type at the keyboard must be enclosed in quotes. In AutoLISP, anything in quotes is known as a *string*. Spaces between a closing quote and the next opening quote aren't necessary, but they make it easier to read your code.

> When you place a command like "ZOOM" in quotes, it's the same as typing it at the command line in AutoCAD followed by a ↵. If you want to include an additional ↵ in the command function, place two quotation marks with nothing between them: "". You need to do this for commands like LAYER, CHPROP, and DONUT to exit the command when you're done with it. If you need the equivalent of the Esc key, place the following line in your code: (command).

) This line is simple: It closes the first parenthesis in the program. Placing it by itself at the end of a program makes it easier for you to see where each program ends and to match it with its opening parenthesis. When you're trying to debug a program, formatting parentheses in this way is very helpful.

The Visual LISP editor does some formatting of your code as you type, and most AutoLISP programmers do even more as they're writing (or *coding*). Use the Format Edit Window button to clean up the whole program when it's done.

> Despite what many people think, computers do only what they're told. You must be specific about what you want a program to do. Before writing any new command, go through the process at the keyboard to make sure you remember each step. Do you need the second ZOOM in this program? Yes you do, but you may overlook it if you don't go through the steps at the keyboard first.

Using the new ZX command

After you create a new command, you have to load it. Then you can type the command name at the keyboard, add it to a toolbar button, or even assign it so that right-clicking the mouse while holding down the Ctrl key will execute the command.

Defining Other New Commands

A cardinal rule of programming is to reuse code (either yours or someone else's) whenever possible. With these three lines, you have the basic syntax to write dozens of new commands. ZA and ZP require only that you simplify the command by replacing E with A and removing the second call to the ZOOM command. Other commands can be substituted for ZOOM, with their own options. Once you understand the format for creating these commands, the sky is the limit.

Improving the CIRCLE command

Try this small improvement in the way a circle is created in AutoCAD (see Listing 8.1). As all designers know, a circle is normally defined by its diameter, not its radius. This program introduces the PAUSE function. For the remainder of this chapter, you can add new programs to one file (make sure each program is enclosed in parentheses) or start a new file for each one. That's up to you.

Each line of this program is described in Table 8.2.

Listing 8.1

circle-dia.lsp

```
(defun C:C()
  (command "._CIRCLE" pause "D")
)
```

If you're wondering why the computer keeps printing the term nil at the end of your programs, don't worry—it's not a statement about your programming ability. Every program has to return a value. If no other value results from running your program, the value nil is returned. The solution is to add a (princ) function just before the last parenthesis of a program. You'll see that line in most AutoLISP programs. After all, who wants to be called "nil" every time they run a program?

Table 8.2	LINE OF CODE	PURPOSE
circle-dia.lsp	(defun C:C()	This line defines a new AutoCAD command named C. Note that this is the alias for CIRCLE, but a loaded AutoLISP function takes precedent over a command alias of the same name.
	(command "._CIRCLE" pause "D")	This line executes the AutoCAD CIRCLE command, pauses so the user can select the center point for the circle, enters the option D for diameter, and stops.
	)	This closing parenthesis matches the opening parenthesis and ends the DEFUN function.

Inserting Drawing Files

Now let's apply what you've learned to a new command that will automatically insert an existing title block drawing into the current drawing (see Listing 8.2). You've already seen almost everything you need in order to understand this. In order to try the program as it's written, you have to place a title block drawing with the name `tbinch.dwg` in `C:\blocks`. When you're done typing, select the Load Active Edit Window tool again.

Each line of this code is described in Table 8.3.

Listing 8.2

`ITB.lsp`

```
(defun C:ITB()
    (command "._INSERT" "c:/blocks/tbinch.dwg" "0,0" "" "" "")
)
```

Table 8.3

`ITB.lsp`

LINE OF CODE	PURPOSE
`(defun C:ITB())`	This line defines a new command named ITB. I use uppercase for command names, but that isn't necessary.
`(command "._INSERT" "c:/blocks/tbinch.dwg" "0,0" "" "" "")`	This line executes the AutoCAD INSERT command, gives the path and name of a file to insert, places it at 0,0, and accepts the next three default settings for X-scale, Y-scale, and rotation.
	Notice anything about the path? You can't use a backslash to separate folders in AutoLISP. You can use a double backslash or a single forward slash.
	The other thing to notice is that using the three pairs of double quotes is equivalent to entering ┘┘┘ at the command line.
`)`	This closing parenthesis matches the opening parenthesis and ends the DEFUN function.

When you try the steps of this program at the command line in AutoCAD, suppress the dialog box that normally pops up by placing a minus in front of the command. -INSERT is the command-line version of INSERT. Do the same for the LAYER command. You don't have to include the dash within your program. AutoLISP understands when not to open a dialog box.

Using Variables

Let's clear up any potential confusion about the term *variables*. AutoCAD has something called *system* variables; these are values that control the appearance or behavior of Auto-CAD in some way. OSMODE is a system variable. You can determine the current setting for any system variable using the GETVAR function with the format (getvar "osmode").

You can also define your own *program* variables. You create these using the SETQ function of AutoLISP. The program variable you define can be used to represent almost anything: numbers, entities, anything typed by the user lists of coordinates, and so on.

To further complicate this distinction, the program variables that you define can be either *global* or *local*. If they're global, then once they're assigned a value of some kind, they keep that value even when your program is finished running. If the same variable name shows up again, it already has a value. To avoid unintended consequences, most users define program variables in AutoLISP programs as local—but not until they finish testing the program to make sure it works.

The program that created ZX required no additional information, either from the drawing or from the user. The ITB program you just wrote doesn't either, but maybe you can improve it. Wouldn't it be nice if the program automatically placed the title block on a particular layer? And wouldn't it be nice if it created the layer automatically after asking the user for a layer name and color? Although you'd probably prefer to put a standard layer name and color into the program by using a template, I'll show you the program in Listing 8.3 anyway, so you'll know how to get input from the user and save it to a program variable.

Listing 8.3

InsertTB.lsp

```
(defun C:InsertTB (/ lname lcolor ss1)
  (setq lname (getstring T "\nDestination layer: "))
  (setq lcolor (getstring "\nLayer Color: "))
  (command "._INSERT" "c:/blocks/tbinch.dwg" "0,0" "" "" "")
  (setq ss1 (entlast))
  (command "._LAYER" "N" lname "C" lcolor lname ""
           "_CHPROP" ss1 "" "LA"      lname ""))
)
```

Each line of this code is described in Table 8.4. An explanation of the new functions follows.

	LINE OF CODE	PURPOSE
Table 8.4 InsertTB.lsp	`(defun C:InsertTB(/ lname lcolor ss1)`	This line defines the new function that will act as a command named InsertTB with three local program variables. Local program variables are added here when you've finished the program and you know it works. Until you place them in this location, they're global program variables, not local.
	`(setq lname  (getstring T "\nDestination layer: "))`	This line sets the variable lname equal to whatever the user types in response to the prompt Destination Layer:. The T after getstring allows spaces to be included in the name. The \n is a control character meaning *new line* that tells AutoCAD to display the prompt on its own line. It must be lowercase.
	`(setq lcolor (getstring "\nLayer Color: "))`	This sets the variable lcolor equal to what the user types in response to the prompt that follows.

LINE OF CODE	PURPOSE
`(command "._INSERT" "c:/blocks/ tbinch.dwg" "0,0" "" "" "")`	This executes INSERT, identifies the path and name of the drawing to insert, gives 0,0 as the insertion point, and accepts the default values of 1, 1, and 0 for the options X-scale, Y-scale, and rotation.
`(setq ss1 (entlast))`	This line uses the function ENTLAST to set variable `ss1` equal to the last object created, which is the inserted title block.
`(command  "_LAYER" "N" lname "C" lcolor lname "" "_CHPROP" ss1 "" "LA" lname "")`	This line creates a new layer if it doesn't already exist, giving it the name stored as a string in `lname` and the color saved in `lcolor`. Then it executes another AutoCAD command, CHPROP, selects the object represented by the variable named `ss1`, issues ↵ to exit the selection prompt, and changes the layer the object is on to the string stored in the variable `lname`.
`)`	This line closes the DEFUN statement.

This program is a little more involved and introduces three new functions:

- SETQ creates program variables so values can be saved and used later in the program. There's a more involved discussion of the SETQ function later in the chapter, but you don't need to know anything else about it for now. Just use it as shown to store data.

- GETSTRING is a function that returns anything the user types at the keyboard. If you want users to be able to type something that contains spaces, you must include the letter T as one argument—`(getstring T "\nName of layer: ")`. The T can be either uppercase or lowercase, but the \n must be lowercase.

- ENTLAST selects the last entity created. Then, that entity can be assigned to a program variable.

Three program variables are created by the program: `lname`, `lcolor`, and `ss1`. I just made up their names. You can give program variables nearly any name, but here are some things to keep in mind:

- Use variable names that will make sense to you a month from now when you may be trying to understand what your program does. I use a consistent naming convention for similar types of program variables. If I have multiple program variables representing selection sets, strings points, angles, distances, radiuses, diameter, and so on, I try to use program variables names like `ss1`, `st1`, `pt1`, `ang1`, `dist1`, `rad1`, and `dia1`. However, this system works only on relatively simple programs. On longer programs, you should use more descriptive names.

- Don't use existing AutoLISP functions as variable names. You'll know you've done so when the name is colored blue instead of black when you type it into the Visual LISP editor. For example, PI, SET, and SETQ are AutoLISP functions and shouldn't be redefined as program variables. Once you've redefined a built-in function, it's no longer interpreted as a function.

- You can use numbers in variable names, but a variable name can't be all numbers. The name must include at least one letter and no spaces; the only other characters allowed are $, _, <, >, and -.

GET Functions

GETSTRING isn't the only GET function. Table 8.5 shows all the functions designed to get information, with a brief description of each. These functions get information from the user, the drawing, or the environment (operating system).

Let's use some GET functions in another program to demonstrate how you can take points apart and put them back together.

Table 8.5

GET functions in AutoLISP

FUNCTION	PURPOSE
GETANGLE	Asks the user for an angle in radians, to be entered by typing or picking two points.
GETCORNER	Asks the user to pick or enter coordinates for the opposite corner of a rectangle.
GETDIST	Returns a real number provided by the user by typing or picking two points.
GETENV	Asks theregistry for the value of an environmental variable, like "username." OS variables aren't case sensitive, but AutoCAD environmental variables are: for example, "Max-Hatch," and "MaxArray."
GETFILED	Asks the user to select a file using a dialog box.
GETINT	Asks the user for an integer, to be entered by typing or through the transparent use of 'CAL or 'QUICKCALC.
GETKWORD	Asks the user for a string that must match a previously defined keyword.
GETORIENT	Similar to GETANGLE, but is always based on a default 0 angle of east.
GETPOINT	Asks the user for a point, to be entered by typing or selecting a point.
GETREAL	Asks the user for a real number, to be entered by typing or through the transparent use of 'CAL or 'QUICKCALC.
GETSTRING	Asks the user for a string—any characters that can be typed.
GETVAR	Asks the drawing or registry for the value of an AutoCAD system variable, such as OSMODE.
INITGET	Establishes acceptable responses to other requests, particularly GETKWORD.
SSGET	Asks the user or the drawing for a selection set of objects.

Creating New Points

Two methods are especially useful for creating new points from user input. The first is to construct new points by calculating an X, a Y, and a Z coordinate, and then putting them into a list of three values using the LIST function. The second is to determine how far and at what angle a point is from another point, using the POLAR function.

Creating Points from Coordinates

In this next program, the user is prompted for two points. The program draws a rectangle using those points as corners and then adds lines across the corners to create an end-section symbol for a piece of structural lumber.

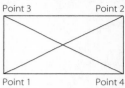

The program in Listing 8.4 asks the user to select the first corner of the rectangle, and then the opposite corner. Once you have those two points, the program uses them to create a new point from the X value of one point and the Y value of the other. The program then creates the fourth point. All these points are saved as program variables, which you then use to draw a rectangle and the two lines.

Listing 8.4

SSECT.1sp

```
(defun C:SSECT (/ pt1 pt2 pt3 pt4)
  (setq pt1 (getpoint "\nFirst corner of rectangle: "))
  (setq pt2 (getcorner "\nDiagonal corner of rectangle " pt1))
  (setq pt3 (list (nth 0 pt1) (nth 1 pt2)))
  (setq pt4 (list (nth 0 pt2) (nth 1 pt1)))
  (command "._RECTANG" pt1 pt2 "._LINE" pt1 pt2 "" "._LINE" pt3 pt4 "")
)
```

Each line of this code is described in Table 8.6.

Table 8.6
SSECT.1sp

LINE OF CODE	PURPOSE
(defun C:SSECT (/ pt1 pt2 pt3 pt4)	This line creates a new command named SSECT and identifies the program variables as local. Local variables retain the value given to them only while the program is running. If you hadn't placed them in the parentheses, they would be global program variables and would retain their values after the program ended. Note the space after the forward slash.
(setq pt1 (getpoint "\nFirst corner of rectangle: "))	This line sets the variable pt1 equal to a point supplied by the user. The quoted string will be displayed at the command line. The \n (must be lowercase) is a control character that means *new line*. If you leave it out, the prompt is placed on the same line in the AutoCAD command window as the last information printed there.
(setq pt2 (getcorner "\nDiagonal corner of rectangle " pt1))	This line sets the variable pt2 equal to the point supplied by the user in response to the prompt for the GETCORNER function. GETCORNER differs from GETPOINT because it displays a rectangle on the screen as the user moves the cursor to select the second point. Note that the first point (pt1) must be referenced in this line either before or after the prompt.
(setq pt3 (list (nth 0 pt1) (nth 1 pt2)))	Working from the inside out, you can say that this line takes the X value of pt1 and the Y value of pt2 and combines them into a new point.
	In AutoLISP, a coordinate point is a list of three values. To create a new point, you need to create a list of at least two values. The function LIST is used to create a new list.

continues

continued

LINE OF CODE	PURPOSE
	To create pt3, you use the X coordinate of pt1 using (nth 0 pt1) and the Y coordinate of pt2 using (nth 1 pt2). The list of two values is assigned to the variable pt3 by the SETQ function.
`(setq pt4 (list (nth 0 pt2) (nth 1 pt1)))`	This line sets the variable pt4 equal to the X value of pt2 (nth 0 pt2) and the Y value of pt1 (nth 1 pt1) and combines them using LIST to create a new list, which is assigned to variable pt3 using the SETQ function.
`(command "._RECTANG" pt1 pt2 "._LINE" pt1 pt2 "" "._LINE" pt3 pt4 "")`	Now that you have program variables representing the four points, the rest is easy. The COMMAND function is used to call up the RECTANG command and feed it pt1 and pt2, which draws a rectangle. While the COMMAND function is open, you can call another AutoCAD command, LINE, and use your four points to create the two lines of the section symbol.
`)`	This closes the DEFUN function, as you've seen before.

Creating Points with Distances and Angles

The POLAR function lets you create a new point from an existing point when you know, or can calculate, how far and at what angle from the existing point you want the next point to appear. The example in Listing 8.5 uses the POLAR function to calculate a point halfway between any two points selected by the user. It then uses the AutoCAD POINT command to place a point at that location. The purpose of the program is to provide a convenient means of adding dimensions to floor plans when the location of walls is determined to their center. Because there's nothing that you can snap to between the lines representing walls, dimensioning them can be tricky. But if you place points there, the Node object snap can be used as the origin of dimensions. If you want a better view of the points, set a new point style by choosing Fomat → Point Style and picking one you like.

This program uses the SETVAR function seen in the first program you wrote; it demonstrates how to change existing system variables and then politely return them to their original form. This program, like all programs, should have error trapping, but I'm leaving that subject for Chapter 9, "AutoLISP by Example: Getting Better."

Each line of this program is described in Table 8.7.

Listing 8.5

`mid.lsp`

```
(defun C:MID (/ pt1 pt2 os ap mid)
  (setq os (getvar "osmode")
        ap (getvar "aperture"))
  (setvar "osmode" 512)
  (setvar "aperture" 3)
  (initget 1)
```

```
        (setq pt1 (getpoint "\nFirst point: "))
        (initget 1)
        (setq pt2 (getpoint "\nSecond point: " pt1))
        (setq mid (polar pt1
                    (angle pt1 pt2)
                    (/ (distance pt1 pt2) 2.0)))
        (command "._POINT" "non" mid)
        (setvar "osmode" os)
        (setvar "aperture" ap)
        (princ)
    )
```

LINE OF CODE	PURPOSE	
`(defun C:MID (/  pt1 pt2 os ap mid)`	Defines the new function that will act as an AutoCAD command. Each variable is made local.	**Table 8.7** `mid.lsp`
`(setq os (getvar "osmode")`	Gets the current value of the OSMODE variable from the drawing and stores it by assigning it to variable os. You do this because the program will change OSMODE, and you want to change it back when the program is complete.	
`ap (getvar "aperture"))`	Gets the current value of the APERTURE variable from the drawing and stores it by assigning it to variable ap. If the aperture is too large, it can be difficult for the user to snap to a line in a cluttered area. Because the program will change the setting for this variable, you need to save the current setting so you can change that back also.	
`(setvar "osmode" 512)`	Sets OSMODE to 512, which is the Nearest osnap.	
`(setvar "aperture" 3)`	Sets APERTURE to 3 pixels to make it small enough to prevent snapping to the wrong line on the drawing.	
`(initget 1)`	Prevents the user from using a ↵ when prompted to select a point. If they do a ↵, they get an "invalid point" error.	
`(setq pt1 (getpoint "\nFirst point: "))`	Prompts the user to select the first point, and then assigns the point they selected to the variable pt1 as a list of three values: X, Y, Z of the point.	
`(initget 1)`	Prevents ↵.	
`(setq pt2 (getpoint "\nSecond point: " pt1))`	Prompts the user to select the second point, and then assigns the point they selected to the variable pt2 as a list. Referencing pt1 after the prompt causes a rubber-band line to be used from pt1 during the selection.	
`(setq mid (polar pt1`	Assigns a value to the variable mid using the POLAR function. That function requires a starting point, which is given in this line as pt1. The next two lines complete the SETQ function that is started here.	
`(angle pt1 pt2)`	Provides the angle needed by the POLAR function by using the ANGLE function to determine the angle from pt1 to pt2.	
`(/ (distance pt1 pt2) 2.0)))`	Provides the last piece of information needed by the POLAR function. The distance is calculated so that variable mid can be assigned a point halfway between pt1 and pt2. To calculate that distance, the / function is used to divide the distance between pt1 and pt2 by the real number 2.0.	

continued

continued

LINE OF CODE	PURPOSE
`(command "._POINT" "non" mid)`	Uses the AutoCAD command POINT to place a point at the location assigned to the variable `mid`. `"non"` is used to temporarily turn off the running osnap so it can't override the location by snapping to an object.
`(setvar "osmode" os)`	Resets the AutoCAD variable OSMODE to the value it had at the beginning of the program.
`(setvar "aperture" ap)`	Resets the AutoCAD variable APERTURE to the value it had at the beginning of the program.
`(princ)`	Prints a clear line at the command prompt to prevent the program from returning the value `nil`.
`)`	Ends the DEFUN function.

Performing Calculations

AutoLISP programs often require mathematical calculations, so this is a good time to reiterate the syntax of all AutoLISP functions. The function always comes first, immediately after the opening parenthesis in AutoLISP. The function is then followed by arguments. AutoLISP uses two kinds of numbers: *integers*, which have no decimal point; and *real numbers* (also known as *floating-point decimals*), which have a decimal point but no other characters. $1.00 isn't a real number, but 1.00 is.

Computational Basics

Let's look at several attempts you might make to write code for performing basic calculations, to see what kinds of pitfalls await you:

- `(3 + 3)` returns `error: bad function: 3`, because 3 isn't a function. Start with the + function.

- `(/ 3 2)` returns the integer `1`, because both arguments are integers.

- `(/ 3.0 2)` returns the real number `1.5`, because one of the arguments is a real number.

- `(* .5 2)` returns `error: misplaced dot on input`, because there is no leading zero.

- `(* 0.5 2)` returns the real number `1.0`, because the leading zero is used.

Math Functions

The following functions perform calculations or conversions with AutoLISP:

- `-` subtracts from the first number those that follow.

- `*` multiplies all numbers listed.

- `+` adds all numbers listed.

- `/` divides the first number by those that follow.

- 1+ adds 1 to a number. It can be used when indexing a list.

- 1- subtracts 1 from a number. It can be used when indexing a list.

- ABS returns the absolute value of a number. (abs -3) returns 3.

- ATAN returns the arc tangent of an angle in radians.

- COS returns the cosine of an angle in radians.

- CVUNIT converts from one system of units to another. (cvunit 25.4 "mm" "inches") returns 1.

- EXPT raises a root to a power. (expt 10 3) returns 10 cubed, or 1000.

- FIX converts a real number to an integer—(fix 34.9) returns 34.

- FLOAT converts an integer into a real number —(float 3) returns 3.0.

- MIN returns the smallest number in a list.

- MAX returns the largest number in a list.

- PI returns the value of ϖ. Don't redefine this variable.

- REM returns the remainder after dividing two numbers. (rem 10 3) returns 1.

- SIN returns the sine of an angle in radians. (sin 45) returns 0.850904.

- SQRT calculates the square root of a number. (sqrt 10) returns 3.16228.

Calculating Within a Program

The program in Listing 8.6 converts from inches to millimeters. As you know, 25.4 millimeters equals 1 inch. After trying this program, see if you can write a program that does the conversion in the other direction—from millimeters to inches.

Each line of this code is described in Table 8.8.

The result of using this program to convert 126.78″ into millimeters is shown in Figure 8.5.

Figure 8.5

Using an alert box in AutoLISP

Listing 8.6

I2M.lsp

```
(defun C:I2M (/ in mm st1 st2)
  (setq in (getdist "\nValue in inches: "))
  (setq mm (* in 25.4))
  (setq st1 (rtos in 2 3))
  (setq st2 (rtos mm 2 2))
  (alert (strcat "Value of " st1 " inches is " st2 " mm"))
  (princ)
)
```

Table 8.8	LINE OF CODE	PURPOSE
I2M.lsp	`(defun C:I2M (/ in mm st1 st2)`	Defines a new command function, and identifies local program variables.
	`(setq in (getdist "\nValue in inches: "))`	Sets the variable in equal to a real number that's either typed or returned by picking two points.
	`(setq mm (* in 25.4))`	Sets the variable mm equal to the result of multiplying the variable in by 25.4.
	`(setq st1 (rtos in 2 3))`	Converts a real number into a string using the AutoLISP function RTOS . The value is reported in an alert box. The integers 2 and 3 used here control the format in which the numerical string is displayed. In this case, it will be in decimal format to a precision of three decimal places. The string is assigned to variable st1.
	`(setq st2 (rtos mm 2 2))`	Performs the same conversion as the previous line for the metric value stored in mm. It's also in decimal format, but only to two decimal places, which is more likely when using metric. This string is assigned to variable st2.
	`(alert (strcat "Value of " st1 " inches is " st2 " mm"))`	Displays a string in a dialog box using the ALERT function. In this case, you have several strings that you want displayed. Because ALERT accepts only a single string as an argument, all the pieces must be added together into one long string. That is what STRCAT does: It concatenates the strings that follow it into one string.
	`(princ)`	Prints a clear line.
	`)`	Closes the DEFUN function.

The values used with the RTOS function to format units are the same values used for the LUNITS system variable in AutoCAD. They're shown in the next section.

String and Number Conversions

A number of functions convert between numbers and strings, in addition to the RTOS function used in the last program. Let's look at the ones you're most likely to use:

- ANGTOS converts an angle, in radians, to a string. I'll address the question "why radians?" in the next section. For now, just accept that ϖ radians = 180 degrees. Like RTOS, this function has modes and precision. The modes are the five kinds of angles you can set under units, starting with the 0 item. Here's the syntax:

    - `(angtos pi 0 3)` uses the decimal degrees mode and returns `"180.000"`.

    - `(angtos pi 1 3)` uses the degrees/minutes/seconds mode and returns `"180d0'0\""`. (The `\"` is necessary to return the literal quotation mark used to represent inches because AutoLISP would interpret a quote as the end of the string otherwise.)

- (angtos pi 2 3) uses the grads mode and returns "200.000g".

- (angtos pi 3 15) uses the radian mode and returns "3.141592653589793r".

- (angtos pi 4 3) uses the surveying mode and returns "W".

- ATOF converts ASCII text into a floating decimal real number. (atof "3.144") returns 3.144.

- ATOI converts ASCII text into an integer. (atoi "3.144") returns 3.

- ITOA converts an integer into ASCII text. (itoa 3) returns "3".

- RTOS converts a real number to string. As I pointed out earlier, both modes and precision can be specified. The modes are the five kinds of units you can set under units, starting with the 1 item (I know, it should have been the 0 item). Here's the syntax:

  - (rtos 6.56 1 3) uses the scientific mode and returns "6.560E+00".

  - (rtos 6.56 2 3) uses the degrees mode and returns "6.560".

  - (rtos 6.56 3 3) uses the engineering mode and returns "6.560\"".

  - (rtos 6.56 4 3) uses the architectural mode and returns "6 1/2\"".

  - (rtos 6.56 5 3) uses the fractional mode and returns "6 1/2".

Converting Between Radians and Degrees

Why do computers use radians? It's faster and more accurate to do complex computations when using radians, so that's what computers use to compute angles. Table 8.9 shows how radians compare to degrees.

WHAT'S A RADIAN?

Geometrically, a *radian* is the angle between two lines drawn from the center of a circle that create an arc with an arc length equal to the radius. One radian is a little less than 57.30 degrees. Why do you have to know this? Because if you think you're giving your AutoLISP program an angular measurement in degrees, but the program interprets it as radians, you can get some odd results.

What do you do when you have a program that rotates objects, but it doesn't give you the results you expect? First, recognize that if you think an object should rotate 90°, and it appears to rotate about 117°, you're probably feeding a value in degrees (90) into a function that expects radians (approximately 1.507). Rotating something 90 radians would require 14.3239 full revolutions. That 0.3239 of a revolution lands at about 117°. Likewise, if you thought you were feeding radians into your program but the result is a rotation of a few degrees, you should probably be using degrees instead.

The sample program in Listing 8.7 rotates a copy of a selection set using a base point and rotation angle provided by the user. You can rotate and copy

Table 8.9

Degrees and Radians Compared

DEGREES	RADIANS
0	0
90	ϖ/2
180	ϖ
270	3ϖ/2
360	2ϖ

with grips, but it involves several steps. In AutoCAD 2006, the ROTATE command has a Copy option,
but if you need this function often, a dedicated command would be helpful.

The following code illustrates the problems new programmers often have with angles. You may think it looks like it will work, but it won't give you the results you probably expect. Try it. When you type **90**, hoping to rotate a copy of the object 90°, you'll get the results shown on the right in Figure 8.6 instead. What's wrong?

Listing 8.7

rc_broken_version.lsp

```
(defun c:rc(/ ss1 pt1 ang1)
  (setq ss1 (ssget))
  (setq pt1 (getpoint "\nBasepoint: "))
  (setq ang1 (getangle "\nAngle of rotation: "))
  (command "._COPY" ss1 "" pt1 pt1
           "._ROTATE" ss1 "" pt1 ang1)
)
```

Each line is described in Table 8.10.

There's a clue in the command line shown with the object in Figure 8.6. When prompted for a rotation angle, I typed in **90**, but the command line shows **1.570796326794897**. That looks like ½ of ϖ. If you look at Table 8.9, 90 = ϖ/2. AutoLISP must have converted the 90 into radians. It did, because I used the GETANGLE function.

Table 8.10	LINE OF CODE	PURPOSE
rc_broken_ version.lsp	`(defun c:rc( ss1 pt1 ang1)`	The new command is named RC.
	`(setq ss1 (ssget))`	The SSGET function prompts the user to make a selection set. The selection in this case is assigned to the variable ss1.
	`(setq pt1 (getpoint "\nBasepoint: "))`	The point provided in response to GETPOINT is saved as variable pt1.
	`(setq ang1 (getangle "\nAngle of rotation: "))`	The angle provided in response to GETANGLE is saved as variable ang1. This creates a problem, because the value is returned in radians. If 90 is typed or selected, 1.570796326794896 is returned. Your objects rotates only about 1.6 degrees when the value is fed to the ROTATE command.
	`(command "._COPY" ss1 "" pt1 pt1`	The selected objects are copied directly on top of themselves. Note that there is no closing parenthesis, so the next line is part of this one.
	`"._ROTATE" ss1 "" pt1 ang1)`	This line is part of the COMMAND function in the previous line. Your original selection set is rotated at the base point by ang1. You expect the results on the left in Figure 8.6, but you get the results on the right.
	`)`	This line ends the DEFUN function.

Figure 8.6

Results of using degrees instead of radians

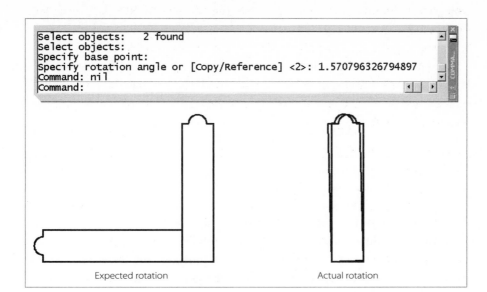

```
Select objects:    2 found
Select objects:
Specify base point:
Specify rotation angle or [Copy/Reference] <2>: 1.570796326794897
Command: nil
Command:
```

Expected rotation   Actual rotation

Oddly enough, this program would have worked fine if I'd used GETSTRING instead of GETANGLE, because the value is supplied to the ROTATE command literally. I didn't use GETSTRING, however, because it doesn't allow the user to pick two points at the prompt. That would make this program behave differently from every other AutoCAD program, which is something you should make every effort to avoid.

Now that you know why your program may be acting up, let's see how you can fix it by creating a new function that can be called in other functions.

CREATING AUTOLISP FUNCTIONS: RTD AND DTR

Before we look at the code required to fix this problem, let's clarify one important AutoLISP concept. There are two different kinds of functions. The kind you've been writing act like AutoCAD commands. Without the C: as part of the function name, it doesn't act like an AutoCAD command, but it can be used as an AutoLISP function. This is pretty potent stuff: You can create your own AutoCAD commands using AutoLISP functions, and you can define your own AutoLISP functions too. Now that's power! Let's solve the conflict between radians and degrees with a new AutoLISP function or two.

You'll find the code in Listing 8.8 in virtually every AutoLISP reference book, because every AutoLISP programmer runs into the radians/degrees problem at some point. Notice that the two new functions are a little different from the programs you've been writing, in two ways: They don't have a C: in front of the function name, and they have a single argument in the parentheses after the function name instead of the name of local program variables. RTD converts radians into degrees, and DTR converts degrees into radians.

Listing 8.8

`angconv.1sp`

```
(defun rtd (r)
    (* 180.0(/ r pi))
)  ;end defun

(defun dtr (d)
    (* pi (/ d 180.0))
)  ;end defun
```

Table 8.11 describes this program.

Because 180° = ϖ radians, the math here is easy. Degrees = (180 × radians)/ϖ. Using the structure of AutoLISP, you'd say "multiply 180 times the result of dividing radians by ϖ." Because functions always come first, the AutoLISP code reads `(* 180 (/ r pi))` where r = radians. Once you write these two conversion functions, they must be loaded before you can use them. You could load them manually each time you want to use them, but there are some automatic ways to load AutoLISP programs so they're always available. In this case, I'd place the functions in a file named `acaddoc.1sp`, which is discussed later in this chapter.

> For clarity, I display most of the programs in this chapter as individual LSP files. It's also possible to combine many AutoLISP programs into a single LSP file. Each one starts and ends with a DEFUN function.

	LINE OF CODE	PURPOSE
Table 8.11 `angconv.1sp`	`(defun rtd (r)`	This line defines a function named RTD. The r is the argument necessary for this function. Any letter can be used. Notice that there's no C: and no /.
	`(* 180.0(/ r pi))`	The value provided, r, is divided by ϖ and multiplied by 180.
	`);end defun`	This line ends the DEFUN function and places a note to that effect to make it easier to find the end of each function in a file that contains multiple AutoLISP programs.
		This is a blank space for clarity, which is OK anywhere in an AutoLISP program.
	`(defun dtr (d)`	This line defines a function named DTR. The d is the argument necessary for this function. Any letter can be used. Notice that there's no C: and no /.
	`(* pi (/ d 180.0))`	The value d provided as an argument is divided by 180 and multiplied by ϖ.
	`);end defun`	This line ends the DEFUN function and places a note to that effect to make it easier to find the end of each function in a file that contains multiple AutoLISP programs.

The two angular conversion functions can be executed at the AutoCAD command prompt using the same format you use in a program: (rtd 2) converts 2 radians into degrees and returns 114.592; (dtr 30) converts 30° into radians and returns 0.523599.

Listing 8.9 shows how the rc.lsp program looks if you use the RTD function to convert the angle from radians to degrees before using it. The RTD function must be loaded before it can be used.

Listing 8.9

rc.lsp

```
(defun c:rc(/ ss1 pt1 ang1)
  (setq ss1 (ssget))
  (setq pt1 (getpoint "\nBasepoint: "))
  (setq ang1 (rtd (getangle "\nAngle of rotation: ")))
  (command "._COPY" ss1 "" pt1 pt1
          "._ROTATE" ss1 "" pt1 ang1)
  )
```

It's a subtle difference. In the fourth line, the RTD function is used before the GETANGLE function, requiring one more set of parentheses. You may find it easier to understand how the RTD function works if I rewrite it to add an additional step. Listing 8.10 adds one more line that redefines the variable ang1. Note the inline annotation that follows the ; in line 5. Don't be surprised to see the program variable ang1 appear twice on that line. That's how program variables are assigned a new value that's based on their existing value. It's very logical.

Listing 8.10

rc2.lsp

```
(defun c:rc(/ ss1 pt1 ang1)
  (setq ss1 (ssget))
  (setq pt1 (getpoint "\nBasepoint: "))
  (setq ang1 (getangle "\nAngle of rotation: "))
  (setq ang1 (rtd ang1));converts ang1 from radians to degrees
  (command "._COPY" ss1 "" pt1 pt1
          "._ROTATE" ss1 "" pt1 ang1)
  )
```

A point about multiple releases: If you think this program could be simplified by using the Copy option of the ROTATE command, you're right. However, prior to AutoCAD 2006, ROTATE had no Copy option. The code as written here (command "._COPY" ss1 "" pt1 pt1 "._ROTATE" ss1 "" pt1 ang1) works in any release, not just those since AUTOCAD 2006. That's good practice when writing code.

Using AutoLISP Functions Transparently

You know that you can execute AutoLISP functions directly from the command line, but you may wonder if the command line has to be empty. It doesn't. You can run an AutoLISP function transparently while you're in a command. Let's create an AutoLISP function that converts inches into millimeters and that you can use on the fly when drawing or editing in AutoCAD. You already created an AutoCAD *command* to do this earlier, so creating a *function* requires only that you modify the program with a little editing; see Listing 8.11.

Listing 8.11

```
ii.lsp

    (defun ii (in)
      (* in 25.4)
    )
```

Let's say you're using the LINE command, and you've selected a start point and established a polar tracking line. You know the length of the line in inches, but you're in a metric drawing. Can you have AutoCAD convert into millimeters while you're drawing the line? Here's how. Once you've loaded the II function, use it in response to a request for input. Just remember to type the parentheses. And if the number is smaller than 1, you must include the leading 0, as shown in Figure 8.7.

> You can't use this system in a dialog box, nor can it follow the @ symbol. But it works great for values that can be entered at the command line; particularly direct distances.

Figure 8.7

Using AutoLISP functions transparently

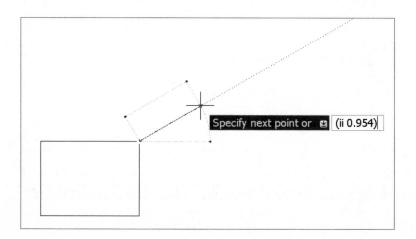

Combining AutoLISP Functions

When you're writing a new program, don't overlook programs that you or others have already written. One of the reasons I use so many examples in this chapter is to provide sample code for you to copy into other programs for a variety of situations.

Let's take an element from rc2.1sp, the Rotate/Copy program, and add it to the structural section program ssect.1sp so the symbol can be drawn at any angle. You'll borrow lines 4 and 5 from rc2.1sp and use them to get an angle for rotating the UCS before calculating the points for the other two corners of the rectangle, as shown in Figure 8.8.

First, copy the RTD function and both programs into a new file—you don't want to mess up programs that already work. Next, open a space in the C:SSECT program and copy the key lines from the C:RC function, which is below it. Delete the entire C:RC function so none of that code interferes with your new program. Then, make a few more changes so you can use the new angle to rotate the UCS; see Listing 8.12. Of course, if your program changes a system variable, don't forget to change it back—see the error-checking section in Chapter 9.

Figure 8.8
Borrowing code

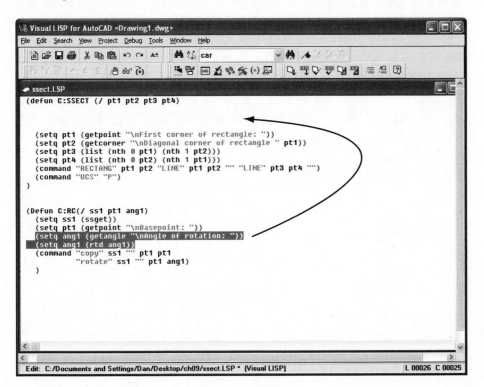

Listing 8.12

structural_section.lsp

```
(defun C:SSECT (/ ang1 pt1 pt2 pt3 pt4)
  (setq ang1 (getangle "\nAngle of structural section: "))
  (setq ang1 (rtd ang1))
  (command "._UCS" "Z" ang1)
  (setq pt1 (getpoint "\nFirst corner of rectangle: "))
  (setq pt2 (getcorner "\nDiagonal corner of rectangle " pt1))
  (setq pt3 (list (nth 0 pt1) (nth 1 pt2)))
  (setq pt4 (list (nth 0 pt2) (nth 1 pt1)))
  (command "._RECTANG" pt1 pt2 "._LINE" pt1 pt2 "" "._LINE" pt3 pt4 "")
  (command "._UCS" "P")
)
```

Figure 8.9 shows the command in action. It would be nice if the rubber-band rectangle rotated with the UCS, but I want to keep this program simple for now. As you can see in Figure 8.10, when the command is used to place the two structural section symbols, you get the result you want.

You may also be thinking that the user should be able to press ↵ to select a default value of 0 for the UCS rotation. Good point. In Chapter 9, I'll show you how to create a default setting using an IF statement.

Figure 8.9

Using C:SSECT

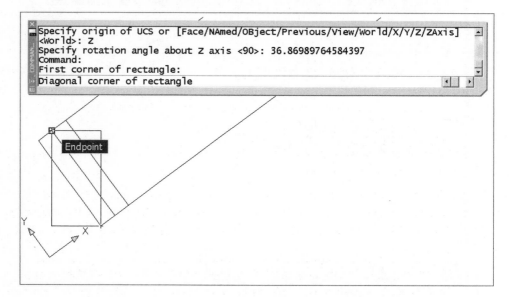

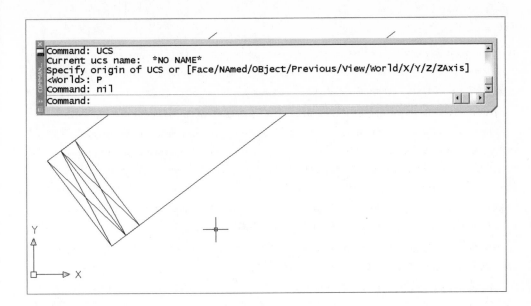

Figure 8.10
Result of C:SSECT

TEN BASIC RULES FOR AUTOLISP PROGRAMMING

I hope this chapter gets you interested in developing your own AutoLISP programs. I chose the programs for this chapter to give you examples of how AutoLISP programs are structured, and how many of the most useful functions can be used. This isn't the whole story, of course. Chapter 9 contains some important additions, including strategies for debugging your programs, techniques for adding error trapping to your programs, methods for annotating programs, and some more advanced examples of functions, including IF, WHILE, and COND functions.

Now that you have a handle on programming, here are some basic rules you should follow:

1. Save your programs as ASCII text files.

2. There must be an equal number of opening and closing parentheses. The last closing parenthesis generally appears alone on the last line.

3. DEFUN means *define function*. It's followed by the name of the function you're defining. If the name includes the C:, you've defined a function that can be used as a new AutoCAD command. If it doesn't, the function can be used in the form (dtr 180) either in another AutoLISP routine or at the command line.

4. Manage your quotation marks. Every opening quote requires a closing quote. If you want to accept a default in a command, " " will do it because it represents a ↵. Don't use this technique with commands whose default values can change; use actual values instead.

continued

continued

5. The backslash has a meaning in an AutoLISP program, and it isn't used to separate subdirectories. (To do that, use a forward slash or a double backslash.) To insert a drawing using AutoLISP, the program line looks like this: `(command "._INSERT" "c:\\dwg\\dsize.dwg" "0,0" "1" "1" "0")`.

6. The parentheses after the DEFUN expression can have two kinds of values: argument names or variable names. When local program variables are included, they must be preceded by both a space and a forward slash. If the parentheses are empty, the function has no arguments and all the program variables in the function are global. Place variable names here only after you know your program works. And don't forget to leave a space after the forward slash. You can check the value of a global variable by typing it at the AutoCAD command line preceded by a exclamation point (`!varname`) or by typing the variable name in the Visual LISP Console.

7. To get a new line for a prompt to the user, always place the characters \n (a lowercase *n*) after the opening quote and before the text of the prompt.

8. Use one or more semicolons before comments.

9. When designing a program, get any values you need from the user or the drawing at the beginning of the program. Use the SETQ function to assign the values to program variables so you can use the values later in the program.

10. Don't get discouraged if a new program doesn't work the first time. It probably won't; that's what makes programming so interesting.

Automatic Loading

Defining functions like RTD and DTR for converting angles—functions that you want always available—brings up the issue of automatic loading. So far, you've been using the Visual LISP editor to both create your programs and load them. Users can automatically load AutoLISP programs by three primary means: add them to the Startup Suite in the APPLOAD dialog box, place the programs in an `acaddoc.lsp` file, or place the programs in an `acad.lsp` file. All of these require that you save the programs in an LSP file.

APPLOAD

We looked briefly at the Load/Unload Applications dialog box earlier in the chapter. It can be used to load all kinds of programs, not just AutoLISP. The file extensions don't always tell you exactly what kind programming language was used to create them, so let's look at them in Table 8.12.

FILE EXTENSION	TYPE OF PROGAM
.lsp	AutoLISP source code. This is the code you've been writing in this chapter. It's open code that can be easily read and altered by anyone.
.fas	Fast-opening machine language code compiled from AutoLISP source code. These files can be created with the Visual LISP editor. Their two advantages over AutoLISP source code are that they load more quickly than text-based LSP files and they're more secure if you want to protect the work you did from being taken by someone else.
.vlx	Files that can also be created from the Visual LISP editor and that are designed to place multiple file types into a single file. These can include Dialog Control Language (DCL) files in addition to compiled AutoLISP code. The Help system indicates that they can include VBA, but I'm not certain that works.
.arx	AutoCAD Runtime Extension. These programs are written in the C++ programming language. They often contain the code for specific commands or groups of commands and are much more sophisticated than AutoLISP.
.dbx	Database Extension. C++ and .NET developers sometimes use these programs to develop third-party applications to read and write to DWG and DXF format.
.dvb	AutoCAD VBA source file written in VBA, another programming language.

Table 8.12

File Types Used by the Load/Unload Applications Dialog Box

Any programs with these file types can be placed in the Startup Suite, but think about what you put in there. You should place program files in the Startup Suite only if you want constant access to them. Suppose you have a complex stair-design program that you use only once in a while. You can use the APPLOAD command to load it only when you want to use it. If you have a complex program to help you design cams, on the other hand, and you use it every day, it should be in the Startup Suite.

Acaddoc.lsp and Acad.lsp Files

AutoCAD doesn't ship with either an acaddoc.lsp file or an acad.lsp file, but if you create either one, AutoCAD recognizes them and automatically loads them on startup. It's like using the Startup Suite, with a difference: The Startup Suite is loaded only for the user who puts files in it. If either an acaddoc.lsp or an acad.lsp file is placed in the AutoCAD search path, its programs load for all users.

> If you want all the users in an office or a company to have the same AutoLISP programs available all the time, put an acaddoc.lsp file in a shared folder and make sure that folder is in the search path for all users. See Chapter 2, "Managing Your System," for more information on adding locations to the AutoCAD search path.

What's the difference between an acaddoc.lsp file and an acad.lsp file, and why are there two of them? Well, for historical reasons. For as long as I've used AutoCAD, it's been possible to place programs in a file named acad.lsp, put the file in the search path of AutoCAD, and have the file automatically load when AutoCAD starts up. But when AutoCAD was updated in AutoCAD 2000 to allow multiple drawings to be opened in a single session, acad.lsp was assigned the behavior of loading *only* for the first drawing opened or created in any one session. The acaddoc.lsp file became an alternative to the acad.lsp file because it loads in each new drawing as it's opened or created.

If you have a file named acad.lsp from an earlier era and want it loaded with every drawing, either rename it acaddoc.lsp or set the variable ACADLSPASDOC to 1. Doing so forces AutoCAD to treat an acad.lsp file as though it's an acaddoc.lsp file.

There is another file that loads AutoLISP programs automatically if you're using a release prior to AutoCAD 2006. The acad.mnl file contains AutoLISP code that is loaded whenever the acad.mns file is loaded. It contains a number of functions that work in conjunction with the menu file. Now, with the CUI, that file exists but contains no code. In its place is a file name acad2007doc.lsp, which loads automatically in each drawing and defines a number of command functions using AutoLISP. I suggest that you avoid editing this file so you don't inadvertently change the behavior of the commands it contains. If you want programs to load automatically, add them to an acaddoc.lsp file.

Managing Your Programs

I hope that after reading this chapter, you want to develop some of your own LSP files. If so, you'll have to decide how to manage them. Do you want them loaded all the time, only once, or only when you need them? As you develop more AutoLISP programs, I recommend you use the following steps:

1. Work on any new program in its own working file in the Visual LISP editor until you've tested it thoroughly, and it works.

2. Decide whether you want to have it available all the time. If not, put it in a folder as a single program and load it using APPLOAD whenever you need it.

3. If you have a program that *only you* want access to, place it in the Startup Suite of the APPLOAD dialog box or in a folder that appears only in your support path.

4. Once you know they work, place all general-access programs into a single file named acaddoc.lsp. That file should be saved in a network folder that's in everyone's support path or in C:\Program Files\AutoCAD 2007\support.

5. If you want a message to be displayed on startup or a program to be loaded only once when a user first starts AutoCAD, place the code for that in an acad.lsp file and place that file in the same path as the acaddoc.lsp file.

S::STARTUP

While we're on the subject of automatic loading, let's look at one special AutoLISP function that is often placed at the beginning of the acaddoc.lsp file. The S::STARTUP function runs an AutoLISP program as soon as acaddoc.lsp is loaded. The user doesn't have to do anything. This can be handy for setting system variables, creating automatic layouts, and adding layers—processes that can also be completed with template files and profiles, of course; but that you may want to automate. The S::STARTUP function is occasionally used for undefining commands so they can be replaced with your own definitions.

Why replace an existing command with a new definition? Maybe you don't like the new-fangled version of a command, and you want it to behave like the old command it replaced. You can undefine the new one and create a new definition that just calls up the old one. The Help system in the Visual LISP editor uses the HATCH and BHATCH commands as an example.

You may also want certain things to happen whenever someone uses a particular command. Perhaps you want all text to be placed on a specific layer. You can undefine the MTEXT command and then define a new one that sets a text layer current. If you want to keep yourself from accidentally placing dimensions in Paper Space, you can replace the standard dimension commands with ones that check to see whether a layout is active before placing dimensions.

> You didn't know that AutoCAD commands can be undefined? Just use the UNDEFINE command followed by the command name you want to undefine. And yes, there is a REDEFINE command.

Listing 8.13 shows an example of how you can use the S::STARTUP function if you want to force yourself to use polylines instead of lines, and you want to make sure polylines are always drawn on the OBJ layer. Note that the REDEFINE command can be used to redefine a native command that has been turned off with UNDEFINE. Note also that placing a period in front of a native command name calls that command even if it's been undefined. That's why you often see the leading period in front of AutoCAD command names in AutoLISP programs.

> The DEFUN-Q function is used only with the S::STARTUP function, although you can use DEFUN instead. DEFUN-Q is a slightly modified version of DEFUN. It permits a startup program to be appended to another startup program, just in case you've used S::STARTUP in more than one automatically loaded file. You won't use DEFUN-Q in any other situation that I'm aware of.

Listing 8.13

startupexample.lsp

```
(defun-q S::STARTUP ()
  (command "._UNDEFINE" "._LINE")
  (Alert
    "The LINE command will draw polylines on Layer OBJ.
    \nType \".LINE\" to use the native LINE command.
    \nUse the REDEFINE command to redefine LINE"
  )
)
(defun c:LINE()
  (setvar "cmdecho" 0)
  (command ".LAYER" "M" "obj" "C" "white" "" "LW" "0.5" "" ""
    ".PLINE")
  (setvar "cmdecho" 1)
)
```

CHAPTER 9

AutoLISP by Example: Getting Better

The AutoLISP examples that I gave you in Chapter 8, "AutoLISP by Example: Getting Started," were simplified, but that doesn't mean they weren't useful. In fact, with only those examples, you can now create hundreds of new and useful AutoCAD commands. But before long, you'll probably want to generate functions that require something more complex than the skeletal AutoLISP structure laid out in the previous chapter. This chapter adds some meat to that skeleton, not only by introducing you to more complex functions, but also by describing two of the most important concepts for your future programming efforts: error handling and annotating.

First, though, let's try to preempt the frustration inherent in creating your own programs. When your program fails to work, how do you figure out what's wrong?

- **Debugging Techniques**

- **Error Handling**

- **Annotation**

- **Selection Sets**

- **IF Function**

- **WHILE Function**

- **COND, INITGET, and GETKWORD Functions**

- **Text and String Manipulation**

- **Getting to DOS**

Debugging Techniques

In chapter 8, the programs you tried were simple enough that you probably had little problem getting them to run. As you start developing more complex programs, however, you'll have to enter the realm of problem-solving known in programming as *debugging*. Before we begin looking at more complex program examples, let's go over some techniques you can use while you're creating new programs. Those techniques include the following:

- Testing sections of code in the Visual LISP Console or at the AutoCAD command prompt
- Finding matching parentheses as you type or after you've typed your code
- Modifying the format of your code so it's easier to read
- Checking your code for structural flaws
- Running code fragments from the Visual LISP editor
- Finding the current value of a variable

> AutoLISP programs deal with two kinds of variables: system variables defined by AutoCAD, such as OSMODE; and program variables defined by you and named by you. Program variables can be either *local*, having a value in only one program, or *global*, holding a value after the program in which it's defined has terminated.

- Stopping the program as it runs so you can see if a problem has developed
- Slowing the program so you can watch it as it runs to see how it's working

> Make sure you saved any open drawing files before you start debugging a program in the Visual LISP Interactive Editing Environment (VLIDE). Have an expendable drawing file open in case AutoCAD stops responding and you have to close it down. It doesn't happen often, but it happens.

Testing Code Sections at the Console

You can test your understanding of the syntax of a function by trying it at the AutoCAD command prompt or in the Visual LISP Console. Suppose, for example, you can't remember the structure of the POLAR function (we looked at that in Chapter 8). POLAR allows you to find a point at a specific distance and angle from an existing point. You know that POLAR requires a starting point, a distance, and an angle. You understand arguments well enough now to know that they must be placed after the function name, but in what order?

If you look up the POLAR function in the Help system (hey, what a great idea!), it gives you the following information:

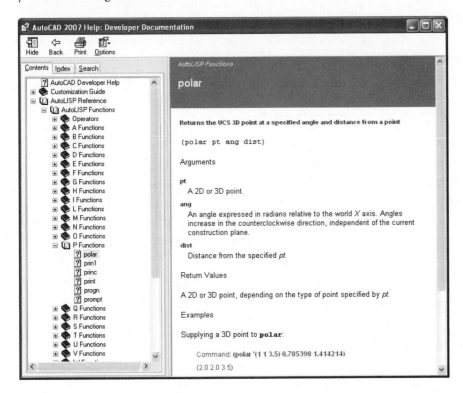

OK, that seems clear enough. You close Help and try the POLAR function by typing it in the Visual LISP Console or at the AutoCAD command prompt exactly as it appears in the Help dialog, and you get the message "error: bad argument type: 2D/3D point: nil."

Of course! The three required arguments must be a point, an angle in radians, and a distance in units. In the Help system, they're represented by pt, ang, and dist. They could be variable names in a program, but until they have a value assigned, they're all nil; therefore, the POLAR function returns an error.

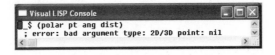

AutoLISP programs often return *nil*, which represents either an empty list or a false condition. Think of it as meaning no value, and don't make the mistake of thinking nil is the same as zero. It's not, since 0 is a value.

You try again, replacing pt with (2 3 0), ang with 45, and dist with 4. Now that you've provided proper arguments, entering the code should return a point that is 4 units away from coordinate 2,3 at an angle of 45°. But it doesn't. Instead, you get a different error message.

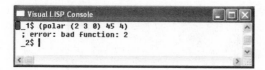

This error message contains a clue, "error: bad function: 2." When you get the bad function error, start looking at open parentheses. The number 2 appears immediately after an opening parenthesis. Remember, there must be a function in that location. Unless you tell AutoLISP not to evaluate the 2 as a function, it tries to do so, only to discover that the function 2 is undefined (or bad). How do you tell AutoLISP not to evaluate the first item in a list? You *quote* the list by adding an apostrophe before the opening parenthesis. The Help system example shows a single quote, but it's hard to notice everything. Now you add an apostrophe and try again, getting the following results.

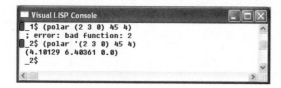

This looks pretty good. At least you got a point, which is to say at least you got a list of three values. But is that point correct? You can't tell for sure, although it looks feasible. How can you check?

Use AutoCAD to find out what the new point should be by drawing a line from the coordinate 2,3 that's 4 units long at an angle of 45°. The coordinates of the new end point are 4.8284,5.8284,0, which aren't the coordinates returned when you entered the function at the Visual LISP Console. You have to try something else.

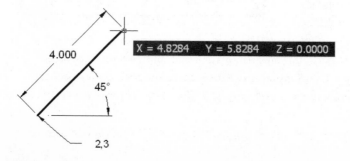

The result is obviously wrong, yet so close to what you expected. Maybe you mixed up the angle and the distance. They're both numbers, so the program would still run. The Help system could be wrong about what comes first, couldn't it? Possible, but unlikely. Look to your code for problems before blaming the Help system.

Let's say you've already checked your code, so you decide to experiment. Maybe the Help system is wrong. You try reversing the values, and type **(polar '(2 3 0) 4 45)**, but that result's not even close. It returns (–27.414 –31.0561 0.0).

In this case, the problem is staring you right in the face. You want an angle of 45°, but the POLAR function thinks you mean 45 radians. It says so in the Help system, but somehow you missed it. Now you try **(polar '(2 3 0) (dtr 45) 4)**, which assumes that DTR (the function you wrote in Chapter 8) is loaded. The results you get from this line of code match the results you get using the ID command—4.8284, 5.8284, 0.

When you're trying to apply a function for the first time, this kind of stumbling around is realistic, even after you've been writing programs for a while. Think of it as a game: Try to have a little fun, even when you're faced with the frustration of getting hung up on the littlest things.

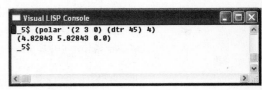

> If you didn't define the function DTR before trying the last code example, do the conversion mathematically. It looks like this: (polar '(2 3 0) (* pi (/ 45 180.0)) 4).

Finding Matching Parentheses and Quotation Marks

When I first started writing AutoLISP programs, I used a program named PQCHECK. It checked AutoLISP code for problems with parentheses and quotation marks, reported the problems, and then identified possible error locations by line number. I had to open the AutoLISP file, go to the identified lines, and then start poking around for trouble.

The Visual LISP editor has improved that process considerably. One of its most appealing features is its ability to keep track of parentheses and double quotes as you type. It also has tools for finding matching parentheses after you type the code.

Let's get double quotation marks out of the way first, because that's easy. With color-coding, the Visual LISP editor displays in magenta any string enclosed in double quotes. This color-coding is applied as you type, so the first quotation mark turns the rest of the file magenta all the way to the next double quote. It stays that way until you place the corresponding closing quotation. If you miss a quotation mark, just go back to where the magenta color begins, and you'll find a double quote. It should be clear where you should place the closing double quote.

Parentheses still cause their share of problems, but the Visual LISP editor contains other tools for solving them.

Jumping Parentheses

As you create the code for a new program, whenever you type a closing parenthesis, your cursor jumps to the corresponding opening parenthesis. If the cursor doesn't jump, this means you have too many closing parentheses: There is no opening parenthesis to jump to. If the program is short, keeping track of the jump is easy. In longer programs, keeping track becomes more difficult, because the cursor goes to a location that's outside the current window.

Double-Clicking on a Parenthesis

The Visual LISP editor solves the problem of tracking cursor jumps with a highlighting feature. Place your cursor directly in front of any opening parenthesis or directly after a closing one, and double-click. The entire contents enclosed by those parentheses will be highlighted. Now you can see where they match up. If you want, you can take advantage of this selected, highlight text and load it to see if it works. I do this all the time while writing or debugging a program. Place your cursor in the location shown, and double-click.

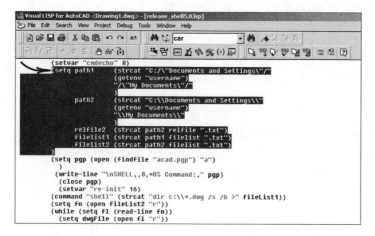

Ctrl+[and Ctrl+]

You can also use the Ctrl key in combination with the open and close bracket keys to move through a document. Place the cursor directly after a closing parenthesis, and press Ctrl+[to go to the matching opening parenthesis. Place your cursor directly before an opening parenthesis, and Ctrl-+] goes to the matching closing parenthesis.

Watch Window

If your new program doesn't run, don't get discouraged—get interested. Start your sleuthing by determining how far your program got before it stopped working. Because most programs, even the simple ones we're using here, use a lot of variables, it's possible to find out where the program stops working by checking to see whether variables have been properly assigned values along the way.

There are three ways to check variables.

- Type **!variableName** (**!pt1**), for example at the AutoCAD command prompt.
- Type **variableName** (**pt1**), for example in the Visual LISP console.
- Add the variables to the Watch window in the Visual LISP editor.

To use the first two methods, it's critical that you avoid making the variables local until you've finished developing the program. Otherwise, the variable values are discarded (returned to nil) when the program ends. Variables become local when they're listed as arguments to the DEFUN function, so you may want to wait until you know the program works before you list them on the DEFUN line.

Adding variables to a Watch window works for both global and local program variables, as long as you set break points in the program. Check the Watch window when the program stops at a break point to see the current values for the listed variables.

To add variables to a Watch window, do the following:

1. Start the Visual LISP editor.

2. Open your AutoLISP program.

3. Place the cursor at a variable name, and right-click.

4. Select Add Watch from the cursor menu.

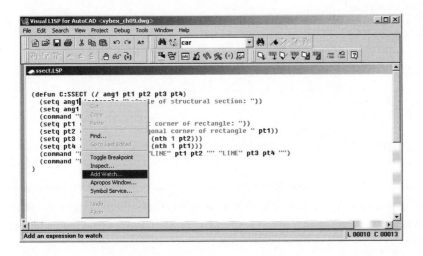

5. Confirm the variable name in the Add Watch dialog box, and click OK. The Watch dialog box opens as shown. The next graphic shows the code for the program that you'll be debugging here. If you want, you can duplicate it in the Visual LISP editor and follow along. Just type it exactly as shown, because it's purposely broken.

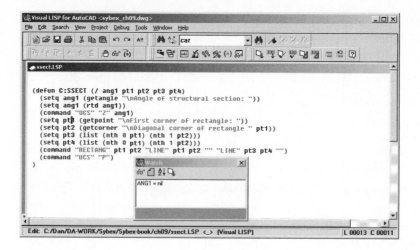

You can add more variables to the Watch window by clicking the Add Watch button (looks like a pair of glasses) on the Debug toolbar. As far as I know, you must add each variable one at a time. All variables in this window are currently nil.

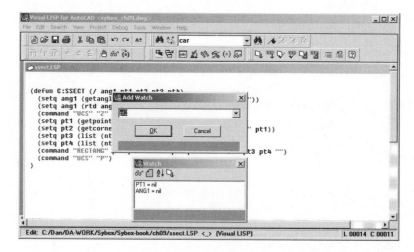

To get values assigned to the variables, you have to run the program; but if you run the program, things happen so fast you can't see the variable values before they're returned to nil. You have to stop the program from running at a few key points. To do that, add some break points.

Remember, there's an error in the SSECT program code that appears in the Visual LISP editor shown in the next graphic. You'll see where it's broken as we go through the debugging procedure.

To place a break point, move your cursor to a location where a break makes sense, right-click, and then select Toggle Breakpoint from the cursor menu. There are four break points in the code. The first break point stops the program after a value is first assigned to ang1 so you can check to see whether it's correct. The second break point stops the program again after the value stored in ang1 is converted from radians to degrees to see if the new value is correct. The third break point stops the program so you can check the list of coordinate values stored in pt1. The last break point, which is placed just before the command function, stops the program so you can inspect the values of pt2, pt3, and pt4.

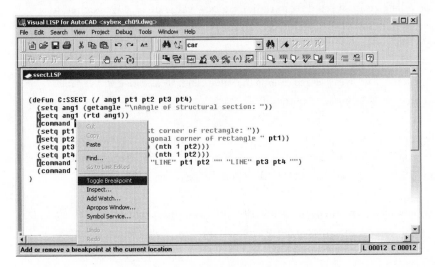

Now that the breaks are in place, load the program using the Load Active Edit Window button, and then click the Activate AutoCAD button and type the new command at the command line. VLIDE switches back to the editor when the break point is reached, so you can check the variable. After starting the program, type **45** in response to the prompt Angle of structural section:. The program stops when it gets to the first break point.

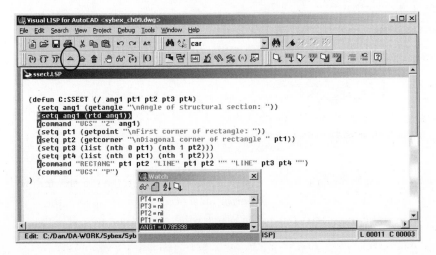

Notice that the variable ang1 now shows a value of 0.785398 in the Watch window—that looks like an angle in radians, and it is. The highlighted line is the expression that will be evaluated next. To continue to the next break point, click the Continue button, which is the one whose button icon is a green triangle.

The program now evaluates the next line. The value of ang1 changes in the Watch window because it's been redefined using the RTD function (if the function is loaded). Once the value of ang1 is converted from radians, a new value of 45.0 is assigned to ang1. Because this matches your intent, you can move on by clicking the Continue button again.

> The SETQ function is used in this line to change the value currently assigned to a variable. This is common practice in AutoLISP programs.

Now the next two lines are evaluated, because the next break point is two lines away. VLIDE switches back to AutoCAD so you can select or enter a point. Type or select 0,0, and the Visual LISP editor opens again, highlighting the next line to be evaluated.

> When you're debugging a program, use points, distances, and angles that allow you to easily predict the results. Once you've gotten the program to work for values like 0,0,0 and 45°, you can test it with more complicated input.

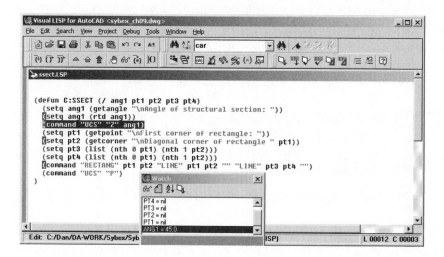

Variable pt1 shows the value (0.0 0.0 0.0), which is correct. So far, the Watch window confirms that the program is working fine. The error must occur somewhere after the break point. Add the other point variables to the Watch window, and continue with the debugging.

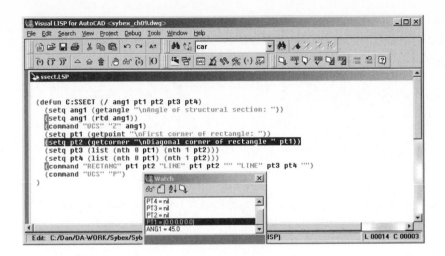

Click the Continue button, and enter **5.5,1.5** at the AutoCAD command line. VLIDE switches back to the editor, and the Watch window now shows the values of pt2, pt3, and pt4. Aha: There's the problem. The variable pt2 shows the correct values of 5.5 and 1.5, but the other two variables have the same values assigned to them. No wonder the program won't work. Two corners of the rectangle have been assigned the same point.

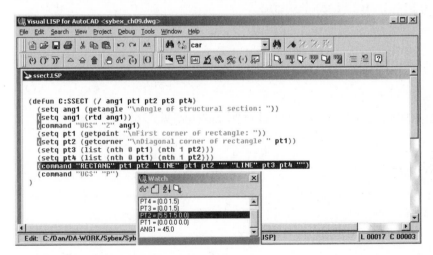

Now that you've found the error, you may be a little perplexed. How could you have made such a mistake? Well, look at the two preceding lines. Because the lines of code are so similar, you undoubtedly copied the first and pasted it to get the second, and then you got distracted and forgot to edit the line. I've done this myself more times than I'd like to admit. Let's fix the problem.

To clear all the break points when you're finished with them, press Shift+Ctrl+F9. If you want to disable the breakpoints while leaving them in place for future debugging, right-click each one, click Breakpoint Service, and click the Disable button in the Breakpoint Service dialog box. There are a number of ways to move through breakpoints:

- ⏶ Continue resumes from the current breakpoint.

- ⏷ Quit stops the current break loop and moves up one level. This is useful only with break loops inside other break loops. The previous example uses only a single break loop, so clicking this button produces the same result as clicking the Reset button.

- ⏶ Reset stops all break loops, even if they're nested.

Animate

When I first found this debugging function, I thought it was fun. Now I don't use it because it takes so long. Try it at least once to see how it works; you may like it.

To turn on animation, use Debug → Animate. Now, load your program, and switch to AutoCAD to try the command. As you follow the prompts for your program, VLIDE switches between the Visual LISP editor and the AutoCAD editor to display the program and highlight the section being evaluated as it moves along. Because this happens so slowly, you can follow along and see where the program hangs up. You may also have time to make coffee and answer your e-mail.

Testing the Program: Final Touches

When your program appears to work flawlessly, it's time to try to break it:

1. If you haven't already done so, add all local program variables to the list of arguments for the DEFUN function.

2. Save the AutoLISP program.

3. Exit the Visual LISP editor, and exit the drawing to clear all stored variables from memory. This step is critical. If you've been debugging one or more programs, it's very likely that some of the variables still have values stored in them.

4. Start AutoCAD, and set up as many variations as possible of how your new function may be applied. To do this for a program like the earlier SSECT command, create a series of lines at different angles—some regular angles like 45 degrees, and others at random angles going in all directions.

5. Use the new command function to create end-section symbols. When prompted for an angle, pick two points on each line. Type some angles. Then, type in some random letters, hit the Esc key, and press the Spacebar to see what happens. In other words, do things that an AutoCAD user *could* do, even if they don't seem logical. This program still has some flaws. See if you can find them.

6. Compare the prompts in your new command to those in AutoCAD to make sure they're similar in form.

Performing these steps with the SSECT program brings up six concerns:

- When the program is running, all the AutoCAD commands and their related prompts are displayed in the command line. You can fix that by turning off the setvar CMDECHO at the beginning of the program and then turning it back on at the end of the program.

- It would be nice if the operator could select a default angle of 0 by pressing Enter. You can fix that with the IF function.

- If you press the Esc key after the UCS is rotated but before the program ends, the UCS never returns to its previous state. You can fix that by adding error handling.

- If you change your mind after creating the new symbol, you have to undo each step used by your program to create the symbol. You can fix that by setting start and end points for UNDO in the program.

- If you pick two points that have the same X or Y coordinates, the rectangle and both lines look like a single line because they're stacked on top of each other. You can fix that, too, but maybe a whole new approach is in order. See the "COND, INITGET, GETKWORD" section below for a different approach to this program.

- When the program is done, nil is printed to the command line. You can prevent that by adding the line (PRINC) to the end of the program.

Running the program as designed prints the following lines to the AutoCAD text screen:

```
Command: SSECT
Angle of structural section <0>:
ucs
Current ucs name:   *WORLD*
Enter an option [New/Move/orthoGraphic/Prev/Restore/Save/Del/Apply/?/World]
<World>: z
Specify rotation angle about Z axis <90>: 0.000000000000000
Command:
First corner of rectangle:
Diagonal corner of rectangle RECTANG
Specify first corner point or [Chamfer/Elevation/Fillet/Thickness/Width]:
Specify other corner point or [Area/Dimensions/Rotation]:
Command: LINE Specify first point:
Specify next point or [Undo]:
Specify next point or [Undo]:
Command: LINE Specify first point:
Specify next point or [Undo]:
Specify next point or [Undo]:
Command: UCS
Current ucs name:   *WORLD*
Enter an option [New/Move/orthoGraphic/Prev/Restore/Save/Del/Apply/?/World]
<World>: P
Command: nil
```

By turning off the setvar CMDECHO at the beginning of the program and then turning it back on at the end of the program, you can reduce the screen text to the following lines:

```
Command: ssect
Angle of structural section <0>:
First corner of rectangle:
Diagonal corner of rectangle
```

Obviously, this is much cleaner. You should wait until you finish testing the program before turning off CMDECHO, because all those lines that are accessible in the Text Window of AutoCAD can be helpful in debugging.

The following code listing shows what the program looks like when it's rewritten to address most of the concerns identified earlier. The core of the program should look familiar, but there are probably a number of things that aren't so familiar. I'll discuss them in later sections of this chapter; you don't have to understand everything right now.

The new version of ssect.lsp is named ssect_xtra.lsp and uses inline annotation—the notes that appear after the semicolon in each line (see Listing 9.1). In the Visual LISP editor shown in Figure 9.1, these comments would be displayed as maroon text on a gray background.

Listing 9.1

ssect_xtra.lsp

```
;;;ssect_xtra.lsp
(defun RTD (r)                     ;function for converting radians
(* 180.0 (/ r pi))                 ;calculates degrees from radians
)                                  ;end DEFUN RTD
(defun LocalError (msg)            ;defines function LocalError
  (command)                        ;cancels active command on error
  (command "UCS" "P")              ;resets UCS to previous on error
  (setvar "CMDECHO" cmd)           ;resets CMDECHO on error
  (setq *error* existError)        ;restores *error* function
  (print "Resetting UCS: ")        ;message to user on error
  (princ)                          ;print a clear line
)                                  ;ends DEFUN LocalError
(defun C:SSECT (/ existError cmd ang1 pt1 pt2 pt3 pt4)
  (setq existError *error*)        ;stores current error function
  (setq *error* LocalError)        ;resets *error* to LocalError
  (command "UCS" "Z" "0")          ;creates a previous UCS
  (setq cmd (getvar "CMDECHO"))    ;gets and stores current CMDECHO
  (setvar "CMDECHO" 0)             ;resets CMDECHO to 0
  (command "UNDO" "be")            ;starts a group for UNDO
  (setq ang1 (getangle "\nAngle of structural section <0>: "))
    (if (= ang1 nil)(setq ang1 0)) ;sets a default value for ang1
  (setq ang1 (rtd ang1))           ;uses RTD to convert to degrees
  (command "UCS" "Z" ang1)         ;rotates UCS around the Z axis
  (setq pt1 (getpoint "\nFirst corner of rectangle: "))
```

```
(setq pt2 (getcorner "\nDiagonal corner of rectangle " pt1))
(setq pt3 (list (nth 0 pt1) (nth 1 pt2)))
(setq pt4 (list (nth 0 pt2) (nth 1 pt1)))
(command "RECTANG" pt1 pt2 "LINE" pt1 pt2 "" "LINE" pt3 pt4 "")
(command "UCS" "P")                 ;restores previous UCS
(command "UNDO" "end")              ;ends the group for UNDO
(setvar "CMDECHO" cmd)              ;resets value of CMDECHO
(setq *error* existError)           ;restores prior *error* function
(princ)                             ;prints a clear line
)                                   ;Ends DEFUN C:SSECT
```

Error Handling

I used error handling in the last program example, because if you cancel the program before it ends you're left with an unexpected UCS. Now let's see how error handling works.

The purpose of error handling is to return the system to its original state if a user presses the Esc key in an attempt to stop a program prematurely. You can see why that would be a problem with programs designed to make changes in order to run—a change in the current coordinate system, for example, or in the value assigned to OSMODE to control running osnaps. You don't want AutoCAD users to be unpleasantly surprised as a result of using your AutoLISP function.

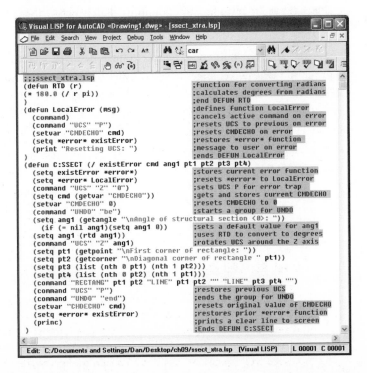

Figure 9.1

ssect_xtra.lsp **program in the Visual LISP editor**

Error-trapping functions are defined the same way as any other AutoLISP function—using DEFUN without the C: in front of the function name. Once you define the error-trapping function, you can use it in any of your other programs by using SETQ to assign it to the AutoLISP variable *error*. The name of that variable does indeed include two asterisks. It's a special variable in AutoLISP, but it has no value until one is assigned using the SETQ function.

There are two kinds of error-trapping strategies: specific and general. The general strategy uses the UNDO command in AutoCAD to set a mark. The error handler rolls AutoCAD back to that mark in response to a program error. This strategy contains potential problems that could have dire consequences, so I won't cover it here. Instead, I recommend that you create a specific error-handling function for any program that changes anything while it's running—system variables, or open files, for example.

I recommend these steps for error handling.

1. Using the BEgin option of UNDO, start an UNDO group at the beginning of any program that creates entities. Doing so allows the user to clear newly created objects with a single UNDO if they don't like the results of using your program.

2. Save the settings of all system variables or environmental variables that are changed in the program by using SETQ to assign them to a program variable.

3. Write an error-trapping function that resets those variables to their original settings in response to an error that occurs while the program is running.

4. Place the error-trapping function immediately before the command function it applies to.

Let's add an error handling function to the mid.lsp program from Chapter 8. The original program made two changes to system variables: OSMODE was changed to 512, and APERTURE was changed to 3. If you recall, the program was polite enough to change the system variables back at the end. That works great as long as nothing goes wrong, but if you cancel the command before it finishes running, you end up with Nearest as the only running osnap. Here's what an error-handling function looks like for a program that changes OSMODE and APERTURE.

```
(defun ErrorMid (message)      ;define function named "ErrorMid"
  (command)                    ;cancel any active command
  (setvar "osmode" os)         ;set "osmode" to saved variable
  (setvar "aperture" ap)       ;set "aperture" to saved variable
  (setq *error* temperr)       ;restore existing *error* function
  (prompt "\nResetting System Variables ")    ;inform user
  (princ)                      ;print a clear line
)
```

This function won't do anything until it's called by another program. Once the error-handling function is written, it must be referenced at the beginning of the C:MID function definition—that means *before* any variables get changed. To use the error-handling function ErrorMid, edit the definition for the C:MID program by adding the following lines:

```
(defun C:MID (/ p1 p2 os ap m)
    (setq temperr *error*)      ;store any current value for *error*
    (setq *error* ErrorMid)     ;re-assign *error* to your function
```

REAL PROGRAMMERS

Even though I've used AutoLISP to solve a lot of problems over the years, I don't consider myself a real programmer. All I want is to get something done, understand how I did it, and avoid surprises when I open the file again later. If it works, I'm happy, even if another programmer could have written it with half as many lines of code. Real programmers, by contrast, strive for a certain artistic flair; they want to create programs that are as efficient and elegant as possible.

Once you get a feel for writing programs, you may want to become a real programmer. So, I asked two pros to give me some guidelines to pass along to you (even if I don't always follow them myself). Here's some advice from Paul Richardson and Scott Danis:

Use variable names that mean something. I tend to use cryptic variable names like p1, p2, and p3 for points. Paul and Scott use names like lineStartPoint and lineEndPoint.

Use "camel case" for variables. Huh? Oh, yeah, camels have humps. If your variable names contain more than one word, use lowercase for the first letter of the first word and uppercase to start each word after that, as in textInsertPoint. No spaces, though. Differentiate functions from variables by using uppercase for all the words when you create a function. The DTR program could look like this: DegreesToRadians. Why? Because it makes debugging code much easier.

Annotate your code. Sometimes I'm really good at this, and other times I'm not. For the two AutoLISP chapters in this book, I've annotated most of the code so you understand what each line does. At the very least, place an explanatory paragraph at the beginning of each AutoLISP program you write. Then, when you open it four years from now, you'll have a clue.

Indent clearly and consistently. Scott uses a full tab for all indents because he finds it makes debugging easier. Paul uses only two spaces for indents to reduce the width of the file when using deeply nested constructs. I use the Visual LISP editor to format my code and then fiddle around with it until it makes sense to me. In other words, my formatting isn't always consistent.

continues

continued

Label every closing parenthesis that completes a section. You can debug programs more efficiently if you can quickly find the end of different sections: for example: `);while`, or `);if`, or `);defun`. Don't forget that the entire line after a semicolon is seen as a comment, so don't try to place annotation anywhere within a line of code. It has to come at the end or on its own line. If you're using the Visual LISP editor, it will be obvious, because everything after the semicolon is color-coded as a comment.

Create functions for actions you can use as part of other functions. The most common examples in AutoLISP are functions that convert from degrees to radians or radians to degrees. Because many other programs have to make these kinds of conversions, you can use the function instead of duplicating the lines of code each time you need them. That makes things a little more elegant, and real programmers like elegant code.

Study programs written by professionals. The best way to study existing code is to try to annotate each line of someone else's program. If you can annotate it, you understand how it works.

Learn to write effective error-handling routines. Because error handling makes programs longer, I omitted it from some of the examples in this book; but you should read the section on error handling carefully and incorporate it into your programs.

Test your code extensively. Have as many other people as possible test it as well, and ask everyone to try to break it on purpose.

Do your research when you have a problem. Web searches, newsgroups, and other programmers can help you sidestep hours of trial and error.

Annotation

Earlier in this chapter, I showed you how a semicolon can be used to add notes to an AutoLISP program. The more notes you add, the easier it will be for you and others to understand your programs later. But too much annotation can make your code harder to read. Find a nice balance.

Annotation should include header material identifying the name of the program, when it was written, who wrote it, what it does, and any limitations you want to put on its use. You (or your employer) own the copyright on any program you write, and so do other people who write code. That's why you shouldn't use programs without permission. I advise you to take a leaf from Autodesk's book. At the beginning of the file, add a line giving people permission to use your program as-is. If you don't want anyone to use your programs, indicate that in the file, and don't pass them around. If you want to protect the code itself from being used by others to write their own program, compile it so it can't be edited. Check the Visual LISP editor Help system to see how.

When you write a program as a subcontractor, make sure all parties agree about who owns the final produce. I retain ownership of my programs, but I give permission for them to be used without express or implied warranty. Why no warranty? Once you hand over a program, you can't anticipate every possible use, or misuse, particularly if you don't compile the programs.

Listing 9.2 is the complete MID.lsp program with annotation and error handling added. To differentiate types of annotation, I varied the number of semicolons used for each section as follows:

;;;;	General header material
;;;	Specific description of the code
;;	Header for individual sections of the program
;	Annotation of individual lines in the code

Listing 9.2

MID.lsp

```
;;;; mid.lsp
;;;; Copyright 2006 by Daniel Abbott. Permission to use,
;;;; copy, modify, and distribute this code for any
;;;; purpose is hereby granted. I provide this program
;;;; "as is" with all faults. I specifically disclaim any
;;;; implied warranty of fitness for any particular use.
;;;; I do not warrant that the program will be error free.

;;;Purpose

;;; This program will place a point between two objects
;;; selected by the user. If parallel lines are selected
;;; point will be centered between them. It is designed as
;;; an aid in adding dimensions between lines that represent
;;; interior walls on floor plans. The points can be used
;;; as dimension origins to locate walls. If points are added
;;; to other dimension origins -- corners, window openings
;;; door openings -- QDIM can be used to quickly add
;;; continuous dimensions by selecting the points using the
;;; FILTER or QSELECT commands.
```

continues

continued

```
;; ----------- PROGRAM CODE STARTS BELOW THIS LINE ---------

;; Error handling function

(defun ErrorMid (msg)              ;define function ErrorTrpMid
  (command)                        ;cancels active command
  (setvar "osmode" os)             ;set "osmode" to os
  (setvar "aperture" ap)           ;set "aperture" to ap
  (setq *error* ExistError)        ;restore existing *error*
  (prompt "\nResetting: ")         ;inform user
  (princ)                          ;print a clear line
);end defun


;; Program Code
(defun C:MID (/ existError p1 p2 os ap m)
  (setq existError *error*)    ;store an existing *error*
  (setq *error* ErrorMid)      ;re-assign *error* to ErrorMid
  (setq os (getvar "osmode"))  ;saves current osnap settings
  (setq ap (getvar "aperture"));saves current aperture setting
  (setvar "osmode" 512)        ;resets "osmode" to  nearest
  (setvar "aperture" 3)        ;resets "aperture" to 3 pixels
  (initget 1)                  ;prevents Enter as a response
  (setq p1 (getpoint "\nFirst point: "))
  (setq p2 (getpoint "\nSecond point: " p1));second point
  (setq m                      ;sets program variable m
    (polar p1                  ;polar starts from p1
      (angle p1 p2)            ;angle from p1 to p2
      (/ (distance p1 p2) 2.0);distance p1 to p2 divided by 2
    );end polar
  );end setq
  (command "point" "non" m)    ;point placed at m with NO osnap
  (setvar "osmode" os)         ;return osmode setting to original
  (setvar "aperture" ap)       ;return aperture setting to original
  (setq *error* existError)    ;return existing error handler
  (princ)
);end defun
```

To save space and simplify the code, some of the remaining program examples in this chapter don't include error handling or annotation. Actual programs should have both.

Selection Sets and Entity Manipulation

In Chapter 8, you saw a list of GET functions—functions designed to get data or objects. Most of them are simple and allow you to prompt users so they know what kind of data you're trying to get. Now let's look at some functions that are more powerful and complex. First I'll show you how your AutoLISP program can get information about entities in your drawing. Once you understand how to get information from an entity, I'll show you how to use that information.

ASSOC, ENTGET, ENTSEL

The ASSOC, ENTGET, and ENTSEL functions show up all the time in AutoLISP programs. They can work together to get a ton of information from an entity in the drawing. You can find out what the entity is, what layer it's on, what linetype it uses, and so on. Enter the following line of code at the AutoCAD command line with an Enter, and then select a circle when prompted. This line will prove extremely useful in future programs:

```
(cdr (assoc 5 (entget (car (entsel)))))
```

The value returned will vary, but it's always a hexadecimal number that represents the entity's *handle*. AutoCAD assigns a handle to each entity as it's created. The handle is permanently associated with that entity.

> Hexadecimal numbers are base 16 numbers, rather than base 10: *hex* (6) + *decimal* (10) are combined to form the word *hexadecimal* (16). Hexadecimals are used in computing because they can represent binary values with fewer characters than are needed for decimal values. To create a base 16 number system, several letters have to be used as though they're digits. To count in hexadecimal, use 0, 1, 2, 3, 4, 5, 6, 7, 8, 9, a, b, c, d, e, f, 10, 11, 12, 13, 14, 15, 16, 17, 18, 19, 1a, 1b, and so on. Entity names and entity handles in AutoLISP are hexadecimal.

You can use the same line with a number other than a 5 to get other information from the entity. Enter the line of code again with a 0, and select the same object; now you'll find out what kind of entity it is:

```
(cdr (assoc 0 (entget (car (entsel)))))
```

For this function, `"CIRCLE"` was returned when I picked a circle. Not too surprising (other entities may not be so obvious). Draw some polylines, dimensions, text, ellipses, and so on, load this line again, and then pick each one. You'll find out what kinds of entity they are.

Now that you know that you can use a 5 or a 0, you've probably guessed that other integers give you different information. These integers are called DXF group codes; and I've listed some of them in Table 9.1, but more on that later. We're not finished with this line of code yet. Let's look at each element of `(cdr (assoc 0 (entget (car (entsel)))))` from the inside out, starting with `(entsel)`. You'll execute each function and then select the same circle, and discuss the results.

CAR, CADR, AND NTH—HUH?

These functions provide a means of identifying items in a list. The function name NTH is logical enough, coming from terms like 4th, 5th, and so on, but don't expect CAR and CDR to make sense. They're both acronyms from the 1950s when they were used to describe the physical location in which computers stored data.

When retrieving items from a list, I find the NTH function more logical, even though the CAR/CDR combinations evaluate more quickly. When used alone, CDR doesn't have an NTH equivalent, so in many situations it's your only choice. The following table describes each function and shows its NTH equivalent, if it has one:

CAR	Returns first element of a list	NTH 0
CADR	Returns second element of a list	NTH 1
CADDR	Returns third element of a list	NTH 2
CDR	Returns a list without the first element	None

CADR and CADDR are both special-case combinations of the two base functions, designed to help manipulate coordinate points, which are lists of three values. But CAR and CDR can be used with each other to get any element of a list no matter how long it is. As a result, you may see some wild combinations as you inspect existing AutoLISP programs. For future reference, this is how these functions are used.

Suppose you write a program that gets a specific block name from a list of seven blocks in a drawing. If the block names each have a single letter, the list consists of seven elements, or *atoms*: A, B, C, D, E, F, and G, for example. Because CAR can return the first item in the list, getting block A is easy. Because CDR returns everything after the first item in the list, applying CAR to the CDR of the list gets the second item, and applying CDR repeatedly eventually gets every item on the list. Let's go seven deep.

In the following examples, the variable `blkList` has been assigned a value consisting of the list A, B, C, D, E, F, and G:

All items	`!blkList` at the command line returns (A B C D E F G)
Seventh item	`(car (cdr (cdr (cdr (cdr (cdr (cdr blkList)))))))` returns G

Let's try getting that seventh item again, this time using the NTH function:

Seventh item   (nth 6 blkList) returns G

See why I like the NTH function? What would it take to retrieve the twenty-seventh item? Generally, I'm willing to sacrifice some speed of execution for simplicity. Oh, and that's not a mistake: The seventh item really is the nth 6 item, because the counting starts with item 0, the nth 0 atom in the list.

(entsel)

The ENTSEL function prompts the user to select a single object. When you use the ENTSEL function, it returns two pieces of information: the entity's name and the coordinates of the point picked to select it. When I selected a circle, (<Entity name: 7ef61ea8> (46.904 22.3015 0.0)) was returned. 7ef61ea8 is the entity *name*, and (46.904 22.3015 0.0) is the selection point.

(car (entsel))

Let's say you want only the entity's name. To eliminate the selection point from the list, use the CAR function, which returns only the first item in a list. (car (entsel)) returns only <Entity name: 7ef61ea8>. As I mentioned earlier in this chapter, I prefer the NTH function for this purpose; but you'll see this process used with CAR at some point, so you should be familiar with it. Use this line of code on your own circle and compare the results.

(entget (car (entsel)))

Now that you have the entity's name, use it with the ENTGET function to get more information. Think of ENTGET as "GET the ENTtity's data." Here's what that function returns from a specific circle. If you enter this line of code in the Visual LISP console it returns all this information on a single, long line similar to the broken lines that follow:

```
((-1 . <Entity name: 7ef61ea8>) (0 . "CIRCLE") (330 . <Entity name:
7ef61cf8>) (5 . "8D") (100 . "AcDbEntity") (67 . 0) (410 . "Model") (8 .
"0") (48 . 2.2222) (100 . "AcDbCircle") (10 51.9761 28.3512 0.0) (40 .
7.95186) (210 0.0 0.0 1.0))
```

If you have a sharp eye, you may notice that the group code 100 shows up twice on this list. Group code 100 is a subclass marker that has no use here. If you want more information, see the article on subclass markers in the Visual LISP editor Help system. And if you want a glimpse of what real programmers deal with, type **ARX↵0↵CL** at the AutoCAD command prompt to see a list of all the AcDb object types in AutoCAD. In other words, don't worry about group code 100.

What you see in this confusing mess is a group of lists—13 of them. They're known as *association* lists because each piece of information is associated with a group code—the integer within each set of parentheses. The period you see with a space on either side is known as a *dot*. If the set of parentheses contains a dot, it's known as a *dotted pair*.

Don't forget about the spaces on both sides of the dot. As you start writing more advanced programs, you'll have to construct your own dotted pairs; leaving out a space will create a problem. The parentheses that have no dot are associations between an integer and another list. The most common list is a list of coordinate points. The list associated with the integer 10, for example, is the center point of the circle—a list of its X, Y, and Z coordinates.

> This dot is *not* a decimal point. Decimal points are distinguished by having no spaces on either side. That's why using a real number that is less than one without a leading zero returns an error message. Dots with spaces aren't decimal points, even if the space is only on one side.

(assoc 0 (entget (car (entsel))))

When you select the same circle after running this part of the function, AutoLISP returns: `(0 . "CIRCLE")`.

The function ASSOC is how you get each association list. You identify the integer as the first argument, followed by an association list. In this case, using 0 with ASSOC returns the dotted pair in which 0 is associated with `"CIRCLE"`. 0 is always associated with the kind of entity you have selected. But in order to use this information, you don't need the 0 or the dot; you just need the string `"CIRCLE"`. To get everything except the first item in the list, use the function CDR.

(cdr (assoc 0 (entget (car (entsel)))))

Now we're back where we started. This function returns `"CIRCLE"`, the single thing you want—the type of entity. What else can you get? You can get the entity name by supplying an argument of -1 in place of the 0. You can get the entity handle by supplying an argument of 5 instead of the 0. Table 9.1 lists some of the integer values that can be associated with an entity in AutoCAD. If you substitute any of them for the 0 and select some entities, you get the data specified. They're known as DXF group codes. If you want the entire list of entities and the group codes most commonly associated with them, use the Visual LISP editor Help system as shown in Figure 9.2. To get the entire list of group codes, search Help for the article "Group Codes in Numerical Order."

GROUP CODE	PURPOSE
−1	Entity name: This is a unique hexadecimal value assigned to each entity in the drawing, but it differs from an entity's handle—the name changes every time you open the drawing. It's used in some situations to get information about an entity.
−4	Conditional operator: This is used to add conditions to the criteria by which a selection set is constructed. See the discussion of conditional operators later in this chapter.
0	Entity type: This is the group code for the object type—a string that tells you what kind of object you have selected. In our case, it was a "CIRCLE".
2	Name: This is different from the entity name. This group code represents a user-defined name for things like block definitions. Only entities that you can name have a group code of 2.
5	Entity handle: It's similar to the name in that it's a unique hexadecimal name, but it differs from the name in one important way—it's permanent. No matter how many times you open or close the drawing, this object always has this handle. It changes only if you insert the drawing or bind an XRef of the drawing into another drawing.
6	Linetype name: Only entities that can have linetypes have this code.
7	Text style name: This is only used for text or mtext objects.
8	Layer name: This is a property of all entities.
10	Primary point: This is a point value, and it means something different for different kinds of entities. For a circle, it's a center. For a line, it's the starting endpoint, and so on.
38	Entity elevation: This code is assigned only to entities with an elevation other than 0. If an entity's elevation is 0, searching for this code returns nil.
39	Entity thickness: Like elevation, this code is assigned only if the entity's thickness isn't 0.
48	Entity linetype scale: This code is assigned only if the entity's linetype scale isn't the default value. If it's the default, searching for this code returns nil. See Listing 9.3 for an example of how to handle a nil return for one of the DXF codes.
62	Entity color: The index color codes are used, with 0 representing color BYBLOCK, and 256 representing color BYLAYER.

Table 9.1

Partial List of DXF Group Codes

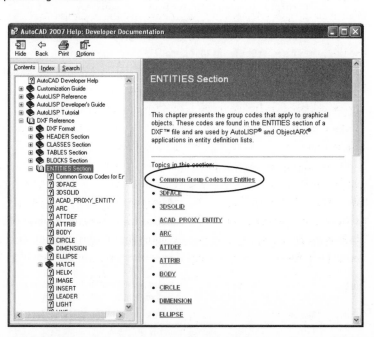

Figure 9.2

Help system listing of group codes

Now that you know some important group codes and how to use them to get information from an entity, let's see how easy it is to apply this approach in another context.

Let's say you want a new command that will allow you to select an entity and apply its linetype scale to other entities. You could do this with MATCHPROP, but that would match all the properties, and you want to match only linetype scale. You can use (cdr (assoc 48 (entget (car (entsel))))) to get the linetype scale of a selected entity, which can then be assigned to a variable. That variable can be used to change the linetype scale of other entities. Once you include error handling, it may look like Listing 9.3.

Listing 9.3

chlts.lsp

```
(defun EtrapCHLTS (message)
  (command)
  (setvar "cmdecho" ce)
  (setq *error* existError)
  (prompt "Reset")
  (princ)
  )

(defun C:CHLTS (/ existError ce source updateEnts lScale)
  (setq existError *error* )
  (setq *error* EtrapCHLTS)
  (setq ce (getvar "cmdecho"))
  (setvar "cmdecho" 0)
  (setq source (entsel "\nSelect source object: "))
  (prompt "\nSelect the objects to update: ")
  (setq updateEnts (ssget))
  (setq ltScale (cdr (assoc 48 (entget (car source)))))
  (if (= ltScale nil) (setq ltScale 1))
  (command "CHPROP" updateEnts "" "S" ltScale "")
  (setvar "cmdecho" ce)
  (setq *error* existError)
  (princ)
  )
```

This program is described in Table 9.2.

Table 9.2	LINE OF CODE	PURPOSE
chlts.lsp **Description**	(defun EtrapCHLTS (message)	Defines the error-handling function to be used with C:CHLTS.
	(command)	Cancels any existing command.
	(setvar "cmdecho" ce)	Resets the system variable to its original setting if something interrupts C:CHLTS.
	(setq *error* existError)	Resets the *ERROR* function to the value assigned to variable existError.
	(prompt "Reset")	Prints the message to the screen.

LINE OF CODE	PURPOSE
`(princ)`	Prints a clear line to the command prompt.
`)`	Ends the DEFUN function.
`(defun C:CHLTS (/ existError` `ce source updateEnts lScale)`	Defines the new command, and identifies local program variables.
`(setq existError *error* )`	Assigns an active error-handling function to the program variable `existError`.
`(setq *error* EtrapCHLTS)`	Sets *ERROR* to the error-handling function defined previously.
`(setq ce (getvar "cmdecho"))`	Assigns the current setting for CMDECHO to the variable ce.
`(setvar "cmdecho" 0)`	Sets the AutoCAD system variable CMDECHO to 0 (turns it off).
`(setq source (entsel "\nSelect` `source object: "))`	Sets the variable `source` equal to a single entity selected by the user. This variable is used later in the program to get information from the selected entity.
`(prompt "\nSelect the objects` `to update: ")`	Tells the user what to do in the next line. The standard `Select objects:` prompt issued by the SSGET function isn't specific enough. You shouldn't use ENTSEL again, because the user may want to select more than one object.
`(setq updateEnts (ssget))`	Sets the variable `updateEnts` to the entity or group of entities selected by the user in response to the prompt `Select objects:` issued by the SSGET function. The operator can use any AutoCAD selection method.
`(setq ltScale (cdr (assoc 48` `(entget (car source)))))`	Uses the functions discussed in the previous section to determine the object's linetype scale. 48 is the DXF group code associated with linetype scale. Once the value is obtained, it's assigned to the variable `ltScale`.
`(if (= ltScale nil)` `(setq ltScale 1))`	Necessary because of a quirk in AutoLISP. Some dotted pairs aren't shown for characteristics that have a default setting. If an entity has a default linetype scale, which is 1, its linetype scale isn't included in an association list. This line assigns a value of 1 to the variable `ltScale` if it's currently assigned a value of `nil`. `ltScale` has a value of `nil` only if the entity selected has a linetype scale of 1. The IF function is discussed later in this chapter.
`(command "CHPROP" updateEnts` `"" "S" ltScale "")`	Uses the CHPROP command to update the selection set obtained with SSGET.
`(setvar "cmdecho" ce)`	Resets the system variable CMDECHO to its original setting.
`(princ)`	Prints a blank line at the command line.
`)`	Ends the DEFUN function.

Using this code as a sample, you can easily modify it to create other new commands that can be used to match any property of an entity to another group of entities. This technique is widely used for managing layers. Just use a different DXF group code to get at the data you want to extract or change.

SSGET

You've seen the SSGET function several times now. It's often used by itself in the form `(SSGET)` when you want the user to create a selection set. The SSGET function has some other options that are worth noting. If you want a program to create a selection set directly from the entities in the drawing, you can modify SSGET as described in Table 9.3.

	SSGET OPTION	PURPOSE
Table 9.3 **Examples of SSGET Options**	`(ssget "X")`	Selects *all* objects in the drawing. If you save the result to a program variable, you can modify all the entities in the drawing.
	`(ssget "X" '((0 . "CIRCLE")))`	Selects *all* circles in the drawing. Notice the single quote preceding the dotted pair. You need that here so the function interprets what follows literally: no function directly follows the open parenthesis. The zero is the group code for entity type. If you want to select objects other than circles, name them instead. If you want more than one type of entity included, use commas to separate them with this format: `(ssget "X" '((0 . "CIRCLE,LINE"))`. To see the entire list of entity types, use the Help system in the Visual LISP editor as shown later in this chapter.
	`(ssget "X" (list (cons 0 "circle")))`	Creates (CONStructs) a dotted pair. This line also selects all circles in a drawing. This is an alternative means of selecting objects. Again, to select other objects, substitute their entity type for `"CIRCLE"`.
	`(ssget "X" '((8 . "0")))`	Uses the group code 8 instead of 0. It selects all objects on layer 0. To get objects on a different layer, put that layer name in double quotes after the dot (don't forget the space). Most of the same DXF group codes can be used with this function as can be used by ASSOC.
	`(ssget "X" '((38 . 10)))`	Selects all objects at an elevation of 10 units. 38 is the DXF group code for ELEVATION.
	`(ssget "W" pt1 pt2)`	Defines a selection set with a window by identifying its corners—in this case, pt1 and pt2. If you can use W, it won't surprise you to know that you can also use C, for a crossing window, P for the previous selection set, and so on. As is true when you're manually selecting entities, they must be visible on the screen to be selected in this way.
	`(ssget pt1)`	Selects all entities that pass through the coordinates assigned to pt1.

SSGET Relational Tests

What if you want to combine properties for a more complex selection set the way you can when using the FILTER or the QSELECT command? Use SSGET with relational operators. These operators are identified in a dotted pair with the group code –4. They're always placed within double quotes. Table 9.4 shows the conditional operators and their meanings.

Let's see an example. To select all text whose height is equal to or greater than .125 but less than .25, use the following syntax (don't forget to leave a space in front of and after each dot in the dotted pairs):

```
(ssget "X" '((0 . "TEXT")(-4 . ">=")(40 . 0.125)(-4 . "<")(40 . 0.25)))
```

Let's take this one from left to right in Table 9.5.

OPERATION	MEANING	
"="	Equal to	Table 9.4
"/=" or "!="	Not equal to	**Conditional Operators for Use with SSGET**
"*"	All	
"<"	Less than	
"<="	Less than or equal to	
">"	Greater than	
">="	Greater than or equal to	

FUNCTION	PURPOSE	
(ssget "X"	The selection set will include all entities that meet the conditions that follow.	Table 9.5
'(	This quotes the following dotted pair so the 0 is interpreted not as a function but as a filter list.	**Application of Conditional Operators**
(0 . "TEXT")	Using the DXF group code for entity type limits the selection set to TEXT entities.	
(-4 . ">=")	The DXF conditional operator code sets the condition greater than or equal to the value that follows.	
(40 . 0.125)	DXF group code 40 is the text height. Only text greater than or equal to 0.125 will be selected.	
(-4 . "<")	This is the conditional operator code for less than the value that follows.	
(40 . 0.25)))	DXF group code 40 is the text height. Only text less than 0.25 will be selected.	

Combining Selection-Set Criteria

Combining selection sets complicates matters somewhat. If you want more control, you can add logical grouping to combine the conditions. The codes for logical grouping are shown in Table 9.6.

OPERATOR	PURPOSE	
"<AND"	Begin the and group	Table 9.6
"AND>"	End the and group	**Logical Grouping Operators**
"<OR"	Begin the or group	
"OR>"	End the or group	
"<XOR"	Begin the either/or group	
"XOR>"	End the either/or group	
"<NOT"	Begin the not group	
"NOT>"	End the not group	

Let's put it all together to create a selection set of all text in the drawing with a height greater than or equal to 3 but less than 6, or text of any height that is not on the text layer.

```
(setq ss1
  (ssget "X"
    '((0 . "TEXT")
      (-4 . ">=")
      (40 . 2)
      (-4 . "<")
      (40 . 6)
      (-4 . "<OR")
      (-4 . "<NOT")
      (8 . "TEXT")
      (-4 . "NOT>")
      (-4 . "OR>")
      )
    )
  )
```

How can you use this code? Let's say you have trouble getting people to use the office standard for text. They always use the right text height of 6 for titles, so you don't want to select any text with that height. Your drawings contain some text labels with a height of 2.5, so you don't want to change those either. But the height used for everything else varies, and the text is often on the wrong layer.

See if the program in Listing 9.4 makes sense. It uses the previous code to select all the text (but not mtext) whose height is between 2 and 6, no matter what layer it's on, and puts it on a text layer at the proper text height of 3 mm without changing its location. If text of any height is on a layer other than the text layer, it's put on the text layer.

Listing 9.4
_____
fixtxt.lsp
_____

```
(defun C:FIXTXT (/ ss1)
  (command "LAYER" "N" "Text" "C" "BLUE" "Text" "")
  (setq ss1
    (ssget "X"
      '((0 . "TEXT")
        (-4 . ">=")
        (40 . 2)
        (-4 . "<")
        (40 . 6)
        (-4 . "<OR")
        (-4 . "<NOT")
        (8 . "TEXT")
```

```
                            (-4 . "NOT>")
                            (-4 . "OR>")
                          )
                      )
                )
            (if (/= ss1 nil)
              (progn
                (command "CHPROP" ss1 "" "LA" "Text" "")
                (command "SCALETEXT" ss1 "" "E" 3)
              )
              (alert "No text found in that range: ")
            )
            (princ)
          )
```

I use AutoCAD commands in these examples because it's easier to understand, but you can directly modify the properties of entities by other means. For more information, read the Help system article on ENTMOD.

LISTS, ATOMS, FUNCTIONS, QUOTES AND SETQ: A SIDE TRIP

Now that you have some real experience with AutoLISP, let's review some concepts I found baffling when I first went in search of help writing Lisp programs. At that time (release 9, for the record), I had a specific and immediate problem, and I wanted to learn just enough to solve it. When I turned to the available references on AutoLISP, I found confusing discussions of functions, atoms, lists, and a host of other new concepts. But I was impatient to start programming and made the mistake of skipping over some important material. Now that you've gotten started programming, let me brief you on some of these concepts.

Lisp is short for List Processing language. When AutoLISP programs run, the Lisp interpreter evaluates each element according to certain rules. There are two kinds of elements: *atoms* and *lists*. An atom is a single object that includes function names (SETQ), numbers (real or integers), program variables, and strings, which are characters enclosed in quotes. You have seen examples of all of these objects earlier in this chapter. A list is a collection of atoms and/or other lists, all of which are contained within parentheses.

In the line (setq ang1 (rtd (getangle "\nAngle of rotation: "))), the entire list consists of an atom, setq; another atom, ang1; and a nested list. The nested list includes an atom, rtd; and another nested list. That nested list includes two atoms: a function, GETANGLE; and a string, "\nAngle of rotation: ".

continues

continued

The parentheses are essential in order for the AutoLISP interpreter to evaluate all these elements in the right order. Be thankful for the Visual LISP editor—it makes keeping track much easier than in the black-and-white days of yore.

Lists are always evaluated from left to right. When AutoLISP encounters an opening parenthesis, it immediately evaluates the first element unless you tell it not to. That first element must be a defined function, or your program fails. If you have a list like (1 2 3 4), your program will crash because the integer 1 isn't a function.

But you can tell AutoLISP not to evaluate the list at all and instead to read it literally. There is a specific function for doing that: QUOTE. You don't see the QUOTE function used often, because it has an alias: a single quotation mark. You can create a list of values by using either one of the following: (quote(3 4 5)) or '(3 4 5).

If you create the function (setq pt3 (quote(3 4 5))) or (setq pt3 '(3 4 5)), AutoLISP returns (3 4 5) and sets that list equal to the variable pt3.

Let's take another look at the SETQ function. Although I often tell people to think of it as meaning *Set Equal to*, that's not how it got its name. It's a combination of two functions: SET and QUOTE. If you assign a value to a variable using the SET function rather than the SETQ function, you have to type it in this format:

(set (quote pt1) '(3 4 5)) or (set 'pt1 '(3 4 5))

SETQ simplifies things by adding a quote to SET, so instead of (set (quote pt1)) you can type (SETQ pt1).

Now let's get back to writing programs.

IF Function

The IF function is often described by programmers as an IF - Then - Else function. It's used all the time to check a condition and have the program respond differently depending on whether the condition is true or false. An IF function has either one or two arguments. If it has one argument, and a condition is true, the function that follows is executed, and the program continues. If the condition is false, the program ignores the next function and continues on.

When an IF statement has two arguments, the first is executed when the IF function returns true, and the second argument is ignored. When the IF condition isn't true, the first function is ignored, and the second function is executed; then the program continues. The best way to understand it is to write a short program to create a toggle.

Creating Toggles

The IF function can be used to toggle a variable—turn it on or off depending on its current state—like a three-way light switch. Let's create a command that turns the UCS icon on if it's off and off if it's on. The visibility of the UCS icon is controlled by the variable UCSICON. Although UCSICON has four settings, you'll use only two of them: 0 to turn it off, and 3 to turn it on and place it at 0,0. See Listing 9.5.

This code described in Table 9.7.

Listing 9.5
ui.lsp

```
ui.lsp
(defun C:UI ()
 (setq uc (getvar "ucsicon"))
 (if (= uc 0)
    (setvar "ucsicon" 3)
    (setvar "ucsicon" 0)
 )
)
```

LINE OF CODE	PURPOSE
(defun C:UI ()	Creates a command function.
(setq uc (getvar "ucsicon"))	Assigns the current value of the system variable UCSICON to the program variable uc.
(if (= uc 0)	Checks to see if there is equality between the value of variable uc and 0. If the two values are equal, the = function returns T (true), and the program executes the next list. If there isn't an equality, the = function returns nil, and the next list is skipped.
(setvar "ucsicon" 3)	The "then" part of the IF function. It's executed *only* if the = function in the last list returns T. If uc is equal to 0, this line is executed, and the value of UCSICON is set to 3.
(setvar "ucsicon" 0)	The "else" part. If uc isn't equal to 0, this line is executed, and the value of UCSICON is set to 0.
)	Ends the IF function.
)	Ends the DEFUN function.

Table 9.7

UCS Toggle Using the IF Function

Creating Default Values

Your newly created AutoCAD commands should behave like every other AutoCAD command. That's why each of the prompts you've used so far starts on a new line and ends with a colon followed by a space. That kind of familiarity makes it easier for AutoCAD operators to use the commands.

Most AutoCAD commands have something else in common: Their prompts list the most likely response as a default that can be selected with an Enter. In AutoLISP programs, you can use the IF function to create defaults. The program in Listing 9.6 shows you how. It creates a circular polyline so you can make circles that have a line width. AutoCAD has a secret circular polyline command: DONUT. But using it requires some calculations. If you want a circle with a diameter of 22 and a width of 0.3, you have to calculate the inside diameter and outside diameter in order to draw it.

Listing 9.6 lets you draw a circle by giving a diameter and a width. While we're at it, let's add a default value. Now you can accept a default width of 0 and worry about editing it later. Of course, if you want all your polycircles to be the same width, you can build that into the program.

The following program uses the DONUT command to create a circular polyline. The width given by the operator is used to calculate the inside and outside diameters of the donut by subtracting it from the diameter to determine the inside diameter and adding it to determine the outside diameter.

Listing 9.6

polycircle.lsp

```
(defun C:CC (/  wid pt1 dia id od)
  (setq wid (getdist "\nWidth of Poly Circle <0>: "))
  (if (= wid nil)
      (setq wid 0)
  )
  (setq pt1 (getpoint "\nCenter of PolyCircle: "))
  (setq dia (getdist "\nDiameter of PolyCircle: " pt1))
  (setq id (- dia wid)
        od (+ dia wid)
  )
  (if (> id 0)
    (command "DONUT" id od pt1 "")
    (alert "Diameter must be positive and larger than width: ")
  )
  (princ)
)
```

The code for polycircle.lsp is described in Table 9.8.

Well, it's nice to have a default value, but in this program it's always 0. Doesn't Auto-CAD normally update the default settings to match the operator input from the last time the command was run? Yes, it does. If you want to do that, define a global program variable for the default width as discussed in the next section.

LINE OF CODE	PURPOSE	Table 9.8
`(defun C:CC (/ wid pt1 dia id od)`	You know what this line does by now. Note that I use CC as a command name because it's easier to type with the left hand than CP or PC. Of course, you can assign the command to a toolbar button.	**Creating Local Default Values**
`(setq wid (getdist "\nWidth of PolyCircle <0>: "))`	Assigns a value provided by the operator to the variable wid. I added a default value in the prompt by enclosing it in <>.	
	This doesn't create a default. It just tells the operator that there is one. An ENTER assigns the value nil to the variable wid. nil means "no numerical value."	
`(if (= wid nil)(setq wid 0)`	Creates the default. If the user responded to the last prompt with an Enter, then the list (= wid nil) returns T for true, and AutoLISP evaluates the next list and assigns a value of 0 to the variable wid. Any value can be used instead of 0.	
	If the operator entered a value for width in the previous line, nil isn't equal to wid and (= wid nil) isn't true, so AutoLISP skips the next list and continues.	
`)`	Ends the IF function.	
`(setq pt1 (getpoint "\nCenter of PolyCircle: ")`	Assigns a point provided by the operator to the variable pt1.	
`(setq dia (getdist "\nDiameter of PolyCircle: " pt1))a`	Assigns a distance provided by operator to the variable dia. Supplying the argument pt1 forces the display of a rubberband tracking line from that point. Notice that the SETQ function is left open for defining multiple variables on the lines that follow.	
`id (- dia wid)`	Sets the variable id to the value stored in dia minus the value stored in wid. This value is used as the inside diameter in the AutoCAD DONUT command.	
`od (+ dia wid)`	Sets the variable od to the value stored in dia plus the value stored in wid. This value is used as the outside diameter in the AutoCAD DONUT command.	
`)`	Ends SETQ.	
`(if (> id 0)`	Checks to see if id is a positive number. If it is, the COMMAND function that follows is executed. If it isn't, the COMMAND function is skipped, and the ALERT function is executed.	
`(command "DONUT" id od pt1 "")`	Creates a donut using the values stored in the variables id, od, and pt1. If the donut inside diameter is equal to its outside diameter, the polycircle has a width of 0.	
`(alert "Diameter must be a positive and larger than width: ")`	Gives the user a warning if id is negative to prevent the program from failing.	
`(princ)`	Prints a clear line.	
`)`	Ends DEFUN.	

Default Settings with a Memory

Earlier in this chapter, I described local program variables. They hold their value only while the program is running and then return to a value of `nil`. (In other words, they're no longer variables.) Using local program variables is good practice if you want to prevent them from being used in another program. But what if you *do* want to use the same variable values again?

In the last program, you saw how the IF function can be used to create a default value. That default value doesn't update, though. No matter what the operator used the last time for a polycircle width, the value 0 shows up each time. If you want the default to be the last value used by the operator, you need a *global program variable*—one that won't return to `nil` when the program ends.

> This type of global default persists only during the current editing session. If the operator starts a new drawing or exits AutoCAD, the values bound to all program variables in AutoLISP are returned to `nil`.

To make a variable global, leave it off the list that follows your DEFUN statement. Be aware that you run the risk of inadvertently using the same symbol as a variable in a different program. To reduce this likelihood, use a variable name that is so specific to the program that it's unlikely to be used in any other. For this program, I use the name `*<>PolyCircWid*`. I can't imagine using this variable in another program, and other programmers almost never use the characters `*`, `<`, or `>`. Besides, how many commands could possibly use `PolyCircWid` as a logical part of a variable name? If you need even more reassurance, make the name even longer, and throw in some random characters.

The program in Listing 9.7 remembers the previous width used for a poly circle and makes it the default setting for future uses of the command. This one asks for a radius rather than a diameter, which makes it behave more like the CIRCLE command.

Listing 9.7

```
polycircle_defaults.lsp

(defun C:CCC (/ str1 wid pt1 rad id od)
  (if (= *<>PolyCircWid* nil)(setq *<>PolyCircWid* 0)
  )
  (setq str1 (rtos *<>PolyCircWid*))
  (setq wid
    (getdist (strcat "\nPolyCircle Width <" str1 ">: ")
    )
  )
  (if (= wid nil)(setq wid *<>PolyCircWid*)
  )
  (setq *<>PolyCircWid* wid)
  (setq pt1 (getpoint "\nCenter of PolyCircle: ")
```

```
        rad (getdist "\nRadius of PolyCircle: " pt1)
        id  (- (* rad 2) wid)
        od  (+ (* rad 2) wid)
      )
    (if (> id 0)
      (command "DONUT" id od pt1 "")
      (alert "Diameter must be positive and larger than width: ")
    )
  (princ)
)
```

Because most of this program was described earlier, let's look only at the lines that create and use the global default in Table 9.9.

LINE OF CODE	PURPOSE	
(defun C:CCC (/ str1 wid pt1 rad id od)	Notice that *<>PolyCircWid* doesn't appear in the list of local program variables.	**Table 9.9** **Polycircle Command with Global Default**
(if (= *<>PolyCircWid* nil)(setq *<>PolyCircWid* 0)	*<>PolyCircWid* is the global program variable this program uses to keep track of the pline width that the operator used the last time a polycircle was drawn. But what if this is the first time the program has been used in this editing session? Because the value of *<>PolyCircWid* will be used later in the program, it can't be nil. This line checks to see if it's nil. If it is, a value of 0 is assigned to it, and that becomes the default. If *<>PolyCircWid* already has a value, that value is retained.	
(setq str1 (rtos *<>PolyCircWid*))	The default setting displayed in the prompt the operator sees when running this program should match the value stored in the variable *<>PolyCircWid*, which has a real number assigned to it. Only a string can be used in a prompt, so this line uses the RTOS function to turn the value of *<>PolyCircWid* into a string and then assigns that string to the variable str1 for use in the prompt in the next line.	
(getdist (strcat "\nPolyCircle Width <" str1 ">: ")	This line creates the GETDIST prompt by joining three strings together using the STRCAT function. The variable str1 is placed between < and > to display the value assigned to the variable *<>PolyCircWid*.	
(if (= wid nil)(setq wid *<>PolyCircWid*)	This IF statement is similar in function to the one in the last version of the program. If the variable wid is nil, the operator used an Enter, which means they want to accept the default setting. If (= wid nil) returns T, the following list is evaluated and the value of wid is assigned to the variable *<>PolyCircWid*. If (= wid nil) returns nil, the operator supplied a number that is used instead of the value stored in the variable *<>PolyCircWid*.	
(setq *<>PolyCircWid* wid)	This line assigns the current value of the variable wid to the variable *<>PolyCircWid* so it's available as the default the next time the operator uses the C:CCC function to create a polycircle.	
rad (getdist "\nRadius of PolyCircle: " pt1)	The only other change to this program is the use of a radius instead of a diameter. This matches the behavior of the AutoCAD CIRCLE command.	

Repeat Function

While programming, you often need to loop through a group of functions—either for a specific number of times, or indefinitely—until some condition changes. When you don't know how many times to repeat, use the WHILE function, which is discussed in the next section; when you do know how many times an evaluation must repeat, use the REPEAT function.

I created this next routine when I was asked to testify in a case in which one company accused another company of using direct copies of several of its drawings to produce an identical product. I wrote a program to determine whether a particular drawing was an original, independent creation or an electronic copy.

The program in Listing 9.8 uses entity handles, which are fixed, to compare the entities in one drawing with the entities in another. Rather than select each entity and use the LIST command to see the handles, I used this program to create a list of the handles for every object in each of the drawings and then write those lists to a text file. When I had finished comparing the files, I felt confident in judging how many entities had been copied from one to the other, and I had documentation to use in the deposition.

This program searches the database of the drawing to determine how many objects it contains and stores that number. Then, it goes through each object in the database and extracts its handle and object type. The handle and object types are then appended to a text file. If multiple sequential entities of the same type have the same hexadecimal name as those in another drawing, they're certainly copies, because handles are assigned to entities in chronological order.

Listing 9.8

handle_file.lsp

```
(defun c:handle_file (/ txtFile userProf fileName selSet1
                        ssLen indexCount entItem entHandle
                        entType entData entFile)
  (setq txtFile (getstring "\nName of file: "))
  (setq userProf (getenv "userprofile")
        fileName
        (strcat userProf "\\My Documents\\" txtFile ".txt")
  )
  (setq selSet1 (ssget "x"))
  (setq ssLen (sslength selSet1))
  (setq indexCount (1- ssLen)
        entFile (open fileName "a")
  )
  (repeat ssLen
    (setq entItem (ssname selSet1 indexCount)
```

```
            entHandle (cdr (assoc 5 (entget entItem)))
            entType (cdr (assoc 0 (entget entItem)))
            entData (strcat entHandle " " entType)
        )
        (write-line entData entFile)
        (setq indexCount (1- indexCount))
    );end repeat
    (close entFile)
    (prompt (strcat "\nData added to " fileName))
    (startapp "notepad" fileName)
    (princ)
);end defun
```

Table 9.10 describes some of the code that appears in `handle_file.lsp`. At this point, you're so familiar with some of these functions that I'll describe just the code that is new.

LINE OF CODE	PURPOSE
`(setq txtFile (getstring "\nName of file: "))`	Assigns a string to the variable `textFile` when it's entered by the user. The program creates a file later in the code using this as the filename.
`(setq userProf (getenv "userprofile"))`	Assigns the profile path for the current user to the variable `userProf`. This will be used to place the file in the My Documents folder of the current user. The SETQ function is left open to evaluate the next line.
`fileName (strcat userProf "\\My Documents\\" txtFile ".txt")`	Uses the SETQ function from the previous line to assign a string to the variable `fileName`. The string is created by using STRCAT to combine the user's profile path, "My Documents", the name of the file assigned to `txtFile`, and the file extension ".txt".
`(setq selSet1 (ssget "x"))`	Assigns all objects in the drawing's database to the variable `selSet1`.
`(setq ssLen (sslength selSet1))`	Counts the number of items using the SSLENGTH function and assigns the value to the variable `ssLen`.
`(setq indexCount (1- ssLen))`	Sets up a means of counting down the number of items stored in `selSet1` by assigning a value to the variable `indexCount` that is one less than the total number of objects. The variable `indexCount` represents the nth value for the last object in the selection set. Don't forget that the first item is the nth 0 item.
`entFile(open fileName "a")`	Opens the file named by the user and stored in `fileName` so that data can be appended to it. If the file doesn't exist, the program creates it. The argument `"a"` means "append" and must be lowercase. The SETQ function then assigns the file to the variable `entFile`.

continues

continued

LINE OF CODE	PURPOSE
`(repeat ssLen`	Begins the REPEAT function. Because there are `ssLen` items in the selection set, you have the program repeat the code that follows `ssLen` times.
`(setq entItem (ssname selSet1 indexCount)`	Begins setting a series of variables. The variable `entItem` is set equal to the value obtained using the function SSNAME, which is the name of the last entity in the selection set assigned to `selSet1`.
	The last item is selected because the value stored in the variable `indexCount` is the number of the last item.
	Before the REPEAT function loops back, the variable `indexCount` will be assigned a new value.
`entHandle (cdr (assoc 5 (ent- get entItem)))`	Uses the open SETQ function from the previous line to assign the handle of `entItem` to the variable `entHandle`. The handle of each entity is one of the two pieces of data you'll print to the open text file represented by `entFile`.
`entType (cdr (assoc 0 (entget entItem)))`	Uses the open SETQ function to assign the entity type of `entItem` to the variable `entType`. The group code 0 represents the entity type.
`entData (strcat entHandle " " entType)`	Uses the open SETQ function to assign the variable `entData` to a combination of the handle, a space, and the object type. The space isn't necessary but it separates the handle from the entity type in the text file and makes it easier to read.
`(write-line entData entFile)`	Writes the string `entData` to the next line of the file.
`(setq indexCount (1- indexCount))`	Sets the variable `indexCount` equal to one less than its current value.
`(close entFile)`	Closes the file represented by the variable `entFile`.
`(prompt (strcat "\nData added to " fileName))`	Informs the user that data was added to the file name stored in the program variable `fileName`.
`(startapp "notepad" fileName)`	Starts Notepad, and opens the file that was just created by this program.

Here are several lines from a file named `Drawing_ent.txt` that was created with this program:

```
17A CIRCLE
17B LWPOLYLINE
17C LINE
17D DIMENSION
18B LWPOLYLINE
18C POINT
18D TEXT
18E MTEXT
18F ELLIPSE
190 SPLINE
191 CIRCLE
```

WHILE Function

To use the REPEAT function, you have to know how many times you want the group of functions to be repeated. In contrast, the WHILE function repeats a series of functions until a specified condition is met. Let's use the WHILE function in the next example, which adds numbers in sequence to a drawing, beginning with whatever value is indicated by the operator. As long as the operator keeps picking points, the program keeps placing numbers. When the operator terminates the program with an Enter, the Spacebar, or a right-click with the mouse, the program exits the WHILE function. See Listing 9.9.

Listing 9.9

Number.lsp

```
(defun C:Number (/  txtStyle numSeq txtInsert str1 str2)
  (setq txtStyle (getvar "textstyle"))
  (command "STYLE" "romans0" "romans" 0 1 0 "N" "N" "N")
  (setq numSeq (getint "\nFirst number in sequence <1>: "))
  (if (= numSeq nil)(setq numSeq 1))
  (setq txtInsert (getpoint "Insertion point:  "))
  (while txtInsert
    (setq str1 (itoa numSeq))
    (setq str2 (strcat "#" str1))
    (command "TEXT" txtInsert "3" "0" str2)
    (setq txtInsert (getpoint "Select insertion point:  "))
    (setq numSeq (+ numSeq 1))
  )
  (setvar "textstyle" txtStyle)
  (princ)
)
```

Table 9.11 describes each of the new functions presented in Number.lsp.

LINE OF CODE	PURPOSE
(defun C:NUMBER (/ numSeq txtInsert str1 str2)	Defines a new command function C:NUMBER with four local program variables.
(setq txtStyle (getvar "textstyle"))	Assigns the current value of the system variable TEXTSTYLE to the program variable txtStyle so it can be retuned when program terminates.
(command "STYLE" "romans0" "romans" 0 1 0 "N" "N" "N")	Creates a new text style with the name "romans0" and a text height of 0.
(setq numSeq (getint "\nFirst number in sequence <1>: "))	Assigns an integer typed by the operator to the variable numSeq.
(if (= numSeq nil)(setq numSeq 1))	Determines whether numSeq is nil, which it is if the user responded to the last prompt with an Enter. If numSeq is nil, the program assigns a value of 1 to numSeq.

Table 9.11
Number.lsp

continues

continued

LINE OF CODE	PURPOSE
`(setq txtInsert (getpoint "Insertion point: "))`	Sets the variable `txtInsert` equal to the point provided by the operator.
`(while txtInsert`	Begins the WHILE function, which repeats the next five lines until the variable `textInsert` is `nil`.
`(setq str1 (itoa numSeq))`	Sets the variable `str1` to the result of converting numSeq from an integer to a string
`(setq str2 (strcat "#" str1))`	Sets the variable `str2` equal to the string "#" combined with the string stored in `str1`. STRCAT is used to combine (concatenate) strings.
`(command "TEXT" txtInsert "3" "0" str2)`	Uses the TEXT command to place the string stored in `str2` to the coordinates stored in `txtInsert` using a height of 3 and a rotation angle of 0.
`(setq txtInsert (getpoint "Select insertion point: "))`	Resets the variable `txtInsert` to the X,Y,Z value of the next point selected or entered by the operator.
`(setq numSeq (+ numSeq 1))`	Resets the variable numSeq to its current value plus 1.
`)`	Closes the WHILE statement.
`(setvar "textstyle" txtStyle)`	Restores the previous text style.
`(princ)`	Prints a clear line.
`)`	Ends DEFUN.

This is a nice little program that you can adapt to any listing situation. In this case, it uses a fixed metric text height suitable for plotting at a 1:1 scale. Do you see any shortcomings? What if you want to use this program for text at different plot scales? Wouldn't it be nice if the text height could scale automatically when placed in a floating viewport?

Listing 9.10 demonstrates a means of placing text and having it automatically scale to a floating viewport. It uses inline annotation. See if you can borrow from it to add automatic scaling capability to `number.lsp`. This example may contain some new concepts, but at this point you should be able to combine elements of these two programs even if you don't completely understand them. Just use copy and paste.

Listing 9.10

Scaletxt.lsp

```
;;;;ScaleTxt.lsp
;;;;Dan Abbott
;;;;March 12, 2005
;;;Places text from a layout into Model Space scaled to the
;;;floating viewport into which it is placed. Text will plot
;;;at the size specified by DIMTXT. Provided "AS IS," with all
;;;faults. You are free to use this code at your own risk in
;;;any way you want.
```

```
;; Error Handling
(defun ScaleTxtError (msg)
  (command)
  (setvar "cmdecho" cm)
  (setvar "dtexted" dtxtEd)
  (alert "Program cancelled.")
  (setq *error* ExistError)
)
;; ScaleTXT command
(defun c:SCALETXT (/ existError cm dtxtEd tm txtInsPt txtHgt
                     txtAngle currentVP viewHgtMS SSVprts
                     selSet viewHgtPS viewScale)
  (setq existError *error*)
  (setq *error* ScaleTxtError)

  (setq cm (getvar "cmdecho"))
  (setvar "cmdecho" 0)
  (setq dtxtEd (getvar "dtexted"))
  (setvar "dtexted" 1)

  (command "style" "romans" "romans" "" "" "" "" "" "")
  (setq tm (getvar "tilemode"))
  (if (= tm 1)
    (progn
      (setq txtInsPt (getpoint "\nLeft Corner of Scaled Text: ")
            txtHgt (getvar "dimtxt"))
      (setq txtAngle (getangle "\Angle of Scaled Text<0>: "
                               txtInsPt))
      (if (= txtAngle nil)(setq txtAngle 0))
      (setq txtAngle (* 180 (/ txtAngle pi)))
    );end progn
    (progn
      (setq txtHgt(getvar "dimtxt")
            currentVP (getvar "cvport")
            viewHgtMS (getvar "viewsize")
            SSVprts   (ssget "X" (list '(0 . "Viewport")
                                       (cons 69 currentVP)))
            selSet (entget (ssname SSVprts 0))
            viewHgtPS (cdr (assoc 41 selSet))
            viewScale (/ viewHgtMS viewHgtPS)
            txtHgt    (* viewScale txtHgt)
            TxtInsPt  (getpoint "\nLeft Corner of Scaled Text: ")
      );end setq
```

continues

continued

```
                (setq txtAngle (getangle "\Angle of Scaled Text<0>: "
                                          txtInsPt))
                (if (= txtAngle nil)
                    (setq txtAngle 0)
                );end if
                (setq txtAngle (* 180 (/ txtAngle pi)))
           );end progn
        );end if
        (command "DTEXT" TxtInsPt txtHgt txtAngle)
        (setvar "DTEXTED" dtxtEd)
        (setvar "cmdecho" cm)
        (setq *error* existError)
        (princ)
    );end defun
```

COND, INITGET, GETKWORD

The COND function behaves like multiple IF functions, but it's much more efficient. It allows you to create a list of multiple conditions and have your program go through them one at a time until it finds one condition that is true. When it finds a true condition, it executes the function that follows but ignores the other conditions in the list.

To illustrate how COND works, let's completely rethink the program for placing an end-section symbol on a piece of structural lumber. The program you wrote earlier is serviceable, but it has some flaws. You can eliminate those flaws by changing your approach. This time, let's force the user to apply the section symbol only in situations that make sense. Because structural lumber in the U.S. comes in the nominal sizes 2×2, 2×3, 2×4, 2×6, 2×8, 2×10, and 2×12, let's require the operator to use this symbol for only those sizes.

Instead of having the program draw out the symbol each time, let's insert a unit-sized block. Actual sizes of lumber are smaller than nominal sizes. Because the actual thickness of all structural lumber is 1.5 inches, you'll create a block that is 1.5×1 units in size. When it's inserted, you'll have the program adjust the X scale factor to match the actual size for the lumber selected by the operator.

To restrict user input, this program applies two GET functions you haven't used yet: INITGET and GETKWORD. INITGET can be used with any of the GET functions to restrict the range of acceptable responses from the user. There are several modes, most of which you won't apply here. Table 9.12 describes them for your information.

CODE	PURPOSE	
(Initget 1)	An Enter isn't an acceptable response.	Table 9.12
(Initget 2)	A zero isn't an acceptable response.	**INITGET Codes**
(Initget 4)	Negative values aren't allowed.	
(Initget 8)	Limit checking won't be used for picking points.	
(Initget 32)	Use dashed lines for rubber band lines and rectangles.	
(Initget "4 6 8")	The response must be one of the keywords in quotes.	

You probably recognize these numbers as bit-codes, except for the keywords defined in the last example. As is true with the setting for the OSMODE system variable, bit codes can be added together to get unique sums:

- (Initget 3) means that neither an Enter nor zero input is allowed (bit code 1 + bit code 2).

- (Initget 40) means that limit checking isn't used and that dashed lines are used for rubberbands (bit code 8 + bit code 32).

- (Initget 1 "4 6 8") means that an Enter can't be used as a response, and that only the keywords "4", "6", and "8" can be used. Those numbers are in quotes to indicate that they're used as keywords.

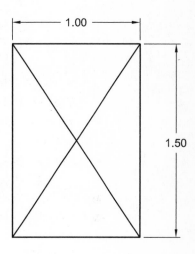

Listing 9.11 shows the new version of the program, complete with keywords. Notice that the program lets you define a default response because it doesn't prevent the use of an Enter. The drawing must contain a block definition named SECTION for this program to work. Define the block from a 1.5 × 1 unit rectangle with diagonal lines, using the lower-left corner as the base point.

Listing 9.11

EndSection.lsp

```
        ;; Radians to Degrees
        (defun RTD (r)
          (* 180.0 (/ r pi))
        )
        ;==========================
        ;;Error handling function
        (defun sectEtrap (msg)
          (command)
          (setvar "cmdecho" cm)
```

continues

continued

```
      (setq *error* existError)
      (Prompt "\Quiting EndSection: ")
      (princ)
  )


;==========================
;;Pogram

(defun C:ENDSECT (/ existEtrap cm blkName size
                    pt1 ro1 xsize)
   (setq existEtrap *error*)
   (setq *error* sectEtrap)
   (setq cm (getvar "cmdecho"))
   (setvar "cmdecho" 0)
   (setq blkName (tblsearch "block" "SECTION"))
   (if (= blkname nil)
     (alert "\nBlock SECTION not found.
   \nCancel and define block: ")
   );end if
   (initget "2 3 4 6 8 10 12")
   (setq size (getkword "\nWidth [2/3/4/6/8/<10>/12]: "))
   (if (= size nil)(setq size "10"))
   (setq pt1 (getpoint "\nInsertion Point: "))
   (setq ro1 (getangle "\nRotation Angle <0>: "))
   (if (= ro1 nil)(setq ro1 0))(setq ro1 (rtd ro1))
   (cond
     ((= size "2") (setq xsize 1.5))
     ((= size "3") (setq xsize 2.5))
     ((= size "4") (setq xsize 3.5))
     ((= size "6") (setq xsize 5.5))
     ((= size "8") (setq xsize 7.25))
     ((= size "10") (setq xsize 9.25))
     ((= size "12") (setq xsize 11.25))
   );end cond
   (command "INSERT" "SECTION" pt1 xsize 1 ro1)
   (setvar "cmdecho" cm)
   (setq *error* existEtrap)
);end defun
```

Table 9.13 describes the lines that use functions that we haven't looked at yet.

LINE OF CODE	PURPOSE	
`(setq blkName (tblsearch "block" "SECTION"))`	Searches the names of symbols in a specified list—in this case, the list of block names. If the block name "SECTION" isn't found in the list, the function TBLSEARCH returns `nil`.	Table 9.13 `endsect.lsp`
`(if (= blkname nil)`	Finds out whether the variable `blkname` is `nil`.	
`(alert "\nBlock SECTION not found.` `\nCancel and define block: ")`	If the variable `blkname` is equal to `nil`, displays the alert box, telling the user that the block required for the program wasn't found.	
`(initget "2 3 4 6 8 10 12")`	Establishes that the only acceptable responses to the next GET function are the keywords 2, 3, 4, 6, 8, 10, and 12.	
`(setq size (getkword "\nWidth [2/3/4/6/8/<10>/12]: ")`	Assigns the user response to the GETKWORD function to the variable `size`. If dynamic input is turned on, the list is displayed at the cursor in addition to the command line. The default value is 10.	
`(cond`	Begins the COND function, which is always followed by a list of conditions. Each of the conditions is searched until one of them returns T or all conditions return `nil`.	
`((= size "2") (setq xsize 1.5))`	The first of the seven conditional statements. If the variable `size` is equal to 2, than the variable `xsize` is set to `1.5` and the program exits the COND function.	
`(command "INSERT" "SECTION" pt1 xsize 1 ro1)`	Inserts the block named "SECTION" at the point given by the user, with an X scale factor equal to the value set in the COND function, a Y scale factor of 1, and the rotation angle entered by the user.	

Text and String Manipulation

Sometimes an AutoLISP program needs to open an existing file, because you want to either read data from it or add data to it. To demonstrate this kind of file management and to show you a little more about handling strings, let's look at a program that solves a small problem with AutoCAD: determining what release format a specific drawing was last saved in.

Every AutoCAD DWG file has a six-character string at the beginning of the file that indicates the format in which the drawing was saved. You can see the code for any AutoCAD drawing by opening the DWG file in a text editor. The rest of the file is unreadable, of course, but you can see those six characters. Except for the first release of AutoCAD (1.1), the first two characters are always *AC*, so the characters that denote the release are the third, fourth, fifth, and sixth.

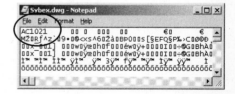

Figure 9.3

GETFILED dialog box

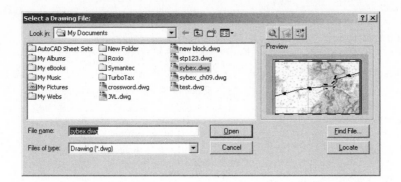

The AutoLISP program in Listing 9.12 uses the GETFILED function to prompt the user to select a DWG file using the dialog box shown in Figure 9.3, and then opens the specified file, reads the key characters, closes the file, sends a message to the screen via the ALERT function, opens a text file, adds the same information to the text file, and finally closes that file. This version refers only to releases R14 through AutoCAD 2007. If you want to go back further than that, see the last program in this chapter. I'm making the assumption here that the current format will be used for at least one more release.

Error handling isn't included in Listing 9.12, but it should be included in the actual program.

Listing 9.12

Release.lsp

```
(defun c:RELEASE (/ path path2 dn fn fl rel str1)
  (setq path (getvar "dwgprefix"))
  (setq dn 1)
  (while (/= dn nil)
    (setq dn (getfiled "Select a Drawing File: " path "dwg" 0))
    (if (/= dn nil)
      (progn
        (setq fn (open dn "r"))
        (setq fl (read-line fn))
        (setq rel (substr fl 3 4))
        (close fn)
        (setq str1 "a format other than 14, 2000, 2004 or 2007.")
        (cond
          ((= rel "1014") (setq str1 "R14/14.01 format."))
          ((= rel "1015") (setq str1 "R2000/2000i/2002 format."))
          ((= rel "1018") (setq str1 "R2004/2005/2006 format."))
          ((= rel "1021") (setq str1 "R2007/2008 format."))
```

```
        );close COND
        (setq str2 (strcat dn " was saved in " str1))
        (setq user (getenv "userprofile")
              path2 (strcat user "\\My Documents\\")
              relfile (strcat path2 "ReleaseNotes.txt")
              fileName (open relfile "a")
        );end setq
        (write-line str2 fileName)
        (close fileName)
        (alert(strcat str2
                      "\n\nRelease format added to file:\n"
                      relfile))
        (setq path dn)
      );close progn
    );close if
  );close while
  (princ)
);close defun
```

I've described the key functions used in this program in Table 9.14. Now that you're pretty savvy with AutoLISP, I don't want to bore you with descriptions of SETQ and DEFUN.

LINE OF CODE	PURPOSE	
(setq dn (getfiled "Select a Drawing File: " path "dwg" 0))	Introduces a new GET function: GETFILED. It displays a File dialog box based on the arguments provided. The prompt Select a Drawing File: appears at the top of the dialog box. The dialog box opens with the path specified by the variable path. Only files with a .dwg extension are displayed. 0 is a bit flag that limits the search to the file type shown.	**Table 9.14** Release.lsp
(if (/= dn nil)	Begins a new IF statement that provides a clean exit from the dialog box. As long as the variable dn isn't nil, the next group of functions is evaluated. If dn is nil, the program exits the IF function and goes to the (PRINC) function at the end of the program.	
(progn	Normally, an IF function executes a single element that follows if it returns T. The PROGN function forces AutoLISP to evaluate everything enclosed in its parentheses. The opening parenthesis on this line is closed near the end of the program.	
(setq fn (open dn "r"))	Opens the drawing file represented by the variable dn, and sets it equal to variable fn. This doesn't open it as a drawing, but rather opens it as a text file. The lowercase r (which must be lowercase) indicates that the file can be read from but not written to. Open files must be closed when your program finishes with them.	

continues

continued

LINE OF CODE	PURPOSE
`(setq firstLine (read-line fn))`	Reads the first line of the opened DWG file and assigns it to the variable `firstLine`, which consists of six characters and a bunch of machine code. You don't need the entire first line, just the four characters that indicate what format the drawing was saved in.
`(setq rel(substr fl 3 4))`	Looks at the line stored in variable `fl` and reads characters starting with the third character and going 4 additional characters. Those indicate the release used to save the file, so they're the ones assigned to the variable `rel`. You'll use it later to determine what release it represents.
`(close fn)`	Any file opened by AutoLISP must be closed. In this case, now that you have the information you need, we can close the file.
`(setq str1 "an unknown or internal release.")`	Later in the program, you'll report the format to the operator, and you'll use a variable named `str1` to store that release information. If the characters read from the drawing file don't match any of the release formats, because the file was saved either long ago or in a noncommercial beta version, this generic message reports that.
`(setq user (getenv "userprofile")`	Saves the user's login profile to the variable `user`, because the plan is to save this information to a file in the user's `My Documents` folder. The GETENV function lets you get environment information from the system registry.
`path2 (strcat user "\\My Documents\\")`	Assigns the variable `path2` to the combination of the user's path with the string "\\My Documents\\" so it can be used as the location for the file being created to hold the release information.
`relfile (strcat path2 "ReleaseNotes.txt")`	Once you have the user's login name, creates a full path for the file by combining `path2` with the string "ReleaseNotes.txt".
`fileName (open relfile "a")`	Creates or opens the file stored in the variable `relfile` so you can append to it in the next line. The *a* must be lowercase. The open file is assigned to the variable `fileName`.
`(write-line str2 fileName)`	Writes the string stored in the variable `str2` to the end of the file represented by the variable `fileName`.
`(close fileName)`	Closes the open file assigned to the variable `fileName`.

Getting to DOS with AutoLISP

Now it's time to pull together a number of different tools. The program in Listing 9.13 was written for a company that deals with various contractors who use a range of AutoCAD releases. The company wanted to generate a list of its drawing files to determine whether any particular file had to be converted to an earlier release before sending it to a contractor. I didn't have to go back to the beginning of AutoCAD to write this program, but I thought it would be interesting, so I included all the commercial versions.

To solve this one, I modified the program from the previous section to search the entire drive and create two text files: one that lists all DWG files, and one that lists all drawings plus the release format in which it was saved. This brings us full circle: To get to DOS, use the external command SHELL from the ACAD.pgp file. For that to work, the bit-flag setting for the SHELL command has to be changed to 0 so the DOS dir command waits to finish making a list of files before returning to AutoCAD. The DOS dir command with the bare switch and the redirection function provides the means to generate the list of all drawing files necessary to complete the program.

I leave it to you to decipher this code based on what you know so far. Note the use of the ;| combination at the beginning and |; at the end of the opening commented section—no need to add all those semicolons. This program may take a long time to run, so be patient. The DOS window stays open until the first file is created.

Listing 9.13

Relshell.lsp

```
;|
relshell.lsp
Dan Abbott
################################################################
The bit flag for the SHELL command in the ACAD.pgp file
must be set to 0 for this program to work. The default setting is
1, so the program adds a line to the end of the file changing it
to 0. This causes no harm, it just forces AutoCAD to wait until the
program finishes its shell function. Use the program when you have
the time to stop using AutoCAD for a while. Depending on the
number of files you have, you may be waiting for some time.
If you use the SHELL command in AutoCAD and want to return the
bit flag setting to 1 when the program terminates, open the
acad.pgp file by typing (startapp "notepad" (findfile "acad.pgp"))
################################################################

    Copyright 2006 by Daniel Abbott.

    You may use, copy, modify, and distribute this software
    for any purpose and without fee. Use it at your own risk.

    Relshell.lsp will search the entire C: drive, create a list
    of all DWG files in all non-hidden directories and then use
    that list to create a file that identifies the release format of
    AutoCAD in which each of those drawings was last saved.

    Two user-named text files are created by this program in
    the My Documents folder of the current user.
    |;
```

continues

continued

```
;;; Error handling function

(defun relShellError (msg)
  (command)
  (if (/= fileOpen nil) (close fileOpen))
  (if (/= fileName nil) (close fileName))
  (if (/= pgp nil)(close pgp))
  (setvar "cmdecho" cm)
  (alert "Program cancelled.")
  (setq *error* old_error)
);end defun

;;;Command definition

(defun c:RelShell(/ fileList relFile path1 path2 fileOpen
          relFile2 fileList1 fileList2 fileName fileLine
          dwgFile rel dwgFileNextLine str1 str2 pgp)
    (alert "The bit flag setting for SHELL will be
          set to 0 in the last line of ACAD.pgp.
          \nPress \"Esc\" now to cancel.")
    (setq cm (getvar "cmdecho"))
    (setvar "cmdecho" 0)
    (setq old_error *error*)
    (setq *error* relShellError)
    (setq fileList (getstring
               "\nDrawing names file <Dwglist>: "))
    (if (= fileList "") (setq fileList "dwglist"))
    (setq relFile (getstring
               "\nRelease Info File <DwgReleaseList>: "))
    (if (= relFile "") (setq relFile "DwgReleaseList"))
    (getstring "\nThis process may take a long time.
               \nPress ENTER to continue, ESC to cancel.")
    (setq path1 (strcat (getenv "userprofile") "/My Documents/")
          path2 (strcat (getenv "userprofile") "/My Documents/")
          relFile2 (strcat path2 relFile ".txt")
          fileList1 (strcat  "\"" path1 fileList ".txt" "\"")
          fileList2 (strcat  path2 fileList ".txt");without quotes
    );end setq
    (setq pgp (open (findfile "acad.pgp") "a"))
    (write-line "\nSHELL,,0,*OS Command:," pgp)
    (close pgp)
    (setvar "re-init" 16)
    (command "shell"
```

```
              (strcat "dir c:\\*.dwg /s /b >" fileList1))
    (setq fileOpen (open relFile2 "a"))
    (setq fileName (open fileList2 "r"))
    (while (setq fileLine (read-line fileName))
      (setq dwgFile (open fileLine "r"))
      (setq dwgFileNextLine (read-line dwgFile))
      (close dwgFile)
      (setq rel (substr dwgFileNextLine 3 4))
      (setq str1 (DrawingRelease rel))
      (setq str2 (strcat fileLine " was saved in " str1))
      (write-line str2 fileOpen)
    );end while
    (close fileOpen)
    (close fileName)
    (prompt "\n-----------------------------------------------")
    (prompt (strcat
                "\nRelease information for all DWG files on
                C:\ has been placed in \n" relFile2)
    );end prompt
    (setvar "cmdecho" cm)
    (setq *error* old_error)
    (princ)
);end defun


;;;;Cond function

(defun DrawingRelease(rel)
  (cond
    ((= rel "0.0 ") (setq rel "R1.1 format."))
    ((= rel "1.2 ") (setq rel "R1.2 format."))
    ((= rel "1.4 ") (setq rel "R1.4 format."))
    ((= rel "1.50") (setq rel "R2.05 format."))
    ((= rel "2.10") (setq rel "R2.10 format."))
    ((= rel "2.20") (setq rel "R2.20 format."))
    ((= rel "2.21") (setq rel "R2.21 format."))
    ((= rel "2.22") (setq rel "R2.22 format."))
    ((= rel "1001") (setq rel "R2.5 pre-release format."))
    ((= rel "1002") (setq rel "R2.6 format."))
    ((= rel "1004") (setq rel "R9 format."))
    ((= rel "1005") (setq rel "R10 pre-release format."))
    ((= rel "1006") (setq rel "R10 format."))
    ((= rel "1007") (setq rel "R11 pre-release format."))
    ((= rel "1008") (setq rel "R11 pre-release format."))
    ((= rel "1009") (setq rel "R11/12 format."))
```

continues

continued

```
          ((= rel "1010") (setq rel "R13 internal format."))
          ((= rel "1011") (setq rel "R13 internal format."))
          ((= rel "1012") (setq rel "R13 format."))
          ((= rel "1013") (setq rel "R14 pre-release format."))
          ((= rel "1014") (setq rel "R14/14.01 format."))
          ((= rel "1500") (setq rel "R2000 pre-release format."))
          ((= rel "1015") (setq rel "R2000/2000i/2002 format."))
          ((= rel "1018") (setq rel "R2004/2005/2006 format."))
          ((= rel "1021") (setq rel "R2007/2008/2009 format."))
          (T (setq rel "an unknown or internal release."))
      );end cond
  );end defun


;;;;;;;;;;;;;;;;;;;;;;;;;;;;;;;;;;;;;;;;;;;;;;;;;;;;;;;;;;;;;;;;;;;;;;;;;;;;
```

Figure 9.4 shows what the user sees at the command line when this program finishes.

In this chapter and the previous one, we've covered a lot of ground, but there's still a lot left to learn about programming if you desire. You may as well plunge right in: Look around the Web, get some books, and start solving problems. Nothing in the AutoCAD realm is quite so satisfying as writing a program, debugging it, having it work, and then watching other people use it effectively.

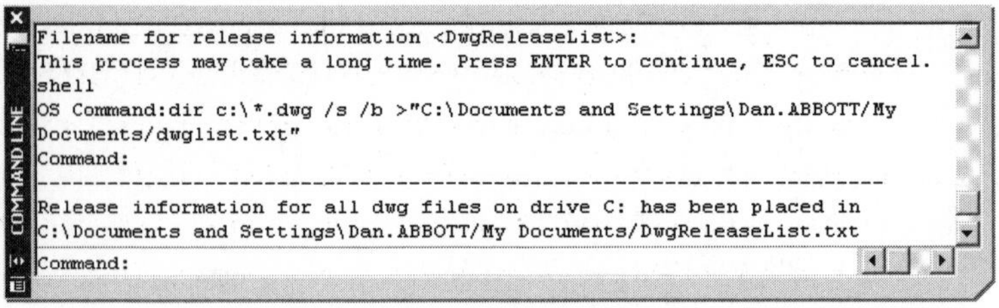

Figure 9.4

Running the Relshell.lsp program

```
Filename for release information <DwgReleaseList>:
This process may take a long time. Press ENTER to continue, ESC to cancel.
shell
OS Command:dir c:\*.dwg /s /b >"C:\Documents and Settings\Dan.ABBOTT/My
Documents/dwglist.txt"
Command:
--------------------------------------------------------------------
Release information for all dwg files on drive C: has been placed in
C:\Documents and Settings\Dan.ABBOTT/My Documents/DwgReleaseList.txt
Command:
```

CHAPTER 10

3D For Everyone

Autodesk first added limited 3D capabilities to Release 2.1 back in the technological olden days of 1985 and then periodically introduced new 3D functions in subsequent releases. But it wasn't until AutoCAD 2007 that 3D came into its own. That release shipped with a huge number of features dedicated to creating and presenting models. AutoCAD was already a very good modeler even before AutoCAD 2007, though, so why haven't more AutoCAD users taken advantage? Three reasons:

- An inaccurate sense that 3D is too hard
- A false perception that AutoCAD is a lousy 3D modeler
- A mistaken belief that 3D modeling isn't worth the time

Let's knock down these reasons one at a time. Is it too hard to learn 3D modeling? No. Even if you've never created a single 3D model in AutoCAD, you know 80 percent of what you need to know: that is, how to create accurate 2D geometry.

Is AutoCAD a lousy modeler? Of course not. It's not as good as some other modelers in certain respects—hence the bad rap. It may not be the gold standard, but so what if Inventor, Architectural Desktop, Mechanical Desktop, VIZ, Revit, and a bunch of other applications have 3D modeling strengths that AutoCAD doesn't have? You paid several thousand dollars for AutoCAD, so why not use everything you paid for? And for you, AutoCAD 3D has one advantage that none of the other software has: familiarity.

Is 3D modeling worth the time? Absolutely. You can produce useful 3D models fairly quickly, as long as you understand some easily mastered basics. Once you've created those models, you can use them for all kinds of things: solving design problems, showing off to customers, laying out views for plotting, exporting for use in other programs, controlling CNC manufacturing processes, and so on.

- ■ **A Brief Overview**
- ■ **Managing Coordinate Systems**
- ■ **Managing Views and Viewports**
- ■ **Creating a Model**
- ■ **Using Existing 2D Geometry**
- ■ **Final Suggestions**

The purpose of this chapter is to introduce you to AutoCAD 3D by helping you understand how to get around in space, how to manage views of your model, and how to use a handful of 3D commands. You'll make a simple model, step by step; you'll look at a strategy for creating a quick perspective line drawing using existing 2D architectural elevations; and you'll see a neat trick for creating a mechanical part with the INTERSECT command.

Overview

You may be surprised, even stunned, by the wide array of individuals and companies that produce useful, professional work with AutoCAD 3D. Let's begin by looking at some projects that were modeled entirely in AutoCAD.

Some Samples

The interior view in Figure 10.1 is an image of the Maine state office building. Meridith Comeau produced this model several years ago for the architectural firm SMRT in Portland, Maine. She imported the AutoCAD model into Autodesk VIZ, added materials, and created a rendered animation to show at a public hearing prior to construction. The firm made several design changes as a result of the feedback from the public and state employees who would be using the building.

The log-home image in Figure 10.2 was created by Paul Richardson for Katahdin Cedar Log Homes in Oakfield, Maine. He didn't model it himself: He wrote the automation program that takes advantage of AutoCAD's modeling capabilities to generate a solid model of every component using input from a designer. The automation program then converts

Figure 10.1
Maine State office building entrance

the DWG file into the CNC code required to select, cut, drill, machine, bar-code, and stack each piece. The entire set of logs is then shipped to a site where it's assembled into a home—the most notable version of which was used on the television show Extreme Makeover Home Edition for a family in Maine.

Meridith Comeau also produced the large dryer unit shown as a rendered image in Figure 10.3. Metso Paper USA designed this device for the tissue-paper industry. The company used the model to demonstrate the unique aspects of its dryer unit. Since then, Metso Paper has manufactured a number of these units for clients around the world. Figure 10.4 shows a hidden view of the AutoCAD model.

Figure 10.2

Katahdin log home

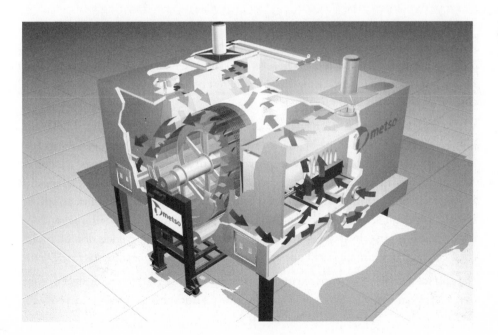

Figure 10.3

Tissue dryer reproduced with the permission of Metso Paper USA, inc.

Figure 10.4

**AutoCAD model of
tissue dryer**

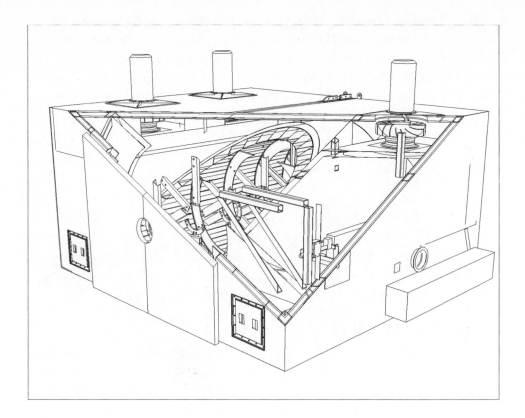

Figure 10.4

AutoCAD model of tissue dryer

Types of 3D Models

You can create and display models in several forms. We'll take a quick look at wireframe, flat surface, and swept-surface models, but the rest of this chapter will be devoted to getting you started with solid modeling.

Wireframe models AutoCAD began as a 2D drawing program in 1982. Its only 3D capabilities were the same as those in board drafting—isometric and oblique drawings that looked like 3D models. The earliest improvements in 3D allowed lines to be created using X, Y, and Z coordinates. The results generated a wireframe model—just the edges existed. It's like bending wire into various shapes: Your object appears in three dimensions, but all the edges are visible from any viewpoint. It's still possible to create wireframe models in AutoCAD, of course, by drawing the edges using lines, but such models don't have many uses. However, wireframe is still one of the most common display options for 3D models.

Flat-surface models A flat-surface model is the equivalent of stretching a sheet of rubber over a wireframe model. You can change an entity's thickness to turn it into a collection of flat surfaces. You can also use the 3DFACE command to cover a wireframe model with surfaces. Those block any lines behind them when VSCURRENT or SHADEMODE has a non-2D setting or the HIDE command is used. The result may look like a solid object, but it isn't. That doesn't mean it's not useful, because you can attach materials to it either in AutoCAD or another program like VIZ or 3ds Max. But it can't be edited like a solid.

Swept-surface models Curved and irregular surface modeling was added in R10 in the form of the RULESURF, TABSURF, REVSURF, and EDGESURF commands. They're still available and are sometimes used for creating quick shapes. The surfaces can be assigned materials that can be rendered—either in AutoCAD directly or by using a program like 3ds Max.

Solid models The most useful form for a 3D model is the solid model. Solid models are easy to make and can be combined with other solids to generate complex shapes. And you can take advantage of techniques that aren't possible with a real-world physical model. For example, you can use a Boolean intersection of two or more models that occupy the same space to make complex shapes. You'll see how to do that later in this chapter.

Managing Coordinate Systems

The most confusing aspect of 3D drawing for most 2D CAD operators is keeping track of their position when viewing or working on a 3D model. To avoid confusion when working in 3D, you must understand how to create, save, and use user coordinate systems. Let's define a few terms to demystify this process. Then, you'll make a simple model.

World Coordinate System

The world coordinate system (WCS) is the default coordinate system in a new drawing. Before AutoCAD 2007, when you started a new drawing, you always saw a plan view of the WCS—that is, looking straight down the Z axis at the ground or floor. In AutoCAD 2007, the plan view is what you see when you start a drawing with the AutoCAD Classic template. A drawing based on the 3D modeling template looks completely different, but the coordinate system is still the WCS. You just have a different view of it. Rather than looking straight down the Z axis, your view is from a point above the X-Y plane, south of the X axis and east of the Y axis.

In a plan view of the WCS, the origin point is always 0,0,0, with the X and Y axes forming a plane at a Z elevation of 0. Any positive value for Z appears above the plane; any negative value is below. You can't modify the WCS, nor would you want to, because it anchors you to one consistent origin point. However, you can and should create as many of your own coordinate systems as you need.

User Coordinate System

Unlike the WCS, a user coordinate system (UCS) can be placed at any origin and in any orientation. Its only restriction is that the three axes are always at 90° angles to each other. They're called user coordinate systems because the user can create them, but there's also a group of predefined user coordinate systems for standard orientations: Top, Bottom, Front, Back, Left, and Right. To use them, turn on the UCS II toolbar, and select them from the drop-down panel. You can add as many others as you want. To save them, use the Named UCS button on the same toolbar, or the DDUCS command (alias UC).

> AutoCAD 2007 has a dynamic UCS option that's controlled by moving the cursor over a face on a model. It's a wonderful tool, but we won't use it here. Instead, you'll create and use static UCSs. That way, this chapter will make sense to all AutoCAD users. But even AutoCAD 2007 users should know how to manage saved UCSs. Use the DUCS button on the status bar to toggle this feature on and off.

> All predefined UCSs have the same origin as the WCS. Don't make the mistake of thinking they'll be on a surface of your model, especially if you haven't placed a corner of your model at 0,0,0.

You have a number of options for creating a new UCS. The standard UCSs are rotated around the X and Y axes. Once you've created a model, the 3 Point option of the UCS command is quick and intuitive. You pick three points: the origin, a point on the positive X-axis, and a point on the positive Y-axis.

The view on the screen is independent of the coordinate system, unless you change the value of the system variable UCSFOLLOW from its default setting of 0 to a setting of 1. You can always match the view to your UCS, by using the PLAN command and selecting **Current**, which is the default option. To get an understanding of the relationship between coordinate systems and your view of them, look at the following figures.

Figure 10.5 shows a simple house shape in both isometric and plan view with one corner at 0,0,0. WCS is the current coordinate system.

> If you always place one corner of your model at 0,0,0, you'll find it easier to locate points on the model.

Figure 10.6 shows the same entity, after the Front UCS has been selected, and the PLAN command was used in the right viewport.

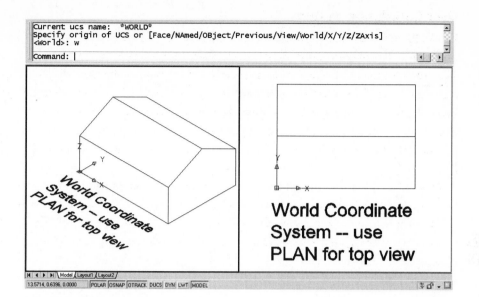

Figure 10.5

World coordinate system

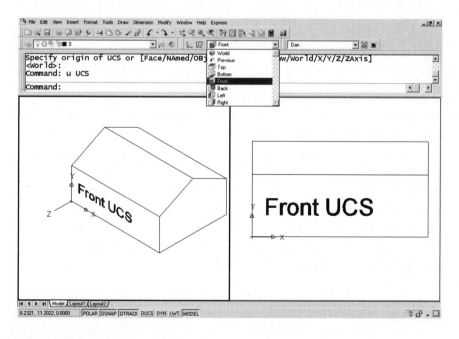

Figure 10.6

Front UCS

The Right UCS is current in Figure 10.7.

Finally, Figure 10.8 shows a UCS created with the 3-point option that sits on one sloped surface of the roof. Because this UCS isn't one that is listed in the toolbar, it was given the name **Angle1** so it can be used again. Note that there are three viewports shown. The upper right viewport shows a plan view in the Angle1 UCS.

Figure 10.7
Right UCS

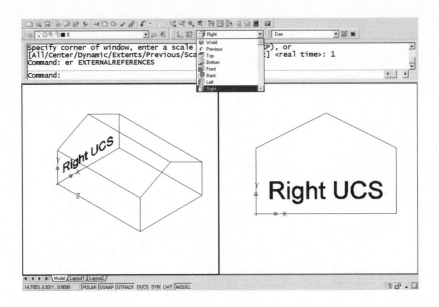

Figure 10.8
3 Point UCS

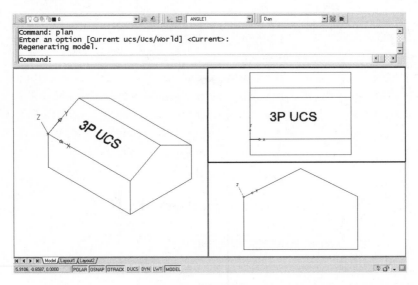

The 3 Point option of the UCS command has been hidden in AutoCAD 2007. You can still use it by typing 3P or 3, but it isn't listed. Instead, the default option for UCS is Specify Origin Of UCS. After your first selection, you're given the option of selecting a point on the X-axis. That in turn gives you the option of selecting a point on the Y-axis. Use object snaps to locate each point. I normally use the NEA OSNAP override to select the X and Y locations so I can zoom in as close as possible to the origin.

Creating a Model

Now that you've seen how UCSs are created, you've had enough preliminaries: Let's make a model. You'll start with a desk organizer. The text on the one you'll create will be recessed rather than raised, but otherwise, when you're done, it'll look like this.

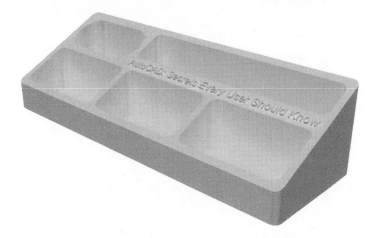

Just in case you want to use them, the dimensions of the desk organizer are shown in Figure 10.9. They're metric.

Before you get going, start a new metric drawing, and set the upper right corner of the limits to 320,120. If you're using AutoCAD 2007, switch to the AutoCAD Classic view in the Workspaces toolbar. If you started with a 3D template file, check the color assigned to the layer you're on. The default color may be hard to see, depending on the background color you use. For this tutorial, most toolbars and all tool palettes are turned off, but

Figure 10.9

Dimensions of the desk organizer

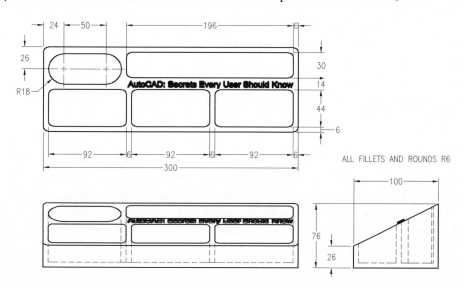

otherwise you'll have either the familiar plan view of the WCS or a screen that looks something like this:

It will look a little different from the classic AutoCAD screen for only a few steps. Whatever view you're starting with, go through the following steps:

1. Display the View toolbar by right-clicking any tool button and selecting View from the pop-up menu. Set a southeast isometric view by selecting the button shown.

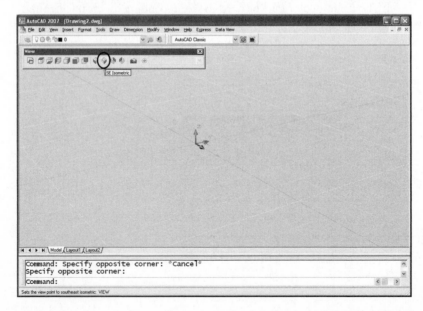

2. Display the two UCS toolbars (UCS and UCS II), and set SHADEMODE to 2D Wireframe. (In AutoCAD 2007, SHADEMODE is an alias for VSCURRENT—visual style current). From the menu, use View → Visual Styles → 2D Wireframe. Your screen will look more like those in the images that follow once you've made these changes.

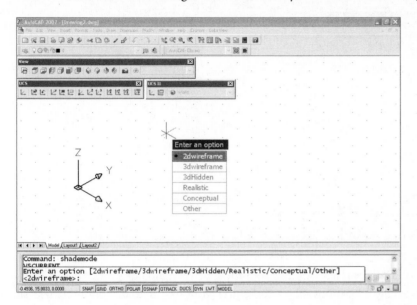

3. Use the UCSICON command to set the properties to 3D with cones, as shown in the next figure. The small square at the intersection of all three axes is displayed only when the WCS is current. If you're in a UCS, the icon has no square. When the UCS icon is at 0,0,0, you see a crosshair at the intersection of the axes (it looks like the axes extend past each other). The crosshair disappears if 0,0,0 is off the screen, but the icon will still be displayed.

You can change the appearance of the icon by selecting the Properties option of the UCSICON command to get the dialog box shown.

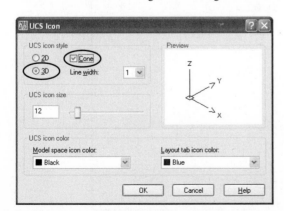

4. Use the UCS II toolbar to set a Right UCS by selecting it from the drop-down list. The UCSICON will change to represent the UCS you select.

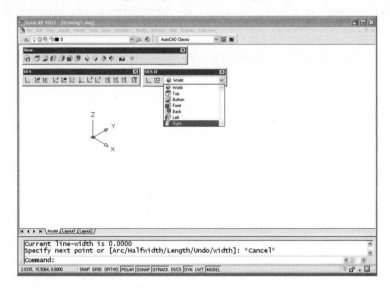

5. Use the PLINE command to draw the profile of the right-side view of the desk organizer, using the dimensions shown earlier in Figure 10.9. Start at 0,0,0, and make sure you close the polyline.

I set DISPSILH to 1 before creating the images for this tutorial. That turns off tessellation lines used to represent curved surfaces on the screen. If DISPSILH is set to 0, you'll see a lot more lines on your model than appear in the images here.

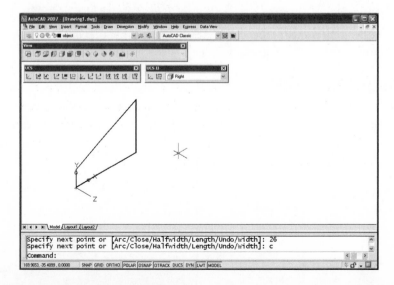

6. Use the EXTRUDE command to extrude the closed polyline 300 units in the positive Z direction by entering an extrusion height of 300. (If you're using a release prior to AutoCAD 2007, you're prompted for a taper angle. Use 0.) You've just created a solid that you'll use to make the desk organizer.

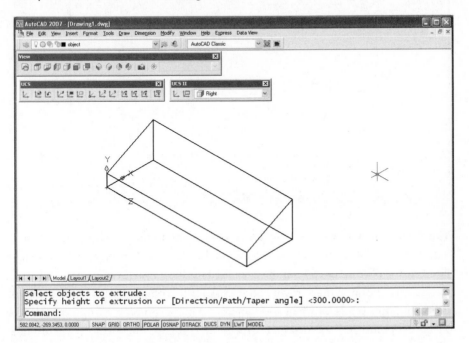

When drawing shapes or creating solids, you can use the same drawing aids you've always used: osnaps, object tracking, polar tracking, temporary tracking, absolute coordinates, relative coordinates, polar coordinates, direct distance entry, and so on. But be careful—it's easy to snap to the wrong end of a line when working in a plan view. The isometric view is often your best bet when snapping to objects.

7. In step 4, when you made the Right UCS current, you probably noticed a number of other typical coordinate systems set up. You need only one additional UCS to complete this project, so let's make it now. Zoom in at the corner of the solid, and either type **UCS**, then **3**, or select the 3 Point button on the UCS toolbar. This is one of the most useful ways to create a new UCS to work on a face of an existing solid.

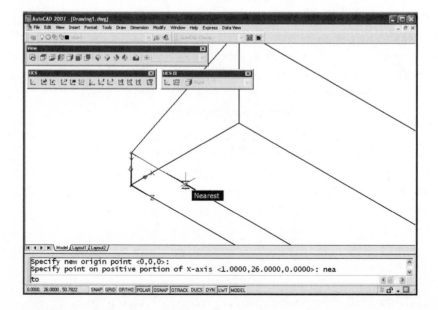

8. You're prompted to specify a new origin point. You can snap to it or type coordinates. After you select the corner of the sloped surface, you're prompted to specify a point on the positive portion of the X-axis. Resist the temptation to zoom out and select the endpoint of the front line. It'll work for this object, but when you're working on multiple solids, or when your objects are more complex, it's easy to snap to the wrong endpoint. Stay zoomed in, use the Nearest osnap, and select anywhere along the line.

9. The next point is on the Y-axis, of course. Use Nearest again to snap to a location on the line. Now you have a new UCS that sits right on the sloped surface so you can place some text on it later.

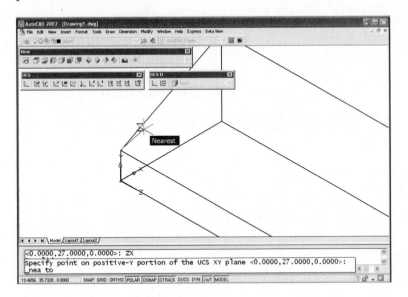

10. Whenever you create a new UCS, save it. You can either type **UCS**, **S** and then type a name for the current UCS, or use the button shown on the UCS II toolbar, which will open the UCS dialog box. Unnamed is listed as the first UCS. Use a slow click, or double-click it, and give it a name that makes sense. Use the name "Slope" for this tutorial.

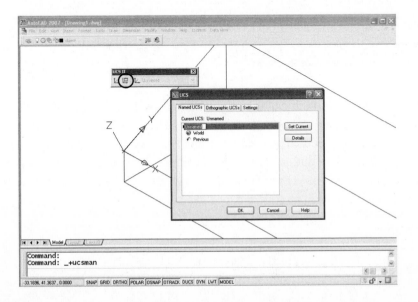

It's easy to lose your bearings when you're working on a 3D model, so you need to give yourself as much help as possible. Now that you have a basic shape and have saved a UCS, let's set up four views so it's easier to keep track of what's happening:

1. Restore the WCS by selecting World from the UCSII toolbar drop-down list.

2. Open the Viewports dialog box. Either type **VPORTS** or use View → Viewports → New Viewports from the menu. (There is also a command-line version, -VPORTS.) Leave the name blank for now—you'll name it after you tweak the views a little. Select Four: Equal in the Standard Viewports pane and 3D in the Setup drop-down list.

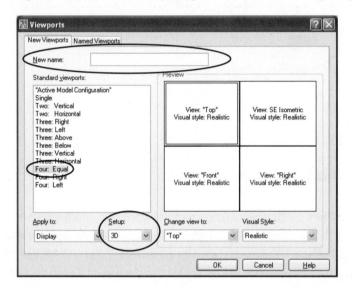

Look at the Preview pane when you set up views. If you don't like the view or style used in each view, you can change them by selecting any of the four viewports and using the Change view to: or Visual Style: drop-downs.

3. When you click OK to exit this dialog box, you have four viewports, each of which has zoomed to the extents of the viewport. Click in the isometric viewport, and type **ZOOM** and then **0.6**. Click in each plan viewport, and type **ZOOM** and then **1**. This is why you set limits earlier. This option of the ZOOM command zooms to the limits, which are a little larger than the object you're creating. After you finish, the three plan views should be displayed at the same scale and look like this:

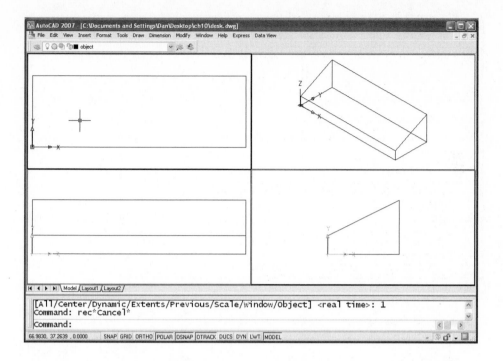

4. Go back to the Viewports dialog box, and give this configuration of views a name. You'll be switching to a full screen to work on any model, so it's much more efficient to restore named viewports than it is to reconfigure them. Notice that the Top, Front, and Right viewports have a plan view of a different UCS. That's the result of creating a 3D setup in the Viewports dialog box. When you make one viewport active and start to draw, you're drawing in the UCS that's active in that viewport.

5. Draw the shape of the pockets, and go through the steps that follow to extrude them the way you extruded the overall shape of the organizer. These shapes have to be closed polylines, circles, or regions. Because the RECTANGLE command creates a closed polyline, use it to create all but one of the shapes. Because the pockets don't go all the way through the object, start the rectangle at a Z-axis value of 6. Because the first rectangular shape is filleted, start with a rectangle that has fillets, and draw it in the Top view. You created the original shape at 0,0, so you can type **6,6,6** to start this rectangle. (You could also temporarily set ELEVATION to 6 and eliminate the Z coordinate, but there's always the danger that you'll forget to set it back to 0.)

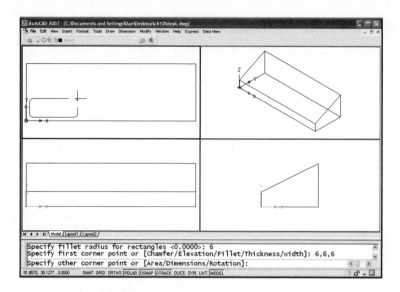

You may try to extrude a polyline that looks closed and get an error. Use the PEDIT command, select the polyline, and see if you can close it. In AutoCAD 2007 you can extrude an open polyline, but the result is an extruded surface, not a solid.

Notice that once the shape is created, you can see it in all four viewports. The Front and Right views show that the rectangle is above the XY plane. If you select the rectangle, it appears highlighted in all four views. You can switch viewports after selecting an entity or starting to create a new entity, but the UCS of the original viewport remains active until you complete the action.

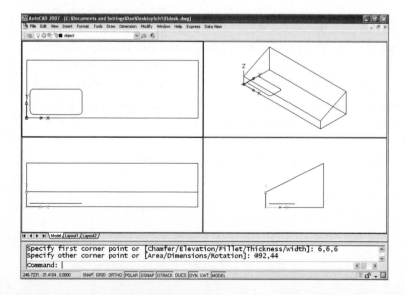

Take advantage of the fact that a polyline is a 2D entity. Once you establish the first vertex, the entire polyline is on the same plane, so there is no danger of drawing something that looks fine in one viewport but extends to a different Z coordinate. If you want a 3D polyline, use the 3DPOLY command.

6. After you draw your first rectangle, copy it twice for the other pockets of the same size. Start the slot by drawing a circle. I used the From osnap in the graphic and typed the offset from the selected corner. Note that this circle should also be at an elevation of 6, so the Z coordinate must be 6.

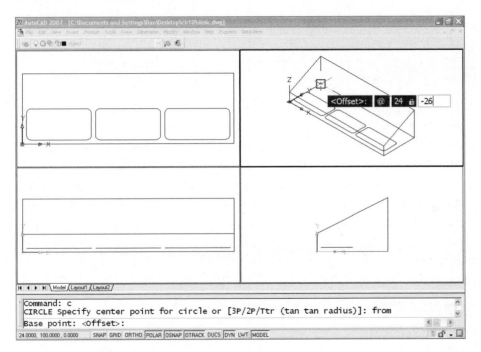

7. Finish the slot by copying the circle 50 units to the right. Add lines between the quadrants of the two circles, trim the circles, and then combine the resulting arcs and lines into a single closed polyline using the PEDIT command.

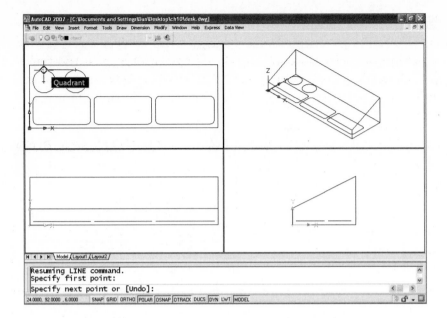

8. Add the last rectangular pocket. The graphic shows the results of selecting the rectangle in one viewport. It's highlighted in all three. Don't be confused by this. You're looking at the same objects in all four viewports, just from different views. If you erase the rectangle in one viewport, it won't exist, so it won't be displayed in any of the others.

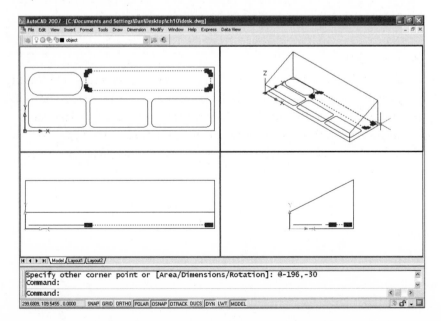

Now that you have all five closed polylines, you can extrude each of them into a solid:

1. Use the EXTRUDE command, and make sure the resulting solids extend beyond the sloped surface of the solid. It doesn't matter how far beyond they go, because you're going to subtract them from the largest solid. You can select all of the objects when prompted for a selection set by the EXTRUDE command and extrude them as a group.

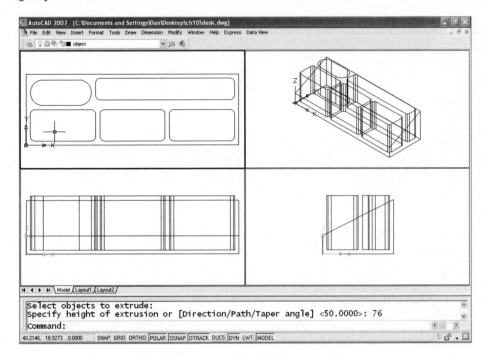

2. Use the SUBTRACT command and select the largest solid when prompted to "Select solids and regions to subtract from…" SUBTRACT is one of the Boolean commands. The others are UNION and INTERSECT. They're used to create shapes from more than one solid or region. You'll see a use for INTERSECT later in the chapter, but the other two are self-explanatory. When you use SUBTRACT, though, you must read the prompts carefully.

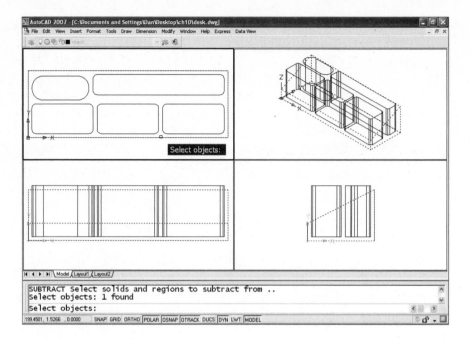

3. After you select the largest solid, you need an ↵ to let AutoCAD know you're finished selecting objects to subtract from. The next prompt asks you to select solids to subtract.

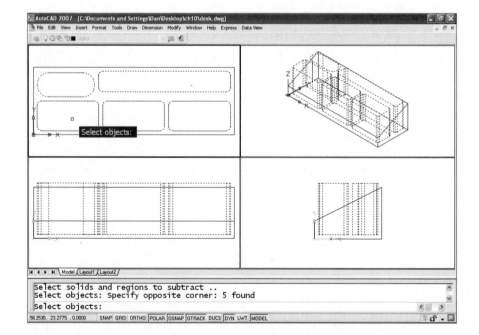

WHY ARE THEY CALLED BOOLEAN COMMANDS?

I'm fascinated by the fact that the two most important influences in the development of CAD were widely read, philosopher-mathematicians born over 200 years apart. Most of us know that Rene Descartes gave us the Cartesian coordinate system in the 17th century, but fewer of us are familiar with George Boole. In the 19th century, Boole developed the system known as Boolean algebra that is the basis for the digital logic used in the design of electronic circuits, without which there would be no computers.

I surmise that these three modeling functions are called Boolean because they resemble the logic of digital switches, which are controlled by AND, OR, and NOT operators.

The SUBTRACT command can deal with two kinds of objects: solids and regions. Regions are 2D, but think of them as 3D objects with no thickness. You can use all three of the Boolean functions on regions in the same way you can with solids. Once you've created a region, you can extrude it, revolve it, or sweep it into a solid.

4. Finally (this won't take as long next time), when you're finished selecting objects, press ↵. Like magic, you've got your desk organizer…almost. I reset DISPSILH to the default value of 0 for this next graphic to show the tessellation lines in the corners of the pockets.

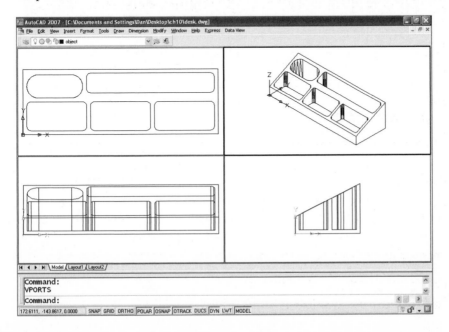

But wait a minute. You can see right through your model, but the mode shown in the previous graphic displays the organizer as a solid in the isometric view. You can choose to display each view of your model in a number of ways. Use the SHADEMODE (VSCURRENT) command, or the Viewports dialog box, or View → Visual Styles, and select any style you want. The next graphic shows the Conceptual visual style in the isometric viewport.

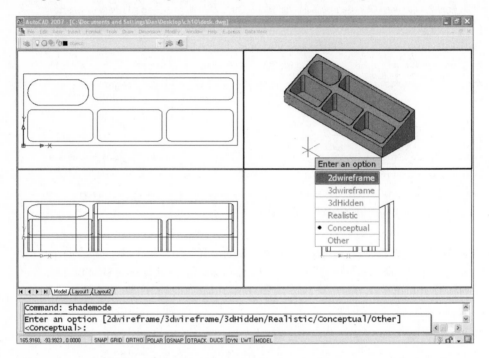

Why not set a Hidden, Conceptual, or Realistic style in all the viewports and leave it that way? Sometimes you can, but it's hard to edit a model if you can't see through it, so set the isometric view back to a 2D wireframe style Let's add some fillets to the corners of the organizer:

1. Use the FILLET command, and select the vertical edges that represent the four corners of the organizer. See why you had to set the isometric viewport back to 2D? The only viewport that displays the edges of all four corners is the isometric view, and you can only get to the back corner if you can reach through your model. Read the prompts carefully. FILLET doesn't work with a solid the same way it does with 2D entities, because you're selecting an edge for filleting on a model rather than two lines.

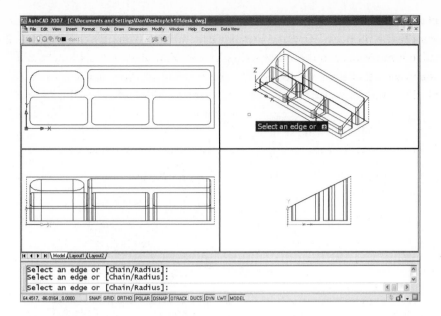

2. Now that you have the entire organizer modeled, you'll add some recessed text to it. This would be easier if your viewports weren't so small, so make one of them larger. Click in the isometric viewport, and display the Viewports toolbar. It has a button that creates a single viewport. Select it. (If you prefer typing, use the SI option of the command-line version of the VPORTS command. You could write a new command for doing this…if only you knew a little AutoLISP programming.)

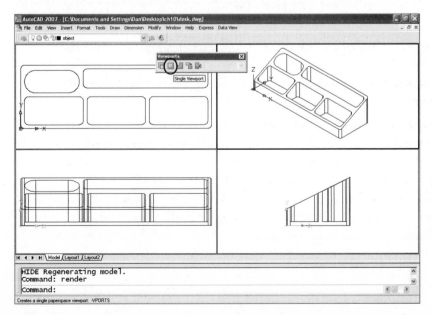

You're making progress. Believe me, skilled 3D AutoCAD users apply these same techniques when designing models far more complex than this one. Although this model is simple, you can make it a little more interesting. I've been asked a few times how to add recessed or raised text to solid objects. The first time I did this, I drew each letter and created polylines that I could extrude, but I've discovered an easier method. In this tutorial you'll place text on the sloped surface, and then create 3D text with the useful, but flawed, Express Tool, TXTEXP. Follow these steps:

1. If you followed all the steps, you have a saved UCS for the sloped surface of the organizer. Make it current.

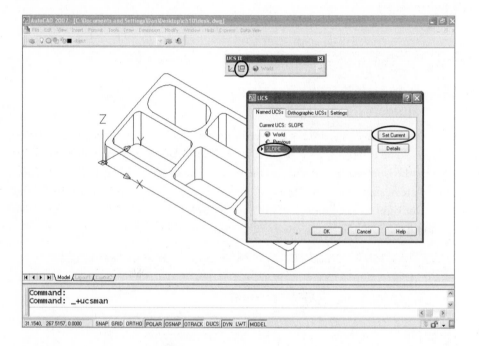

2. After you make the Slope UCS current, you can draw on it. But it's easier to place text when you're looking straight at the surface it's being placed on. Use the PLAN command.

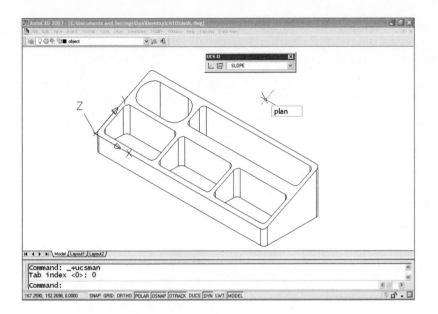

3. Now you're looking straight down on the sloped surface. Zoom in so you can see what you're doing, use the HIDE command to clear up the view, and then use the DTEXT or MTEXT command to place some text. Make sure the text is based in a TrueType font. I use Arial in this example. Make your choice, and then use Express → Text → Explode Text and select the text. If you don't have Express Tools loaded, you'll have to skip a few steps. You can still add some text as a 3D surface model though. Use an SHX font, and give it a thickness using the Properties palette.

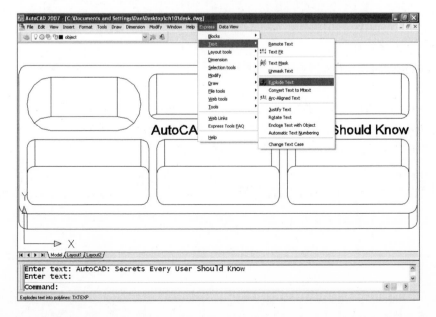

Express Tools aren't native commands and aren't supported by Autodesk. They don't always work flawlessly. Although it's worked well for me, there have been a number of reports of problems with the TXTEXP Express Tool, the command used here to explode the text. If the text disappears when you use TXTEXP, do a ZOOM Extents to find it and move it back into place. If it has been scaled, use the Reference option of the SCALE command to change it back to the correct height. Although the problems are annoying, they're a small price to pay for solid text if you ever need it.

4. When the text is exploded, it's replaced with a large number of closed polylines. The closed polylines in the next image are about to be extruded negative four (–4) so they can be subtracted from the model. If you prefer, you can give the text a positive extrusion and union it to the model instead of subtracting.

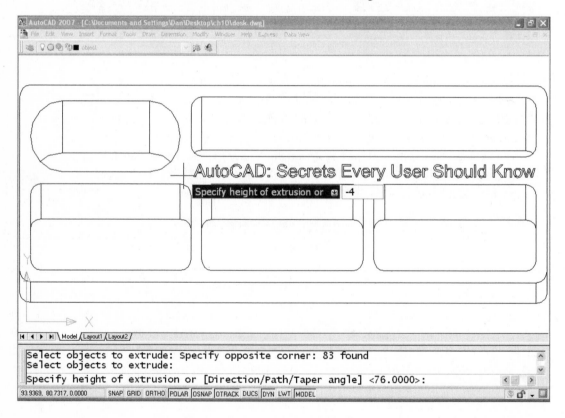

5. After extruding the closed polylines, subtract them from your model. You may find that you get better results if you UNION them together to form a single 3D solid first and then subtract the result from your organizer. The desk organizer should now be one object. Restore the group of four viewports and the organizer should appear as follows:

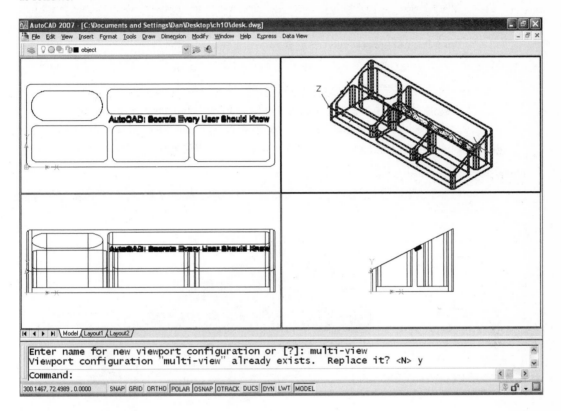

You've been able to change your view of the organizer with several methods:

- Using the PLAN command
- Setting up viewports
- Selecting the SE Isometric button on the View toolbar

3DORBIT (the alias is 3DO) allows you to rotate your view (not the object) using the mouse. You can type that command or its cousin 3DCORBIT (continuous orbit), or find it on the AutoCAD 2007 menu using View → Orbit → Continuous Orbit. Earlier releases have it listed directly under View. Before you use it, make a few changes:

1. Create a single viewport for your isometric view.

2. Change the color of the model's layer to red (it looks better than white or black in this next step).

3. Set the visual style for the view to Realistic in AutoCAD 2007, or change SHADEMODE to gOuraud+edges (type an **o**) if you're using an earlier release.

4. Issue the 3DORBIT command, and play around with it. It's very intuitive. Hold the left mouse button while moving the mouse.

5. Right-click to bring up the 3DORBIT menu and change to a perspective view. In releases before AutoCAD 2007, you have to select the Projection option first to get to the Perspective View option, but in AutoCAD 2007 you can select Perspective directly as shown.

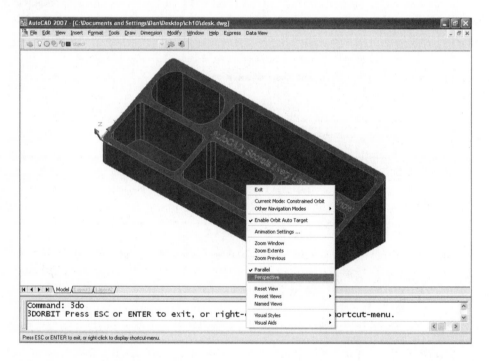

When you select Perspective and start moving the mouse, you're suddenly looking at a different view of the object.

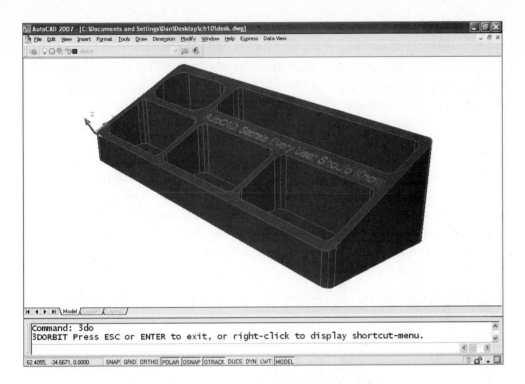

If you want this organizer to look as though it's made of marble, glass, or wood, or if you want a graphic image applied to it, you can attach materials and render it. That process is very different in AutoCAD 2007 than it is in earlier releases. A lot of books cover the 3D features of AutoCAD 2007 thoroughly, and a little searching on the Web will bring up tutorials and other material.

Using Existing 2D Geometry

I'll end this chapter with two examples, one architectural and one mechanical, of how to use existing geometry to generate models fairly quickly. The first example uses solid models to produce a perspective line drawing from existing elevations of a residence. The second example uses an existing multiview drawing of a mechanical part to create a solid model quickly. You don't have to invest a huge amount of time in learning 3D to get something worthwhile out of it.

Quick Perspective Line Drawing

When I first started using AutoCAD, I did a perspective drawing of a new church. At the time, I had a special drafting table for doing perspective drawing, but I wanted to see how well AutoCAD was suited for the task. So, I laboriously drew a plan view and eleva-tions, and then set up a picture plane, horizon line, ground line, true-height line, station point, and three vanishing points in AutoCAD. In other words, I created a perspective drawing using the same tools I would have used for board drafting. Although I did use viewports to place the two vanishing points closer together, I'd have been better off at the board for all the time I invested. The building committee loved it…and asked for two other views. I declined.

That experience prompted me to look into the 3D tools in AutoCAD. After a little experimenting, I realized that I could make a 3D mass model in AutoCAD and paste the 2D elevations I already had onto the surfaces. I couldn't get rendered output, but I could create quick perspective line drawings that would give people a much better picture of a building. If you have some existing 2D elevations, try this technique. It'll give you some practice with 3D modeling. and you may find that the return on your investment of time is much greater than the time required to create a rendered fly-around.

Let's start with the elevations. Suppose you've drawn a front and right side view of a residence, as shown in the simplified version here:

Use the following steps to create a 3D model using the elevations:

1. Create block definitions of the elevations. Don't use all the entities in each elevation; include only the entities that would be on a single plane of the final model. The gable-end block should show the siding and the windows, but not the roof overhang or the side of the dormer. The side of the dormer should be a separate block definition. The front elevation looks like this:

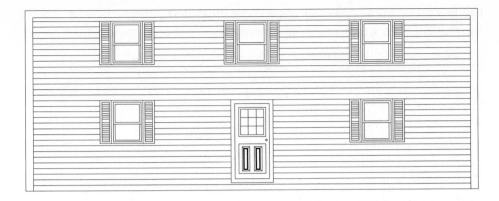

2. After you produce all the necessary blocks, create a solid model of the house and a separate solid model of the roof system. (You practiced with all the tools you need in the desk-organizer exercise.) Use the same dimensions you used for the 2D elevations. The house with a separate roof system is shown in the next image. It doesn't look like much right now.

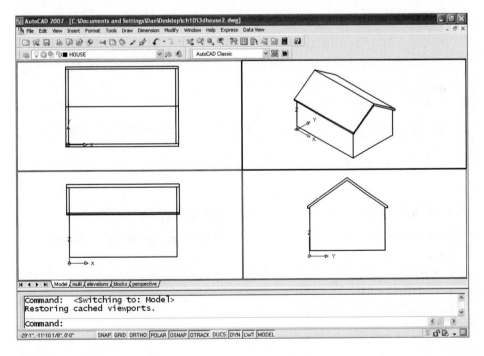

3. Make the Front UCS active, and insert your front elevation onto the front of the mass model. Do the same for the other surfaces. The dormers are added in the next image.

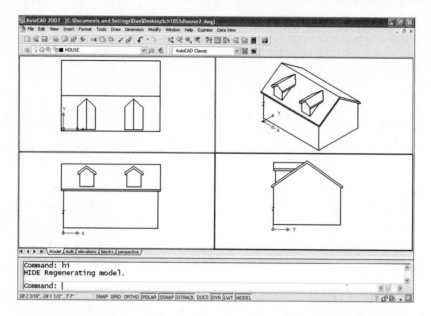

4. Set each UCS for placing the other 2D blocks. The gable-end block requires a Right UCS. So does the near side of the dormers. If you want to paste elevations on the back of the house, use the Back UCS. The next image shows the front block being placed.

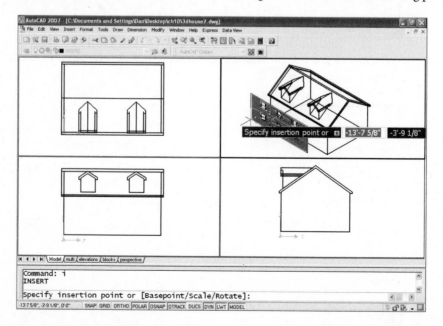

5. Create a UCS for each roof plane using the 3P option of the UCS command, and add a hatch pattern (I use AR-RROOF at a scale of 24) to simulate roofing. To place the hatch, create a closed polyline, and use Add: Select Objects to select the boundary—picking a point inside a boundary doesn't work well in 3D. For the roof, outline the area you want to hatch with a rectangle that starts at the origin (0,0,0) of your roof UCS. After adding the porch details and perhaps a foundation and chimney, you have something similar to the next image.

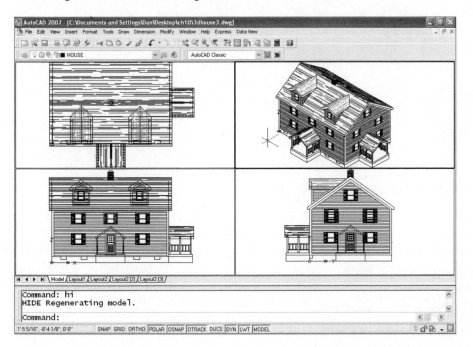

6. You have two choices for getting a perspective view: 3DORBIT or DVIEW. Because you're familiar with creating a perspective view with 3DORBIT, use that method in a single viewport. Now you have a credible perspective line drawing that you can plot and use for presentation purposes. Or, you can plot it out and trace over it by hand to create a true hand rendering in a lot less time. Some clients still love to see those hand-made illustrations. The screen display may drop some lines, as it did in the next figure. That won't affect how this view plots.

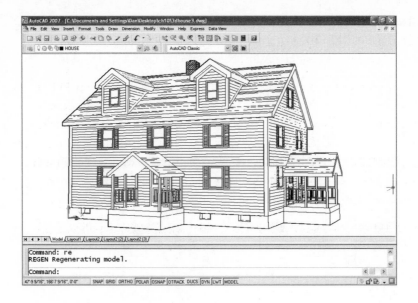

Solid Model from 2D Multiviews

Here's another strategy for using existing work, this one involving a mechanical part. You'll use a simple part here, but you can use this strategy to get a fairly complete model even with much more complex parts. I understand that a selling point used by one of the parametric 3D modeling programs is that it can convert 2D drawings into a 3D model, which implies that you can't do that in AutoCAD. Well, here's how you can, and I bet the resulting model is just as good.

Let's look at the three-view orthographic drawing with dimensions.

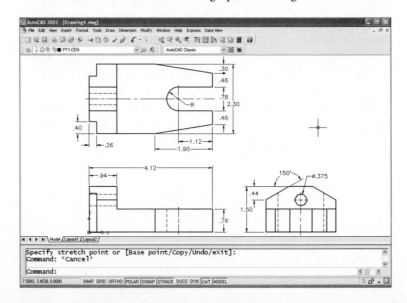

Use these steps to turn this 2D multiview drawing into a solid model:

1. Make the object layer current, and freeze all the other layers (-LAYER → F → * does that quickly).

2. Delete all interior features except the hole in the Right view, and then use the PEDIT command to convert the lines into polylines. (Or use the BOUNDARY command to pick a point and have closed polylines or regions placed on top of the lines.) Use the REGION command to convert the closed polyline and circle in the Right view, and subtract the circle from the polyline. This generates a single region with a hole through it. (If you're using AutoCAD 2006 or 2007, you don't have to use PEDIT to convert the lines into a closed polyline before creating a region.)

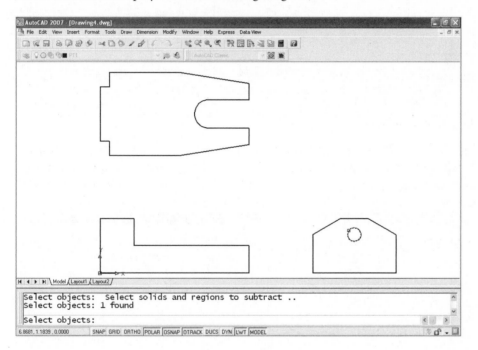

3. Switch to a SE Isometric view, and move each of the polyline profiles so the common origin of each is at 0,0,0. Note that for the Top view, this common origin is a projected intersection, while it is a corner for the front and right side views.

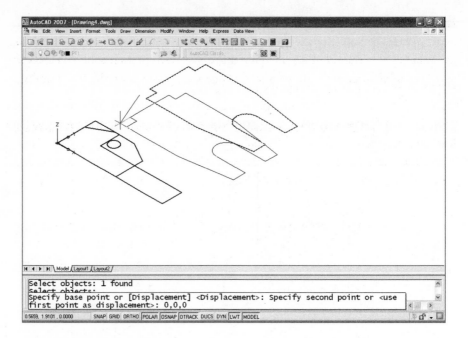

4. Use the ROTATE3D command to rotate the Front and Right profiles into their proper positions. You can leave the WCS current. Select two points to establish an axis for rotation.

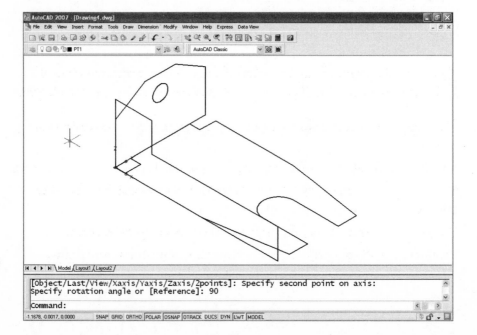

5. Extrude each of the profiles to its proper length. You can either type those values or select a point (two points prior to AutoCAD 2007). The Front view requires a negative value (−2.3). The result is something that defies physics: three solid objects occupying the same space at the same time. Not possible in the real world, but it works in AutoCAD.

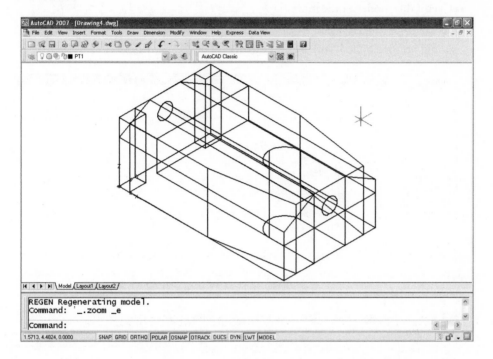

6. Now comes the magic. Use the INTERSECT command to create a solid from the mass that is common to all three objects. Select the objects, then ↵, and don't blink.

At this point, you've completed the model. If you want to edit it, you can do so in several ways:

- Add fillets or chamfers to some of the edges.
- Use SOLIDEDIT or the AutoCAD 2007 3D editing tools to modify faces or shell the object.
- Use the SLICE command to cut though the model, using any three points.
- Use the SECTION command to create a 2D section through any three points. The result can be moved off the object and hatched when creating views.

- Place another solid and subtract that shape. A cylinder created with the CYLIN-DER command can be subtracted to create a hole.

- Add features by using the UNION command to combine this solid with other solids.

Let's edit this model a little more:

1. Use **SOLIDEDIT** → **Body** → **Shell** → *select the model* → ↵ → **0.05**↵ → **X** → ↵ → ↵. The model should become hollow with a wall thickness of 0.05.

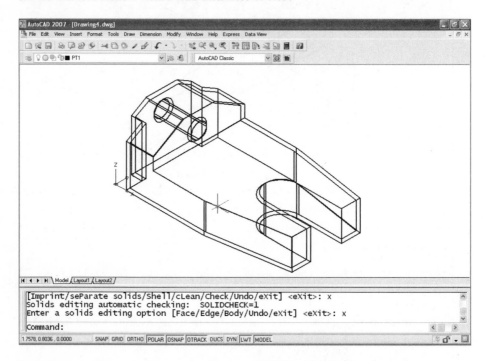

2. Let's slice it. You'll return to this point later, so use the Mark option of the UNDO command to place a mark before slicing the model. Use the SLICE command, and select the model. To cut it down the middle, select three midpoints, and select the piece in the background when prompted to Specify a point on desired side or [keep Both sides] <Both>:.

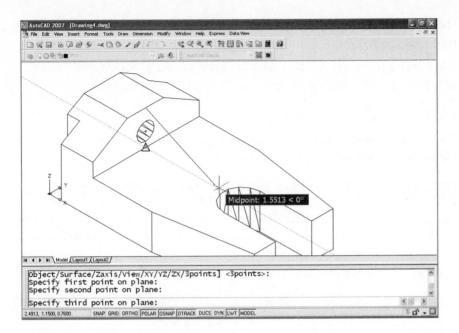

3. Change the color of the object's layer to red, and then use 3DCORBIT (3D continuous orbit) to display it realistically and move it around. Once you get it going, it appears to spin on its own. Press Esc to stop it, and ZOOM Previous to get back to your starting view.

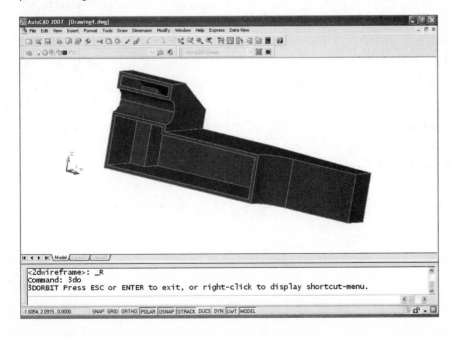

Let's end this section by setting up a layout with four engineering views of the presliced model you just created:

1. Undo back to a point before you used the SLICE command but after you used SOLIDEDIT to shell the object. If you set a mark, type **UNDO** and then **B**.

2. Set Visual Style to 2D.

3. Select a Layout tab.

4. Erase any viewports it contains.

5. Create a page setup for an A-sized sheet.

6. There are a couple of ways to set up drawing views of a model. You could use SOLVIEW, but in this example use **MVSETUP** → **Create** → **Create Viewports** → **2**, and select two corners for the four views. Then, type **0** → **0** → **Scale Viewports**, select all four viewports, and press ↵. Now select the default values Uniform, 1.0 and 1.0. Lock the display of all four viewports. You should have four views that look like this:

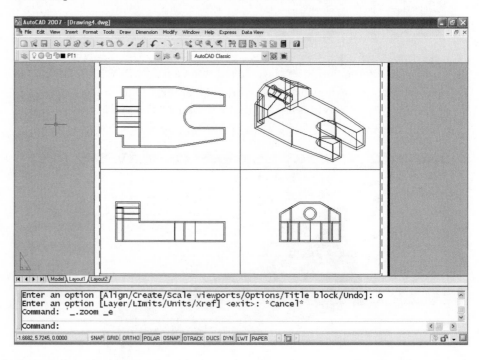

To finish, let's generate 2D profiles that display hidden linetypes in each of your views:

1. Activate the isometric view.

2. Type **SOLPROF**, and then select the model in the Top viewport.

3. Answer Yes to all three questions with ↵, ↵, ↵. Doing so creates hidden profile lines on a separate layer, projects the profile forward onto a flat plane, and prevents tangents from being represents by a line.

4. Repeat step 3 in each of the other three views.

5. Freeze the layer the model is on. Your sheet may not look any different, but you're no longer looking at a 3D model, you're looking at lines. Using the HIDE command will have no effect. What's the point? This gives you a line drawing that can be dimensioned reliably.

6. Look at the Layer Properties Manager. You have eight new layers, four of which start with PH, four with PV. The PH layers have the lines that are hidden and the PV layers have the lines that are visible. Note that in each viewport, six of these layers are frozen by viewport.

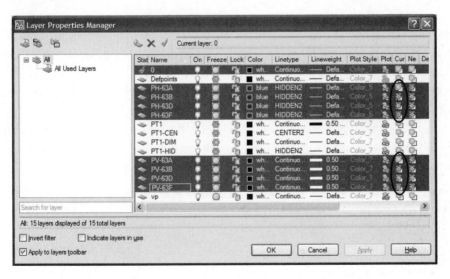

7. Change all the PH- layers to a Hidden2 linetype and a different color.

8. Change the lineweight of all the PV- layers to 0.4 or 0.5, and exit the Layer Properties Manager.

Your sheet should now look like this:

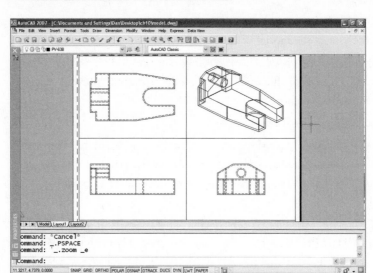

In each view, you have two anonymous block references (their names begin with *), one for visible lines and one for hidden lines. The isometric view doesn't display lines as hidden until you explode the block it contains, but you don't normally show hidden lines in an isometric view anyway; freeze that layer (or erase the block reference). The other views show the hidden lines correctly, but some of them require editing because they're so close to visible lines that they interfere with them. Explode the block to edit them.

In the following image, I erased the hidden lines in the isometric view, erased a few hidden lines that were too close to visible lines, and changed the linetype scale of two of the hidden lines so that they intersect properly with another hidden line.

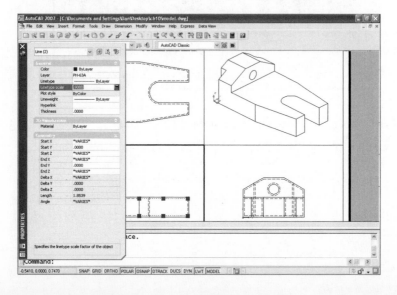

Final Suggestions

Now that you understand coordinate systems and can create 3D models, try modeling something for fun. Maybe you can make a model of the interior of your home with the furniture in each room. The next time someone in the family wants to rearrange the furniture, do it on the computer first—it may save you some back strain and scratched floors. Or maybe you've got an invention in the back of your mind and want to know how it would look. Or, even better, create a model of something for the workplace, and show the people you work for how useful it can be. You may have to produce the first one on your own time, but your ingenuity may make you the one person your department can't live without.

I'll close with a handy tip sheet for 3D modeling.

- Anchor your model by placing one corner or the center at 0,0,0.

- Whenever you create a new UCS, save it with a logical name.

- Use viewports in Model Space during the modeling process, and save the useful configurations with names. You can restore these named configurations in a layout using the MVIEW command.

- Use the VIEW command to save views that you particularly like. It takes a little time to set up a perspective view that looks good, and specific views are hard to duplicate exactly using 3DORBIT.

- Use the BOUNDARY command to quickly create closed polylines or regions.

- If you want to move multiple solid objects into place as a group, don't union them together just for that purpose. Use the GROUP command. I've seen a lot of people make a single model using UNION, only to regret it later when they want to move or edit one of the original 3D solids.

- If you use 3D models for 2D line drawings as you did in the architectural exercise, make all your blocks in the WCS and insert them onto the surfaces. Don't try to define blocks on the surface of a model. You'll run into pitfalls constantly.

- When you're working with multiple models, place each one on its own layer.

- If you plan to animate a model, don't UNION parts that move independently.

- Create the most distinctive or complex shapes as closed polylines, and extrude them to reduce the amount of work you'll have to do later.

- Don't overuse the commands that create primitive solids. You can use the CYLINDER and BOX commands for creating holes and getting a model started, but you seldom need the others if you extrude your most complex shapes from closed plines or regions. (I've seen the torus used to create an o-ring groove, though, so don't forget those other commands entirely.)

- If your files start getting too large, consider the surface modeling commands. If they can do the job, they'll reduce your file sizes. If you have an assembly consisting of multiple models, bring them together in a master drawing as XRefs.

- If you want to take advantage of all the 3D features, particularly in AutoCAD 2007, you may need to upgrade your video card.

- There are modeling commands you didn't use in this chapter. Look at the REVOLVE command and the Path option of the EXTRUDE command in all releases.

- In AutoCAD 2007, look at SWEEP and HELIX, which can be used together to create springs or threads by drawing a cross section and sweeping it along a helix.

- Also in AutoCAD 2007, try the POLYSOLID command. It's like a 3D polyline, creating slabs with straight lines and arc segments. It can also be used to convert existing 2D objects into solids.

- You can get volume information about a solid with the MASSPROP command.

- DISPSILH determines how models will look when the HIDE command is used. If you set DISPSILH to 0, tessellation lines are shown; if you set it to 1, they aren't.

- The ISOLINES variable controls the smoothness with which solids are displayed on the screen.

- The FACETRES variable controls the smoothness with which models are displayed when rendered. It's multiplied by the setting for VIEWRES. The higher you set both variables, the smoother curved objects look when you render them. (VIEWRES also controls the screen resolution of arcs and circles, which are unaffected by FACETRES.)

- The UCS command has some options that you didn't use for the exercises in this chapter. The most useful is the option that lets you rotate the current UCS around any axis by typing **X**, **Y**, or **Z** at the UCS prompt.

Speaking of rotating the UCS, you'll see the *right-hand rule* discussed in a lot of references as an aid to determining whether an angle should be positive or negative when working in 3D. Instead of puzzling over the rule, try typing in a value to see if it goes in the right direction. If you guess wrong, there's UNDO, the most frequently used command in AutoCAD (at least, by me).

- The 3DORBIT command can be used to set clipping planes for viewing objects. You can hide the portion of an object in front of one plane and behind another so you can work more easily on the interior of a complex model.

CHAPTER 11

AutoCAD Puzzlers

Over the years, I've gotten a lot of phone calls, e-mails, questions at workshops, and other sorts of queries from people stymied by something in AutoCAD. Because I teach at a public college, I consider answering these questions to be part of my job; but in truth, I like being an unofficial help desk. Troubleshooting other people's problems keeps me up to date, and there is something really satisfying about sleuthing on other users' behalf. This book is, in large part, the result of all that problem solving.

The 35 puzzlers in this final chapter don't result from bugs or glitches that inevitably occur in any software program. On the contrary, they result from *normal* AutoCAD behavior—that is, behavior that poses a problem either because you've never encountered it before or because you don't understand how you're causing it to happen.

See how many puzzlers you can solve. If you've read this book carefully, you should have all the tools you need. I've discussed all the solutions at some point in this book, and you may also find alternative solutions. I'll provide mine—but you have to turn to the pages at the end of the chapter to find them. How much fun would it be otherwise?

- ■ **The Puzzlers**

- ■ **The Solutions**

The Puzzlers

Each of these puzzlers came to me as an actual question by an AutoCAD user; many came from multiple sources. In some cases, the user who asked the question was merely perplexed, but in others they were really frustrated—sometimes to the point of panic. After all, things tend to go wrong when you're faced with a killer deadline. I can usually figure out the source of the problem, but not always. In the cases where I find a solution to the problem but no clue as to how it occurred, maybe you have a theory to share with me. I hope so.

Puzzler 1: Disappearing Preview

You open the Dimension Style Manager dialog box, and no dimensions are displayed in the preview pane. Do you need a new video card?

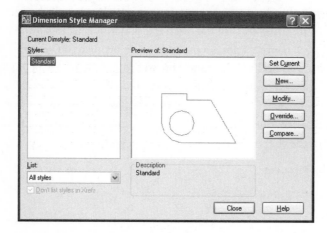

Puzzler 2: Broken Absolute Coordinates?

Your office upgraded to AutoCAD 2007, and suddenly it seems like you can't draw anymore. When did they eliminate absolute coordinate entry? And why? What could be more fundamental to AutoCAD than absolute coordinates? How can you get them back?

Puzzler 3: Lost Hatch Boundary

You place a hatch pattern at the wrong scale, so you erase it. (You could have used HATCHEDIT, but you didn't think of it.) The hatch boundary disappears with the pattern. You can always create a new hatch pattern, but how do you stop this from happening again?

Puzzler 4: Hatch Edit Problems

You try to move an island in a hatch pattern, but the hatch pattern won't change with it. Such hatch patterns always changed before. Did you get a virus somehow?

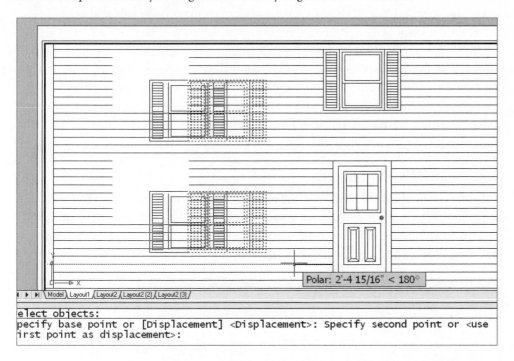

Puzzler 5: Entities Stuck on a Layer

You select an object and try to change its layer by picking a new one from the Layer drop-down list. Nothing happens. You check to see if the object's current layer is locked. It isn't. Maybe the object is a block reference? Not this time. What's going on?

Puzzler 6: Disabled Viewport Locking

You select a floating viewport and right-click so you can lock the display. The menu pops up, but the Display Locked option isn't there. You check the right-click behavior settings in the Options dialog box, but nothing you do there brings back the one thing you want on that menu. How do you get your menu option back?

Puzzler 7: Broken Delete Key

You always use the Delete key to erase objects, but suddenly it doesn't work. You assume the Delete key is broken, but a new keyboard doesn't help. What will?

Puzzler 8: Once and Done

You select one entity and then try to select another, but the first entity is no longer highlighted. Your office mate advises you to hold down the Shift key. That works, but you never had to do that before. How do you make sure you never have to do that again?

Puzzler 9: Dense Hatch

You're using the MATCHPROP (PAINTER) command to match all the properties of one hatch to another with a different pattern. When you select the second hatch pattern, its layer changes, but not the pattern. You get the following error message: Hatch spacing too dense, or dash size too small. Select destination object(s) or [Settings]:. You don't want to edit the hatch, so what do you do?

Puzzler 10: Missing Folders

You want to create a custom linetype, so you try to open the acadiso.lin file. But you can't find it. You know it exists, because your linetypes work, so it must be in the Auto-CAD path. The Options dialog box shows the following support path (except that your user name shows up after Documents and Settings):

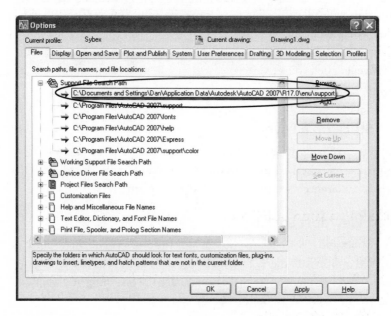

Where's the C:\Documents and Settings*user name*\Application Data folder?

Puzzler 11: What Working Set?

While working on a drawing, you try to select some objects and get the message that they're ...not in the working set. Nothing you do seems to help, so you decide to save the drawing and restart AutoCAD—normally a pretty good idea. Unfortunately, things go from bad to worse. After getting the Save Drawing As dialog box and clicking the Save button, you get the following message:

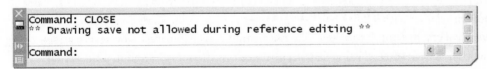

```
Command: CLOSE
** Drawing save not allowed during reference editing **
Command:
```

You aren't doing any reference editing, at least not intentionally, so you close without saving and resign yourself to redoing the lost work. How could you have avoided losing all that work?

Puzzler 12: Broken AutoLISP Program

Your office finally upgraded to the latest release of AutoCAD, and you hope all your custom settings and commands will still work. Things go smoothly until you try to use an old standby named JOIN. It's defined in an AutoLISP program that you've used for years to convert lines into polylines and join them together. It doesn't work. Even the prompts for the command have changed. When you examine the program, it looks like it always did:

```
(defun C:JOIN(/ ss1)
  (setq ss1 (ssget))
  (command "PEDIT" ss1 "Y" "J" ss1 "" "")
  (princ)
)
```

What changed?

Puzzler 13: AutoLISP Program Still Broken

You rewrite the previous program (as indicated in the solution at the end of this chapter), and the new command works fine—for a while. But one day it breaks again, giving you the message Invalid option keyword. ; error: Function cancelled. It's a good thing the latest version of AutoCAD has so many improvements, or this upgrade business would start to look like a bad idea. What do you do now?

Puzzler 14: The 30-Inch Building

You open a file that contains the floor plan from an old project. After making some changes, you begin to add dimensions. Instead of 120′, as you expect, the dimension reads 2′6″. You realize this mistake must have something to do with dimensioning in Paper Space, but that's what you always do, and the numbers have always been right. Why are they wrong now?

Puzzler 15: Mysterious Line Lengths

Your civil engineering firm asks you to use a contractor's drawing to locate a treatment plant. You check some existing distances between entities only to find that they're far greater than you expect. Some of them are longer than the entire property. How can that be?

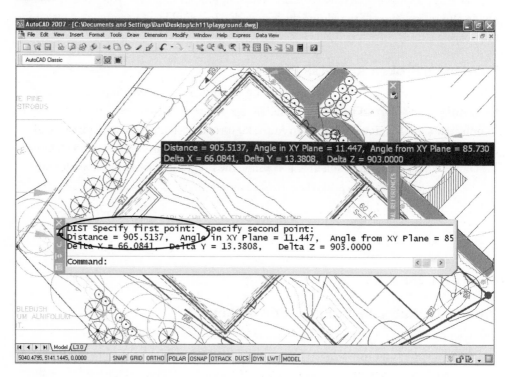

Puzzler 16: Missing Linetypes

After making a series of polylines to represent contours, you use the Spline option of PEDIT to smooth out the lines. The polylines are on a layer with a hidden linetype. Everything else with a hidden linetype looks fine, but your contour lines are continuous. How can you fix them?

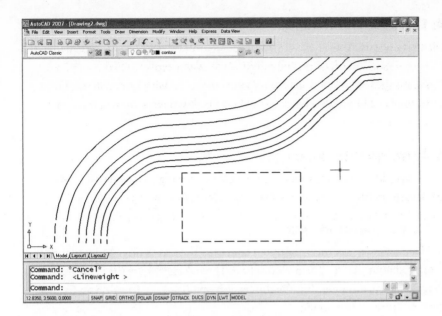

Puzzler 17: Blocks Scale Themselves

After you design a building, the builder asks you to add a playground. On your playground drawing, when you place your standard title block as an XRef, it's much too small. You assume someone else in the office changed the original title-block drawing, but when you open it to check, it's still 35 × 22.5, the same size it's always been. Why did it scale itself?

Puzzler 18: What Came First?

Returning to a drawing after a month away, you discover several different versions of the same design, each on its own layer. You wish you'd used better layer names, because you can't remember which design was done when. Is there any way to tell which design is most recent?

Puzzler 19: Can't Turn on Toolbars

To get more drawing space, you closed all your toolbars. But now you want to turn one of them back on. Oops, you don't have a toolbar button available to right-click. So, you try View → Toolbars, but that opens the Customize User Interface dialog box; you can't find any place to turn on a toolbar. If you have no buttons displayed, how do you turn on a toolbar?

Puzzler 21: Tiny Dimensions

After you place some dimensions, the tick marks are too small, there's no gap on the extension lines, and you can't even find the text. What's the secret?

Puzzler 22: Tiny Dimension Text

This time you place a dimension on a floor plan, and only the text is tiny—unreadable, in fact. Everything else about the dimension looks fine: The tick marks are the right size, and there's a gap for the extension lines. But the dimension text is a dot. How do you fix this without making everything else too big?

Puzzler 23: Sideways Text

Your office uses a vertical title block, and the new in-place text editor in AutoCAD 2006 forces you to turn your head 90° when you try to edit any text in it. Can you get the old editor back?

Puzzler 24: Can't Select a Viewport

You want to unlock a viewport in a layout, but you can't select it. You can see it—and its layer isn't locked, frozen, or turned off—but you can't pick it. You suspect the problem has something to do with the Defpoints layer, but you can't find out because you can't select the viewport to put it on a different layer. What do you do next?

Puzzler 25: No Warnings

You define a new block with no problems and suddenly remember that you already have a block defined with the same name. You're certain you never got a warning about redefining the original block, but now the old definition has been replaced with the new. Why was there no warning?

Puzzler 26: Which File Format?

Your office works with clients and contractors who use older releases of AutoCAD. They frequently ask you to send them DWG files, and you have to keep track of what release they use, open the DWG file, and save it as their release. How can you determine the format used to save a DWG file?

Puzzler 27: Unextrudable Polyline

When trying to extrude a polyline that you know is closed, you keep getting the following error: `Cannot sweep or extrude a self-intersecting curve` (prior to AutoCAD 2007, it would say `Unable to extrude the selected object`). What can you do to make the polyline extrudable?

Puzzler 28: Which Variable Changed?

You're writing a program that requires the name of the system variables controlled by checking Specify Plot Offset Relative To and Hide System Printers in the Plot And Publish tab of the Options dialog box. Why aren't the variable names displayed in the dialog box? How can you find them?

Puzzler 29: Blown-Up Batting

You've carefully added insulation to a drawing using the Batting linetype. When you go to a Layout tab and set up a floating viewport, the batting is much too large. How can you control its size?

Puzzler 30: Dimension Nightmare

While working with a drawing provided by a client, you discover that one of the dimensions looks odd. Sure enough, the dimension value has been overridden and the geometry is wrong. Now you don't know which dimensions you can trust and which ones you can't. Do you have to check each dimension to find out if it's been overridden?

Puzzler 31: Entities upon Entities

After taking care of the overridden dimensions on the drawing from the previous puzzler, you find out why there were so many. This drawing is a mess: lines on top of lines, and lots of places where short segments are connected in what looks like a single line. With too many objects snaps in the way, the client figured that typing in the correct dimension was quicker than fixing the drawing. How can you clean it up at this point?

Puzzler 32: Overkill in AutoLISP

You decide to use the OVERKILL command on all drawings from outside contractors. Using AutoLISP, you begin to create your own OK command, using the following code:

```
(defun C:OK()
(command "OVERKILL" "ALL" "" "")
)
```

When you try to use the OK command, it returns `nil`. When you test the code by typing `(command "OVERKILL")`, you get the error message: `overkill Unknown command "OVERKILL"`. How can it be an unknown command when you can type it at the command line?

Puzzler 33: No CHSPACE

Your office doesn't have the Express Tools loaded, and you haven't upgraded to AutoCAD 2007 yet, so CHSPACE isn't a native AutoCAD command. How can you move entities from Paper Space into Model Space? And while you're at it, how can you scale them so they appear to be the same size?

Puzzler 34: Invisible Block Reference

You try to insert a block reference, but it doesn't show up. You've selected the Specify On-Screen Insertion Point option, so you know the block reference isn't being placed off the screen at 0,0. The Explode check box isn't checked, so the block reference isn't being exploded on insertion. You've made that mistake before and found the entities on their original layer after thawing the layer. This time, you checked everything, and yes, the current layer is on. Where's your block?

Puzzler 35: Bound XRef Blows Up

You decide to bind an external reference from another office to its host. The XRef looks great. The dimensions are perfect, the text meets your standards, and things are going smoothly.

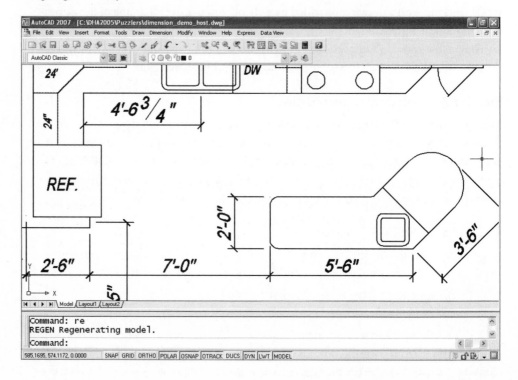

But when you bind the XRef, the text changes to that ugly font. How annoying. Then, when you explode the bound XRef, the dimensions completely blow up. What a mess. How could you have avoided this?

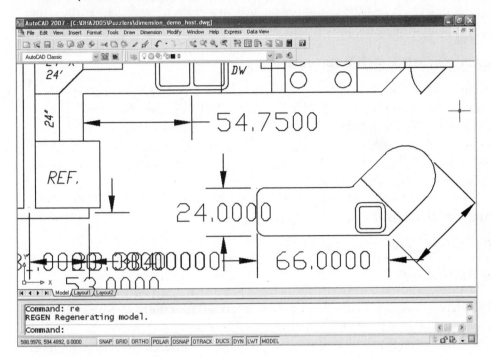

The Solutions

Here are the answers to the questions posed by each puzzler, and my solutions.

Puzzler 1: Disappearing Preview

No, you don't need a new video card. The current layer is turned off. Turn it back on.

Turning off the current layer can cause other puzzling behaviors too, including being able to create entities on the layer without knowing you're doing it. In this case, you turned off the layer to make it easier to select items on other layers, got distracted, and then tried to modify a dimension style. No new video card needed.

Puzzler 2: Broken Absolute Coordinates?

You can get them back by settting DYNPICOORDS to 1.

This isn't a problem for those of you who stuck with the command line; but by default, coordinates entered in AutoCAD's dynamic input window are relative, not absolute. That can be a surprise if you've been using an earlier release.

This behavior makes sense for most users, because we use relative coordinates far more often than absolute. If you want to enter absolute coordinates, precede them with the pound sign, as in #4,3. If you want to go back to the behavior of earlier releases, change the value of DYNPICOORDS to 1. If you can't remember the name of that variable, type DYN and start pressing the Tab key until it shows up.

Puzzler 3: Lost Hatch Boundary

You can stop it from happening by setting PICKSTYLE to either 0 or 1.

PICKSTYLE is saved in the registry, so it affects every drawing. It has four settings and controls how groups and hatch boundaries are selected. You can toggle it between two of the settings using Ctrl-H or Ctrl-Shift-A, but that affects only the group-selection behavior, not the hatch behavior. This problem can be solved with a variable setting, but I'm not certain what caused it in the first place. It may have been the result of running an AutoLISP program that didn't have error trapping, but I can't confirm that. I just know it happens.

Puzzler 4: Hatch Edit Problems

You don't have a virus; you need to set HPASSOC to 1.

HPASSOC controls the associativity of hatch patterns. If it gets turned off, you no longer have the ability to edit islands and boundaries and have the hatch pattern update. How does it get turned off? My best guess is that it happens in the Hatch And Gradient dialog box when someone accidentally clears the Associative option. HPASSOC must be on at the time the hatch is created.

Puzzler 5: Entities Stuck on a Layer

You need to set PICKFIRST to 1.

PICKFIRST is another system variable that causes headaches. It was added long ago to allow selection of objects with either a Verb/Noun or Noun/Verb syntax. You normally select an object and then select a destination layer from the Layer toolbar control window. That won't work with PICKFIRST set to 0. Without Noun/Verb selection turned on, AutoCAD needs the command (the verb) before you can select the entity (the noun).

Puzzler 6: Disabled Viewport Locking

Set PICKFIRST to 1.

You also can't lock a floating viewport using the right-click menu without Noun/Verb selection turned on, because you have to select an object first to get it to open. There are two alternatives to the right-click menu. You can use the Properties palette to unlock the display, or you can use the Lock option of the MVIEW command; but if you don't normally do that, you may not remember how.

Puzzler 7: Broken Delete Key

There's no guarantee you'll never have to do it again, but set PICKFIRST to 1.

This is the last PICKFIRST puzzler, honest—but yes, this puzzler has the same solution. Lots of users routinely select objects and then press the Delete key to erase them, but the Delete key isn't a command. You can't press the Delete key and then select objects to erase; and with PICKFIRST turned off, you can't select an object first and then delete it.

How does PICKFIRST get turned off? Perhaps you accidentally cleared it in the Selection tab of the Options dialog box. If the Noun/Verb check box is cleared, PICKFIRST gets turned off. But I doubt that's it. I long suspected that an AutoLISP program was the culprit, but I couldn't confirm my hunch…until recently.

My Delete key stopped working. I immediately used UNDO to back up one step at a time, hunting for the moment when PICKFIRST got turned off. When I got to that point, I checked the text screen. Aha: The only thing I had done was run the MVSETUP command! But then I couldn't duplicate the problem, so I opened the `mvsetup.lsp` file and searched for *pickfirst*. I found this line of code: `(if (/= 0 mv_oas) (setvar "pickfirst" 0))`. I haven't yet figured out what I did while running MVSETUP to sneak past the error handler, but I know I did something. Hey, someday I'll try to solve *that* puzzler.

Puzzler 8: Once and Done

Set PICKADD to 1.

When PICKADD has been set to 0, you have to hold down the Shift key to add objects to a selection set. This happened a lot when the Properties palette first showed up. Inexplicably, there is a PICKADD toggle in the Properties palette. Why would you need it, and how often would you change it on purpose? Probably never. But because it looks a little like the Close icon in all the other windows in AutoCAD, you may accidentally select it while trying to close the Properties palette without noticing that the button icon then changes from a plus sign to the number 1.

Puzzler 9: Dense Hatch

Increase the value of MaxHatch.

MaxHatch is an environment variable, not a system variable, so it behaves a little differently. How you change it depends on whether you're using AutoCAD or AutoCAD LT. The default setting for this variable is *10000* and it controls how dense a hatch pattern can be.

AutoCAD format: `(setenv "MaxHatch" "10000000")`. That's right. To change an environment variable, you need to use an AutoLISP function, SETENV. This particular variable is case sensitive (not all environment variables are). If you want to know what the current setting is, use this format: `(getenv "MaxHatch")`.

AutoCAD LT format: `setenv MaxHatch`. You omit the parentheses and the quotation marks, but it's still case sensitive, so it must be typed as shown.

Puzzler 10: Missing Folders

The folder is hidden, but you don't need it. Type **(startapp "notepad" (findfile "acad.lin"))**.

OK, I didn't tell you where the missing folder is. For that, go back and look at Chapter 2, "Managing Your System." The `Application Data` folder is hidden by default, and that chapter shows you how to unhide it. But you can open any file in the AutoCAD support path by typing a couple of AutoLISP functions at the command line as shown in the solution. If you want to open a different file, change the filename.

Puzzler 11: What Working Set?

You could have avoided losing all that work by typing the command REFCLOSE.

This problem is more likely in AutoCAD releases prior to AutoCAD 2006, but it can still happen in the current release. It's caused when you double-click a block (pre-AutoCAD 2006) or an XRef (any release), pick the OK button in the Reference Edit dialog box, and then close the resulting Refedit toolbar thinking that will exit the command. It doesn't. AutoCAD thinks you're editing the block or XRef.

Why click OK in a dialog box without really looking at it? Hey, you're busy; you just want to get rid of the thing. When this happens, type **REFCLOSE** or issue the REFEDIT command so the toolbar appears, and click the Cancel button. The person who called me about this really did close the drawing, by the way. Luckily, he'd been saving regularly and had only about an hour's work to do. So much for being in a hurry.

Puzzler 12: Broken AutoLISP Program

What changed is the addition of a new native AutoCAD command. Edit the AutoLISP file to rename your JOIN command.

There's a command named JOIN as of AutoCAD 2006, and it'll win the "native command vs. AutoLISP function" battle every time. Although you could use the UNDEFINE command to undefine the native version of JOIN, I don't recommend such drastic action here. Open your AutoLISP program, and rename this command to something other than JOIN. How about JJ? Now your program looks like this:

```
(defun C:JJ(/ ss1)
  (setq ss1 (ssget))
  (command "PEDIT" ss1 "Y" "J" ss1 "" "")
  (princ)
)
```

But…that leads to the next puzzler.

Puzzler 13: AutoLISP Program Still Broken

Rewrite the program again, this time taking PEDITACCEPT into account.

Although changing the command name got past the JOIN command problem, it allowed another intermittent problem to emerge—the error message Invalid option keyword.... This problem is the PEDITACCEPT registry variable, which was added to AutoCAD 2004. Apparently you turned it on. If so, you're no longer asked whether you want to turn an object into a polyline when you use the PEDIT command and select a line or an arc. If AutoCAD doesn't ask that question, the "Y" in your program has no meaning, and the program sees it as an unknown command.

Your original LISP program was written with the assumption that it will be used only with lines, so it includes the "Y" option as a response to the question Object selected is not a polyline. Do you want to turn it into one? <Y>. If you want the program to work no matter how the PEDITACCEPT variable is set, rewrite it again, this time as follows:

```
(defun c:JJ(/ ss1 peAccept)
  (setq peAccept (getvar "PEDITACCEPT"))
  (setvar "PEDITACCEPT" 0)
  (setq ss1 (ssget))
  (command "pedit" ss1 "y" "J" ss1 "" "")
  (setvar "PEDITACCEPT" peAccept)
  (princ)
)
```

It's sometimes a challenge, but try to write AutoLISP programs that work in any release of AutoCAD. This one does that by temporarily turning off the PEDITACCEPT variable and then resetting it at the end of the program. You can do two other things to improve this program. First, add an error handler to reset the variable PEDITACCEPT in case of an error. That's discussed in detail in Chapter 9, "AutoLISP by Example: Getting Better." Second, have the program determine whether the objects you select are already polylines. The program can contain one function for objects that are already polylines and a different function for objects that aren't.

Puzzler 14: The 30-Inch Building

The dimensions are wrong now because it's an old drawing. Set DIMASSOC to 2.

You opened a drawing that was created before AutoCAD 2000. Back then, dimension associativity was controlled by the DIMASO system variable, which had only two settings. The variable DIMASSOC was added to AutoCAD 2000, and it has three settings: 0, 1, and 2. If you open an older drawing, its DIMASO value is probably 1, and that is used as the setting for DIMASSOC.

Unfortunately, a setting of 1 for DIMASSOC means that Paper Space dimensions aren't associated with their underlying geometry. Any dimension you add in Paper Space reflects the measured distance on the sheet of paper, *not* the actual distance in model space.

Puzzler 15: Mysterious Line Lengths

Lines can be longer than they appear if the ends have different Z-axis values. Use the FLATTEN Express Tool.

I have gotten some form of this question surprisingly often. It's possible to snap to objects that are at different elevations, even though in plan view everything appears to be on the same plane. With only one view, you can't see the elevation differences. If you read the command line carefully, you'll find clues. You'll see an angle from the XY plane, and the Delta X and Delta Y are much smaller than the Distance.

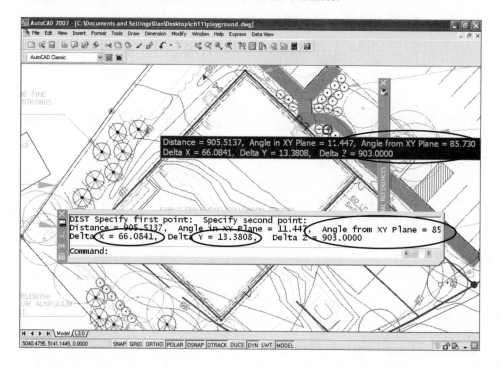

FLATTEN converts the drawing into a 2D model. Now everything moves to an elevation of 0, including endpoints of lines that are currently at different elevations.

You may wonder if the Properties palette can be used to do the same thing. It can't. Elevation isn't a listed property when you select multiple types of objects. CHANGE can change elevations of multiple objects, but if the endpoints of lines have different Z-axis coordinates, CHANGE won't flatten it.

You may also wonder if the FLATSHOT command in AutoCAD 2007 will take of this problem, but that won't work either. FLATSHOT uses solids or surfaces to create a 2D block.

Puzzler 16: Missing Linetypes

Enable linetype generation for the contour lines using the Properties palette.

By default, linetype generation is turned off for polylines. If a polyline has a linetype other than continuous, the linetype is generated between the vertices of each segment. A segment that is too short for the specified definition displays as continuous. A lot of short segments, which is common with a spline-fitted polyline, look continuous.

You can either set PLINEGEN to 1 before creating polylines so they have linetype generation turned on, or change the properties of individual polylines using the Properties palette. I recommend adjusting linetype generation using the Properties palette so you don't get unintended consequences that you don't notice, like missing corners of hidden rectangles.

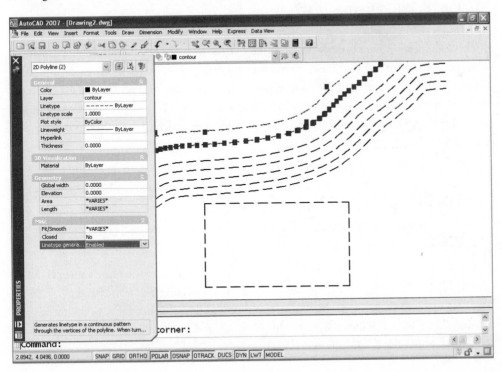

Puzzler 17: Blocks Scale Themselves

It scaled itself because you told it to. To fix it, change insertion units to Inches.

You didn't intentionally tell the block to scale itself, of course. Although it's often overlooked, the Drawing Units dialog box contains an Insertion Scale section with a pane for selecting the Units To Scale Inserted Content. If you're drawing a playground using decimal feet, you may be tempted to select Feet as the insertion units.

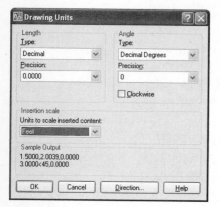

That would be helpful when you insert a drawing of a swing set that was drawn in inches. With insertion units set to feet, the swing set automatically scales 1:12 to become just the right size. That's great.

The surprise comes when you externally reference or insert your standard title block, which was also drawn in inches. It's ½ the size you want it to be. This problem also shows up sometimes when a drawing with units set to millimeters is inserted into a drawing done in inches. In that case, you may discover that it's been scaled twice: once automatically, and once by you. You can even get this problem if you set the Insertion Scale to Unitless.

Puzzler 18: What Came First?

There is a way to tell what came first. Create a DXF file, and compare the handles.

The real question here is, how can you find out the order in which entities in a drawing were created? Assuming that the drawing was opened (not inserted and then exploded), you can find out by creating a DXF file. Open it with Notepad, and you'll see a list of every object in the order in which it was created—if you know how to interpret the mysterious text. How is each entity identified, and how do you know which one it refers to in your drawing?

- Use the LIST command to find the handles of key objects on each layer, and make a note of them. Each handle consists of a few characters—either numbers or letters. You may find that the handle of an object is 10A.

- Search for those handles in the DXF text file. The objects that come later in the file should be more recent.

Be careful, though. The handles are hexadecimal numbers, and the same value can be used in a different context. Any handle in a DXF file is on a line below the header 5. The following segment from a DXF file shows two pieces of data: the header 0, which designates object type (in this case a lightweight polyline); and the header 5, which designates the handle of that object (in this case is 10A):

```
    0
LWPOLYLINE
    5
10A
```

Puzzler 19: Can't Turn On Toolbars

When no buttons are displayed, you can turn toolbars on with the -TOOLBAR command.

It used to be easy before the CUI was added to AutoCAD 2006. View → Toolbars opened a list of toolbars with check boxes, and you set their visibility. And the TOOLBAR command doesn't help, because it opens the CUI, and there's no visibility checklist there.

So, use the command-line version by preceding the command with the minus sign. The prompt for the -TOOLBAR command is Enter toolbar name or [ALL]:, so you try the ALL option. You have plenty of toolbar buttons now, but you have to close everything you don't want. I recommend typing a toolbar name instead. Don't know their names? After entering the -TOOLBAR command, type **Standard ↵ Show**. Now you can right-click any of the Standard toolbar buttons and select to your heart's content.

You can also use the -TOOLBAR command when you know a toolbar is turned on but you can't find it. That sometimes happens with multiple toolbars—one of them gets shoved aside or buried under another. For example, if you lose your Viewports toolbar, type **-TOOLBAR ↵ Viewports ↵ Float ↵ 0,0**, and it will display in the upper-left corner of your screen.

If you've defined a workspace that includes toolbars, you can make it current using the WORKSPACE command.

Puzzler 21: Tiny Dimensions

Set DIMSCALE to 0 or the reciprocal of your plot scale.

If nothing about the dimensions is the right size, setting DIMSCALE to 0 (which happens when you select Scale Dimensions To Layout in the Fit tab of the Modify Dimension Style dialog box) automatically scales the dimensions based on the zoom magnification of a floating viewport in a layout. See Chapter 6, "Plotting," for more information. You can also set a specific scale factor for DIMSCALE if you know the plot scale that will be used.

Puzzler 22: Tiny Dimension Text

Fix the height problem by setting the text style height to 0.

If only the text in a dimension is too small, the problem is the text style used for the dimension. If it's defined as having a fixed height, it'll always have that height. If dimensions are placed in Model Space and plotted at any scale other than 1:1, the height of the text will be wrong. In an architectural or civil field, the text will be tiny.

Dimensions in Paper Space won't have this problem.

Puzzler 23: Sideways Text

You can get the old editor back. Set MTEXTED to OldEditor.

AutoCAD 2006 introduced the in-place text editor, and, for the most part, users like it—except when text isn't in a horizontal position. If you use AutoCAD 2006 (problem fixed in AutoCAD 2007) and want the old editor back, set MTEXTED to OldEditor. When you decide you want the in-place editor back, set MTEXTED to Internal or type a period. Or, you can upgrade to a newer release.

Puzzler 24: Can't Select a Viewport

Turn on and/or thaw layer 0.

If you turn off or freeze layer 0, you can't select anything on the Defpoints layer. You've probably been putting objects on the Defpoints layer for years. After all, it used to be the only nonplot layer in AutoCAD, and it still works great for that purpose, so that's where you put floating viewports. That way, you can still select them—usually—but they don't plot. What does layer 0 have to do with it? The Defpoints layer exists to hold defpoints contained in dimensions, which are anonymous block references. The Defpoints layer has several characteristics that no other layer has, including a peculiar relationship with layer 0.

Puzzler 25: No Warnings

There was no warning, because you're an expert. If you want a warning set EXPERT back to 0.

OK, you may not know everything, but zero? The EXPERT variable setting determines when you get a warning about things like overwriting drawing files, block names, layer names, dimension styles, and so on. You've probably come to rely on those warnings and can't believe it's possible to turn them off, but it is. There are six levels of EXPERT. A setting of 0 issues all prompts. Users don't set this variable to anything else while they're drawing, at least not on purpose, but sometimes it gets turned off by an AutoLISP program, a menu macro, or a script. Why? So the program can redefine something without stopping at a prompt that requires user input, such as `Block "a" already exists. Redefine it? [Yes/No] <N>:`. If a program sets EXPERT to a value other than 0, it should be set back, but that doesn't always happen.

As you learned in Chapter 9, a polite AutoLISP program restores changed settings for variables using error handling. If you run a program without error handling and stop it before it's finished, it may set EXPERT to something other than 0 and leave it that way.

The good news is that the setting is never saved. It'll haunt you only during that editing session. Of course, you should still find out how EXPERT got changed in the first place and fix the problem.

Puzzler 26: Which File Format?

Open the DWG file in Notepad, and read the first line.

No, a DWG file isn't a text file, but yes, you can open one in Notepad (or any text editor). Most of it's unreadable, but the first line contains a code that indicates the format in which it was saved. The relationship between the code and the release format isn't obvious, so the following table describes the most likely of the 24 possibilities:

Code	Release
AC1004	9
AC1006	10
AC1009	11 and 12
AC1012	13
AC1014	14 and 14.01
AC1015	2000, 2000i, 2002
AC1018	2004, 2005, 2006
AC1021	2007 (and probably, 2008, and 2009)

See Chapter 9 for two programs that are helpful in determining release information. One of them searches your hard drive for all DWG files, creates a list of them, and then creates a file indicating the format in which each was saved.

Puzzler 27: Unextrudable Polyline

You don't have to make the polyline extrudable, if you use BOUNDARY to create a new polyline.

If there is even the smallest overlap or duplicate segment in a polyline, it can't be extruded. Sometimes it's small enough to be hard to find. Don't bother looking. Using the BOUNDARY command, select a point inside the shape you want to extrude, and create a new shape that is either a closed polyline or a region. Either of these entities can be extruded.

Puzzler 28: Which Variable Changed?

You can find most variable names by clicking the Help button in the Plot And Publish tab.

Variable names aren't displayed in dialog boxes because they would clutter them up. To find the names, use the Help button in that tab. When each element of the tab is discussed, the variable name is given. According to the Help system, the variable PLOTOFFSET controls plot offset. Great—but wait a minute. If that's true, why doesn't the Help system tell you the name of the variable that changes when you select Hide System Printers? Because it's not a system variable.

Some of the variables that control AutoCAD are environment variables. You saw MaxHatch in an earlier puzzler. They're harder to find than system variables, because there's no listing in AutoCAD. Try your favorite internet search engine. In the meantime, here's how to set a few printing-related environment variables, including HideSystemPrinters:

```
(setenv "HideSystemPrinters" "1")
(setenv "PrinterConfigDir" "r:\\plotters")
(setenv "PrinterDescDir" "r:\\plotters\\pmp files")
```

Puzzler 29: Blown-Up Batting

You can control it's size by changing the line's linetype scale property in a floating viewport.

This is a tough one. The Batting linetype looks like a great idea, but it's scaled in Paper Space because PSLTSCALE is on. That means the Batting linetype gets larger by the reciprocal of the plot scale used in the floating viewport. That behavior is great for all the other linetypes you use, but unfortunately, PSLTSCALE affects all lines in the layout. You can't turn it off for just one line.

You have two choices. Edit the linetype scale of the line used after you've set up a layout, or create batting using block references that you array at an angle. I use the second choice, but if you want to use the Batting linetype, here's what you have to do:

1. Leave LTSCALE, CELTSCALE, and PSLTSCALE set to 1.

2. Draw a line down the center of the area where you want the insulation symbol.

3. Place the line on a layer with the linetype set to Batting.

4. With an LTSCALE of 1 in a drawing that uses Imperial units, the batting linetype is 0.8 inches wide. (In a metric drawing, it's 20.3mm.) To use it as insulation, you have to calculate a new linetype scale. If you're using it in a cavity that is 9.25″ at a scale of ¼″=1′ (which is a scale factor of 1:48), here's how the math looks:

   Linetype scale = 9.25/(0.8 × 48) = 0.24

5. If you use it for a cavity that is 5.5″ at a scale factor of ⅛″=1′, it looks like this:

   Linetype scale = 5.5/(0.8 × 96) = 0.07.

Puzzler 30: Dimension Nightmare

You don't have to check each dimension. Use the Express Tool DIMREASSOC.

DIMREASSOC highlights only the dimensions that have override values so you can be prepared for the ugly truth of how bad a drawing really is. You can then decide whether to restore the default values. Hey, maybe there's only one bad dimension.

Puzzler 31: Entities upon Entities

You can clean up the drawing by using the Express Tool OVERKILL.

It's not perfect, but this Express Tool makes a big dent in this problem. It cleans up three problems. However, you'll get the best results if you don't try to clean up everything at once. Run OVERKILL once for polylines, once for overlapping lines, and once for end-to-end line segments.

Puzzler 32: Overkill in AutoLISP

OVERKILL isn't like other AutoCAD commands. To use it, put the macro ^c^c-OVERKILL;ALL;; on a toolbar button.

OVERKILL isn't a native AutoCAD command; it's an AutoLISP function defined in overkill.lsp. You can't call it up with the AutoLISP command function the way you can the LINE command. If you want to modify its behavior so you don't have to respond to the prompts manually, you have to modify the original program. It's much easier to call it from a toolbar button. See Chapter 3, "Customizing AutoCAD's Interface," to see how to create a new command with this macro.

Puzzler 33: No CHSPACE

With no CHSPACE command, you can Copy/Paste, and use 'SPACETRANS to scale.

Thankfully, CHSPACE is now a command in AutoCAD 2007, so this won't be a problem once you upgrade. But you don't need CHSPACE to move entities from Paper Space to Model Space. Just do this:

1. Select the entities.

2. Use the COPYBASE command (Ctrl-Shift-C, or right-click and select Copy With Base Point from the cursor menu) to place them on the clipboard. If the entities are dimensions, select the origin point used for one of them as the base point.

3. Activate the floating viewport where you want to place the entities.

4. Use the PASTEBLOCK command (Ctrl-Shift-V) to paste the entities using the base point you selected when copying them to snap to the desired location.

5. Issue the SCALE command.

6. Select the entities using the L selection option.

7. Select the base point using the @ symbol.

8. Type 'SPACETRANS to start the command transparently.

9. Enter **1** when prompted to Specify Paper Space Distance.

5. Erase the originals when you're happy with the copy.

Unless the floating viewport has a scale of 1:1, the entities appear to be larger or smaller than they did in Paper Space. They haven't changed size, but they appear that way because of the zoom magnification of the floating viewport. That's why you needed to scale them.

Use this technique to copy entities from one layer to another.

Puzzler 34: Invisible Block Reference

Your block's right where you inserted it, but you'll need to redefine the block to see it.

It's possible to define a block with a name and insertion point but no entities. You get a warning message, but AutoCAD is perfectly happy to let you create a block out of nothing. You don't remember defining a block as nothing. So how did it happen? Impatience or fatigue, probably. You had a slight memory lapse and tried to use BLOCK when you meant to use INSERT. You blew right by that warning and kept picking points for insertion, until you unintentionally defined a block. Because you didn't select any entities, your block is empty.

Puzzler 35: Bound XRef Blows Up

You could have avoided this problem by binding the XRef with the Bind option, not the Insert option.

If a host drawing and an inserted drawing use the same name for a text style or a dimension style, the host drawing *always* wins if you explode the drawing. When a good-looking drawing suddenly displays the ugly text and even uglier dimensions, Standard was probably used as the name for the text style and dimension style. When an XRef is bound to its host, it becomes an inserted block, and the text style matches that of the host, not the original XRef. Once the block is exploded, the dimension style follows suit.

To preempt this problem, don't use the name Standard. In this case, the external reference is already in the drawing. To avoid the naming conflict when binding an XRef, select Bind, not Insert, as the type. Then, if you need to explode the bound XRef, its text style and dimension style won't have the same name as those in the host drawing.

When a bind-type is used for a bound XRef, all named objects in the drawing, including the text style and the dimension style, have the XRef drawing name as a prefix. With no conflict between the names, the dimensions won't blow up on you.

Index

Note to the Reader: Throughout this index **boldfaced** page numbers indicate primary discussions of a topic. *Italicized* page numbers indicate illustrations.